THE SCOTT AND LAURIE OKI SERIES IN ASIAN AMERICAN STUDIES

THE SCOTT AND LAURIE OKI SERIES IN ASIAN AMERICAN STUDIES

From a Three-Cornered World:
New and Selected Poems
by James Masao Mitsui

Imprisoned Apart:
The World War II Correspondence of an Issei Couple
by Louis Fiset

Storied Lives:
Japanese American Students and World War II
by Gary Y. Okihiro

Phoenix Eyes and Other Stories
by Russell Charles Leong

Paper Bullets: A Fictional Autobiography
by Kip Fulbeck

Born in Seattle:
The Campaign for Japanese American Redress
by Robert Sadamu Shimabukuro

Confinement and Ethnicity: An Overview
of World War II Japanese American Relocation Sites
by Jeffery F. Burton et al.

CONFINEMENT AND ETHNICITY

An Overview of World War II Japanese American Relocation Sites

JEFFERY F. BURTON   MARY M. FARRELL   FLORENCE B. LORD   RICHARD W. LORD

With a new Foreword by Tetsuden Kashima

An essay by Eleanor Roosevelt

Cartography by Ronald J. Beckwith

A contribution by Irene J. Cohen

UNIVERSITY OF WASHINGTON PRESS

Seattle and London

Confinement and Ethnicity was originally published in 1999
as Publications in Anthropology 74 of the Western Archeological
and Conservation Center, National Park Service,
U.S. Department of the Interior, and
reprinted with corrections in August 2000.

First University of Washington Press edition,
with corrections, published in 2002
Foreword by Tetsuden Kashima © 2002
by the University of Washington Press
Printed in the United States of America

Library of Congress Cataloging-in-Publication Data
Confinement and ethnicity : an overview of World War II
Japanese American relocation sites / by Jeffery F. Burton . . . [et al.] ;
with a new foreword by Tetsuden Kashima ;
an essay by Eleanor Roosevelt ;
cartography by Ronald J. Beckwith
and a contribution by Irene J. Cohen.
p. cm.
Includes bibliographical references.
ISBN 0-295-98156-3 (alk. paper)
1. Japanese Americans—Evacuation and relocation, 1942–1945.
2. World War, 1939–1945—Japanese Americans—Housing.
3. World War, 1939–1945—Concentration camps—United States.
4. Historic sites—United States.   I. Burton, Jeffery F.
II. Roosevelt, Eleanor, 1884–1962.   III. Cohen, Irene J.
D769.8.A6 C57 2001   940.54'7273—dc21   2001033288

The paper used in this publication is acid-free and recycled from 10 percent
post-consumer and at least 50 percent pre-consumer waste. It meets the
minimum requirements of American National Standard for Information
Sciences—Permanence of Paper for Printed Library Materials,
ANSI Z39.48-1984. ♾ ♺

This book is published
with the assistance of a grant from the
Scott and Laurie Oki Endowed Fund
for the publication of Asian American studies.

Abstract

This report provides an overview of the tangible remains currently left at the sites of the Japanese American internment during World War II. The main focus is on the War Relocation Authority's relocation centers, but Department of Justice and U.S. Army facilities where Japanese Americans were interned are also considered. The goal of the study has been to provide information for the National Landmark Theme Study called for in the Manzanar National Historic Site enabling legislation. Archival research, field visits, and interviews with former internees provide preliminary documentation about the architectural remnants, the archeological features, and the artifacts remaining at the sites. The degree of preservation varies tremendously. At some locations, modern development has obscured many traces of the World War II-era buildings and features. At a few sites, relocation center buildings still stand, and some are still in use. Overall the physical remains at all the sites are evocative of this very significant, if shameful, episode in U.S. history, and all appear to merit National Register of Historic Places or National Historic Landmark status.

強制収容と民族性
第二次世界大戦下の日系人強制収容所 概観

この報告書は、第二次世界大戦中の日系人強制収容所跡に現存する史料について、概観を試みるものです。
本書では、戦時転住局管轄の収容所を中心に、司法省や米陸軍管轄の収容施設にも光をあてていきます。
当調査研究は、マンザナ国定史跡の文化財指定を目指して、国定文化財委員会に資料を提供するために進められました。
建物跡や考古学的史料、史跡に残された物品については、古書、実地検証、体験者談話を補足資料として調査を行い
ました。保存の程度は実に様々です。第二次大戦当時の建造物跡は、近年の開発によってほとんど消滅している所も
あるかと思えば、現役で使用に耐えている場所もあるのです。収容所跡の物理的な遺物は全て、この重要かつ不面目な
米国史のひとコマを後世に伝える大切な史料であり、国定史跡登録 (National Register of Historic Places) または
国定文化財 (National Historic Landmark) の評価に値すると思われます。

Acknowledgments

As would be expected with a project taking nearly six years to complete, the authors are indebted to many. Three of the authors (Mary, Dick, and Flo) volunteered hundreds of hours of their time. Partial funding for the senior author was provided by Manzanar National Historic Site. The support, encouragement, and patience of former park superintendent Ross Hopkins is gratefully acknowledged. George Teague supervised the project. AutoCAD maps were prepared by Ron Beckwith. Uncredited photographs in the report were taken by the authors. Translations were furnished by James Honeychuck and Shoko Fujita-Ehrlich. The authors would also like to thank the following persons and institutions for their help and encouragement:

Tom Akashi
Joe Allman
Mary Blackburn
Jane Beckwith
Birt Bedeau
Tink Borum
James Bryant
Daniel Burton
Irene Cohen
John Collins
Roger Daniels
Craig Dorman
Phyllisa Eisentraut
John Ellington
Jim Erickson
Terry Hendricks
Gerald Gates
Jane Goldstein
Rosalie Gould
Elizabeth Greathouse
Farrell Hatch
Gary Hathaway
Dale Heckendorn
Gordon Hirabayashi
Taro Hirama
John Hopper
Mas Inoshita

Destry Jarvis
Kent Just
Tetsuden Kashima
Neil King
Erik Kreusch
Jim Kubota
Signa Larralde
Cliff Logan
Frank Makamura
Nathan Mayo
Bill Michaels
Jim McDonald
Lynne McDonald
Jean McDowell
Jim McKie
Angela Nava
Joe Norikane
Rose Ochi
John Pelton
Tom Pittman
Garth Portillo
Nicole Ramos
Mary Robertson
Raoul Roko
Roger Roper
Rusty Salmon
Yosh Shimoi

Thomas Shiratsuki
Ann King Smith
Kenji Taguma
Susumu Toyoda
Priscilla Wegars
Sue Wells
James West

Archaeological Research Services
Arizona Chapter JACL
Arizona Daily Star
Bancroft Library
Coronado National Forest
Crystal City Town Hall
Eastern California Museum
Franklin D. Roosevelt Library
Great Basin Museum
Heart Mountain Memorial
    Foundation
Kenedy Chamber of Commerce
Klamath National Wildlife
    Refuge
Lordsburg Information Center
Los Angeles County Fairplex
Los Angeles Times
Mack Alford Correctional
    Center

Manzanar Advisory
    Commission
Mayer Public Library
Museum of Northern Arizona
North Dakota State Historical
    Society
Prescott National Forest
Prescott Public Library
Puyallup Fair
Santa Anita Racetrack
Seattle Times
Sharlott Hall Museum
Topaz Museum Foundation
Trans-Sierran Archaeological
    Research
UCLA Special Collections
Tule Lake National Wildlife
    Refuge
Twin Falls Chamber of
    Commerce
United States National Archives
University of Arizona Special
    Collections
Yuba County Library

Contents

Foreword

Ethnicity and confinement—words that capture the essence of an epochal American tragedy that unfolded between 1942 and 1945. The United States then incarcerated behind barbed-wire fences almost an entire ethnic group living within its continental borders. Without formal charges, trials, findings made, or sentences passed, nearly 120,000 persons of Japanese ancestry were held in crude prison camps situated mainly in dusty and desolate areas of the United States. Places such as Manzanar, Tule Lake, Minidoka, Heart Mountain, Poston, Gila River, Topaz, Jerome, Granada, Rohwer, Camp Harmony, Santa Anita, and Tanforan are well known as World War II incarceration centers. In 1982 a congressional commission, after hearing testimony and examining the Japanese American and Aleut incarceration experiences, published its findings in the book *Personal Justice Denied.*[1] This influential report concluded that the root cause of the removal and incarceration was not military necessity, as the U.S. government had claimed, but a combination of racism, inadequate political leadership, and wartime hysteria. Partly as a result of the commission's work, subsequent congressional action led to a presidential apology with symbolic monetary redress given to each surviving person of Japanese ancestry and each Aleut affected by the presidential order (Executive Order 9066) that made the incarceration possible. The incarceration catastrophe is now recognized as an important epoch in U.S. history.

Before the publication of *Confinement and Ethnicity,* most studies of the removal and imprisonment of persons of Japanese ancestry in the United States during World War II focused on two types of incarceration camps: the fifteen holding areas called "assembly cen-

ters" (run by the U.S. Army's Wartime Civil Control Administration [WCCA]) and ten "relocation centers" (created by the War Relocation Authority [WRA]). Less well known are numerous internment camps created by the Justice and War Departments that coexisted with the WRA and WCCA camps and held seventeen thousand persons of Japanese ancestry. Between 1941 and 1947 each of these internment camps held from a few dozen to more than 1,500 such persons who had lived in Latin American countries, the territories of Hawaii and Alaska, and the contiguous United States. These internees were kept in places such as Crystal City, Seagoville, and Kenedy, Texas; Fort Stanton, Lordsburg, and Santa Fe, New Mexico; and Bismarck, North Dakota. The basic rationale for their internment was the 1798 Alien Enemies Act, by means of which the U.S. government confined designated nationals of countries with which it was at war. Besides persons of Japanese ancestry, some eleven thousand persons of German ancestry, three thousand of Italian ancestry, and two hundred "others"—for a combined total of nearly thirty-two thousand internees—were held by the Justice Department.

Earlier writings paid scant attention to these camps for several main reasons. First, the incarceration camps that received the most attention held more inmates, most of whom were American citizens. The abrogation of civil rights was obvious. Second, for decades after the war, official information and documents about the internment camps were difficult to obtain. Many U.S. agencies involved with the operation of such camps placed security classifications on their files, thereby hampering access to information. Only recently has it become possible to examine some of these materials. And third, former internees were reluctant to speak about their experiences. Only now, with the passage of time, has some of this reluctance waned.

Confinement and Ethnicity makes two significant contributions to the literature on the World War II imprisonment experience. First, it focuses attention on the previously neglected internment camps. Without acknowledgment of the existence, scope, and operation of these camps, documentation of the Japanese American World War II experience was incomplete. The second and more obvious contribution of this book is the unique visual perspective provided through tangible evidence of the camps' wartime conditions and use, and through photographs of present-day settings and landscapes. A pictorial record of this scope and breadth has never before been attempted; this comprehensive volume captures the camp experience in magnificent detail.

The significance of visual documentation will increase as the years pass and preservation of the camps' physical environment—both impressionistic and realistic—becomes more difficult. Time wreaks havoc on documents, photographs, and physical sites if they are not captured in some way or if they are left unprotected. The sites themselves continue to be changed by erosion, development, floods, malicious mischief, and removal of material by souvenir hunters. This volume preserves images of important pieces of the physical record that face inevitable disintegration.

What remains of the camps, which from 1941 to 1947 contained rows and rows of tar-paper shacks, guard towers, mess-halls, administrative buildings, and agricultural work-projects? It was reported in 1988 that at the site of the Manzanar WRA incarceration camp, in the foothills of California's Sierra Nevada, "Nothing remains . . . but a graveyard with a single bold monument; nothing remains of it but the memories of those who were detained there, some documents, some photographs, and a quest for justice as yet denied."[2] This may be figuratively true, but reminders of the confinement experience do exist at Manzanar and at virtually all of the camps that imprisoned persons of Japanese ancestry during those difficult and dark days. Such reminders are documented meticulously—often poignantly—in *Confinement and Ethnicity.*

A few earlier pictorial and artistic interpretations of the imprisonment experience are available, many of them of the WRA Manzanar camp. Although the WRA prohibited the taking of photographs by inmates, it did allow outside-media representatives restricted access to some individuals.[3] Photographers Dorothea Lange and Ansel Adams are known for their pictorial essays on this camp. The WRA hired Lange in April 1942 to photograph selected Japanese Americans before and during their expulsion from their homes and during their journey to the "assembly" center and to the Manzanar camp. Her portraits capture eloquently the injustices suffered by her subjects.[4] Adams entered Manzanar as a friend of the camp director in 1943. His stark portraits and images of perseverance under the dismal and difficult conditions at Manzanar record dramatically a key moment in time.[5]

This volume provides an expanded temporal view of the imprisonment experience and makes use of a variety of media: historical and new photographs; written descriptions of relics and structural remains; Japanese transliterations and English translations of writings on artifacts; analysis of relics; charts; maps; blueprints; and a contemporary written reflection, in the form of an essay by Eleanor Roosevelt. The section on the Manzanar center, for example, contains a few photographs by Lange and Adams as well as many other photographs, from numerous sources, that reflect utilitarian concerns rather than artistic ones. WRA documentary shots of undeveloped building sites as well as photographs of extant concrete foundations, fence posts, inmate-constructed drainage ditches, and foundations or parts of buildings provide a sense of the architectural setting. Other memorabilia emphasize the human dimension by documenting inmates' efforts to maintain a sense of selfhood, often with humor or with suppressed anger at the injustices they were forced to suffer. Inscriptions written on wet concrete during construction of the water reservoir read, "I Love Myself—Tommy Muraoka" and (in Japanese) "Peace." The other camps are treated in like fashion. Included are lesser-known WRA centers such as Moab, Utah; Leupp, Arizona; Cow Creek and Tulelake (separate from the Tule Lake camp), California; and Antelope Springs, Utah. Understanding the purpose of these latter centers helps us comprehend the entire WRA story.

Eight Department of Justice internment camps and four U.S. Army facilities that held mainly Japanese nationals and others virtually kidnapped from Latin American countries are included, along with prisons: Catalina Federal Honor Camp, Arizona; Leavenworth Federal Penitentiary, Kansas; and McNeil Island Federal Penitentiary, Washington. One learns here that the Catalina camp is now the Gordon Hirabayashi Recreation Site and that Japanese American resisters served prolonged prison terms for protesting their military draft and their parents' incarceration behind guarded fences. The material on internment camps and prisons alone is an important and unique contribution to the literature.

This landmark work is the culmination of prodigious research that has admirably accomplished the goals of the study: "[To] identify, evaluate, and nominate as national historic landmarks those sites, buildings, and structures that best illustrate or commemorate the period in American history from 1941 to 1946 when Japanese Americans were ordered to be detained, relocated, or excluded pursuant to Executive Order 9066, and other actions."[6] As of 2001, seven WRA centers and a Department of Justice camp are listed on the National Register of Historic Places and others are recognized as National Historic Landmarks or are identified with local historical markers. It is hoped that other sites will be so designated.

Confinement and Ethnicity is an invaluable resource. Visitors to World War II imprisonment sites can learn about what they see, and armchair travelers can view relics without making an arduous trek to each camp. Writers, scholars, students, artists, and descendants of those who were imprisoned will appreciate the images of camps during the war years and today.

In viewing *Confinement and Ethnicity* from a larger perspective, we see that it quietly but powerfully makes the point that this is not so much a Japanese American saga as it is an American story: the majority of those imprisoned were American citizens, the decisions to imprison them were made by other Americans, the imprisonment sites were located within the United States, and the U.S. government transferred persons of Japanese ancestry from other countries and confined them in the Americas. This larger context is vital to recall because the imprisonment experience is part of the warp and woof of U.S. race-relations history. As Gunnar Myrdal pointed out a half century ago, there exists in the United States an "American dilemma"—the intertwining of the nation's highest ideals of equality, liberty, and justice with a social reality based on perceived racial inequality.[7] Examination of this tragic era in our nation's history is necessary, not for purposes of self-mortification but rather to ensure that our eyes and actions move toward the highest principles. We can do this only by knowing the reality of our nation's past.

TETSUDEN KASHIMA
Seattle
October 2001

NOTES

1. Commission on Wartime Relocation and Internment of Civilians, *Personal Justice Denied* (Washington, D.C.: Government Printing Office, 1982; reprint, Seattle: University of Washington Press, 1997).

2. John Armor and Peter Wright, *Manzanar* (New York: Times Books, 1988: xv). Emphasis in the original.

3. Despite the WRA rule, exceptions were made. Toyo Miyatake, a professional photographer from Los Angeles incarcerated in the WRA Manzanar center, fashioned a homemade camera. He could set up a photographic shot but the actual picture had to be taken by a WRA official. Later he was allowed to click his own shutter. Photographs by camp residents are presented in Jack T. Yamaguchi, *This Was Minidoka* (Tacoma, Wash.: Pollard Printing Group, 1989); and Residents of the Minidoka Relocation Center, *Minidoka Interlude* (Hunt, Idaho: Residents of the Minidoka Relocation Center, 1943; reprint, Gresham, Ore.: T. Takeuchi, 1989).

4. See Ben Clarke, ed., *Image and Imagination: Encounters with the Photography of Dorothea Lange* (San Francisco: Freedom Voices, 1997); Maisie and Richard Conrat, *Executive Order 9066: The Internment of 110,000 Japanese Americans* (San Francisco: California Historical Society, 1972).

5. Ansel Adams, *Born Free and Equal* (New York: U.S. Camera, 1944); Armor and Wright, *Manzanar*. For a contemporary photographic essay, see Frank Iritani and Joanne Iritani, *Ten Visits: Brief Accounts of Visits to All Ten Japanese American Relocation Centers* (San Mateo, Calif.: Japanese American Curriculum Project, 1994) ; and the excellent volume by Gary Okihiro, with photographs by Joan Myers, *Whispered Silences: Japanese Americans and World War II* (Seattle: University of Washington Press, 1996).

6. U.S. Public Law 102-248, 102d Congress, 1st sess. (15 May 1991), 2.

7. Gunnar Myrdal, *An American Dilemma: The Negro Problem and Modern Democracy* (New York: Harper & Brothers, 1944).

Confinement and Ethnicity

Evacuee barracks at Tule Lake ca. 1943

(John D. Cook photograph, Bancroft Library, University of California, Berkeley)

Chapter 1

Sites of Shame
An Introduction

In 1942, almost 120,000 Japanese Americans were forced from their homes in California, western Oregon and Washington, and southern Arizona in the single largest forced relocation in U.S. history. Many would spend the next 3 years in one of ten "relocation centers" across the country run by the newly-formed War Relocation Authority (WRA). Others would be held in facilities run by the Department of Justice and the U.S. Army (Figure 1.1). Since all Japanese Americans on the west coast were affected, including the elderly, women, and children, Federal officials attempted to conduct the massive incarceration in a humane manner (Figure 1.2). However, by the time the last internees were released in 1946, the Japanese Americans had lost homes and businesses estimated to be worth, in 1999 values, 4 to 5 billion dollars. Deleterious effects on Japanese American individuals, their families, and their communities, were immeasurable.

During World War II the relocation was justified as a "military necessity." However, some 40 years later, the United States government conceded that the relocation was based on racial bias rather than on any true threat to national security. President Ronald Reagan signed the Civil Liberties Act of 1988 which provided redress for Japanese Americans. The following year President George Bush issued a formal apology from the U.S. government. Many histories describe the political, economic, legal, and social aspects of the relocation (see, for example CWRIC 1982, Daniels 1989; Daniels et al. 1991; Irons 1983, 1989; Spicer et al. 1969). This report, in contrast, provides an overview of the physical remains left at the sites of the Japanese American relocation. The main focus is on the architectural remnants, the archeological features, and the artifacts remaining at the relocation centers themselves, although other sites where Japanese Americans were held during World War II are also considered.

One of the relocation centers, Manzanar, was designated a National Historic Site in 1992 to "provide for the protection and interpretation

1

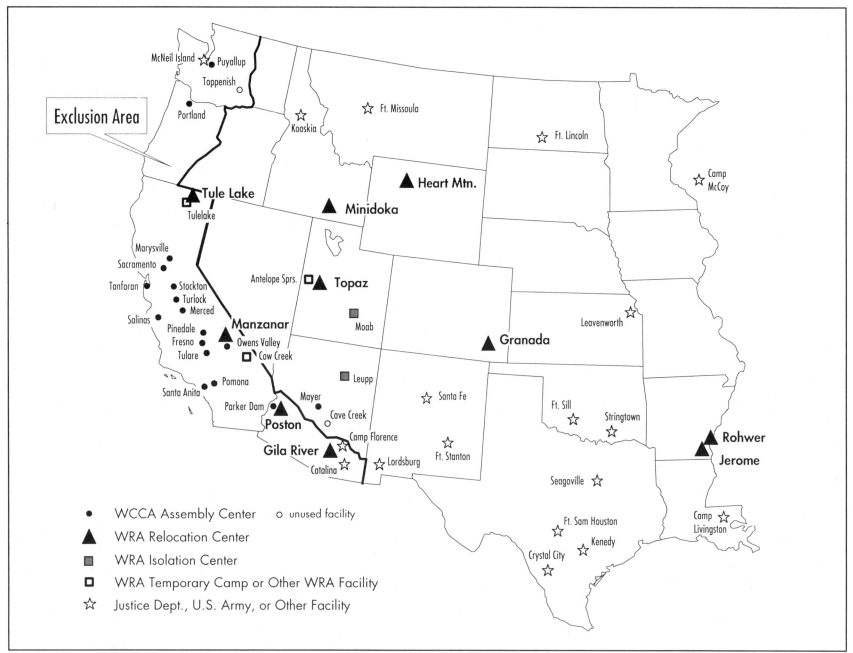

Figure 1.1. Sites in the western U.S. associated with the relocation of Japanese Americans during World War II.

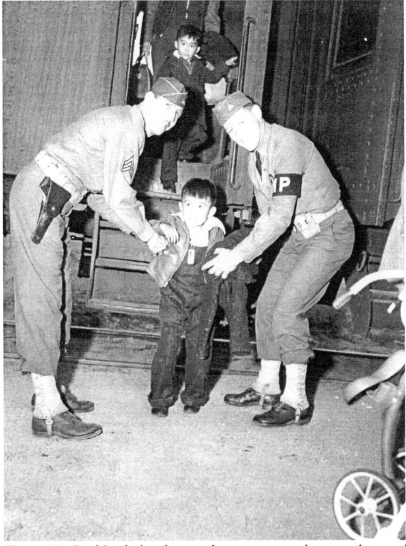

Figure 1.2. In this obviously posed government photograph armed military police lend a helping hand, Manzanar 1942 (National Archives photograph).

of historic, cultural, and natural resources associated with the relocation of Japanese Americans during World War II" (Public Law

102-248). But there are nine other relocation centers, and numerous other facilities associated with the relocation and internment. Most of the Japanese Americans were first sent to one of 17 temporary "Assembly Centers," where they awaited shipment to a more permanent relocation center. Most of those relocated were American citizens by birth. Many were long-term U.S. residents, but not citizens, because of discriminatory naturalization laws. Thousands of these "aliens" were interned in Department of Justice and U.S. Army facilities.

This report describes what is left at places where Japanese Americans were incarcerated during World War II, to the extent possible given the many facilities associated with the relocation. The present work is part of the National Landmark Theme Study called for in the Manzanar National Historic Site enabling legislation, to "...identify, evaluate, and nominate as national historic landmarks those sites, buildings, and structures that best illustrate or commemorate the period in American history from 1941 to 1946 when Japanese Americans were ordered to be detained, relocated, or excluded pursuant to Executive Order Number 9066, and other actions" (Public Law 102-248, March 3, 1992).

Methods included both archival research and field inspections, as well as informal interviews with former evacuees. Many primary sources were consulted, such as the relocation center newspapers (available on microfilm), blueprints and photographs from the National Archives, and materials in special collections at university libraries. Information was also solicited from federal land-managing agencies where sites associated with the relocation were located (the Bureau of Reclamation, the Bureau of Land Management, and the Forest Service), from State Historic Preservation Offices, and from the California Historic Resources Information System centers. USGS topographic maps, relevant archaeological reports, and National Register of Historic Places nominations were also consulted. Secondary sources used include a wealth of published books, articles, agency reports, and

Figure 1.3. Topaz Relocation Center in 1943 (National Archives photograph).

Figure 1.4. Site of the Topaz Relocation Center today.

unpublished manuscripts.

Field work included visits to all of the facilities run by the WCCA (Wartime Civilian Control Agency) and the WRA (War Relocation Authority) associated with the relocation, including relocation centers, isolation centers, and assembly centers. Many of the other sites where Japanese Americans were held that were run by the Department of Justice and the U.S. Army were visited as well. The current landscape was compared with old maps, blueprints, and photographs, to discover which of the existing features were present during the Japanese American internment (Figures 1.3 and 1.4).

The primary documentation for this project consists mostly of photographs, both color and black and white. Maps were prepared for features where access and time allowed. Former evacuees and local residents often provided useful information, and many times accompanied us in the field to point out and explain different features. Additional information was obtained from local museums and historical societies; many of these institutions have photographs, artifacts, documents, and even structures from the relocation centers. Chambers of Commerce and visitor information centers near the sites also provided tips on local resources.

The degree of preservation at the sites visited varied tremendously. At some, modern development has obscured most traces of the World War II-era buildings and features. Other sites have been protected by their isolation, or their location on undeveloped private or tribal lands. At a few sites relocation center buildings still stand, some abandoned and decrepit, but some still in use. Table 1.1 gives a general summary of the features remaining at each relocation center site; Table 1.2 lists the standing buildings and major structures present. Table 1.3 provides general information about the presence of features at each Assembly Center. Other facilities are considered in Table 1.4.

Figure 1.5. Hospital heating plant at the Heart Mountain Relocation Center.

Current Interpretation and Recognition

Six of the relocation centers and two other facilities (the Moab Isolation Center and the Fort Missoula Internment Camp) are listed on the National Register of Historic Places for their association with events that have made a significant contribution to the broad patterns of U.S. history (Criterion A) (Table 1.5). For Moab and Fort Missoula the relocation was only part of the significant historic association cited in their nominations. Although the relocation centers did not meet the minimum of 50 years age requirement at the time of listing, they were deemed to be of exceptional importance (Criterion G). The Manzanar Relocation Center and the memorial cemetery at the Rohwer Relocation Center also have National Historic Landmark status. All of the assembly centers in California are state historic landmarks.

All ten of the relocation centers have historical markers. These range from a single plaque at some of the sites to memorial parks at Heart Mountain and Rohwer.

At the Gila River Relocation Center there is a historical plaque at the site of Canal Camp and a historical plaque and memorial plaque at Butte Camp. However, access to the sites, which are on tribal land, is restricted. There are exhibits about the relocation center at the nearby tribal cultural center.

The Granada Relocation Center, also called Amache, has a recent memorial monument at the relocation cemetery. An interpretive drive and walk are planned. The site is now owned by the nearby town of Granada.

In the former administration area at the Heart Mountain Relocation Center there is a small memorial park which includes several plaques and the foundation of a mess hall chimney. To the north three buildings remaining from the relocation center hospital complex are still intact and may someday be used to house exhibits (Figure 1.5).

The central portion of the Jerome Relocation Center is owned by a single family who farms the land. There is a large historical marker along the highway at the site, placed with the landowners' permission.

Manzanar has a state of California historical marker, a National Landmark plaque, and a Blue Star Memorial Highway marker at the original relocation center entrance. The site is now administered by the National Park Service, which plans to rehabilitate the relocation center auditorium on site for use as an interpretative center. Other plans call for a loop tour road, outdoor interpretative displays, and a reconstructed barracks and watch tower.

Table 1.1. Summary of Relocation Center Features.

	Central Area													Security				Agriculture							Support Facilities							Interpretation				
	Administration/Staff	Warehouse/Factory/Garage	Hospital	Barracks	Police Station/Jail	Fire Station	High School	Other Schools	Churches	Sports Fields and Facilities	Ponds and Gardens	Victory Gardens	Trees and other Vegetation	Watch Towers	Sentry Post/Entrance	Perimeter Fence	Military Police Compound	Farm Kitchen	Chicken Farm	Turkey Farm	Hog Farm	Cattle Ranch/Dairy	Agricultural Fields	Irrigation Canals	Outlying Warehouse/Depot	Water Tank/Reservoir	Wells/Pumping Plant	Sewage Disposal	Landfill	Disposal Pits	Cemetery (on site)	Monument (historic)	Monument (recent)	Local Museum Exhibit	Directional Signs (highway)	Cemetery (relocated)
Gila River - Butte Camp	●	●	●	●		●	●	○	○		●		○		X				X		X	X	○	○		●		●	●			●	●	●		
Gila River - Canal Camp	●	●	●	●		●	○	○	○	○	●		○	X	X		●						○	○	○	○	●					●	●			
Granada	●	●	○	●		●	●	●	●	○	○	○		●	●	○	●	●	●	○		X	○	○	●	●	●	●	●	●	●	●	●			○
Heart Mountain	●	●	●	X	X		○	X	X	○	X	X	X	X	X	○	X		X		X		○	○		●	●	X			X	●	●	●	●	●
Jerome	○	○	●	X	X	X	X	X	X	X	X	X	X	X	X	○	X	X	X	X			○	○		●	●	●						●		
Manzanar	●	●	●	●	○	●	●	○	○	●	●	●	●	●	●	●	○		●		●		●	●	○	●	●	●	●	●	●	●	●	●	●	
Minidoka	●	●	X	X	X	●	X	X	X	X	○	X	○	X	●	○	○	○	X		X		○	●	○	●	○	○	○	○	○	●	●	○	X	X
Poston 1	●	○	X	X	X	X	○	●	X	X	X		●		X		○	X		X			○	○	●	X	○	●				●	●	●		
Poston 2	○	○		X	X	X	X	X	X	X	X	X							X				○	○	X		●							●		
Poston 3	X	X		X	X	X	X	X	X	X	X		X						X				○	○	X		●							●		
Rohwer	○	○	●	○		●	X	X	X	X	X		X	X	X	○	X						○	○		●	●	●				●	●	●		●
Topaz	●	●	●	●	●	○	●	●	○	●	○	○	○	●	X	○	○	●	●	●	●	●	○	○	○	○						●	●	●		
Tule Lake	●	●	○	○	●	X	○	X	X		X			X	○	○	●	●	●	●	○		●		○	○	●	●	●	●	○	X	●	○	●	●

● = substantial remains (standing buildings, foundations, and other features); ○ = minor remains (foundations and other features); X = no remains (destroyed or buried); shaded box = not applicable; empty box = no information.

Table 1.2. Standing Buildings and Major Structures Remaining at Relocation Centers.

Gila River – Butte
Honor Roll Monument
Sewage Treatment Plant

Gila River – Canal
Sewage Treatment Plant

Granada
Cemetery Monument
Outlying Farm Buildings (pre-WRA construction, most still in use)
Co-op Store Storage Room
Water Tank

Heart Mountain
Honor Roll Monument
Hospital Boiler Room
Hospital Mess
Hospital Warehouse
Reservoir
Root Cellar
High School Storage Room
Staff Apartment

Jerome
Hospital Smokestack
Sewage Treatment Plant
Water Tank

Manzanar
Auditorium (still in use)
Cemetery Monument
MP Police and Internal Police Sentry Posts
Reservoir
Sewage Treatment Plant

Minidoka
Fire Station (still in use)
Garage (½, still in use)
Irrigation Canal Drops (numerous still in use)
Root Cellar
Sentry Post and Waiting Room at Entrance
Staff Apartment (2, relocated on site, still in use)

Poston I
Auditorium and Classrooms
Garage/Shop (still in use)
Sewage Treatment Plant

Poston II
Sewage Treatment Plant
Hospital Building (relocated on site, still in use)

Poston III
Sewage Treatment Plant

Rohwer
Cemetery Monuments, Headstones, and landscaping
Hospital Smokestack
Sewage Treatment Plant
Water Tank

Topaz
Outlying Farm Buildings (most are pre-WRA construction, some still in use)

Tule Lake
Farm Kitchen
Stockade Jail
Military Police, Administration, and Staff Buildings (numerous still in use)
Sewage Treatment Plants (2)
Warehouses (several still in use)

Table 1.3. Summary of Features at Other WRA Facilities and Assembly Centers.

	WRA					Assembly Centers (WCCA)														
	Antelope Springs	Cow Creek	Leupp	Moab	Tule Lake	Fresno	Marysville	Mayer	Merced	Pinedale	Pomona	Portland	Puyallup	Sacramento	Salinas	Santa Anita	Stockton	Tanforan	Tulare	Turlock
Pre-WW II Construction	●	●	●	●	●	?	?	X		X	●	●	●	?	●	●	?	X	●	●
WW II-era Construction	?	shaded	?		○	○	shaded		X	○	X	X	?	X	X	X	X	X	X	X
Dump or Scattered Artifacts	○			○			●													
Historical Marker				●					●		●	●	●	●		●	●			
Garden, Ramada, or Sculpture													●	●	●					
Local Museum Exhibit				●																

● = substantial (standing buildings, foundations, or other features); ○ = minor (foundations or other features); ? = possible (unknown); X = none (destroyed or buried); shaded box = not applicable; empty box = no information.

Table 1.4. Summary of Features at Justice Department, U.S. Army, and Prison Facilities.

	Justice Department								U.S. Army												Prisons		
	Crystal City	Kenedy	Kooskia	Fort Lincoln	Fort Missoula	Fort Stanton	Santa Fe	Seagoville	Camp Florence	Camp Forrest	Camp Livingston	Camp Lordsburg	Camp McCoy	Fort Meade	Fort Richardson	Fort Sam Houston	Fort Sill	Honouiuli	Sand Island	Stringtown	Catalina	Leavenworth	McNeil Island
Pre-WW II Construction	X	X	○	●	●		X	●									●			●	○	●	●
WW II-era Construction	●	○					X					●											
Historical Marker	●	●			●		A														B		
Local Museum Exhibit					●																		

● = substantial (standing buildings, foundations, or other features); ○ = minor (foundations or other features); A = under consideration; B = under construction; X = none (destroyed or buried); shaded box = not applicable; empty box = no information.

Table 1.5. Sites Associated with the Relocation of Japanese Americans During World War II Listed on the National Register of Historic Places.

Site	Date Listed
Ft Missoula Internment Center	April 29, 1987
Granada Relocation Center	May 18, 1994
Heart Mtn Relocation Center	December 19, 1985
Manzanar Relocation Center	July 30, 1976
Minidoka Relocation Center	July 10, 1979
Moab Isolation Center	May 2, 1994
Rohwer Relocation Center	July 30, 1974
Topaz Relocation Center	January 2, 1974

Figure 1.6. Elementary school auditorium at the Poston Relocation Center.

At the entrance to the Minidoka Relocation Center there are several plaques. A museum at the nearby town of Jerome has an interpretive exhibit and plans are underway for a more extensive exhibit in a former barracks at a different museum location.

Along the highway at the site of the Poston Relocation Center there is a large memorial monument and an information kiosk with interpretative displays. Just northwest of the monument there is an adobe-walled auditorium and other buildings left from the relocation center. The auditorium building, built by the Japanese American residents, is in disrepair, but in general retains substantial architectural integrity and is relatively accessible, suggesting it could make an excellent interpretative center (Figure 1.6).

At the Rohwer Relocation Center cemetery is a recent historic monument and a National Landmark plaque. The cemetery also includes two large monuments built during the relocation, as well as numerous graves (Figure 1.7).

At the Topaz Relocation Center there is a parking area and a large historical monument. In the nearby town of Delta there is another monument with directional information, and the local museum has brought in and rehabilitated a barracks, which it uses to display artifacts and information about the relocation center.

At the Tule Lake Relocation center there is an ornate rock and concrete pedestal and wall built to display a state of California historical marker. Numerous buildings from the relocation center remain at the site, including the infamous stockade jail, located just north of the historical marker.

Figure 1.7. Memorial park at the Rohwer Relocation Center.

Two other facilities used by the WRA are interpreted for the public. Use of the Dalton Springs CCC Camp as an isolation center is mentioned in a museum exhibit in the nearby town of Moab and a historical marker was placed at the site in 1995. The temporary use of the Cow Creek CCC Camp at Death Valley National Park is the subject of interpretive talks and a booklet sold at the Park visitor center.

Seven of the WCCA assembly centers have commemorative markers on site. One also has a fenced memorial garden (Salinas), one has a ramada (Figure 1.8; Sacramento), and one has a sculpture (Puyallup).

Two of the Department of Justice internment camps, Crystal City and Fort Missoula, have commemorative markers on site. At Fort Missoula one of the original internment barracks has been returned to the site and will be used to house interpretive displays about the internment (Figure 1.9). The internment camp at Kenedy is mentioned on a

Figure 1.8. Historical marker and ramada at the site of the Sacramento Assembly Center.

Figure 1.9. Reconstructed barracks on the grounds of the Fort Missoula History Museum.

historical marker located in downtown Kenedy. In addition to these three sites, efforts are presently underway to place a marker at the Santa Fe Internment Camp. None of the U.S. Army facilities that held Japanese Americans have plaques.

Of the three Federal prisons that held Japanese American during World War II, two are still being used as prisons. The third is located on U.S. Forest Service land (Catalina Federal Honor Camp) and was abandoned in the 1970s. The site is now a Forest Service recreation site named in honor of Dr. Gordon Hirabayashi, one of the most famous figures associated with the prison and the Japanese American relocation. Future plans for the campground include interpretative signs or brochures about the Japanese American relocation experience, as well as that of Hopi Indians, Jehovah's Witnesses, and others who were sent to the prison for their beliefs.

Remnants of Architecture and Archeology

Beyond the monuments, many of the facilities associated with the relocation are intact, from an archeological standpoint. That is, although most buildings have been removed or destroyed, there remains a wide range of artifacts and features which evoke the distinct aspects of confinement and ethnicity. Other remaining features, such as hospitals, schools, and sewage treatment plants, reflect the requirements of a large concentration of people in previously sparsely populated areas (Figure 1.10).

The most abundant archeological remains were noted at the relocation centers and other sites used by the WRA. Continued use of many of the other facilities has erased most evidence of their former use. The best examples of these are those that were abandoned soon after World War II. These include the Department of Justice camps at Crystal City and Fort Missoula, and the U.S. Army internment camp at Lordsburg (Figure 1.11).

Of the assembly centers the most significant archeological remains discovered were those of an eroding dump at Marysville. Of the three Federal prisons, two are still in use and retain much of their original character. Numerous foundations and other features remain at the abandoned Catalina Federal Honor Camp (Figure 1.12).

Remnants of watchtowers and fences are visible at several of the relocation center sites. At Manzanar five of eight watchtower foundations are still in place, and recent archaeological work has revealed evidence of the remaining three. All the watchtower foundations at Granada and Topaz are still visible in their original locations (Figure 1.13); at Tule Lake some are in place and some have been pulled out of the ground and left nearby. At Jerome, watchtower foundation remnants can be seen discarded in a ditch.

Figure 1.10. Hospital smokestack at the Jerome Relocation Center.

At the other camps, watchtower foundations have been removed or possibly buried by sediments. At one of the former Department of Justice facilities (Fort Missoula) portions of two guard towers have been preserved and are on display.

Stone sentry posts are still standing at the entrances to Manzanar and Minidoka (Figure 1.14); the less-substantial sentry posts at the other camps have not survived. Perimeter fences at Manzanar and Granada are still mostly intact, with many of the original fence posts of the 5-foot high, five-strand barbed wire fences still in place. At Manzanar, the top and bottom strands of barbed wire have been removed for its current role as a range fence. Heart Mountain, Minidoka, Rohwer, and Topaz retain some sections of perimeter fence; of these Heart Mountain's is the most substantial, with an added top section. Portions of the 6-foot-high chain link and barbed wire fence that was constructed when the Tule Lake Relocation Center was converted to a Segregation Center are still intact. None of the other sites investigated had evidence of their former security fences.

The effectiveness of the perimeter fences at the relocation centers can be seen in the artifact distribution: all trash at most of the relocation centers was disposed of in centralized trash dumps. The only exception was the unfenced Gila River Relocation Center in Arizona, where small trash scatters outside the central area of the relocation center are as abundant as at any contemporary town.

One of the most conspicuous symbols of the internment still remaining is the jail constructed for the Tule Lake Segregation Center (Figure 1.15). Of durable concrete, the jail stands abandoned within a highway maintenance yard, a visible reminder of the heightened security at Tule Lake. Tule Lake also has evidence of the largest and most substantial military police compound, with many of its buildings still standing. Six other relocation centers have foundations and other features remaining from their associated military police compounds,

Figure 1.11. Remains at the site of the Lordsburg Internment Center.

Figure 1.12. Rock and concrete steps in the staff housing area at the Catalina Federal Honor Camp.

Figure 1.13. Watch tower foundation blocks at the Granada Relocation Center.

Figure 1.14. Sentry post and waiting room at the entrance to the Minidoka Relocation Center.

with the Gila River and Granada relocation centers retaining the most features and suffering the least disturbance.

Confinement was not, however, absolute. Evacuees at most of the relocation centers were allowed to leave the fenced areas to work in the center farms, to collect landscaping materials, or even to recreate. Evidence of some of these outlying facilities remains. For example, some of the relocation center farm buildings at Topaz and Granada are still standing; features remain at a CCC camp used by evacuees at the Topaz relocation center (Antelope Springs); and some picnic features are located outside the fenced central area at Manzanar. Evacuees at Tule Lake (probably before it was converted to a segregation center) visited a nearby prehistoric rock art site at Lava Beds National Monument, and chiseled their names into the cliff faces and neighboring boulders.

The WRA and even some within the Japanese American community hoped the evacuation, removal, detention, and eventual relocation would further acculturation with white America (e.g. Masaoka 1944). However, confinement may have had the opposite effect. Although the Japanese language was banned or proscribed in the centers, Japanese writing can be seen both in concrete features in outlying areas and in more public areas. At Manzanar, Japanese writing in concrete is most common outside the fenced central area. Possibly it was harder to circumvent the ban on Japanese writing under the closer scrutiny of camp confines. The ban did not apply to the dead: memorials at the cemeteries at Manzanar, Rowher, and Granada contain Japanese writing, as did headstones at Tule Lake and Heart Mountain (Figure 1.16).

Even though the Japanese Americans were imprisoned because of their ethnic background, they did not hide their Japanese heritage: ceramics include numerous rice bowls, tea cups, and other "Made In Japan" objects in the trash dumps at most of the facilities where such deposits

Figure 1.15. Jail at the Tule Lake Relocation Center.

Figure 1.16. Cemetery monument at the Manzanar Relocation Center.

were found. At Manzanar, fragments of saki bottles and "Go" gaming pieces were found during archaeological testing, and faint traces of Japanese baths were noted at a few latrine slabs (Burton 1993).

Evacuee-constructed features, such as landscaping, gardens, ponds, and irrigation systems, also reflect the Japanese heritage (Figure 1.17). Remnants of these features are most evident at the Manzanar and Gila River relocations centers, but historical photographs indicate they were common at the other relocation centers as well. The Judo house at Manzanar and the Sumo wrestling arena at Gila River also indicate the maintenance of traditional Japanese culture. As mentioned above, at Granada, Heart Mountain, Manzanar, Rohwer, and Tule Lake, the cemetery monuments and grave stones have prominent Japanese inscriptions. Even the evacuee-constructed sentry buildings at Manzanar and Minidoka show a distinct Japanese influence. However, evacuees also constructed facilities that could be considered typically "American:" at Gila River, Manzanar, and Topaz there is still evidence of the baseball fields that played an important role in evacuee life.

Interestingly, there are fewer archaeological correlates of ethnicity at the Tule Lake Segregation Center, the isolation centers, and internment camps where the supposedly "more Japanese" Japanese Americans were held. This probably reflects the tighter security and control at these camps: perceived troublemakers were not allowed to bring their dishes or other comforts of home and were not likely to be allowed outside the camps to collect landscaping materials.

Comparing the remaining features of the relocation centers raises questions. For example, why do landscaping features such as ponds and walkways seem more substantial at Gila River and Manzanar than the other relocation centers? Did the evacuees who built ponds at these centers feel a relatively greater sense of permanence that encouraged their efforts to beautify their bleak surroundings with landscaping? Was Japanese landscaping a symbolic form of resistance?

Even between Manzanar and Gila River there are suggestive differences in landscaping. At Manzanar, there are large gardens associated with most of the communal mess halls. At Gila River, most ponds and landscaping appears to be associated with single barracks, rather than whole blocks. Do the large gardens at Manzanar reflect an usually high degree of cohesiveness? Many of the evacuees at Manzanar came from geographically restricted areas such as Terminal Island or other Los Angeles neighborhoods, where they had been neighbors before the relocation.

Many of the relocation centers have substantial archaeological remains and the potential for buried features. Overall, the physical remains at all the sites are evocative of this very significant, if shameful, episode in U.S. history. Each appears to have intrinsic historic value, meriting National Register or National Landmark status. Certainly all of the sites associated with the Japanese American relocation are eligible for the National Register under criterion A (associated with events that have made a significant contribution to U.S. history). Many would also be eligible under criterion D (data potential): the Marysville Assembly Center, the Leupp and Moab isolation centers, the Crystal City, Lordsburg, and Kooskia internment camps, the Catalina Federal Honor Camp, and all of the relocation centers except possibly Jerome.

In addition, all of the sites associated with the relocation may be eligible for the National Register of Historic Places as traditional cultural properties. They continue to serve an important function in the Japanese American community: they are visited regularly by former evacuees, their families and supporters, and members of the civil rights community, in formal reunions and pilgrimages. These events, along with less formal, smaller group visits, serve as springboards for community discourse about the internment and Japanese American history, in particular, and about the struggle for civil rights and fairness and justice in the United States' multi-cultural society, in general.

Figure 1.17. Small concrete pond at the Gila River Relocation Center.

Of the relocation centers only Jerome lacks the high degree of integrity required for National Landmark designation. Particularly noteworthy for Landmark status are the stockade jail and possibly other features at Tule Lake, the school auditorium at Poston I, the remaining hospital buildings and administration area at Heart Mountain, the sentry post, waiting room, and other features at Minidoka, and the entire sites of Gila River, Granada, and Topaz.

Of the assembly centers, the Santa Anita Racetrack retains the most integrity. Still present are the horse stables that were used for internee housing, the grandstand that was used for bachelor housing and camouflage net production, and other buildings (such as the one used as the hospital). National Landmark status seems warranted for this site: in addition to having the best remaining features, it was the longest occupied assembly center, housed the greatest number of internees, and is arguably the most well-known.

The Moab and Leupp isolation centers, the Crystal City, Lordsburg, Fort Lincoln, and Fort Missoula internment camps, and the Catalina Federal Honor Camp also merit National Landmark status because each of these sites still include significant features that tell a critical part of the relocation story.

Report Structure
In this report Chapter 2 is a first-hand contemporary report of one relocation center by an outside observer: Eleanor Roosevelt visited the Gila Relocation Center in 1943 to investigate charges that the evacuees were being "coddled." Roosevelt, whether by design or chance, did happen to visit the relocation center with slightly more substantial construction than most, but could not find any evidence of coddling. Chapter 3 is a brief overview of the history of the relocation and internment. Chapters 4 through 13 summarize the individual history at each relocation center, the physical layout, and the current condition and access. Chapter 14 discusses the Moab and Leupp

Isolation Centers; Chapter 15 describes other temporary facilities operated by the War Relocation Authority. Chapter 16 describes the assembly centers. Chapter 17 describes Department of Justice and U.S. Army internment camps where non-citizen Japanese Americans were held. Chapter 18 discusses three Federal prisons where a few hundred Japanese American citizens were incarcerated for protesting the relocation.

Terminology
The War Relocation Authority used euphemisms such as "relocation center" and "evacuees." The relocation centers certainly fit the dictionary definition of a concentration camp and use of that term for the relocation centers has many historical precedents (Uyeda 1995:57). However, the term "concentration camp" has since become almost synonymous with Nazi death camps. Even the use of the relatively benign term "internees" in reference to Japanese Americans has resulted in controversy (e.g., Baker 1994:23-24). When discussing the relocation centers this report to a great extent uses the terminology originally coined by the War Relocation Authority. In this we follow the use of the terms used by the National Park Service in its interpretation at Manzanar National Historic Site (Manzanar Committee 1998:iii-iv). The terms are not presumed to be an accurate definition of the events, attitudes, or facts of the relocation. They are used because they are most common in the historical records and may reflect the contemporary subjective context.

Chapter 2

To Undo a Mistake is Always Harder Than Not to Create One Originally

Eleanor Roosevelt

This essay is a draft of an article that had been written for Collier's Magazine by Eleanor Roosevelt. Mrs. Roosevelt visited the Gila River Relocation Center in Arizona in 1943 in response to charges that the Japanese American evacuees there were being "coddled" (Figures 2.1 and 2.2). The manuscript, courtesy of the Franklin D. Roosevelt Library (Hyde Park, New York), was published in a revised form October 10, 1943. It is reproduced here from the original draft with only minor editorial changes.

We are at war with Japan, and yet we have American citizens, born and brought up in this country whose parents are Japanese. This is the essential problem. A good deal has already been written about it. One phase, however, I do not think as yet has been adequately stressed. To really cover it, we must get the background straight first.

In this nation of over one hundred and thirty million, we have 127,500 Japanese or Japanese Americans. Those who have lived for a long time in the Midwest or in the east and who have had their records checked by the FBI, have been allowed to go on about their business, whatever it may be, unmolested. The recent order removing aliens from strategic areas, of course, affects those who were not citizens, just as it affects other citizens, however.

112,000 Japanese of the total 127,500 lived on the West Coast. Originally they were much needed on ranches, and on large truck and fruit farms, but as they came in greater numbers, people began to discover that they were not only convenient workers, they were competitors in the labor field, and the people of California began to be afraid of their own importation, so the Exclusion Act was passed in 1917. No people of the Oriental race could become citizens of the United States, and no quota was given to the Oriental nations in the Pacific. They were marked as different from other races and they were not treated on an equal basis. This happened because in one part of our country they were feared as competitors, and the rest of our country knew them so little and cared so little about them that they did not even think about the principle that we in this country believe in – that of equal rights for all human beings.

We granted no citizenship to Orientals, so now we have a group of people, some of whom have been here as long as fifty years who have not been able to become citizens under our laws. Long before the war, an old Japanese man told me that he had great grand-children born in this country and that he had never been back to Japan, all that he cared about was here on the soil of the United States, and yet he could not become a citizen.

The children of the Japanese born in this country, however, were citizens automatically and now we have about 42,500 native born Japanese who are known as Issei, and about 85,000 native born Japanese American citizens, known as Nisei. Some of these Japanese Americans have gone to our American schools and colleges and have never known any other country or any other life than the life here in the United States. Sometimes their parents have brought them up, as far as family life is concerned, in the old Japanese family tradition. Age has its privileges and the respect that is due the elders in a family is strongly emphasized in Oriental life. So for a young Japanese American to go against his parents is more serious than for other children. As a rule in the United States we do not lay undue emphasis upon the control of the older members of the family, or the respect and obedience that is due to mere age.

This large group of Japanese on the West Coast preserved those family traditions, because since they were feared they were also discriminated against. Japanese were not always welcome buyers of real estate. They were not always welcome neighbors, or participators in community undertakings. As always happens with groups that are discriminated against, they gather together and live among their own racial group. The younger ones made friends in school and college and became a part of the community life, and prejudices lessened against them. Their elders were not always sympathetic to the changes thus brought about in manners and customs.

Figure 2.1. Mrs. Eleanor Roosevelt, accompanied by WRA National Director Dillon S. Myer, visits the Gila River Relocation Center (WRA photograph, Bancroft Library, University of California, Berkeley).

There is another group in this number of American born Japanese called the Kibei. The parents of this group had kept complete loyalty to Japan and some of them were acting as agents of that government in this country. Some of them longed for the day when they could return and live at home in Japan, so they sent their children, born in this country, back to Japan for their education. Some of these young people returned to this country in 1938 and 1939. They saw war coming in Japan and apparently were not loyal enough to Japan to want to go to war on the Japanese side, and neither did they have enough loyalty to the United States, since they did not grow up here, to serve this country. They form a group which is given scant respect either by their elders who are loyal to Japan or from the Japanese who are loyal to the United States.

Enough for the background. Now we come to Pearl Harbor, December 7, 1941. We see the problems which faced the Pacific coast from this date on. There was no time to investigate families, or to adhere strictly to the American rule that a man is innocent until he is proven guilty. These people were not convicted of any crime, but emotions ran too high, too many people wanted to reek vengeance on Oriental-looking people. Even the Chinese, our Allies, were not always safe on the streets. A few of the Japanese had long been watched by the FBI and were apprehended on the outbreak of war and taken into custody.

In an effort to live up to the American idea of justice as far as possible, the Army laid down the rules for what they considered the safety of our West Coast. They demanded and they supervised the evacuation. A civil authority was set up, the War Relocation Authority, to establish permanent camps and take over the custody and maintenance of these people, both for their own safety and for the safety of the country.

To many young people this must have seemed strange treatment of American citizens, and one cannot be surprised at the reaction which manifests itself not only in young Japanese American, but in others who had known them well and been educated with them, and who bitterly ask: "What price American citizenship?"

Figure 2.2. Representatives of Councils greet Mrs. Roosevelt, Gila River Relocation Center (WRA photograph, Bancroft Library, University of California, Berkeley).

Nevertheless most of them recognized the fact that this was a safety measure. The army carried out its evacuation on the whole with remarkable skill and kindness. The early situation in the camps was difficult. They were not ready for occupation. Sufficient water was not available, food was slow in arriving. The setting up of large communities meant an amount of organization which takes time, but the Japanese proved to be patient, adaptable and courageous for the most part.

Many difficulties have had to be met, but the War Relocation Authority and the Japanese themselves have coped with these remarkably well. There were unexpected problems and one by one these were discovered and an effort made to deal with them fairly. For instance, these people had property they had to dispose of, often at a loss. Sometimes they could not dispose of it and it remained unprotected, so as the months go by it is deteriorating in value. Some business difficulties have arisen which had to be handled through agents, since the Japanese could not leave the camps.

In reading the various accounts which have been written it struck me that practically no one has recognized what a tremendous variety of things the War Relocation Authority has had to develop to meet the innumerable problems created by the removal of a great group of people from one small section of the country and their temporary location in other parts of the country. When I read the accusations against the Authority for acquiring quantities of canned goods, and laying in stocks of food, I realized there was a lack of understanding of one basic fact, namely, that government authorities such as this have to live up to the law, and if it is the law of the land that we are rationed, we are rationed everywhere – in prisons, in hospitals, in camps, wherever we may be, individuals are rationed and even the War Relocation Authority cannot buy more than is allowed for the number of people they have to feed.

The Armed Services in camp here in this country are probably exempt, but even they are now being put on short rations and I have had many complaints from boys that they were given field rations, which probably comes nearer to approximating the civilian ration. It is logical that in the Armed Forces, men who are undergoing training, physical and mental, should require more food that the civilian population. It is for that reason that civilian goods grow scarcer and we accept rationing in a desire to see that all civilian goods are more equitably distributed to all of us.

But no government authority dealing with civilians is free from the laws of the country as a whole. I think that is something that should be borne in mind when we read attacks as to the manner in which the relocation camps are run, and then see the government officials obliged to deny or explain how they happened to have a certain amount of this or that on hand. If you have a city of 14,000 people living in a camp such as the one I went to in Arizona, even in these days, you have to have more on hand than the average small community (Figures 2.3-2.5).

In these transplanted communities, schools have had to be established, hospitals have had to be equipped and manned. At Gila, the land is rented from the Indian Reservation and no special buildings could be erected to accommodate either schools or hospitals. The buildings are just barrack buildings, adapted as well as human ingenuity can do it, to the needs for which they are used. Those of us who are familiar with the type of migratory labor camp which was gradually developed in different parts of the country during the past few years will understand what these relocation camps are like. They have certain familiar arrangements, such as a central washing unit for laundry and for personal cleanliness, and a central mess hall where the people gather for their meals. These are located in every barrack block containing about two hundred and fifty people.

The day I was at Gila there was no butter and no sugar on the tables. The food was rice and fish and greens. There was some milk for the children and some kind of pudding on the table. Neither in the stockrooms, or on the tables did I notice any kind of extravagance.

Except for the head doctor in the hospital who was an American, the other doctors are Japanese. One had been a surgeon and had had a large Caucasian practice, he is now earning $19.00 a month, the standard pay for all work except for those who are working under Army or Navy contracts.

Ingenuity has been used in the schools. The class in typing only had two typewriters, so they worked out a key-board of card board with holes for the keys and on this the class prac-

Figure 2.3. Residential area at the Gila River Relocation Center (WRA photograph, Bancroft Library, University of California, Berkeley).

ticed. The typewriters were rationed, ten minutes use a day to each member of the class.

In the nursery school the toys were quite obviously homemade, and the children stretched out on the floor for their midday rest, with little makeshift covers under them which they folded up when the rest period was over.

Contractors, building army camps or any other type of camp, apparently level off the land in the quickest possible way, taking out any tree or any bush that may stand in the way of their building operations. The desert has few trees, but the scrub growth which usually holds down the land to a certain extent is completely removed around the camps I have seen. This makes a high wind a pretty disagreeable experience as you are enveloped in dust. It chokes you and brings about irritations of the nose and throat and here in this climate where people go to recover from respiratory ailments, you will find quite a number of hospitals around the camps, both military and non-military, with patients suffering from the irritations that the swirling dust cannot fail to bring.

Around the barrack buildings at Gila, a great effort has been made to ameliorate this condition by using scrap lumber and burlap bags for makeshift porches and awnings. They are now getting screens for protection against the insects. They have made small gardens, some with vegetables and some with flowers and shrubs from the surrounding desert, to beautify the barren streets.

At Gila there is a big farm where the Japanese who worked on the land, but perhaps grew

Figure 2.4. Buddhist Church at the Gila River Relocation Center (WRA photograph, Bancroft Library, University of California, Berkeley).

only one type of vegetable, are now learning to cultivate as a complete farm enterprise and they care for cattle, chickens and grow a variety of foodstuffs. If some are never able to go back to the West Coast, they will be better able to learn a living on a general farm. Others work in various activities necessary to the life of the community. Since the formation of a Japanese division in the Army, it has been possible for Japanese American young men who have been checked and found loyal to the United States to volunteer for this division, and many of the Japanese American girls asked me if they would have an opportunity to serve in the same way in the Auxiliary Military Services.

Under the living conditions which exist in these camps it is natural that some of the most difficult problems faced are problems of morality. This is neither strange nor new, since overcrowding and restraint of free and normal living always bring up such problems, but crimes of violence or of theft have been remarkably low. A small force of Japanese policemen does the policing of the camps and has apparently few difficulties with which to contend.

We can be grateful that everyone has work, for work is a great panacea in all difficult human relationships.

There is perhaps a higher percentage of people with college degrees here than in the average community of the same size. They are taken from every background and yet must work in unfamiliar occupations, and one can realize that the close living quarters must create great problems.

I can well understand the bitterness of people who have lost loved ones at the hands of the

Japanese military authorities, and we know that the totalitarian philosophy, whether it is in Nazi Germany or Fascist Italy or in Japan, is one of cruelty and brutality. It is not hard to understand why people living here in hourly anxiety for those they love have difficulty in viewing this problem objectively, but for the honor of our country the rest of us must do so. These understandable feelings are aggravated by the old time economic fear on the West Coast and the unreasoning racial feeling which certain people, through ignorance, have always had wherever they came in contact with people who are different from themselves. This is one reason why many people believe that we should have directed our original immigration more intelligently. We needed people to develop our country, but we should never have allowed any groups to settle as groups where they created a little German or Japanese or Scandinavian island and did not melt into our general community pattern. Some of the South American countries have learned from our mistakes and are now planning to scatter their needed immigration.

To undo a mistake is always harder than not to create one originally but we seldom have the foresight. Therefore we have no choice but to try to correct our past mistakes and I hope that the recommendations of the staff of the War Relocation Authority, who have come to know individually most of the Japanese Americans in these various camps, will be accepted. Little by little as they are checked, Japanese Americans are being allowed on request to leave the camps and start independent and productive lives again. Whether you are a taxpayer

Figure 2.5. Group of Japanese American children at the Gila River Relocation Center, August 1943 (National Archives photograph).

in California or in Maine, it is to your advantage, if you find one or two Japanese American families settled in your neighborhood, to try to regard them as individuals and not to condemn them before they are given a fair chance to prove themselves in the community.

"A Japanese is always a Japanese" is an easily accepted phrase and it has taken hold quite naturally on the West Coast because of fear, but it leads nowhere and solves nothing. A Japanese American may be no more Japanese than a German-American is German, or an Italian-American is Italian, or of any other national background. All of these people, including the Japanese Americans, have men who are fighting today for the preservation of the democratic way of life and the ideas around which our nation was built.

We have no common race in this country, but we have an ideal to which all of us are loyal: we cannot progress if we look down upon any group of people amongst us because of race or religion. Every citizen in this country has a right to our basic freedoms, to justice and to equality of opportunity. We retain the right to lead our individual lives as we please, but we can only do so if we grant to others the freedoms that we wish for ourselves.

Chapter 3

A Brief History of Japanese American Relocation During World War II

On December 7, 1941, the United States entered World War II when Japan attacked the U.S. naval base at Pearl Harbor. At that time, nearly 113,000 people of Japanese ancestry, two-thirds of them American citizens, were living in California, Washington, and Oregon. On February 19, 1942, President Franklin D. Roosevelt signed Executive Order No. 9066 empowering the U.S. Army to designate areas from which "any or all persons may be excluded." No person of Japanese ancestry living in the United States was ever convicted of any serious act of espionage or sabotage during the war. Yet these innocent people were removed from their homes and placed in relocation centers, many for the duration of the war (Davis 1982:27). In contrast, between 1942 and 1944, 18 Caucasians were tried for spying for Japan; at least ten were convicted in court (Uyeda 1995:66).

To understand why the United States government decided to remove Japanese Americans from the West Coast in the largest single forced relocation in U.S. history, one must consider many factors. Prejudice, wartime hysteria, and politics all contributed to this decision (CWRIC 1982; Hirabayashi and Hirabayashi 1984).

West Coast Anti-Asian Prejudice

Anti-Asian prejudices, especially in California, began as anti-Chinese feelings. The cultural and economic forces that led to the anti-Japanese feelings are discussed in detail by Daniels (1989:2-25), and summarized here. Chinese immigration to the U.S. began about the same time as the California gold rush of 1849. During the initial phases of the economic boom that accompanied the gold rush, Chinese labor was needed and welcomed. However, soon white workingmen began to consider the Chinese, who in 1870 comprised about 10 percent of California's population, as competitors. This economic competition increased after the completion of the trans-continental Union-Central Pacific Railroad in 1869, which had employed around 10,000 Chinese

Figure 3.1. Japanese American family harvesting their strawberry field near San Jose, April 5, 1942 (Dorothea Lange photograph, Bancroft Library, University of California, Berkeley).

Figure 3.2. Japanese store, Penryn, California (Francis Stewart photograph, Bancroft Library, University of California, Berkeley).

laborers. Chinese labor was cheap labor, and this economic grievance became an ideology of Asian inferiority similar to existing American racial prejudices. Discrimination became legislated at both the state and federal level, including a Chinese immigration exclusion bill passed in 1882 by the U.S. Congress.

The experiences of Chinese immigrants foreshadowed those of Japanese immigrants, who began arriving about the same time the Chinese exclusion bill was passed. Japanese immigrants were called Issei, from the combination of the Japanese words for "one" and "generation;" their children, the American-born second generation, are Nisei, and the third generation are Sansei. Nisei and Sansei who were educated in Japan are called Kibei. The Issei mostly came from the Japanese countryside, and they generally arrived, either in Hawaii or the mainland West Coast, with very little money. Approximately

half became farmers, while others went to the coastal urban centers and worked in small commercial establishments, usually for themselves or for other Issei (Figures 3.1 and 3.2).

Anti-Japanese movements began shortly after Japanese immigration began, arising from existing anti-Asian prejudices. However, the anti-Japanese movement became widespread around 1905, due both to increasing immigration and the Japanese victory over Russia, the first defeat of a western nation by an Asian nation in modern times. Both the Issei and Japan began to be perceived as threats. Discrimination included the formation of anti-Japanese organizations, such as the Asiatic Exclusion League, attempts at school segregation (which eventually affected Nisei under the doctrine of "separate but equal"), and a growing number of violent attacks upon individuals and businesses.

The Japanese government subsequently protested this treatment of its citizens. To maintain the Japanese-American friendship President Theodore Roosevelt attempted to negotiate a compromise, convincing the San Francisco school board to revoke the segregation order, restraining the California Legislature from passing more anti-Japanese legislation and working out what was known as the "Gentlemen's Agreement" with the Japanese government. In this, the Japanese government agreed to limit emigration to the continental United States to laborers who had already been to the United States before and to the parents, wives, and children of laborers already there.

In 1913, California passed the Alien Land Law which prohibited the ownership of agricultural land by "aliens ineligible to citizenship." In 1920, a stronger Alien Land Act prohibited leasing and sharecropping as well. Both laws were based on the presumption that Asians were aliens ineligible for citizenship, which in turn stemmed from a narrow interpretation of the naturalization statute. The statute had been rewritten after the Fourteenth Amendment to the constitution to permit naturalization of "white persons" and "aliens of African descent." This exclusionism, clearly the intent of Congress, was legitimized by the Supreme Court in 1921, when Takao Ozawa was denied citizenship. However, the Nisei were citizens by birth, and therefore parents would often transfer title to their children. The Immigration Act of 1924 prohibited all further Japanese immigration, with the side effect of making a very distinct generation gap between the Issei and Nisei.

Many of the anti-Japanese fears arose from economic factors combined with envy, since many of the Issei farmers had become very successful at raising fruits and vegetables in soil that most people had considered infertile. Other fears were military in nature; the Russo-Japanese War proved that the Japanese were a force to be reckoned with, and stimulated fears of Asian conquest – "the Yellow Peril." These factors, plus the perception of "otherness" and "Asian inscruta-bility" that typified American racial stereotypes, greatly influenced the events following Pearl Harbor.

Preparing for War with Japan

While the Japanese attack of Pearl Harbor came as a shock to most Americans, the U.S. government had already investigated possible actions to take in case of war with Japan. Japanese Americans also had speculated on what would happen to them, fearing as early as 1937 that they would be "herded into prison camps – perhaps we would be slaughtered on the spot" (Daniels 1989). Some Nisei emphasized their loyalty and Americanism, which led to generational conflict with their Issei parents. The Japanese American Citizens League (JACL), an influential all-Nisei organization, represented this pro-American attitude in their creed. The JACL creed, an optimistic, patriotic expression written by Mike Masaoka in 1940, was published in the Congressional Record for May 9, 1941 (Daniels 1989:24-25):

> I am proud that I am an American citizen of Japanese ancestry, for my very background makes me appreciate more fully the wonderful advantages of this nation. I believe in her institutions, ideals and traditions; I glory in her heritage; I boast of her history; I trust in her future. She has granted me liberties and opportunities such as no individual enjoys in this world today. She has given me an education befitting kings. She has entrusted me with the responsibilities of the franchise. She has permitted me to build a home, to earn a liveli-hood, to worship, think, speak and act as I please – as a free man equal to every other man.

> Although some individuals may discriminate against me, I shall never become bitter or lose faith, for I know that such persons are not representative of the majority of the American people. True, I shall do all in my power to discourage such practices, but I shall do it in the American way – above board, in the open, through courts of law, by education, by proving myself to be worthy of equal treatment and consideration. I am firm in my belief that American sportsmanship and attitude of fair play will judge citizenship and

patriotism on the basis of action and achievement, and not on the basis of physical characteristics. Because I believe in America, and I trust she believes in me, and because I have received innumerable benefits from her, I pledge myself to do honor to her at all times and all places; to support her constitution; to obey her laws; to respect her flag; to defend her against all enemies, foreign and domestic; to actively assume my duties and obligations as a citizen, cheerfully and without any reservations whatsoever, in the hope that I may become a better American in a greater America.

At the same time as the JACL creed was written, the United States government was preparing for war. The Alien Registration Act of 1940 required the registration and fingerprinting of all aliens over fourteen years of age. The Federal Bureau of Investigation (FBI) compiled a list of dangerous or subversive German, Italian, and Japanese aliens who were to be arrested or interned at the outbreak of war with their country. In November 1941, President Franklin Roosevelt received a secret report on the West Coast Japanese Americans by Curtis B. Munson, a well-to-do Chicago businessman who gathered intelligence under the guise of being a government official (CWRIC 1982:52). In his report Munson concluded that most of the Japanese Americans were loyal to the United States and that many would have become citizens if they had been allowed to do so. Moreover, the report stated that most of the few disloyal Japanese Americans hoped that "by remaining quiet they [could] avoid concentration camps or irresponsible mobs." However, Munson also noted that the West Coast was vulnerable to sabotage, since dams, bridges, harbors, and power stations were unguarded; Munson wrote "There are still Japanese in the United States who will tie dynamite around their waist and make a human bomb out of themselves. We grant this, but today they are few." Response to the report by Army Intelligence, although never sent to Roosevelt after the confusion following Pearl Harbor, argued that "widespread sabotage by Japanese is not expected ... identification of dangerous Japanese on the West Coast is reasonably complete" (Daniels 1989:28).

Figure 3.3. Aliens at the Camp Sharp Detention Station prior to transfer to internment camps (Clem Albers photograph, Bancroft Library, University of California, Berkeley).

In the Aftermath of Pearl Harbor

Beginning December 7, the Justice Department organized the arrests of 3,000 people whom it considered "dangerous" enemy aliens, half of whom were Japanese (Figure 3.3). Of the Japanese, those arrested included community leaders who were involved in Japanese organizations and religious groups. Evidence of actual subversive activities was not a prerequisite for arrest. At the same time, the bank accounts of all enemy aliens and all accounts in American branches of Japanese banks were frozen. These two actions paralyzed the Japanese American community by depriving it of both its leadership and financial assets.

In late January 1942 many of the Japanese arrested by the Justice Department were transferred to internment camps in Montana, New Mexico, and North Dakota. Often their families had no idea of their whereabouts for weeks. Some internees were reunited with their families later in relocation centers. However, many remained in Justice camps for the duration of the war.

After Pearl Harbor, the shock of a sneak attack on American soil caused widespread hysteria and paranoia. It certainly did not help matters when Frank Knox, Roosevelt's Secretary of the Navy, blamed Pearl Harbor on "the most effective fifth column work that's come out of this war, except in Norway." Knox apparently already realized that the local military's lack of preparedness far overshadowed any espionage in the success of the attack but did not want the country to lose faith in the Navy (Daniels 1989:35). This scapegoating opened the door to sensationalistic newspaper headlines about sabotage, fifth column activities, and imminent invasion. Such stories had no factual basis, but fed the growing suspicions about Japanese Americans (J.A.C.P. 1973). In fact, as far as Japanese attacks on the mainland were concerned, the military had already concluded that Japanese hit-and-run raids were possible, but that any large-scale invasion was beyond the capacity of the Japanese military, as was any invasion of Japan by the U.S. military.

"Military Necessity"

After the attack on Pearl Harbor martial law was declared in Hawaii and all civilians were subject to travel, security, and curfew restrictions imposed by the military. Japanese fishing boats were impounded and individuals considered potentially dangerous were arrested (Ogawa and Fox 1991).

Politicians called for the mass incarceration of people of Japanese ancestry in Hawaii. But the military resisted: one-third of the Hawaiian population was of Japanese ancestry and the military didn't have enough soldiers to guard them or enough ships to send them to the mainland (Weglyn 1976:87-88). More importantly, their labor was crucial to the civilian and military economy of the islands (Daniels 1993:48). In the end fewer than 1,500 (out of a population of 150,000)

were confined and eventually removed to the mainland.

One of the key players in the confusion following Pearl Harbor was Lt. General John L. DeWitt, the commander of the Western Defense Command and the U.S. 4th Army. DeWitt had a history of prejudice against non-Caucasian Americans, even those already in the Army, and he was easily swayed by any rumor of sabotage or imminent Japanese invasion (Daniels 1989:36).

DeWitt was convinced that if he could control all civilian activity on the West Coast, he could prevent another Pearl Harbor-type disaster. J. Edgar Hoover of the FBI ridiculed the "hysteria and lack of judgment" of DeWitt's Military Intelligence Division, citing such incidents as the supposed powerline sabotage actually caused by cattle.

Nevertheless, in his Final Report (1943), DeWitt cites other reasons for the "military necessity" of evacuation, such as supposed signal lights and unidentified radio transmissions, none of which was ever verified. He also insisted on seizing weapons, ammunition, radios, and cameras without warrants. He called these "hidden caches of contraband," even though most of the weapons seized were from two legitimate sporting goods stores (Hersey 1988:22).

Initially, DeWitt did not embrace the broad-scale removal of all Japanese Americans from the West Coast. On December 19, 1941, General DeWitt recommended "that action be initiated at the earliest practicable date to collect all alien subjects fourteen years of age and over, of enemy nations and remove them" to the interior of the country and hold them "under restraint after removal" (Daniels 1989:39). On December 26, he told Provost Marshall General Allen W. Gullion that "I'm very doubtful that it would be commonsense procedure to try and intern 117,000 Japanese in this theater ... An American citizen, after all, is an American citizen. And while they all may not be loyal, I think we can weed the disloyal out of the loyal and lock them up if necessary" (Daniels 1989:40).

With encouragement from Colonel Karl Bendetson, the head of the Provost Marshall's Aliens Division, on January 21, DeWitt recommended to Secretary of War Henry Stimson the establishment of small "prohibited zones" around strategic areas from which enemy aliens and their native-born children would be removed, as well as some larger "restricted zones" where they would be kept under close surveillance. Stimson and Attorney General Francis Biddle agreed, although Biddle was determined not to do anything to violate Japanese Americans' constitutional rights.

However, on February 9, DeWitt asked for much larger prohibited zones in Washington and Oregon which included the entire cities of Portland, Seattle, and Tacoma. Biddle refused to go along, but President Roosevelt, convinced of the military necessity, agreed to bypass the Justice Department. Roosevelt gave the army "carte blanche" to do what they wanted, with the caveat to be as reasonable as possible (Hersey 1988:42).

Two days later, DeWitt submitted his final recommendations in which he called for the removal of all Japanese, native-born as well as alien, and "other subversive persons" from the entire area lying west of the Sierra Nevada and Cascade Mountains (Hersey 1988:43). DeWitt justified this broad-scale removal on "military necessity" stating "the Japanese race is an enemy race" and "the very fact that no sabotage has taken place to date is a disturbing and confirming indication that such action will be taken" (Hersey 1988:44).

On February 17, Biddle made a last ditch effort to convince the President that evacuation was unnecessary. In addition, General Mark Clark of General Headquarters in Washington, D.C., was convinced that evacuation was counteractive to military necessity, as it would use far too many soldiers who could otherwise be fighting. He argued that "we will never have a perfect defense against sabotage except at the expense of other equally important efforts." Instead, he recommended protecting critical installations by using pass and permit systems and selective arrests as necessary.

Meanwhile, the Japanese American community, particularly the Nisei, were trying to establish their loyalty by becoming air raid wardens and joining the army (when they were allowed to). Since so many in the Issei leadership had been imprisoned during the initial arrests, the Nisei organizations, especially the JACL, gained influence in the Japanese American community. The JACL's policy of cooperation and appeasement was embraced by some Japanese Americans but vilified by others.

At first, there was no consistent treatment of Nisei who tried to enlist or who were drafted. Most Selective Service boards rejected them, classifying them as 4-F or 4-C (unsuitable for service because of race or ancestry), but they were accepted at others. The War Department prohibited further Nisei induction after March 31, 1942, "Except as may be specifically authorized in exceptional cases." The exceptions were bilingual Nisei and Kibei who served as language instructors and interpreters. All registrants of Japanese ancestry were officially classified as 4-C after September 14, 1942. (USDI 1946).

While the military debated restrictions on Japanese Americans and limited their involvement in the war, public opinion on the West Coast was growing in support of confining all persons of Japanese ancestry (J.A.C.P. 1973). The anti-Japanese American sentiment in the media was typified by and editorial in the *Los Angeles Times*: "A viper is nonetheless a viper wherever the egg is hatched — so a Japanese American, born of Japanese parents — grows up to be a Japanese, not an American" (Hersey 1988:38).

Despite opposition by Biddle, the JACL, and General Mark Clark, on February 19, 1942, President Roosevelt signed Executive Order 9066, authorizing the Secretary of War "to prescribe military areas in such places and of such extent as he or the appropriate Military Commander may determine, from which any or all persons may be excluded, and with respect to which, the right of any person to enter, remain in, or leave shall be subject to whatever restrictions the Secretary of War or the appropriate Military Commander may impose in his discretion. The Secretary of War is hereby authorized to provide for residents of any such area who are excluded therefrom, such transportation, food, shelter, and other accommodations as may be necessary in the judgement of the Secretary of War or said Military Commander... ."

In mid-February Congressional committee hearings headed by California congressman John Tolan were held on the West Coast to assess the need for the evacuation of Japanese Americans. The overwhelming majority of the witnesses supported the removal of all Japanese, alien and citizen, from the coast. California Governor Culbert L. Olson and State Attorney General Earl Warren supported removal of all Japanese Americans from coastal areas, stating that it was impossible to tell which ones were loyal (Drinnon 1987:31-32). As *de facto* spokesmen for the Japanese community, JACL leaders argued against mass evacuation, but to prove their loyalty pledged their readiness to cooperate if it were deemed a military necessity.

Other events in California contributed to the tense atmosphere. On February 23 a Japanese submarine shelled the California coast. It caused no serious damage but raised fears of further enemy action along the U.S. coast. The following night the "Battle of Los Angeles" took place. In response to an unidentified radar echo, the military called for a blackout and fired over 1,400 anti-aircraft shells. Twenty Japanese Americans were arrested for supposedly signaling the invaders, but the radar echo turned out to be a loose weather balloon (Davis 1982:43; Webber 1992).

Even prior to the signing of Executive Order 9066, the U.S. Navy had begun the removal of Japanese Americans from near the Port of Los Angeles: on February 14, 1942, the Navy announced that all persons of Japanese ancestry had to leave Terminal Island by March 14. On February 24 the deadline was moved up to February 27 (Daniels 1989:86). Practically all family heads (mostly fisherman) had already been arrested and removed by the FBI (Weglyn 1976:301) and the 500

Figure 3.4. The Shibuya family at their Mountain View, California, home (Dorothea Lange photograph, Bancroft Library, University of California, Berkeley).

families living there were allowed to move on their own anywhere they wanted. Most stayed in the Los Angeles area until they were again relocated by the U.S. Army.

Evacuation

Even after Executive Order 9066, no one was quite sure what was going to happen (Figures 3.4 and 3.5). Who would be "excluded," where would the "military areas" be, and where would people go after they had been "excluded"?

General DeWitt originally wanted to remove all Japanese, German, and Italian aliens. However, public opinion (with a few vocal dissenters) was in favor of relocating all Japanese Americans, citizen and alien alike, but opposed to any mass evacuation of German or Italian aliens, much less second generation Germans or Italians. Provost Marshall Gullion, who had always supported relocation of Japanese Americans, had only figured on males over the age of fourteen – about 46,000 from the West Coast and 40,000 from Hawaii.

As the military negotiated possibilities, the Japanese American community continued to worry. Most followed the lead of the JACL and chose to cooperate with evacuation as a way to prove their loyalty. A few were vocally opposed to evacuation and later sought ways to prevent it, some with court cases that eventually reached the Supreme Court.

DeWitt issued several Public Proclamations about the evacuation, but these did little to clear up confusion; in fact, they created more. On March 2, Public Proclamation No. 1 divided Washington, Oregon, California, and Arizona into two military areas, numbered 1 and 2. Military Area No. 1 was sub-divided into a "prohibited zone" along the coast and an adjacent "restricted zone."

Figure 3.5. Newspaper headline (Dorothea Lange photograph, Bancroft Library, University of California, Berkeley).

Ninety-eight smaller areas were also labeled prohibited, presumably strategic military sites. The announcement was aimed at "Japanese, German or Italian" aliens and "any person of Japanese ancestry," but it did not specifically order anyone to leave. However, an accompanying press release predicted that all people of Japanese ancestry would eventually be excluded from Military Area No. 1, but probably not from Military Area No. 2 (Daniels 1989:84).

At this time, the government had not made any plans to help people move, and since most Issei assets had been frozen at the beginning of the war, most families lacked the resources to move. However, several thousand Japanese Americans voluntarily did try to relocate themselves. Over 9,000 persons voluntarily moved out of Military Area No. 1: of these, over half moved into the California portion of Military Area No. 2, where Public Proclamation No. 1 said no restrictions or prohibitions were contemplated. Later, of course, they would be forcefully evacuated from Military Area No. 2. Somewhat luckier were the Japanese Americans who moved farther into the interior of the country: 1,963 moved to Colorado, 1,519 moved to Utah, 305 moved to Idaho, 208 moved to eastern Washington, 115 moved to eastern Oregon, 105 moved to northern Arizona, 83 moved to Wyoming, 72 moved to Illinois, 69 moved to Nebraska, and 366 moved to other states (DeWitt 1943:107-111). But many who did attempt to leave the West Coast discovered that the inland states were unwilling to accept them. The perception inland was that California was dumping its "undesirables," and many refugees were turned back at state borders, had difficulty buying gasoline, or were greeted with "No Japs Wanted" signs.

On March 11 the Army-controlled Wartime Civilian Control Administration (WCCA) was established to organize and carry out the evacuation of Military Area No. 1. Public Proclamation No. 2, on March 16, designated four more military areas in the states of Idaho, Montana, Nevada, and Utah, and 933 more prohibited areas. Although DeWitt pictured eventually removing all Japanese Americans from these areas, these plans never materialized.

Public Law No. 503, approved on March 21, 1942, made violating restrictions in a military area a misdemeanor, liable up to a $5,000 fine or a year in jail. Public Proclamation No. 3, effective March 27, instituted an 8:00 pm to 6:00 am curfew in Military Area No. 1 and listed prohibited areas for all enemy aliens and "persons of Japanese ancestry." Public Proclamation No. 3 also required that "at all other times all such persons shall only be at their place of residence or employment or traveling between those places or within a distance of not more than five miles from their place of residence."

Voluntary evacuation ended March 29, when Public Proclamation No. 4 forbade all Japanese from leaving Military Area No. 1 until ordered. Further instructions established reception centers as transitory evacuation facilities and forbade moves except to an approved location outside Military Area No. 1.

The first evacuation under the auspices of the Army began March 24 on Bainbridge Island near Seattle, and was repeated all along the West Coast. In all, 108 "Civilian Exclusion Orders" were issued, each designed to affect around 1,000 people (Figure 3.6). After initial notification, residents were given six days in which to dispose of nearly all their possessions, packing only "that which can be carried

PROHIBITED AREA

EXCLUSION ORDER No. 108

WESTERN DEFENSE COMMAND AND FOURTH ARMY

This Map is prepared for the convenience of the public; see the Civilian Exclusion Order for the full and correct description.

Figure 3.6. Map included with Civilian Exclusion Order 108 (Tulare County, California).

by the family or the individual" including bedding, toilet articles, clothing and eating utensils. The government was willing to store or ship some possessions "at the sole risk of the owner," but many did not trust that option. Most families sold their property and possessions for ridiculously small sums, while others trusted friends and neighbors to look after their properties.

By June 2, 1942, all Japanese in Military Area No. 1, except for a few left behind in hospitals, were in army custody. The image of the Japanese Americans is that they passively accepted evacuation. There is a Japanese philosophy "shikataganai" – it can't be helped. So, indeed the vast majority of the Japanese Americans were resigned to following the orders that sent them into the assembly centers which for many was a way to prove their loyalty to the U.S.

But a few cases of active resistance to the evacuation occurred. Three weeks after he was supposed to evacuate, Kuji Kurokawa was found, too weak to move due to malnutrition, hiding in the basement of the home where he had been employed for 10 years. He decided that he would not register or be evacuated, "I am an American citizen," he explained (JACP 1973:18). In another story, perhaps apocryphal, Hideo Murata, a U.S. Army World War I veteran, committed suicide at a local hotel rather than be evacuated (Davis 1982:57).

Three Japanese-Americans challenged the government's actions in court. Minoru Yasui had volunteered for military service after the Japanese attack on Pearl Harbor and was rejected because of his Japanese ancestry. An attorney, he deliberately violated the curfew law of his native Portland, Oregon, stating that citizens have the duty to challenge unconstitutional regulations. Gordon Hirabayashi, a student at the University of Washington, also deliberately violated the curfew for Japanese Americans and disregarded the evacuation orders, claiming that the government was violating the 5th amendment by restricting the freedom of innocent Japanese Americans. Fred Korematsu changed his name, altered his facial features, and went into hiding. He was later arrested for remaining in a restricted area (Davis 1982:118). In court, Korematsu claimed the government could not imprison a group of people based solely on ancestry. All three lost their cases. Yasui spent several months in jail and was then sent to the Minidoka Relocation Center, Hirabayashi spent time in jail and several months at a Federal prison in Arizona, and Korematsu was sent to the Topaz Relocation Center.

According to one author, the only act of "sabotage" by a Japanese American was a product of the relocation process. When told to leave his home and go to an assembly center, one farmer asked for an extension to harvest his strawberry crop. His request was denied, so he plowed under the strawberry field. He was then arrested for sabotage, on the grounds that strawberries were a necessary commodity for the war effort (Hersey 1988:5). No one was allowed to delay evacuation in order to harvest their crops and subsequently Californians were faced with shortages of fruits and vegetables. Japanese Americans grew 95 percent of the state's strawberries and one-third of the state's truck crops (JACP 1973:20-21).

Even though the justification for the evacuation was to thwart espionage and sabotage, newborn babies, young children, the elderly, the infirm, children from orphanages, and even children adopted by Caucasian parents were not exempt from removal. Anyone with 1/16th or more Japanese blood was included. In all, over 17,000 children under 10 years old, 2,000 persons over 65 years old, and 1,000 handicapped or infirm persons were evacuated (Uyeda 1995:32).

Assembly Centers

After reporting to collection points near their homes, each group was moved to hastily contrived reception or assembly centers (Figures 3.7 and 3.8; Table 3.1). Two centers on vacant land, at Parker Dam and in the Owens Valley, were originally intended for use as "Reception Centers" to expedite the voluntary evacuation. Both would later become WRA-run Relocation Centers as well (Poston and Manzanar).

The Parker Dam Reception Center was on the Colorado River Indian Reservation in Arizona. Permission from the Department of Interior was contingent on the center being a "positive program ... not merely ... a concentration camp" (Daniels 1989:88). The Owens Valley Reception Center was on land leased from the City of Los Angeles.

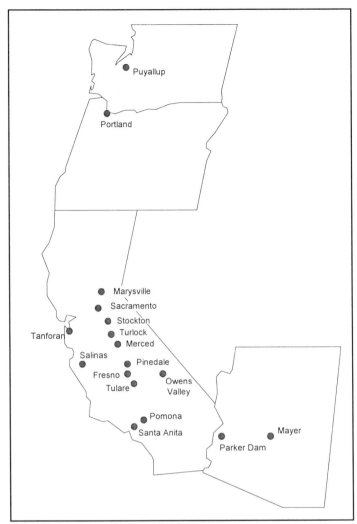

Figure 3.7. Assembly Centers.

Generally, the first to arrive at the reception centers were volunteers, mainly JACL leaders and their families. Since the Owens Valley and Parker Dam centers could only hold a small fraction of the West Coast Japanese and little time was available for additional large-scale construction, existing facilities were converted into temporary assembly centers.

Eleven of the assembly centers were at racetracks or fairgrounds. Others were at the Pacific International Livestock Exposition Facilities (Portland, Oregon), a former mill site (Pinedale, California), migrant workers camps (Marysville and Sacramento, California), and an abandoned Civilian Conservation Corps (CCC) Camp (Mayer, Arizona) (Thomas 1952:84).

Two additional assembly centers were partially readied. Toppenish, in eastern Washington, ultimately was not used because of unsuitable sanitation facilities, and because there was enough room in the California assembly centers for the evacuees. A refurbished CCC camp at Cave Creek, Arizona, was not needed due to considerable voluntary migration from the southern part of the state (DeWitt 1943:152).

Living conditions at the assembly centers were chaotic and squalid. Existing buildings were used, and supplemented with temporary "Theater of Operations"-type army barracks, 20-ft-by-100-ft buildings divided into five rooms. These barracks were originally designed for temporary use by combat soldiers, not families with small children or elderly people (USDI 1946).

At the racetracks, stables had been hastily cleaned out before their use as living quarters, but the stench remained. Still, the converted stables were described as "somewhat better shelter than the newly constructed mass-fabricated houses" (McWilliams 1942:361). At the Santa Anita Assembly Center, 8,500 of the total population of over 18,000 lived in stables. At the Portland Assembly Center over 3,000 evacuees were

The Owens Valley was (and still is) a major source of water for Los Angeles. City officials were worried that the evacuees would poison the water supply, but were assured that they would be kept under heavy guard (Daniels 1989:88).

Table 3.1.
WCCA Assembly Centers (Tajiri 1990:107, 116; Thomas 1952:84).

Center	Date of first arrival	Peak population	Date of last departure	Primary Destination
Fresno, California	5-6-42	5,120	10-30-42	Jerome, Gila River
Owens Valley, California	3-21-42	9,666	5-31-42	same*
Marysville, California	5-8-42	2,451	6-29-42	Tule Lake
Mayer, Arizona	5-7-42	245	6-2-42	Poston
Merced, California	5-6-42	4,508	9-15-42	Granada
Parker Dam, Arizona	5-8-42	11,738	5-31-42	same*
Pinedale, California	5-7-42	4,792	7-23-42	Tule Lake, Poston
Pomona, California	5-7-42	5,434	8-24-42	Heart Mtn.
Portland, Oregon	5-2-42	3,676	9-10-42	Heart Mtn., Poston
Puyallup, Washington	4-28-42	7,390	9-12-42	Tule Lake, Minidoka
Sacramento, California	5-6-42	4,739	6-26-42	Tule Lake
Salinas, California	4-27-42	3,594	7-4-42	Poston
Santa Anita, California	3-27-42	18,719	10-27-42	Poston, six others
Stockton, California	5-10-42	4,271	10-17-42	Rohwer, Gila River
Tanforan, California	4-28-42	7,816	10-13-42	Central Utah
Tulare, California	4-20-42	4,978	9-4-42	Gila River
Turlock, California	4-30-42	3,662	8-12-42	Gila River

* administration transferred to WRA

housed under one roof in a livestock pavilion that was subdivided into apartments (DeWitt 1943:183).

The atmosphere in the assembly centers was tense. Many of the evacuees were demoralized, convinced that America would never accept them as full-fledged Americans. Some Nisei who had been very patriotic became very bitter and sometimes pro-Japanese. Most tried to do everything possible to make living conditions better, organizing newsletters and dances and planting victory gardens. Jobs were available in the assembly centers, but the decision was made that no evacuees should be paid more than an Army private (which was then $21 per month) to combat charges of coddling. Initially, unskilled laborers were paid $8 per month, skilled laborers $12, and professionals, $16. These were later raised to $12, $16, and $19, respectively.

Evacuees worked as cooks, mechanics, teachers, doctors, clerks, and police. At the Santa Anita and Manzanar assembly centers, camouflage net factories, managed by a private company under military contract, were set up. Only citizens could be employed on this war-related work.

Figure 3.8. Arrival at Salinas Assembly Center, April 29, 1942 (Clem Albers photograph, Bancroft Library, University of California, Berkeley).

Privacy at the assembly centers was next to non-existent, with communal lavatories and mess halls and thin walls in the barracks. Families were crowded into small apartments, usually 20 ft by 20 ft. The evacuees fixed up their new homes as best they could with salvaged lumber and other supplies that they could find, in an attempt to make them more liveable.

Shortages of food and other material and deplorable sanitation were common at many of the centers (Weglyn 1976:80-82). The 800 Nisei working at the net factory at Santa Anita conducted a sit-down strike complaining about weakness due to lack of food as well as low pay and unfair production quotas (Weglyn 1976:81).

Some opportunities for leaving the assembly centers were available. California educators made an effort to allow college-age Nisei to attend school outside of the prohibited area. Many colleges refused to accept them, but around 4,300 students were eventually released from the assembly and relocation centers to attend school (Daniels 1989:99-101). The war had created a massive labor shortage, so the WCCA agreed to allow seasonal agricultural leave for those they deemed loyal. Over 1,000 evacuees were granted temporary leave to harvest cotton, potatoes, and sugar beets.

The evacuees for the most part took their hardships in stride. However, the effects of overcrowding and stress became apparent at the Santa Anita Assembly Center on August 4, 1942. On that day a routine search for contraband (including Japanese language books and phonograph records), and an unannounced confiscation of hot plates turned violent. Rumors and complaints spread as crowds gathered. The internal police and suspected informers were harassed and one suspected informer was severely beaten. In the end 200 military police were called in to silence the 2,000 protesters (Davis 1967:79). That night the residents were confined to their barracks and no meals were served. The military patrolled inside the center for three days (Lehman 1970).

Setting up the Relocation Centers

To reduce the diversion of soldiers from combat, a civilian organization, the War Relocation Authority (WRA), had been created on March 19, 1942. Once the military made the decision to relocate Japanese Americans en masse from Military Areas No. 1 and 2, this civilian agency was left to figure out how to implement this policy. Milton S. Eisenhower, then an official of the Department of Agriculture, was chosen to head the WRA. Eisenhower initially hoped that many of the evacuees, especially citizens, could be resettled quickly. He expected that evacuees could be either directly released from the assembly centers and sent back to civilian life away from the military areas, or sent to small unguarded subsistence farms.

However, after meeting with the governors and other officials from ten western states on April 7, Eisenhower realized that anti-Japanese racism was not confined to California. No governor wanted any Japanese in their state, and if any came, they wanted them kept under guard. The common feeling was expressed by one of the governors: "If these people are dangerous on the Pacific coast they will be dangerous here!" (Daniels 1993:57). But, their chief concern was that the Japanese would settle in their states and never leave, especially once the war was over. However, at a meeting with local sugar beet growers on the same day, a different view prevailed. Desperate for labor, S.J. Boyer of the Utah Farm Bureau said that farmers "don't love the Japanese, but we intend to work them, if possible" (Daniels 1989:94).

Eisenhower was forced to accept the idea of keeping both the Issei and

Nisei in camps for the duration of the war. The idea of incarcerating innocent people bothered him so much, however, that he resigned in June 1942. He recommended his successor, Dillon S. Myer, but advised Myer to take the position only "if you can do the job and sleep at night" (Myer 1971:3).

Relocation Centers

The relocation centers were located in isolated areas, most in deserts or swamps, perhaps unwittingly following newspaper columnist Henry McLemore's vitriol, "Herd 'em up, pack 'em off and give them the inside room of the badlands. Let 'em be pinched, hurt, hungry and dead up against it" (McLemore 1942).

The assembly centers at Manzanar and Poston were redesignated relocation centers and eight new sites in seven states were selected (Figure 3.9; Table 3.2). Over 300 possible sites were reviewed; primary consideration was given to locations with railroad access and agricultural potential (Madden 1969:23-25). Site selection was made by the WRA, but site acquisition was left to the War Department. The Relocation Centers were primarily on unused or underutilized federal lands. With the exception of the California Relocation Centers, all were in sparsely populated areas, making them some of the largest "communities" in their respective states.

The Tule Lake Relocation Center in California, the Minidoka Relocation Center in Idaho, and the Heart Mountain Relocation Center in Wyoming were located on undeveloped federal reclamation projects. The Jerome and Rohwer Relocation Centers in Arkansas were partially on land meant for subsistence homesteads under the Farm Security Administration; the balance of the site at Rohwer was bought from local farmers.

The Colorado River (Poston) and Gila River Relocation Centers in

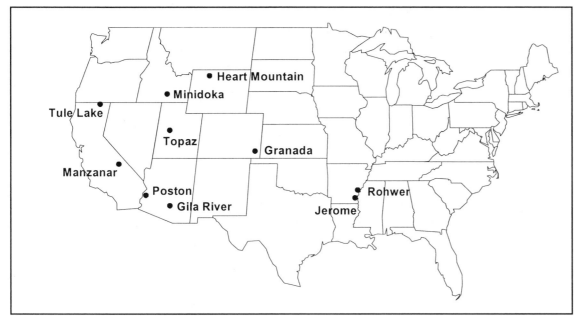

Figure 3.9. Relocation Centers.

Evacuees at assembly centers which had only pit latrines or which presented a fire hazard were the first priority for transfer to the relocation centers (DeWitt 1943:280). In theory, evacuees would be sent to the relocation center with the climate most similar to their home, and each relocation center would have a balance of urban and rural settlers. Evacuees were transferred from the assembly centers to the relocation centers by trains; this mass movement was carefully choreographed to avoid interrupting major troop movements.

The transfer process lasted from early June to October 30. Following the transfer of evacuees and supplies to the relocation centers all but two of the assembly and reception centers were turned over to various Army agencies or the U.S. Forest Service (Table 3.3).

Arizona were both on Indian Reservations. Both Tribal Councils opposed the use of their land on the grounds that they did not want to participate in inflicting the same type of injustice as they had suffered, but they were overruled by the Army and the Bureau of Indian Affairs (BIA). In fact, in a verbal agreement Eisenhower had turned over administration of the Colorado River Relocation Center to the BIA. The WRA later resumed control of the center when Dillon Myer became WRA director.

The Central Utah Relocation Center (Topaz) had been part public domain, part county owned, and part privately owned. The Granada Relocation Center in Colorado had been privately owned and was purchased by the Army for the WRA (Daniels 1989; USDI 1946). The Manzanar Relocation Center was located on unused land held by the City of Los Angeles for its water rights.

Concurrently with the transfers from the assembly centers, the military decided to remove all Japanese Americans from the remainder of California. The eastern portion of California had been designated Military Area No. 2, and was not supposed to be as sensitive as Military Area No. 1, where all Japanese had already been removed from their homes to assembly centers. But, within the California portion of Military Area No. 2 there remained two concentrations of Japanese Americans immediately adjacent to Military Area No. 1, vital military installations, and important forests (DeWitt 1943:360). Over 9,000 people were directly moved from this area to the Tule Lake, Poston, and Gila River relocation centers between July 4 and August 11. This included many who had voluntarily moved out of Military Area No. 1 prior to Public Proclamation No. 4. Alaskan Japanese who were not picked up by the Department of Justice after the attack on Pearl Harbor

Table 3.2.
WRA Relocation Centers (Daniels 1993:131; Thomas 1952:88).

Center	Date of first arrival	Peak population	Date of peak population	Date of last departure
Gila River	7-20-42	13,348	12-30-42	11-10-45
Granada	8-27-42	7,318	2-1-43	10-15-45
Heart Mountain	8-12-42	10,767	1-1-43	11-10-45
Jerome	10-6-42	8,497	2-11-43	6-30-44
Manzanar	3-21-42	10,046	9-22-42	11-21-45
Minidoka	8-10-42	9,397	3-1-43	10-28-45
Poston	5-8-42	17,814	9-2-42	11-28-45
Rohwer	9-18-42	8,475	3-11-43	11-30-45
Topaz	9-11-42	8,130	3-17-43	10-31-45
Tule Lake	5-27-42	18,789	12-25-44	3-20-46

were airlifted to Washington and then moved to Minidoka. Of the 151 people of Japanese ancestry removed from Alaska, about 50 were seal- and whale-hunting half-Eskimo or half-Aleut (Weglyn 1976:57).

Relocation Center Layout and Building Design

General plans for the construction of the relocation centers were developed prior to the establishment of the WRA. Initial facilities were constructed by the War Department, which also procured the initial equipment. Per capita construction costs ranged from $376 at Manzanar to $584 at Minidoka. The total construction cost, for all centers, was over $56 million.

The relocation centers were designed to be self-contained communities, complete with hospitals, post offices, schools, warehouses, offices, factories, and residential areas, all surrounded by barbed wire and guard towers. Since the centers were supposed to be as self-sufficient as possible, the residential core was surrounded by a large buffer zone that also served as farmland. As at the assembly centers, the Military Police (MPs) had a separate living area adjacent to the relocation center, to reduce fraternization. The civilian employees also had living quarters available at the camp, but these were usually supplemented by whatever housing was available in the nearby towns.

The layout of the relocation centers varied, but certain elements were fairly constant. The perimeter was defined by guard towers and barbed wire fences. There was generally a main entrance leading to the local highway, and auxiliary routes to farming areas outside the central core. Some of the major interior roads were paved, but most were simply dirt roads that were dusty or muddy depending on the weather.

The layout of the two Arizona relocation centers differed from the others. Located on dead-end roads, rather than along a major highway, there were no watch towers and little or no barbed wire. The Poston Relocation Center consisted of three separate camps at five-mile intervals (Poston I, II, and III) and the Gila River Relocation Center consisted of two separate camps (Butte Camp and Canal Camp).

Plans were based on a grid system of blocks. Block size varied in the non-residential areas such as the administrative area, warehouses, and hospital. The remainder of the central cores were made up of residential blocks separated by empty fire breaks. Each residential block consisted of ten to fourteen barracks, a mess hall, latrines for men and women, a laundry, and a recreation hall (Figure 3.10). Eventually, large sewage systems were built; sometimes these modern facilities (necessary because of the population density of the centers) aroused the ire and envy of the local rural residents who relied on septic systems or outhouses.

The design of buildings for the relocation centers presented a problem since no precedents for this type of housing existed. Permanent buildings were not desired. The military had available plans for semi-permanent "Cantonment"-type buildings and temporary "Theater of Operations"-type buildings. A set of standards and details was developed by the Army, modifying the "theater of operations"-type buildings to make them suitable for housing women, children and elderly people while still meeting the requirements of quick construction, low cost, and restricted use of critical materials.

These standards and details of construction were put in place by the WCCA on June 8, 1942, and provided for uniform construction after that date. However, Manzanar, Tule Lake, Poston, and Gila River were already under construction. Construction also varied because different local Engineer Divisions interpreted the rather vague standards differently, and these local offices were responsible for developing or contracting out the plans and specifications for each center.

Local craftsmen were used, but the requirements were not always stringent; in Millard County, Utah, near the Topaz Relocation Center, the term "Topaz Carpenter" is still a derogatory term, since anyone who showed up at the site with a hammer would be hired. Supplies were also difficult to come by in such large quantities during wartime.

Table 3.3.
Disposition of Assembly Centers (from DeWitt 1943:184).

Center	Transfer Date	New Using Agency
Fresno	11/9/42	4th Air Force Training Command
Marysville	6/16/42	VII Army Corps
Mayer	6/27/42	Forest Service
Merced	9/30/42	4th Air Service Area Command
Pinedale	8/6/42	4th Air Force
Pomona	9/4/42	Ordnance Motor Transport
Portland	9/30/42	Portland Port of Embarkation
Sacramento	7/30/42	Signal Corps
Puyallup	9/30/42	9th Service Command
Salinas	7/24/42	VII Army Corps
Santa Anita	11/30/42	Ordnance
Stockton	10/30/42	4th Air Service Area Command
Tanforan	10/27/42	Northern Calif. Sector, WDC
Tulare	9/15/42	VII Army Corps
Turlock	8/24/42	9th Service Command

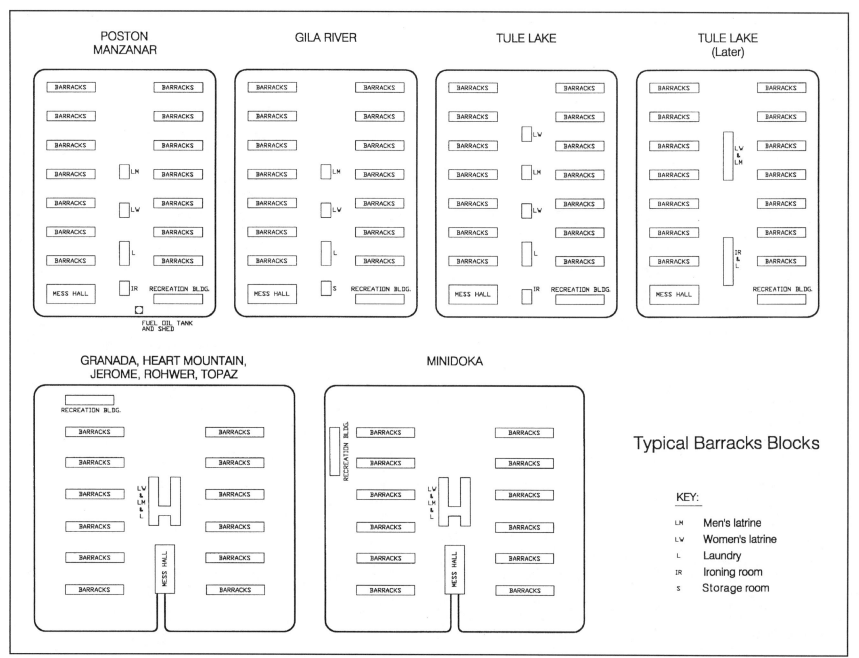

Figure 3.10. Typical layouts of relocation center evacuee residential blocks.

In addition, some suppliers were reluctant to use valuable resources for "Japs," making construction somewhat makeshift at times.

The five-room 20 ft by 100 ft plan of the assembly center barracks was supplanted by 20 ft by 120 ft barracks plans with six variably-sized rooms. The barracks thus built followed standard plans, with different-sized apartments to accommodate different-sized families and groups of single people. Each barracks had two apartments at each of the following sizes: 16 ft by 20 ft, 20 ft by 20 ft, and 24 ft by 20 ft. Partitions between the apartments extended only to the eaves, leaving a gap between the walls and the roof. Each apartment had a heating unit, either coal, wood, oil, or natural gas. Furnishings included a single drop light, army cots, blankets, and mattresses.

The exterior walls and roofs of the barracks were generally of boards covered with tarpaper on frames of dimension lumber. In the colder climates wallboard was provided for insulation. The raised floors were wooden boards, which quickly shrank and allowed dust and dirt to fly all over the barracks. Eventually, "Mastipave" flooring was provided for use at the Tule Lake, Manzanar, Gila River, and Poston Relocation Centers to help seal the drafty floors. The window configurations varied, but were typically either sliding square windows or double hung, with divided lights. The gabled ends of the buildings had rectangular vents – a standard Army construction detail.

Barracks construction varied only at the Granada and the Arizona centers. At Granada the barracks had weatherized wallboard exterior walls and brick floors. The barracks at the Arizona centers had double roofs for insulation and the Gila River Center even had white wallboard exterior sheathing. Clearly the Gila River Relocation Center, visited by Eleanor Roosevelt in April 1943, was a showplace (Inoshita 1995).

Most other buildings were variations on the same theme. Recreation halls and community buildings were basically the same as barracks, but 20 ft by 100 ft and without interior partitions. Mess halls were 40 ft by 100 ft, and included a kitchen, store room, and scullery.

Block latrine and laundry facilities at the earlier constructed relocation centers differed little from that of the assembly centers. At Manzanar, Poston, Gila River, and Tule Lake there were three separate buildings in each residential block for the men's bathroom, women's bathroom, and laundry. These army-type facilities had no toilet partitions or bathtubs and very little hot water. A separate ironing room was added as an afterthought after numerous power outages. At Tule Lake later-constructed blocks had a combined laundry and ironing room and a combined men's and women's bathroom.

Block latrine and laundry facilities at the relocation centers built after the WCCA standards were established consisted of a large centralized H-shaped structure. One side of the building contained the block laundry, the other side contained the men's and women's bathrooms. The crossbar of the H contained the hot water heater. In addition to the standard toilets, sinks, and communal showers provided in the earlier constructed facilities, the women's bathroom was equipped with toilet stalls and four bathtubs.

Administration buildings were similar to evacuee barracks, but with white clapboard exteriors rather than tarpaper. Staff housing, also with clapboard exteriors, was divided into self-contained one, two, or three bedroom apartments each with its own kitchen and bathroom.

Community buildings such as schools and churches were left to be constructed by the evacuees, who initially used empty barracks for these functions. Often entire blocks of barracks were devoted to schools. The block recreation halls, originally intended for use by that block, were usually converted to other general community purposes, such as churches or cooperative stores.

Buildings that were later designed or built by the evacuees were often far more individualistic, and often built of more permanent materials. For instance, school buildings at Poston were built of adobe brick made by the evacuees. These later buildings were typically set at acute angles to the uniformly gridded relocation center roads.

evacuee crews recycled fats, metal, and other material considered vital to the war effort.

The WRA intended to have industries supporting the war effort at the relocation centers, but these plans were thwarted by industries and

Table 3.4.
Relocation Center Agricultural Enterprises, June 1944 (W.R.A. 1944).

| | Field Acreage | | Number of | Number of | Number of | Number of |
	Vegetables	Field Crops	Hogs	Chickens	Egg Hens	Cattle
Gila River		1400	1106	3332	5252	1377
Granada	505	2185	1017	4712	2210	456
Heart Mtn	427	573	873	1437	8918	30
Jerome	123	-	701	-	-	-
Manzanar	242	126	469	3869	4669	87
Minidoka	312	425	611	3249	3627	-
Rohwer	202	375	411	1150	-	-
Poston	1462	819	565	4275	5285	-
Topaz	242	990	887	62	1285	377
Tule Lake	305	856	532	-	-	-

Agricultural enterprises at all of the centers provided much of each center's food, with surpluses sent to the other relocation centers. However, over 40 percent of the rice produced in the U.S. went to the relocation centers (Smith 1995:185). Most of the centers also had hog and chicken farms, and beef or dairy cows were raised at Gila, Granada, Topaz, and Manzanar (Table 3.4).

The relocation centers were subject to the same rationing as the rest of the country. Victory Gardens supplemented the rations and

unions who feared unfair competition. The only venture that enjoyed even a modest degree of success was the short-lived manufacture of camouflage nets at three of the centers (Figure 11; Smith 1995:176). The Manzanar net factory, supervised by the Corp of Engineers, was closed following a December 1942 riot. Privately run net factories at the Poston and Gila River relocation centers were discontinued in May 1943 after the completion of their original contracts.

Other war-related industries at the relocation centers included a ship model factory at Gila that produced models for use in training Navy pilots and a poster shop at Granada. Other planned industrial projects were put on hold, due to outside pressures and to encourage relocation out of the centers.

Industry for internal use included garment factories at Manzanar, Heart Mountain, and Minidoka, a cabinet shop at Tule Lake, sawmills at Jerome and Heart Mountain, and a mattress factory at Manzanar. In addition, factories for the processing of agricultural products were common at all of the centers. For instance, Manzanar made all the soy sauce it used (Smith 1995:244).

Figure 3.11. Camouflage net factory at the Manzanar Relocation Center (National Archives photograph).

difference between inside and outside the camps, freedom and confinement. Even a WRA report admits this: "... the contrast between the barbed wire and the confinement within Manzanar and the observable freedom and motion for those immediately outside, is galling to a good many residents" (W.R.A. 1943).

The weather was another element that greatly affected the evacuees' lives. Both contemporary and later accounts stress dust, mud and extremes in temperature that came as great shocks to West Coast residents used to much more temperate climates. The dust, caused by the massive disturbance of the soil from construction of hundreds of buildings at once, eventually settled, but the harshness of the climate stayed the same.

Life in the Relocation Centers

The physical surroundings, while not having as profound an impact as political and philosophical issues, had a great effect on everyday life. When the evacuees arrived at the camps, they found identical blocks of identical flimsy barracks (Figure 3.12). They quickly improved and personalized their new lodgings, first to make them habitable, and later to make them into homes. The physical changes the evacuees made in their environment were important ways of taking control over their own lives. The changes also helped personalize the identical barracks, to relieve the monotony.

Physical elements could also be reminders of their lack of freedom. The guard towers and especially the barbed wire fences delineated the

Originally, block leaders were appointed by the relocation center director. But, the WRA decided that the evacuees should participate in governing their own communities as much as possible. WRA policy called for a community council with one elected representative from each block, an executive committee, and a judicial committee. Issei were not eligible to hold an elective office. Manzanar was the only center that never elected a council. Instead it relied on elected block leaders who served as an advisory group for the center director (Myer 1971:39-40; Smith 1995:253).

Some conflicts within the Japanese American community were caused by relocation, while others were merely brought to the surface. Many Japanese Americans had supported the United States and were loyal and patriotic until their government decided that they were untrustworthy and guilty until proven innocent. Their feelings of betrayal sometimes caused formerly loyal citizens to renounce their citizenship, in extreme cases, or merely to sympathize with the Japanese government. It was probably most difficult for the Issei, who often still had feelings of loyalty to Japan, even though they also felt American. Other Japanese Americans continued to feel loyal to their country, even though they had lost their homes and freedom. Their major goal was to find ways to prove their loyalty to the outside world.

Inter-generational tension was also a major problem in the relocation centers, especially since Issei and Nisei were very distinct generations. There was a large shift in the balance of power from the Issei to the Nisei, for many reasons. The

Figure 3.12. Evacuee barracks at the Manzanar Relocation Center (WRA photograph, National Archives).

majority of the Issei leadership had been arrested after Pearl Harbor, and the Nisei gained power and influence, both within families and in general. Once the relocation centers were set up, many of the Issei were released to join their families in the centers. However, use of the Japanese language was very restricted: all meetings had to be conducted in English, and all newsletters and other publications were in English. Since many Issei did not speak English, or were not very fluent, this was a further handicap. The Issei also often lost more in the arrests and relocation, since they usually had established farms or businesses. The Nisei usually had less to lose, and some saw the entire experience as an adventure or merely a temporary setback.

Resistance within the relocation centers took many forms. Ethnic churches, Japanese language schools, and unofficial unions flourished. More overt resistance came in the form of strikes and protest demonstrations. How far these went depended on whether an acceptable compromise could be reached (Okihiro 1974).

In November 1942 Heart Mountain was beset by protests over the erection of a barbed wire fence and watchtowers around the relocation center. A petition signed by over half of the adults in the center stated that the fence was an "insult to any free human being." The fence stayed, but the protests continued (Daniels 1989:115).

That same month Poston came close to open revolt. When two suspected informers were beaten, administration officials arrested two Kibei men. Crowds demanded they be freed, workers went on strike, and the police station was picketed. Demonstrators flew flags that from a distance resembled the Japanese flag. However, the protest ended peacefully as the Issei leaders of the protest saw things getting quickly out of hand and a compromise settlement was reached.

The most serious disturbance erupted at Manzanar in December 1942, following months of tension and gang activity between Japanese American Citizens League (JACL) supporters of the administration and a large group of Kibei. On December 6, a JACL leader was beaten by six masked men. Harry Ueno, the leader of the Kitchen Workers

Table 3.5.
Relocation Center Population Statistics (Tajiri 1990:117).

Number Arriving From		Number Departing To	
WCCA Assembly Centers	90,491	West Coast	54,127
Direct Evacuation	17,915	Other U.S. Areas	52,798
Births	5,981	Japan	4,724
Department of Justice Camps	1,735	Department of Justice Camps	3,121
Seasonal Workers (WCCA)	1,579	U.S. Military	2,355
Institutions	1,275	Deaths	1,862
Hawaii	1,118	Institutions	1,322
Voluntary Residents	219	Unauthorized Departures*	4
Total	120,313	Total	120,313

* Smith (1995:419) characterizes these four people who left the centers without permission as three persons with a history of mental problems who disappeared and one person under suspicion of murder who likely fled.

Union, was arrested for the beating and removed from the center. Soon afterward, 3,000 to 4,000 evacuees held a meeting, marched to the administration area, and selected a committee of five to negotiate with the administration. In exchange for a promise of no more demonstrations, the center director agreed to bring Ueno back to the relocation center jail.

However, when Ueno was returned a crowd formed again. Fearing the worst, the director called in the military police, who then used tear gas to break up the crowd. When a truck was pushed toward the jail, the military police fired into the crowd, killing one and wounding at least ten others (one of whom later died).

A group of 65 "outspoken patriots" (Myer 1971:64) who supported the Manzanar administration were on a reported death list, including the JACL leader who had been beaten. For their protection, these evacuees were removed to an abandoned CCC Camp in Death Valley. Sixteen alleged troublemakers, including Ueno, were removed to local jails and then to another abandoned CCC Camp at Moab, Utah. This so-called "Isolation Center" was later moved to an Indian boarding school at Luepp, Arizona, in April 1943.

Others from Manzanar and other relocation centers were also sent to the Isolation Center, some for "crimes" as minor as calling a Caucasian nurse an old maid (Drinnon 1987:104). No formal charges had to be made, transfer was purely at the discretion of the relocation center director (Myer 1971:65). At Luepp, the military police outnumbered the inmates 3 to 1.

The Minidoka Center was continually plagued by strikes and protests. The evacuees organized a labor council, termed the Fair Play Committee, to represent them. The main objection was the low wage scale and the difference in wages between the evacuees and the Caucasian staff. A strike by evacuee coal workers was broken by employing other evacuees from the center who volunteered, and a strike by hospital workers was broken by sending the strike leaders to Luepp. Similar conflicts later arose with block maintenance staff, mail carriers, gatekeepers, telephone operators, warehouse workers, and other groups. A never-finished gymnasium stood as a reminder of administration-evacuee conflict. The construction crew walked out over a dispute about work hours and no volunteers could be found to replace them (Sakoda 1989:263).

Even with suspected troublemakers shipped out at a moment's notice, a crisis could erupt at anytime, as at the Topaz Relocation Center. On Sunday, April 11, 1943, 63-year-old James Hatsuaki Wakasa was fatally shot just before sunset by military police. Either distracted or unable to hear or understand the sentry's warnings, he was near the perimeter fence about 300 feet from the watchtower, when he was shot in the chest. The sentry, a disabled veteran of Pacific combat, claimed that Wakasa was trying to crawl through the fence and that he warned him four times before firing a warning shot (guards had fired warning shots on eight previous occasions).

The relocation center residents were shocked and outraged by the killing and a general alert was called by the military in case of trouble.

However, relative calm prevailed as both the administration and the Topaz Japanese American leadership wanted to avoid a confrontation. After a brief work stoppage, compromises on the funeral location (near, but not at, the spot of death) and limits placed on military police were reached. The military were subsequently restricted in their use of weapons, no MPs would be allowed inside the center, and Pacific veterans would be withdrawn and no more would be assigned. Nevertheless, a little more than a month later, a sentry fired at a couple strolling too close to the fence (Taylor 1993:141).

Indefinite Leave Clearance

One of the goals of the War Relocation Authority was to determine which evacuees were actually loyal to the United States, and then to find places for them to work and settle away from the West Coast, outside of the relocation centers. At first, each case had to be investigated individually, which often took months, since each person had to find a job and a place to live, while convincing the government that they were not a threat. Eventually, to streamline the process, every adult evacuee was given a questionnaire entitled "Application for Indefinite Leave Clearance" whether or not they were attempting to leave. Unfortunately, these questionnaires had originally been intended for determining loyalty of possible draftees, and were not modified for the general population, which included women and Japanese citizens. The controversial questions were Numbers 27 and 28:

No. 27: Are you willing to serve in the armed forces of the United States on combat duty, wherever ordered?

No. 28: Will you swear unqualified allegiance to the United States of America and faithfully defend the United States from any and all attack by foreign or domestic forces, and foreswear any form of allegiance or obedience to the Japanese Emperor, or any other foreign government, power, or organization?

The first question was a bit strange for women and the elderly, but otherwise relatively straightforward. However, the ambiguity of the second question was especially inappropriate. For Issei, who were not allowed to become American citizens, saying yes effectively left them without a country. On the other hand, some of those who already felt loyal to the United States considered it to be a trick question. No one was sure what the consequences would be, but each family debated how to answer these questions.

Many of the relocation center directors saw the dilemma in the loyalty questionnaire and got permission from the Washington Office to change the wording. At Manzanar the wording was changed to "Are you sympathetic to the United States and do you agree faithfully to defend the United States from any attack by foreign or domestic forces?" With this change many Issei at Manzanar answered "yes" (Smith 1995:292-293).

However, even with the changed wording controversy remained. While some of the "no-no boys" were truly more loyal to Japan than to the United States, in many cases people compromised to keep families together. Others answered "no" as a way of protesting the injustice of the entire relocation rather than suggesting loyalty to Japan. Some did not want to imply that they wanted to apply for leave, since now that they were settled in the relocation centers, they considered them to be a safe haven and did not want to be forced out into the unknown. The questionnaire and segregation was one of the most divisive events of the entire relocation.

Those who answered "yes" to the loyalty questionnaire were eligible to leave the relocation centers, if they found a sponsor. One of the largest single sponsors, Seabrook Farms, was also one of the largest producers of frozen vegetables in the country. The company, experiencing a labor shortage due to the war, had a history of hiring minorities and setting them up in ethnically segregated villages. About 2,500 evacuees went to Seabrook Farms' New Jersey plant. They worked 12-hour days, at 35¢ to 50¢ an hour, with 1 day off every 2 weeks. They lived in concrete block buildings, not much better than the relocation center barracks, and had to provide for their own food and cooking (Seabrook 1995).

Through the indefinite leave process, the overall population of the relocation centers was reduced. On June 30, 1944, the Jerome Relocation Center was converted into a POW camp for Germans, after the 5,000 residents remaining were transferred to other centers. This closure not only saved administration costs, but also was used to show that the relocation program was working. Over 18,000 evacuees moved out of the relocation centers in 1944. By the war's end over 50,000 Japanese Americans had relocated to the eastern U.S. (Table 3.5).

Canada, Latin America , and the Caribbean

The mass evacuation of Japanese Americans from the West Coast was only part of the removals undertaken throughout much of the Western Hemisphere. At the outbreak of World War II there were some 600,000 ethnic Japanese living in the Americas (Daniels 1991:132).

Canada, already at war with Germany and Italy, declared war on Japan within hours of the attacks on Pearl Harbor and British Hong Kong. Of the 23,000 people of Japanese ancestry in Canada, 75 percent were Canadian citizens. In the beginning, only Japanese aliens were arrested, but over 1,200 Japanese-Canadian fishing vessels, all owned by citizens, were impounded and later sold to finance the relocation (Figure 3.13; Daniels 1989:182-184).

By January 14, 1942, all Japanese alien males over 16 years of age had been removed from Pacific coast areas. When British Columbia politicians learned of the U.S. decision to evacuate all people of Japanese ancestry, including U.S. citizens, from the West Coast they demanded Canada do the same (Hirabayashi 1991).

A total evacuation was ordered on February 24. However, exceptions were made for those married to non-Asians (Daniels 1989:185). On March 16, eight days before the first evacuation of Japanese Americans by the U.S. Army, the removal of all Japanese-Canadians in British Columbia began. Over 21,000 were sent through the Hastings Park clearing station, the Canadian equivalent of an assembly center. From Hastings Park, half of the Japanese-Canadians were sent to Interior Housing Centers at six abandoned mining towns. The remaining were relocated to sugar beet farms, lumber camps, road construction camps, and other work camps in interior Canada (Figure 3.14). Even after the war, the Japanese-Canadians were not allowed to return to British Columbia until April 1949.

In Mexico people of Japanese ancestry along the Pacific Coast and the U.S. border were required by the Mexican government to liquidate property and move inland to resettlement camps (Weglyn 1976:57). They were eventually required to resettle in Mexico City or Guadalajara (Daniels 1991:132).

Figure 3.13. Seized fishing boats impounded on the Fraser River (Public Archives of Canada, Adachi 1976).

The U.S. pressured many Central and South American counties, even those not at war with Japan, to turn over Japanese immigrants and nationals to U.S. authorities for transportation to the U.S. (Weglyn 1976:57). The U.S. cited the safety of the Panama Canal as the rationale for this removal, but the use of the Japanese as pawns for exchange was not overlooked. During the early part of the war some 7,000 U.S. citizens had been captured by Japanese forces in the Philippines, Guam, Wake Island, and China.

In all, 2,264 Japanese were sent to the U.S. from Latin American and Caribbean counties; over 1,000 were from Peru (Gardiner 1991). Brazil's 300,000 Japanese, the largest population outside of Hawaii, were left largely alone (Daniels 1991:132), as were persons of Japanese ancestry in Chile and Argentina. Cuba incarcerated all adult male Japanese.

The first transfer to the U.S. occurred in April 1942. Most of the Japanese sent to the U.S. from Latin America were confined at Crystal City, Texas, a special family facility operated by the U.S. Immigration and Naturalization Service.

During the war the Swedish ship *Gripsholm* made two voyages to exchange 2,840 Japanese for American citizens. Nearly half of the Japanese exchanged were from Latin America. Alarmed at the number of Japanese being sent to the U.S. and with the exchange of citizens with Japan at a standstill, the Department of Justice ended the deportations to the U.S. in early 1943 (Weglyn 1976:63-64). After the war, many of the deportees were denied reentry to their sending country, and as a result many returned to Japan or stayed in the U.S. In 1946 many went to work at Seabrook Farms in New Jersey.

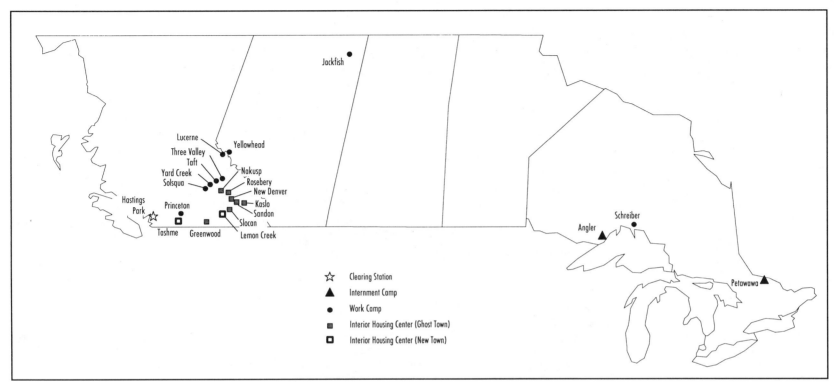

Figure 3.14. Japanese Canadian relocation sites.

Tule Lake Segregation Center

Those who answered "no" to the loyalty questions were considered "disloyals." In response to public and congressional criticism, the WRA decided to segregate the disloyals from the "loyals." One of the Poston camps was originally chosen, but eventually, the disloyals were segregated to the relocation center at Tule Lake, which already housed the highest number of disloyals.

The half of the original evacuees at Tule Lake who answered "yes" to the loyalty questions were supposed to choose another relocation center to make room for more disloyals at Tule Lake. But 4,000 loyals at Tule Lake chose to stay; some didn't want to leave California and others were just tired of being pushed around (Myer 1971:77), so the loyal and disloyal remained together. The 1,800 disloyals at Manzanar could not be moved to Tule Lake until the Spring of 1944, when additional housing was completed.

Ray Best, who had run the Isolation Centers at Moab and Luepp, was named the new director of Tule Lake. The 71 inmates at Luepp were transferred to Tule Lake (Myer 1971:77). Additional troops were assigned to Tule Lake, including eight tanks (Drinnon 1987:110). A "manproof" fence around the relocation center perimeter and more guard towers were eventually added as well.

The Tule Lake Segregation Center maintained the same internal democratic political structure as at the relocation centers, and the new arrivals became active in center politics (Figure 3.15 and 3.16).

A tragic accident set off a chain of events that fueled dissension in the center, and culminated in the Army taking over control of the Tule Lake Segregation Center. On October 15, 1943, a truck transporting evacuees from agricultural fields overturned, killing one evacuee. The center administration was blamed since the driver was underage, and evacuees were outraged that the widow's benefits amounted to only two-thirds of $16, the deceased's monthly wage.

A massive public funeral was conducted without administration approval and ten days later agricultural workers decided to go on strike. The strikers did not want to harvest food destined for other centers. They saw themselves as the "loyals" and the pro-U.S. Japanese Americans at the other centers as traitors to Japan.

Figure 3.15. Residents of the Tule Lake Center post signs to welcome the arrival of transferees from other centers (Charles E. Mace photograph, Bancroft Library, University of California, Berkeley).

The administration brought in 234 Japanese Americans from other relocation centers to harvest the crops. For their protection, the "loyals" were housed outside the center at a nearby former CCC camp. Further inciting the strikers, the strike breakers were paid $1 per hour rather than the standard WRA wages of $16 per month (Weglyn 1976:162).

When WRA Director Dillon Myer made a routine visit to Tule Lake on November 1, a crowd assembled in the administration area. During the assembly a doctor was beaten and some cars were vandalized. A group-appointed "Committee of 17" met with Myer, but all of their demands (including removal of director Best) were rejected. Further, future evacuee meetings in the administration area were forbidden. On November 4 the administration began work on a fence between the administration and evacuee areas.

That evening a crowd of around 400 tried to prevent trucks from being used to take food to the strike breakers (Weglyn 1976:163) and later the mob headed towards the director's residence. The Army, arriving with tanks and jeeps mounted with machine guns, used tear gas to disperse crowds throughout the center. Many evacuees were arrested and a curfew was established. The next day schools were closed and most work was stopped.

When an assembly called by the Army on November 14 was boy-cotted, more evacuees were arrested and martial law was declared. On November 26 a center-wide dragnet was conducted to find the leaders, who had been hidden by sympathetic evacuees.

A stockade was built in the administration area to house those arrested. The stockade had 12-ft-high wooden walls to obstruct the view and prevent communication with the rest of the center popula-tion. By December 1 the last of the leaders turned themselves in to authorities in a show of solidarity with those already arrested. On January 1 those incarcerated in the stockade initiated the first of three hunger strikes.

Within the rest of the cen-ter, however, the protests waned. On January 11, while over 350 dissident leaders were in jail, the center residents voted to end the protests. The vote was close (and one block refused to vote) but the moderates had retaken control. In response to the vote martial law was lifted on January 15. The center administration, except for the stockade, was returned to the WRA.

The April 18 Tokyo Declaration, in which the Japanese government officially protested the treatment of the disloyals, provided some recognition to those within the stockade. Shortly thereafter, 276 were released from the stockade and on May 23, 1944, Army control of the stockade was turned over to the WRA.

Figure 3.16. Demonstration at Tule Lake (WRA photograph, National Archives).

Eventually, over 1,200 Issei were removed from the Tule Lake Segregation Center to Justice Department internment camps at Bismarck, North Dakota, and Santa Fe, New Mexico (Culley 1991; Myer 1971:90). But tension still ran high. On May 24, James Okamoto was shot and killed during an altercation with a guard, and in June the general manager of the Business Enterprise Association, one of the most stable elements in the evacuee community, was murdered.

On August 19, 1944, soon after the American Civil Liberties Union (ACLU) demanded to see those in the stockade, all were suddenly released and the fence removed. The stockade jail was used again for a short period in June 1945 when five teenagers were sentenced by the center director to the stock-ade for blowing bugles and wear-ing Japanese-style clothing.

Nisei in the Army

The initial aim of the registration questionnaire had been to deter-mine loyalty of draft-age males before calling for volunteers for the army, and then to reinstate the draft for Japanese Americans. In early 1943, President Roosevelt declared that " ... Americanism is not, and never was, a matter of race or ancestry ... Every loyal American should be given the opportunity to serve this country wherever his skills will make the greatest contribution – whether it be in the ranks of our armed forces, war production, agriculture, government service, or other work essential to the war effort." While the initial call for volunteers resulted in a much smaller group than initially expected by the government, approximately 1,200 Nisei volunteered from the

Figure 3.17. Japanese American women in the armed forces (Japanese American Historical Society, San Francisco).

relocation centers at the initial registration (Figures 3.17-3.19).

These volunteers and the later draftees became the 442nd Regimental Combat Team. The 442nd combined with the 100th Infantry Battalion of the Hawaii National Guard, which had originally been transferred to the mainland and given only wooden guns to train with. The government had hoped creating a predominantly Japanese American unit would help impress the general public with Nisei patriotism and bravery, but some Japanese Americans opposed joining the army in a segregated unit.

The combined 100th and 442nd became the most decorated unit of its size in American history, with 18,143 individual decorations and 9,486 casualties in a regiment with an authorized strength of 4,000 men (Chuman 1976:179; Uyeda 1995:73). Both units fought in Italy and France, and were responsible for the rescue of the "Lost Battalion" of the 36th Texas Division. Ironically, the 522nd battalion of the 442nd Regiment discovered and liberated the Dachau Concentration Camp, but were ordered to keep quiet about their actions (Noguchi 1992; Uyeda 1995:75). The next day, another American battalion arrived and "officially" liberated the camp.

In addition, more than 16,000 Nisei served in the Pacific and in Asia, mainly in intelligence and translation, performing invaluable and dangerous tasks. Not only were there normal risks of combat duty, they risked certain death if captured by the Japanese. Nisei women also served with distinction in the Women Army Corps, as nurses, and for the Red Cross.

In general, the initial Japanese American opposition to serving in the Army turned into pride in their accomplishments, partly through the efforts of the soldiers' families. Almost every camp built "Honor Rolls" listing men who were serving in the Army and many windows displayed service flags. Awareness of the accomplishments of the 442nd/100th outside the camps varied according to how closely one followed the news, but those who followed military progress closely

Figure 3.18. Japanese American soldiers in Italy (U.S. Army photograph, National Archives).

Figure 3.19. Honor roll at the Minidoka Relocation Center (WRA photograph, Bancroft Library, University of California, Berkeley).

were impressed by the accomplishments of the 442nd "Go For Broke" Regiment and the 100th Battalion.

While many Nisei joined the Army as a method of proving their loyalty, others resisted volunteering and the draft to protest the relocation. Nationwide, 293 interned Japanese Americans were tried for draft resistance (Daniels 1993:64). The resisters did not oppose the draft itself, but hoped that their protest would clarify their citizenship status. The best organized draft resistance was organized by the Fair Play Committee at the Heart Mountain Relocation Center, where 54 of 315 potential draftees did not show up for physicals (Daniels 1989:125). Committee leader Kiyoshi Okamota was branded disloyal and transferred to Tule Lake. Another leader, Isamu Horino, was arrested as he tried to walk out the front gate to dramatize his lack of freedom. Horino was also sent to Tule Lake. A third leader, Paul Nakadate, was sent to Tule Lake after an administration interrogation determined his disloyalty.

The 54 draft resisters, and nine additional people who counseled the resisters, were arrested. All 63 were found guilty in the largest mass trial for draft resistance in U.S. history. Seven members of the Fair Play Committee were found guilty of conspiracy, as well. However, the verdicts did not silence the resistance: 22 more Heart Mountain evacuees were later arrested for draft evasion. In all, 85 evacuees at Heart Mountain were convicted of draft evasion and were sent to federal prison. However, at Heart Mountain more than 700 evacuees did report for physicals, and 385 were inducted. Of these, 63 were killed or wounded in combat (Daniels 1989:128).

Supreme Court Cases

The constitutional questions raised by the relocation of Japanese Americans were left to the U.S. Supreme Court to decide. The

Hirabayashi, Korematsu, and Endo cases respectively dealt with the curfew, evacuation, and detention (tenBroek et al. 1954:211-223).

In *Hirabayashi v. United States* on June 21, 1943, the court unanimously decided that due to "the gravest imminent danger to the public safety" the military did have the right to enforce a curfew for a specific group of people, on the grounds of military necessity. They ruled that the curfew was not motivated by ethnic identity or race, but by an actual threat.

The final two cases were decided December 18, 1944. In *Korematsu v. United States*, in a split decision, the court upheld the government's right to exclude people of Japanese ancestry from the West Coast based on military necessity. "Military necessity" was purposely not defined – if the military did it, it must have been necessary.

In *Endo v. United States* it was unanimously decided that Mitsuye Endo, a loyal U.S. citizen, should be released unconditionally, that is, without having to follow the indefinite leave procedure established by the WRA. The court stated that the WRA "has no authority to subject citizens who are concededly loyal to its leave procedure." The government therefore did not have the right to confine any loyal Japanese American. While sidestepping the constitutional question of the right of government to hold citizens without cause in wartime, it did in effect free all loyal Japanese Americans still held in Relocation Centers. The WRA had simply exceeded its authority.

Closing the Relocation Centers

During the war, the Japanese American evacuees had wondered what would be the ultimate fate of the relocation centers. Some expected them to close when the war ended, while others, particularly the elderly, felt the government owed them a place to stay, now that they had been forcibly removed from their own homes. Anticipating the

Supreme Court decisions, on December 17, 1944, the War Department announced the lifting of the West Coast exclusion orders, and the WRA simultaneously announced that the relocation centers would be closed within one year. Initial reactions of the evacuees varied: some immediately returned to the West Coast, some at the other end of the spectrum vowed never to leave the centers.

Some of the first to return to the West Coast encountered violence and hostility and difficulty finding housing and jobs. Others had more success and encouraged people to leave the camps and return. Many who feared returning to the West Coast found refuge in other parts of the country, especially Denver, Salt Lake City, and Chicago.

Evacuees had to relocate on their own. The WRA provided only minimum assistance: $25 per person, train fare, and meals on route for those with less than $500 in cash. Many left when ordered and by September over 15,000 evacuees a month were leaving the various centers. But many had no place to go, since they had lost their homes and businesses because of the relocation. In the end the WRA had to resort to forced evictions.

At the Minidoka Relocation Center, laundries, latrines, and mess halls were progressively closed until the few remaining people had to search for food to eat. Evacuees were given 2-week, 3-day, and 30-minute eviction notices. If they still did not leave on their own, the WRA packed their belongings and forced them onto trains (Sakoda 1989).

Eventually the centers were emptied out, and all were finally closed by the end of 1945. The Tule Lake Segregation Center operated longer, until March 20, 1946, because many evacuees there had renounced their citizenship.

Enacted on July 1, 1944, Public Law 504 had allowed U.S. citizens to renounce their citizenship on U.S. soil during time of war. Of the

Figure 3.20. Abandoned evacuee barracks at the Tule Lake Center (Bureau of Reclamation photograph, Mid-Pacific Regional Office, Sacramento).

5,700 Japanese Americans requesting renunciation, 95 percent were from Tule Lake. A third of all those interned at Tule Lake applied for repatriation to Japan; 65 percent of those requesting repatriation were born in the U.S. (Daniels 1989:116). On February 23, 1946, the first 432 repatriates set sail for Japan. Over 4,000 would follow. However, over the next five years all but 357 would apply for a return of their U.S. citizenship (Smith 1995:444).

Figure 3.21. Transporting building materials from the Manzanar Relocation Center (Los Angeles Times Photograph).

After the last internees were released, the Tule Lake facility was placed on standby use during the Cold War for potential McCarran Act detainees, but was never used (Roger Daniels, personal communication, 2000). All the other relocation centers lay abandoned. If the land had been privately owned, the original owners were generally given the option to re-purchase the land. Otherwise, the land reverted to the control of the previous land-managing agency (Table 3.6). Buildings were sold to veterans, auctioned off, or given to local schools and hospitals (Figures 3.20 and 3.21). On May 15 the last WRA field office was closed and on June 30, 1946, the WRA was officially disbanded.

Retrospect

Six of the former relocation centers are listed on the National Register for their historical significance. Two sites are also National Historic Landmarks: Manzanar, and the memorial cemetery at Rohwer. Plaques and small monuments are the only memorials. People still debate whether the exclusion orders and the relocation centers were just, reasonable, constitutional, or justifiable responses to war (Baker 1991, 1994; Smith 1995; Uyeda 1995). However, in 1982 the California legislature passed a bill to provide $5,000 restitution to 314 Japanese Americans who were fired from their state jobs in 1942. Significantly, the three Japanese Americans who had been convicted of violating curfew and not reporting to the relocation centers were exonerated. Evidence surfaced that the War Department and the Justice Department had altered blatantly racist reports and submitted false information to the Supreme Court about the potential danger posed by the Japanese Americans. With this newly discovered information Federal District Courts overturned Fred Korematsu's conviction in 1984, Minoru Yasui's conviction in 1985, and Gordon Hirabayashi's conviction in 1986 (Figure 3.22). In 1989 the U.S. government officially apologized and granted redress of $20,000 to each surviving evacuee.

Figure 3.22. Fred Korematsu, Minoru Yasui, and Gordon Hirabayashi.

Table 3.6.
Disposition of WRA Centers (Myer 1971:348).

Center	date of release	Agency designated for Disposal
Gila River	2/23/46	Government Land Office
Granada	1/26/46	Farm Credit Administration
Heart Mtn.	2/23/46	Bureau of Reclamation
Jerome	10/1/44	War Department
Manzanar	3/9/46	Government Land Office
Minidoka	10/1/44	Bureau of Reclamation
Poston	3/9/46	U.S. Indian Service
Rohwer	3/9/46	Government Land Office
Topaz	2/9/46	Farm Credit Administration
Tule Lake	5/4/46	Bureau of Reclamation

Chapter 4

Gila River Relocation Center

The Gila River Relocation Center was located about 50 miles south of Phoenix and 9 miles west of Sacaton in Pinal County, Arizona. The site is on the Gila River Indian Reservation, and access to the site today is restricted. The post office designation for the center was Rivers, named after Jim Rivers, the first Pima Indian killed in action during World War I. The relocation center included two separate camps located 3½ miles apart, Canal Camp (originally called Camp No. 1) in the eastern half of the Relocation Center reserve, and Butte Camp (Camp No. 2) in the western half. When the Gila River Relocation Center was in operation it was the fourth largest city in Arizona, after Phoenix, Tucson, and the relocation center at Poston.

The Gila Relocation Center lies within the broad Gila River Valley, and the Gila River flows southeast to northwest about 4 miles northeast of the reserve boundary. Just 3 miles south of the reserve, the rocky Sacaton Mountains rise 700 feet above the valley floor. Two main irrigation canals roughly follow the contours of the Sacaton Mountains' north and east bajada, and most of the relocation center reserve lies between these two canals (Figure 4.1). The South Side Canal, at about 1350 feet elevation, is near the southern boundary; the Casa Blanca Canal, at about 1225 feet elevation, forms the northern boundary. Interstate 10 now cuts through the eastern portion of what once were farm fields of the reserve. Most of the relocation center is on flat or very gently sloping sandy alluvial loam, but the rocky outcroppings of Sacaton Butte are just west and north of Butte Camp. The Sonoran desert vegetation of the area is dominated by mesquite trees, creosote and bursage bushes, and cactus.

Before the Gila River site was chosen for a relocation center, other potential sites in Arizona were considered, including Cortaro Farms near Tucson, Fort Mohave on the Colorado River, and Beardsley near Phoenix. These sites were rejected as either too costly to build or too

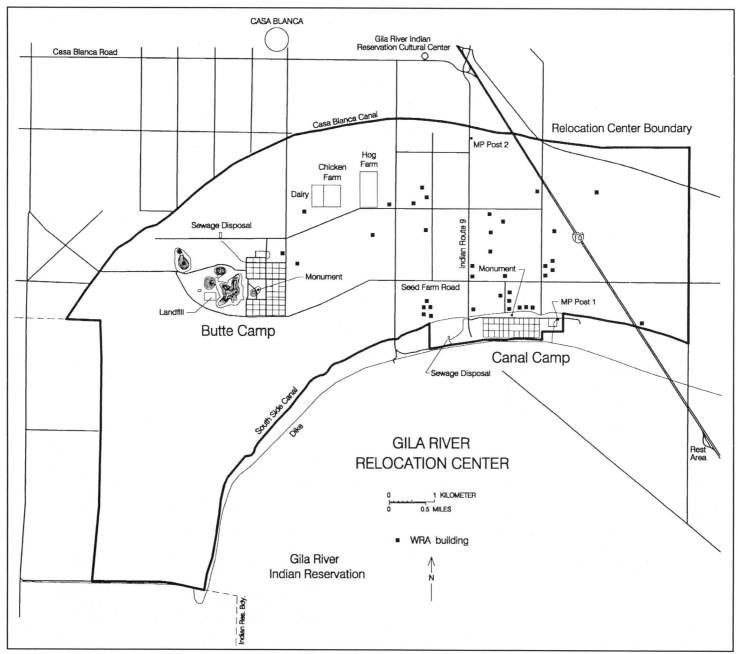

Figure 4.1. Gila River Relocation Center.

close to sensitive military areas. The Gila River site was approved, in spite of objections by the Gila River Indian tribe, on March 18, 1942. Plans were soon expanded to accommodate 14,000 instead of 10,000 at Gila River to make up for a relocation center site in Nebraska which was rejected at the last minute (Madden 1969). The construction of brand-new cities for 10,000 people would, of course, require a prodigious amount of resources even during peace time. The copper necessary for the transmission line that would have had to be constructed for the Nebraska facility simply was in short supply during the war, and it was more feasible to expand other centers.

The WRA leased the 16,500 acres for the relocation center reserve from the Bureau of Indian Affairs under a five-year permit. Under the terms of the permit, the WRA agreed to develop agricultural lands and build roads to connect the relocation center with state highways to the north and south. Construction of the relocation center began on May 1, 1942, with 125 workers; by June over 1,250 were employed (Weik 1992). On July 10, the first advance group of 500 Japanese Americans arrived to help set up the relocation center. Groups of 500 Japanese American started to arrive each day the following week. By August the evacuee population was over 8,000. The maximum population, 13,348, was reached in November 1942 even before major construction was completed, which was not until December 1, 1942.

The evacuees at Gila River were mainly from the Tulare, Turlock, Stockton, and Fresno assembly centers, but nearly 3,000 were sent directly from Military Area 2 (southern San Joaquin Valley) without first staying in an assembly center. Canal Camp housed mostly rural people from the Turlock Assembly Center and Military Area 2, while Butte Camp housed mostly urban people from the Tulare and Santa Anita Assembly Centers.

The evacuee barracks at the two camps were constructed of wood frame and sheathed with lightweight white "beaverboard." Roofs were

Figure 4.2. Typical barracks at the Gila River Relocation Center (National Archives photograph).

double, to provide protection from the heat of the desert, with the top roofs sheathed with red fireproof shingles (Figure 4.2). Another extra feature to help deal with the heat at the Gila River Relocation Center was the use of evaporative coolers. Clearly the Gila River Relocation Center was a showplace. Soon after his arrival at the center anthropologist Robert F. Spencer noted "The center is rather attractive as compared with the others. The white houses with their red roofs can be seen from miles away" (Spencer 1942). In April 1943, Eleanor Roosevelt, along with WRA director Dillon Myer, made a surprise visit to the Gila River Relocation Center, spending 6 hours inspecting facilities (see Chapter 2; Figure 4.3).

However, in spite of the model appearance of the camps, there were problems with the infrastructure. There were chronic water shortages, and for a time parts of Butte Camp ran out of water by nightfall. Use of evaporative coolers was curtailed and other water conservation

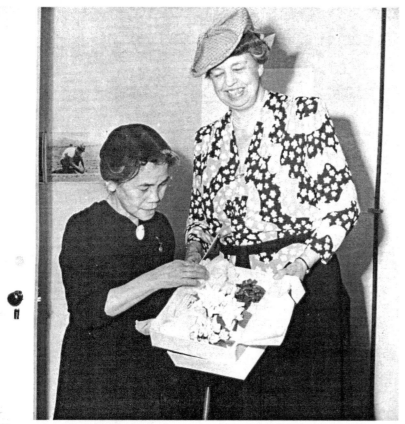

Figure 4.3 Eleanor Roosevelt at the Gila River Relocation Center, April 23, 1943 (Francis Stewart photograph, Bancroft Library, University of California, Berkeley).

measures were enforced. An existing natural gas line just east of Canal Camp provided fuel to heat the mess halls and hospital, but barracks were heated with fuel oil due to a limited supply of natural gas (Madden 1969).

Only one watch tower was ever erected at the Gila River Relocation Center. Located at Canal Camp, it was reportedly torn down because staffing it would have imposed a serious burden on the small military police detachment (Madden 1969). Within 6 months the perimeter

Figure 4.4. Model ship building shop (National Archives photograph).

barbed wire fences around each camp were removed as well. At Butte Camp a camouflage net factory run by Southern California Glass Company employed 500 evacuees. But, the factory was discontinued after 5 months. A model ship building shop at Canal Camp provided models for use in military training (Figure 4.4).

Supplies for the relocation center were originally shipped by train to Casa Grande and transported the last 17 miles to the camps by truck. In 1943 a loading and warehouse facility for the center was built at a railroad siding at Serape, only 11 miles away.

Canal Camp covered a narrow 210-acre area three blocks north-south and slightly more than nine blocks east-west in the eastern part of the reserve at the southern boundary (Figure 4.5). Bounding the camp on the north was the South Side Canal; on the south was a raised earthen dike that had been constructed to protect the canal from flash floods. The camp was separated by firebreaks into three groups of nine blocks each. The blocks were numbered from 1 to 27, starting in the

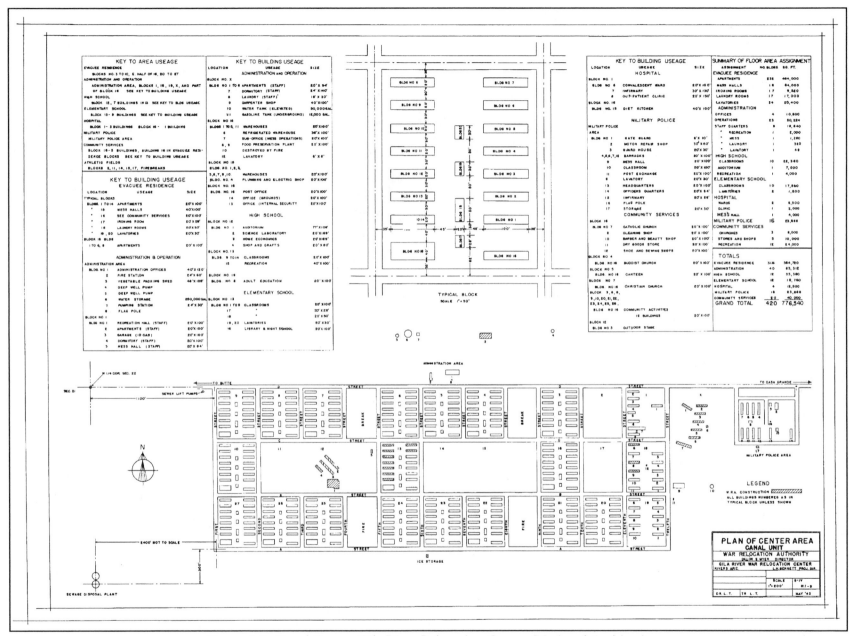

Figure 4.5. Canal Camp, Gila River Relocation Center (National Archives).

Figure 4.6. Water tank at Canal Camp (National Archives photograph).

Figure 4.7. Administration building at Canal Camp (National Archives photograph).

Figure 4.8. Auditorium under construction at Canal Camp (WRA photograph, Bancroft Library, University of California, Berkeley).

northeast corner and proceeding west to Block 9. The next row began with Block 10 just south of Block 9, with numbers ascending back to the east to 18. The southernmost row started with 19 at the east edge, increasing to 27 at the southwest corner. The firebreaks were not numbered. North-south streets were numbered from west to east, east-west streets were lettered with "A" on the south and "D" on the north. "D" Street led west to Butte Camp and east to Casa Grande.

The military police were housed in a compound just east of Canal Camp. The 15 buildings in the compound included five barracks, a mess hall, a classroom, a post exchange, a latrine, a headquarters building, an officers' quarters, an infirmary, a storage building, a guardhouse (jail for military personnel), and a motor vehicle repair shop. Along "D" Street northeast of the military police compound there was an 8-foot-by-10-foot sentry post. Another sentry post was located well north of the two camps along the road to Phoenix.

Canal Camp itself included 404 buildings, 44 of which were devoted to administration and hospital use. Most of the administration and hospital buildings were located in the three blocks (1, 18, and 19) along the eastern edge of the camp. Block 1 had an apartment building, a dormitory, a recreation hall, a mess hall, a ten-car garage, and the hospital. The hospital included a convalescent ward, an infirmary, and an out-patient clinic. The hospital also ran a "diet kitchen" in Block 16. Between Block 1 and the military police compound the evacuees constructed six apartment buildings, a dormitory, and a laundry for additional staff housing. South of Block 1, in Blocks 18 and 19 there were 12 warehouses, a refrigerated warehouse, an office, two food preservation plant buildings, a plumbing and electrical shop, and a latrine. East of these blocks there was a carpenter shop, an underground gas tank, and a 50,000-gallon elevated water tank (Figure 4.6).

Centrally located north of Block 5, between the evacuee residential area and the South Side Canal, there was a 40 foot by 120 foot administration office building and a fire station (Figure 4.7). North across the canal from the administration office building were two deep water wells, a pumping station, a 250,000-gallon water storage tank, and an evacuee-constructed vegetable packing shed. The post office and two additional administration offices were located in buildings within Block 16. An evacuee-constructed ice storage building was south of Block 23, between the evacuee residential area and the protective dike. Canal Camp had its own sewage treatment plant ½ mile west of the residential area. A sewage pumping station west of Block 9 pumped sewage to the plant, which was about 20 feet higher in elevation.

The 360 buildings at Canal Camp devoted to evacuee residential uses included 232 Barracks, 17 mess halls, 17 ironing rooms, 17 laundry rooms, 34 latrine and shower buildings, 24 school buildings, and 20 community service buildings. Each of the 17 evacuee residential blocks included fourteen 20 foot by 100 foot barracks, a mess hall, a men's latrine and shower building, a women's latrine and shower building, a laundry room, an ironing room, a recreation building, and a 1,000-gallon fuel oil tank. The recreation buildings and some of the barracks were used for churches, meeting rooms, classrooms, libraries, and other community services. The ironing rooms were reportedly never used for their intended purposes, and all were eventually converted to storage rooms for mess hall supplies.

The evacuees ameliorated the harshness of their surroundings by planting gardens, building fish ponds, and planting trees for shade. Small canals were excavated to provide irrigation. Block 13, in the middle of the evacuee residential area, was used for elementary and high schools. An outdoor stage was located in the northeast corner of the firebreak west of Block 13. In Block 12, a vacant block to the west of the schools, the evacuees constructed an auditorium/gym (Figure 4.8), a science laboratory, a home economics building, and a vocational arts (shop/crafts) building. Athletic fields were located in the remaining vacant blocks (Blocks 2, 11, 14, 15, 17) and in firebreaks.

The larger of the two camps at the Gila River Relocation Center, Butte Camp, covered 790 acres at the base of Sacaton Butte 3½ miles west of Canal Camp (Figure 4.9). At Butte Camp east-west streets were numbered, 1st on the south to 14th on the north; north-south streets were lettered "A" Street on the east to "G" Street on the west. The main entrance to the camp was along the east side, at 9th street. The blocks were numbered from 28 to 81, beginning at the southeast corner and wrapping west, then east, row by row to the north. There were two narrow east-west firebreaks, one just south of 9th Street and one between 4th and 5th Streets.

There were 821 buildings in all at Butte Camp. Administration offices, warehouses, and staff housing were in the northeastern quarter of the developed area. The 22 buildings in the administration area (Blocks 69 and 70) included five office buildings, the post office, two ten-car garages, mimeograph buildings, nine warehouses, a police office, a court, and the staff canteen. Staff housing in Block 75 included a mess hall, recreation building, 5 dormitories, and a laundry. To the east and north, in Blocks 76 and 81, were 12 staff apartments, a water filtration plant, a refrigerated warehouse, a laundry, and a gas station; all but the gas station and four of the apartments were built by the evacuees (Figure 4.10).

The warehouse area (Blocks 67 and 68) included 22 warehouses, two of which were built by evacuees. North of the warehouse blocks, in areas designated Blocks 77 and 78, were two carpenter shops, a warehouse, a planer shed, a plumbing and electrical shop, an ice house, and a 37-by-108-foot machine shop, the latter two buildings built by evacuees.

The motor pool and a camouflage net factory were located west of Blocks 61 and 72 in the northwestern portion of the camp. There were four buildings for the net factory, one 60 feet by 400 feet in size, two 26 feet by 250 feet, and one 25 feet by 200 feet (Figure 4.11). The net

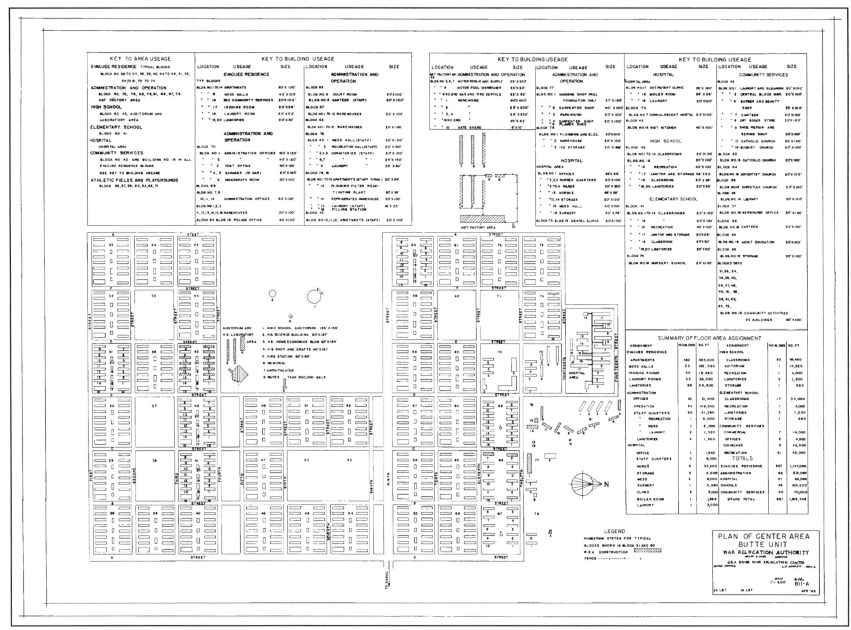

Figure 4.9. Butte Camp, Gila River Relocation Center (National Archives).

66

Figure 4.10. Staff housing at Butte Camp (National Archives photograph).

Figure 4.11. Camouflage net factory at Butte Camp (National Archives photograph).

factory was enclosed by a fence and had an 8-foot-by-10-foot guard house at the entrance. From the net factory one could access the motor pool, located to the west. The motor pool buildings included a 22-foot-by-60-foot office, a 22-foot-by-82-foot shop, and three 26-foot-by-250- foot repair and supply buildings.

The Butte Camp hospital, which served both Butte and Canal Camps, was located north of the administration area. In addition to the hospital's 18 interconnected buildings, there was a dental clinic in Block 73 and a convalescent hostel in Block 74.

The evacuee residential area, comprising 36 developed blocks, was located to the south and west of the administration area. The evacuee residential area wrapped around two small knolls. On the higher knoll there was a 300,000-gallon water tank supplied by a deep water well. On the other knoll the evacuees built a servicemen's memorial. On

the slope below the memorial they built an outdoor stage and amphitheater (Figure 4.12). A fire station was located east of the knolls at the west end of 6th Street (west of Blocks 46 and 51).

The WRA map lists 627 evacuee residential buildings, 46 of which were used as schools, 6 for churches, and 29 for other community services. All of Block 41 was an elementary school. Block 42 was used for community services including offices, churches, a shoe repair shop, a sewing shop, a laundry and dry cleaners, a barber shop, a beauty shop, a canteen, a store, and a "diet kitchen." Four buildings in Block 42 were used for staff apartments. Block 43 was used for a high school. To the north of Block 43 the evacuees built an auditorium and three classroom buildings for science, home economics, and vocational arts (shop/crafts).

Vacant blocks (35, 37, 38, 50, 53, 62, and 71) were used for athletic

Figure 4.12. Water tank and outdoor stage at Butte Camp (National Archives photograph).

fields, playgrounds, and other facilities. Butte Camp also featured what has been called the WRA's finest baseball diamond (Hansen 1997). Designed by professional baseball player Kenichi Zenimura it included dugouts, bleachers, and other features and could accommodate up to 6,000 spectators.

In 1935 about 7,000 acres of the area that would become the relocation center reserve had been leveled, irrigated, and planted with alfalfa for grazing. Water for irrigation was supplied from San Carlos Reservoir upstream on the Gila River. By August 1942, 500 acres of the grazing land were converted into vegetable farms, growing beets, carrots, celery, and other vegetables (Figure 4.13-4.17). Local farmers rented the remaining grazing land until the WRA started their own livestock program (Madden 1969). Partly to provide access to the farm fields, 13 miles of oil-surfaced roads with box culverts and bridges and 10-plus miles of graded roads were constructed.

At its peak during the 1943-1944 harvest season agricultural production at the Gila Relocation Center employed nearly 1,000 men and women. In the first nine months of operation, 84 train carloads of food were shipped from Gila to the other relocation centers. Twenty percent of the food used at all of the relocation centers across the county was produced at the Gila River Relocation Center. Evacuees also produced 150 acres of flax, cotton, and castor beans as war crop production. To expedite the shipping of crops, a second warehouse was constructed in 1944 at the railroad siding at Serape.

A seed farm was started due to shortages of seeds, and two nurseries grew seedlings for flowers, shrubs, and trees for landscaping. By 1943 over 1,600 acres north of Canal Camp and east of Butte Camp were under cultivation. The Gila River Relocation Center was the only relocation center to make use of its waste water: there was a 10-acre small "sewer farm" located to the west of each of the two sewage treatment plants, where effluent was used to irrigate grains and livestock feed.

In May 1943 a livestock program was started with 36 dairy cows, 720 Mexican steers, 50 young female hogs (gilts) from California, and 2,000 meat and egg chickens. Evacuees built shelters and pens for the hogs and dairy cows (Figure 4.18 and 4.19). The dairy included a 36-foot-by-105-foot milking barn, a 20-foot-by-60-foot milk house, a 20-foot-by-100-foot feed warehouse, and 16 feed lots with concrete troughs. The meat animals were shipped to Phoenix for slaughter and processing until a butchering plant was built at Gila River. By the end of the year there were 1,377 cattle, 1,106 hogs, and 8,584 chickens, and the farm program supplied 60 hogs and 60 cattle a week to the mess hall kitchens (Madden 1969).

Canal Camp was closed on September 28, 1945, and Butte Camp soon followed on November 10, 1945. The last to leave the Gila River Center were 155 Hawaiian Japanese. In December many of the

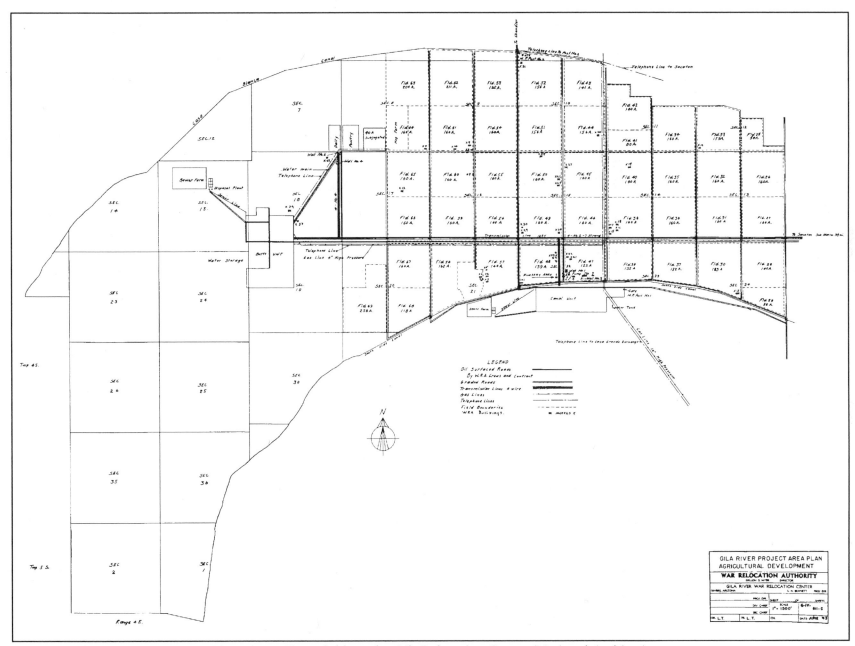

Figure 4.13. Farm fields at the Gila Relocation Center (National Archives).

Figure 4.14. Harvesting cucumbers at the Gila River Relocation Center (Francis Stewart Photograph, Bancroft Library, University of California, Berkeley).

Figure 4.16. Growing carrot seeds at the Gila River Relocation Center (Francis Stewart Photograph, Bancroft Library, University of California, Berkeley).

Figure 4.15. Growing experimental plants at the Gila River Relocation Center (Francis Stewart Photograph, Bancroft Library, University of California, Berkeley).

Figure 4.17. Harvesting daikon at the Gila River Relocation Center (Francis Stewart Photograph, Bancroft Library, University of California, Berkeley).

Figure 4.18. Feeding dairy cows at the Gila River Relocation Center dairy farm (National Archives photograph).

Figure 4.19. Feeding calves at the Gila River Relocation Center dairy farm (WRA photograph, Bancroft Library, University of California, Berkeley).

buildings at the relocation center were allocated and moved to educational institutions throughout the state. The City of Mesa bought the Butte high school auditorium (Hansen 1997). The WRA auctioned off the barracks and other property in August 1946, and sealed bids to purchase the remaining buildings and utilities continued until March of 1947 (Weik 1992).

Recent archaeological studies for the Gila Farms expansion have provided additional information on the past history and current condition of some of the features associated with Butte Camp. In 1983 a sample survey of lands surrounding Butte Camp was conducted for the farm expansion. No relocation center remains were encountered in that survey, but the report recommended that the area immediately adjacent to Butte Camp be thoroughly examined before development commenced, because of the potential for significant remains associated

with the relocation center (Effland and Green 1983).

In 1987, a 2,230-acre area north of Butte Camp and seven randomly-selected quarter sections (1,280 acres) south of Butte Camp were intensively surveyed. Relocation-center-era remains recorded in the northern survey area included the Butte Camp sewage treatment plant and adjacent sewer farm, the relocation center dairy, a small scatter of medical supplies, and an expansive area adjacent to the north and east edges of Butte Camp encompassing numerous small trash dumps. About 1½ miles west of Butte Camp a small relocation-center-era trash dump surrounded by a light scatter of artifacts covering 7½ acres was recorded. Somewhat surprisingly, none of these sites was considered eligible for the National Register on their own merits or as contributing elements of a larger property that would include other remains of the relocation center. No further consideration of the sites was recommended in the original report (Sullivan et

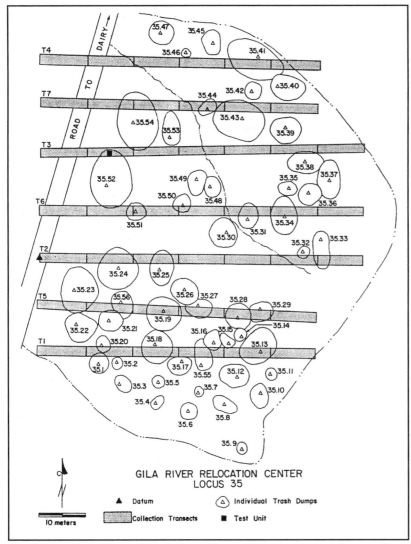

Figure 4.20. Trash concentration (Locus 35) near Butte Camp (from Sawer-Lang 1989).

In 1989 further archeological work was conducted around Butte Camp to define and characterize the trash scatter surrounding Butte Camp. These investigations included surface collection, excavation, and survey of approximately 2,000 acres south of Butte Camp (Sawyer-Lang 1989). Two pet graves and 37 discrete trash loci were identified within the previously-recorded trash scatter. One of the loci (Locus 35) included 56 distinct trash clusters (Figure 4.20). Although not recognized as such at the time, remnants of the Zenimura baseball field were recorded just east of the southeast corner of evacuee residential area. Surface collections were made at each of the 37 loci and eight were tested. It was determined that the remains probably dated to the last days of the relocation center when organized trash disposal had ceased.

A 1993 supplemental study included a detailed analysis of the artifacts collected in 1989, as well as archival research and oral history interviews (Tamir et al. 1993). While noting the constraints of the collection (most notably the fact that it dates to the end of the camp occupation), the artifact assemblage was described, oddly enough, as "ordinary." That is, with the exception of Japanese ceramics, the material could have been discarded by any contemporary American community (Russell 1995). However, even a cursory comparison of the Butte Camp collection with other sites demonstrates the dearth of artifacts associated with typical American pastimes such as cars, guns, and alcohol. Most of the features recorded in their studies have since been destroyed by agricultural developments, but still remaining are some small trash dumps immediately north of Butte camp and a pet grave left in an orchard to the southeast of Butte Camp.

Canal Camp

Canal Camp is located along what used to be the main highway between Phoenix and Casa Grande. The portion of this road north of Canal Camp was built by the WRA as part of their lease agreement

al. 1987). However, subsequent government review of the project resulted in the recommendation that more archeological work would be needed in order to mitigate the effects of the farm expansion.

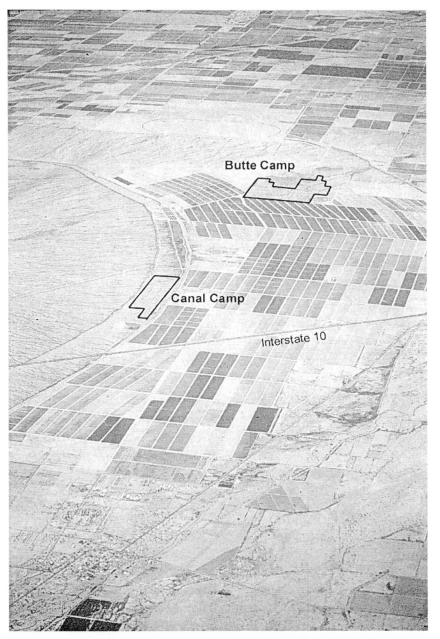

Figure 4.21. Oblique aerial view of the Gila River Relocation Center area today (north to right).

Figure 4.22. Old highway bridge over the South Side Canal.

with the BIA. The highway was superseded by Interstate 10, and now, the road is closed south of the bridge over the South Side Canal (Figures 4.21 and 4.22). Canal Camp is in fairly pristine condition. No buildings remain, but all of the camp roads are still passable. Abundant remains are present, including the concrete slabs of administration buildings, warehouses, the high school, and latrines, many pier footing blocks from the evacuee barracks and other buildings, landscaping, traces of irrigation ditches (Figure 4.23), and most features of the sewage treatment plant. Abundant artifacts occur throughout the administration and evacuee residential area as well as the surrounding area (Figure 4.24).

Administration, Hospital, and Warehouse Areas
In the central portion of the camp, between the residential area and the South Side Canal, the concrete slab foundations of the administration building and fire station are intact (Figure 4.25). Both building slabs have names and dates in the concrete (Table 4.1). There is also

Figure 4.24. Vehicle licence plate at Canal Camp.

an eight-sided concrete base that apparently held a flagpole (Figure 4.26). Culverts southeast and southwest of the administration area and along "D" street have several inscriptions that include the official post office name for the relocation center (Rivers, Ariz.) and a 1943 date (Figures 4.27 and 4.28). In the eastern portion of Canal Camp, there is little evidence of the staff housing or hospital buildings. However, the 21 concrete slab foundations from the warehouses still remain (Figure 4.29).

Evacuee Residential Area
Within the evacuee residential blocks the locations of latrines, storage (ironing), and laundry rooms are marked by their concrete foundation slabs (Figures 4.30-4.32). The main impact to the site appears to have been from the salvage of cast iron pipe. Apparently the concrete slabs of all of the latrines and laundries were broken up to remove the pipes below. An interesting feature in each residential block is an underground concrete tank accessed by a manhole (Figure 4.33). These

Figure 4.23. Remains of irrigation ditch at Canal Camp.

Figure 4.25. Concrete slab of the Canal Camp fire station.

Table 4.1. Inscriptions at Canal Camp.

Inscription	Location
~1943~ RIVERS	Administration Area
T. NAGAI 9.4 1943 A RIVERS, ARIZ.	Administration Area
YUTAKA HANDA MAR 3, 1943	Administration Area
S. Handa YAS S. Handa 3/3/43	Fire Station
HHM	Block 3 sidewalk
43 Sa...aki Handa	Block 4
• 8-1-A • K. KUNISUYE •	Block 8 entry
In Japanese: "Showa 17 (1942) August Sakuyuki (surname)"	Block 8 pond
8-26-03 (?)	Block 13
Y. KODA Feb 6, 1944 *In Japanese:* "KODA"	Block 25 entry
KOODA–BROS 25-6-D 2/6/44 BY PORKY R.O. CARDS–JRS	Block 25 entry

Figure 4.26. Flagpole base in administration area at Canal Camp.

Figure 4.27. Inscription in administration area at Canal Camp.

Figure 4.28. Inscription in administration area at Canal Camp.

Figure 4.29. Concrete slab of warehouse at Canal Camp.

Figure 4.30. Concrete slab of latrine and shower building at Canal Camp.

cisterns were most likely used to store water for fire fighting because the regular water system proved to be undependable. They would have to have been filled by hose or water truck, since there are no pipe fittings apparent below ground level.

Footing pier blocks are still in place for most of the evacuee barracks (Figure 4.34), and there are numerous infilled basements evident, some with concrete steps still in place (Figures 4.35 and 4.36). There are abundant remains of landscaping around the former barracks (Figures 4.37-4.40). Many incorporate recycled materials such as concrete and clay pipe and tin cans, rather than rock.

Also present in the evacuee residential area are dozens of small ponds. Most are associated with individual barracks rather than mess halls or other communal buildings (Figures 4.41-4.49). The Block 23 mess hall, however, sported the largest pond. Either for aesthetic reasons or cooling many of the ponds were situated so as to be partially under a barracks. The ponds are chiefly made of concrete, however a few use apparently salvaged material such as cement pipe. Very little native rock was used. Many of the ponds have whimsical shapes; two are heart-shaped. Inscriptions in the concrete at Canal Camp are normally kept covered with sand as a protection measure. They are uncovered and highlighted with charcoal for special events such as reunions. The inscriptions consist mostly of names, dates, and addresses, some in Japanese characters (see Table 4.1, Figures 4.50-4.53).

Other Areas

Foundations of the evacuee-built auditorium and other high school buildings are still present in the open area north of Block 25 (Figure 4.54), but nothing remains of the outdoor theater that was northeast of the high school. A wooden home plate (Figure 4.55) and wooden pitcher's "rubber" marks a baseball field in the firebreak between Blocks 24 and 25.

Figure 4.31. Laundry room slab.

Figure 4.33. Cistern manhole.

Figure 4.34. Barracks footings at Canal Camp, protective dike in background.

Figure 4.32. Latrine grease trap.

Figure 4.35. Barracks basement depression.

Figure 4.36. Barracks basement.

Figure 4.37. Exterior faucet in evacuee residential area.

78

Figure 4.38. Posts remaining from shade canopy at Block 10 mess hall, Canal Camp.

Figure 4.39. Landscaping at Canal Camp.

Figure 4.40. Sidewalk and landscaping at Canal Camp.

Figure 4.41. Evacuee-built pond at Canal Camp.

Figure 4.42. Evacuee-built pond and other landscaping at Canal Camp; note barracks footing block within pond.

Figure 4.43. Evacuee-built pond at Canal Camp.

Figure 4.44. Evacuee-built pond at Canal Camp.

Figure 4.45. Evacuee-built pond at Canal Camp.

Figure 4.46. Evacuee-built pond at Canal Camp.

Figure 4.47. Evacuee-built pond at Canal Camp.

Figure 4.48. Evacuee-built pond at Block 23 mess hall, Canal Camp, note footing block within pond.

Figure 4.49. Japanese inscription on pond edge at Canal Camp.

Figure 4.50. Inscription at Canal Camp.

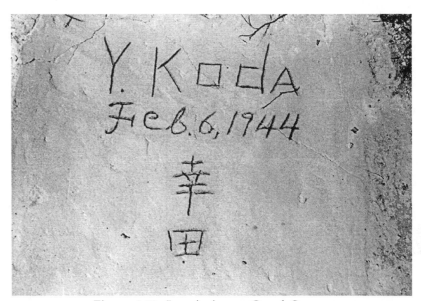

Figure 4.51. Inscription at Canal Camp.

Figure 4.52. Inscription at Canal Camp.

Figure 4.53. Inscription at Canal Camp.

Figure 4.54. Foundation at Canal Camp high school.

Figure 4.55. Wooden home plate at Canal Camp.

Figure 4.56. Foundation of ice house at Canal Camp.

Figure 4.57. Clarifier and digester at the Canal Camp sewage treatment plant.

Figure 4.58. Control room at the Canal Camp sewage treatment plant.

Figure 4.59. Headworks at the Canal Camp sewage treatment plant.

The ice house located south of Block 23 is marked by a raised concrete foundation (Figure 4.56). There are several small relocation-center-era trash dumps west of Canal Camp. Further west, the sewage treatment plant includes substantial remains of the digester, clarifier, control room, sludge beds, and sewer farm (Figures 4.57-4.59). Across the canal north of the Canal Camp administration building, several foundations and a well remain from the camp water system.

Butte Camp

Butte Camp is surrounded on three sides by recently planted orange and olive groves irrigated by the Central Arizona Project (see Figure 4.21). There are no buildings left at Butte Camp; the most visible

remains are those of the servicemen's honor roll monument located on a small butte. Besides the monument, there are concrete slab foundations, footing pier blocks, manholes, cisterns, ditches, ponds and other landscaping features, and large tamarisk trees. The most substantial remains are at the former hospital, warehouse area, high school, and fire station.

As at Canal Camp, foundation slabs have been broken open to remove the cast iron pipe below. However, in addition a number of foundation slabs have been broken up completely and placed in piles (Figure 4.60). This work was likely done in anticipation of clearing the camp area itself for farming, a project since abandoned due to the now-recognized significance of the site. Many of the roads are still

Figure 4.60. Piled concrete rubble at Butte camp.

Figure 4.61. Irrigation ditch at Butte Camp.

passable and many areas within the camp are covered with abundant recent trash, apparently from drinking parties and garbage dumping. In contrast to Canal Camp, not all roads within Butte Camp are driveable. Some have eroded into small washes and others have been covered with sediments and revegetated. On the other hand, some of the roads still have traces of asphalt pavement. Along some of the roads can be seen traces of irrigation ditches and remnants of culverts (Figure 4.61).

Administration, Hospital, and Warehouse Areas
In Block 70, the L-shaped concrete slab foundation of the administration building is still apparent, although it has been partially broken up (Figure 4.62). Footing pier blocks also remain at some of the other administration building sites in this block. Most of the slab foundations for the administrative offices and warehouses in Block 69 are still intact, although two slabs in the northwest portion the block have been broken up. In the Block 76 staff housing area there is an up-turned cistern (Figure 4.63).

In the hospital area numerous footing piers and concrete entries mark the locations of offices and wards (Figures 4.64 and 4.65). Many of the footing piers are over 18 inches high. At either end of the hospital complex there is a large concrete-walled rectangular vault sunk into the ground that appears to have been a grease trap (Figure 4.66). South of the hospital wards, concrete slab foundations remain at the laundry room and heating plant locations (Figures 4.67 and 4.68). Between the two foundations there is a large square cistern (Figure 4.69). Northwest of the hospital area there are two incinerators made of poured concrete (Figure 4.70). They were likely used for the disposal of hazardous hospital waste.

East of the hospital, in the staff housing area, there are four 20-foot-by-94-foot concrete slab foundations of apartment buildings (Figure 4.71). Eight other staff apartment buildings built by the evacuees apparently did not have slab foundations. Large tamarisk trees and concrete entry steps remain at one of the building locations. A 16-foot-by-20-foot slab is likely from a laundry room (Figure 4.72).

Figure 4.62. Foundation of administration building at Butte Camp.

Figure 4.63. Overturned cistern at Butte Camp.

Figure 4.64. Entry and footing blocks at the Butte Camp hospital.

Figure 4.65. Footing blocks at the Butte Camp hospital.

Figure 4.66. Foundation remains at the Butte Camp hospital.

Figure 4.67. Foundation of heating plant at the Butte Camp hospital.

Figure 4.68. Foundation of laundry building at the Butte Camp hospital.

Figure 4.69. Cistern at the Butte Camp hospital.

Figure 4.70. Incinerators northwest of the Butte Camp hospital.

Figure 4.71. Foundation of staff apartment building at Butte Camp.

Figure 4.72. Foundation of staff laundry room at Butte Camp.

Figure 4.73. Foundation of warehouse at Butte Camp.

Figure 4.74. Foundation of refrigerated warehouse at Butte Camp.

Figure 4.75. Foundation of ice house at Butte Camp.

Figure 4.76. Foundation of mess hall at Butte Camp.

Figure 4.77. Concrete threshold at Butte Camp mess hall.

Figure 4.78. Landscaping in the evacuee residential area at Butte Camp.

Figure 4.79. Landscaping in the evacuee residential area at Butte Camp.

Figure 4.81. Evacuee landscaping at Butte Camp.

Figure 4.80. Saguaro cactus and scattered rock work in the evacuee residential area at Butte Camp.

All of the concrete slab foundations in the warehouse blocks are still intact. Several of the slabs in the northeast portion of Block 67 are currently being used as form foundations for pouring small steel reinforced-concrete slabs used for canal bridges and diversions (Figure 4.73). Across the road to the north of the warehouse blocks there is a concrete gas pump island, a 30-by-100-foot slab from a refrigerated warehouse (Figure 4.74), four 20-foot-by-100-foot concrete slabs from shops and warehouses, a 37-foot-by-168-foot perimeter foundation from a never-completed machine shop, and a raised concrete foundation from an ice house (Figure 4.75). On a low hill west of the ice house foundation there is a modern steel water tank.

Evacuee Residential Area

Concrete slab foundations of the latrines, laundry rooms, and storage room are still present, although broken up with the cast iron pipes removed. Unlike Canal Camp, the mess halls at Butte Camp had

Figure 8.82. Saguaro cactus and rock work in the evacuee residential area.

Figure 4.83. Detail of garden in the evacuee residential area.

Figure 4.84. Concrete entry at the front of an evacuee barracks.

Figure 4.85. Inscription at Butte Camp.

Figure 4.87. Evacuee-built pond at Butte Camp.

Figure 4.86. Inscription at Butte Camp.

Figure 4.88. Evacuee-built pond at Butte Camp.

concrete slab foundations. These foundations have been broken up to remove the pipe below and some (in Blocks 30-31, 72, and 73) have been completely broken up and placed in piles. An interesting feature of the mess hall foundations are door thresholds molded into the concrete slabs (Figures 4.76 and 4.77).

Concrete cisterns remain in each block, as do footing piers for barracks and some depressions from basements. There are remains of numerous evacuee-built improvements around the former barracks, including concrete entries, gravel and concrete walkways, elaborate rock-outlined gardens, including two with saguaros (Figures 4.78-4.84). Very few inscriptions in the concrete are present (Table 4.2, Figure 4.85 and 4.86).

There are fewer, but generally larger, ponds at Butte Camp than at Canal Camp (Figures 4.87-4.90). Most are in the western portion of the residential area with the greatest number in Block 61, which also has the largest pond at the relocation center. In general, there appears

to have been less concrete and more native rock used in the Butte Camp ponds than those at Canal Camp. This is not surprising since abundant rock is readily available from the hillsides adjacent to Butte Camp.

Other Areas

Between 8th and 9th Street, in the firebreak south of Block 56 there is a low square earthen mound identified by Minoru Inoshita (personal communication, 1998) as the sumo arena built by his father (Figures 4.91 and 4.92).

At the high school location, there are concrete slab foundations from the wings on both sides of the auditorium, footing piers of the auditorium, and footing piers and entry steps for other buildings (Figure 4.93 and 4.94). Two inscriptions in the concrete (initials and a proclamation of love) were noted (see Table 4.2, Figure 4.95). North of the high school, the fire station area includes a large concrete slab (Figure 4.96), which included three different building episodes, and an

Figure 4.89. Evacuee-built pond at Butte Camp.

Figure 4.90. Evacuee-built pond at Butte Camp.

Figure 4.91. Sumo wresting arena, November 1942 (Francis Stewart photograph, Bancroft Library, University of California, Berkeley).

asphalt driveway.

The camouflage net factory and motor pool, located on the west side of the camp, has been heavily disturbed. Remains at the largest building (60 foot by 400 foot in size) consist of portions of the perimeter foundation, a small intact concrete slab, and piled rubble (Figure 4.97). Linear piles of concrete rubble remain at six of the other building locations (Figure 4.98). Another building location is now marked by a large pit partially filled with rubble.

Figure 4.92. Area of the sumo arena today.

The Butte Camp sewage treatment plant, basically identical to the one at Canal Camp, includes remains of the digester, clarifier, control room, sludge beds, and sewer farms (Figure 4.99).

The most eminent feature at Butte Camp is the honor roll monument located on a knoll overlooking the camp (Figure 4.100). The memorial was built by the evacuees to honor those Japanese Americans from the Gila River Relocation Center who served in the military during World War II (Figure 4.101) and included a reflecting pool and a ramada with concrete benches. The ramada, flagpole, and wooden facade of the monument that held the list of names are now gone. A dirt road provides access to the monument and recent trash abounds. Once covered with abundant graffiti, the monument has been recently painted (Figures 4.102 and 4.103). The foundation of the camp water tank is on a higher knoll just west of the monument (Figure 4.104). There is little evidence of the outdoor theater, once located on the slope below the monument.

Figure 4.93. Remains at Butte Camp high school auditorium.

Figure 4.94. Footing blocks at the Butte Camp high school.

Figure 4.95. Inscription at the Butte Camp high school.

Figure 4.96. Foundation of the Butte Camp fire station.

Figure 4.98. Concrete rubble at the camouflage net factory.

Figure 4.97. Concrete slab at the camouflage net factory.

Figure 4.99. Butte Camp sewage treatment plant today.

Figure 4.100. Monument on knoll at Butte Camp.

Figure 4.101. Servicemen's monument at Butte Camp in 1944 (National Archives photograph).

Figure 4.102. Detail of Butte Camp monument.

Figure 4.103. Monument at Butte Camp prior to repainting.

Table 4.2. Inscriptions at Butte Camp.

RH 44	High School
RALPH OSADA X ROSIE	High School step
HOME SWEET HOME June 12, 1944	Block 63 entry
74-1-C	Block 74 entry
May 29, 19..	Block 72 garden

Figure 4.104. View towards Butte Camp high school from the water tank foundation.

Figure 4.105. Foundation of the military police vehicle repair shop.

Figure 4.107. Sidewalk at the military police compound.

Figure 4.108. Abandoned ditch in the evacuee farm area.

Figure 4.106. Flagpole base at the military police compound.

95

Security Features

No remnants of the military police sentry posts at the north and south entrances to the relocation center reserve or of the temporary watch tower are visible today. Notable, however is the excellent condition of the former military police compound. The large foundation of the vehicle repair shop remains (Figure 4.105). In addition, there are other foundation remnants, gravel walkways, rock alignments, and an impressively landscaped flagpole base (Figures 4.106-4.107).

Outlying Area

The fields once farmed by the evacuees are still under cultivation and most of the outlying developments of the relocation center, such as the chicken, hog, and dairy farms, were located within what are now irrigated fields and orchards (see Figure 4.21). Some abandoned ditch segments located in areas farmed by the evacuees may be left from the relocation center use (Figure 4.108).

Prior to being converted into a farm field the site of the relocation center dairy was documented by Sullivan et al. (1987). They recorded the foundations of three substantial buildings (Figure 4.109). These consisted of a 36-foot-by-105-foot milking barn, a 20-foot-by-100-foot feed warehouse, and a five-room 14½-foot-by-55-foot milk house. The feed warehouse and milking barn were connected by a 20-ft-long walkway. The milking barn had a multi-level floor that was tilted to the north to facilitate washing. It had an inscription made into the wet concrete that read "Sam Okada" or "Sam Okara." The floor of the milk house was noted as broken open to remove underlaying pipes. Other features at the dairy

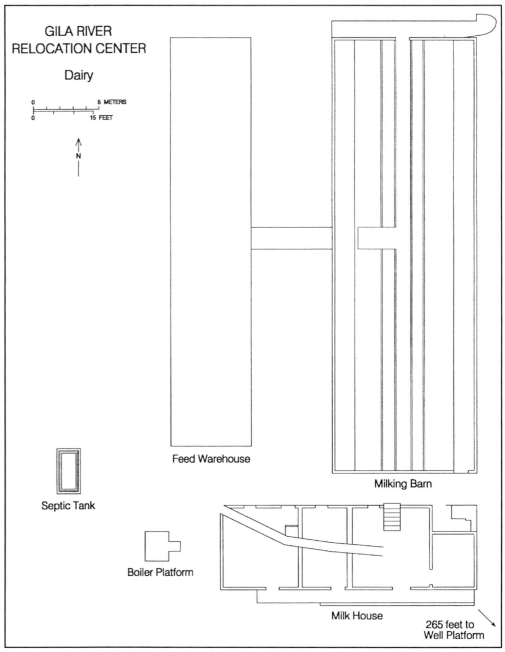

Figure 4.109. Gila Relocation Center Dairy farm (adapted from Sullivan et al. 1987).

Figure 4.110. Pet grave southeast of Butte Camp in 1994 (orange trees are now over 10 feet tall).

Figure 4.111. Foundation of water tank north of the Canal Camp administration area.

site included a boiler platform, a well platform, and a septic tank. No artifacts beyond construction materials were found during the 1987 recording.

The location of Zenimura's elaborate baseball field just outside the southeast corner of Butte Camp is now an olive grove. Several features of the ballfield were apparently recorded by Sawyer-Lang (1989; Locus 12), including remains of the dugouts and backstop. None of these features remain today.

At least one of two pet graves identified by Sawyer-Lang (1989) still remains. Located in an orange grove southeast of Butte Camp, from Sawyer-Lang's description it appears to have been refurbished (Figure 4.110). It includes inscriptions written in the wet cement in both Japanese and English. The English text reads: "'Guard upon/all livings'/Dog, Kookey Yokogama/Died Jan 14th 1945," the Japanese

text reads "Guard upon all livings/The Spirit of Kookey." The other pet grave had both English and Japanese inscriptions as well. The English text read "HERE LIES CHUBBY/FUJIYAMA/ OCT 19, '43"(Sawyer-Lang 1989). It could not be relocated.

As mentioned above, there are substantial remains at both the Canal Camp and Butte Camp sewage treatment plants. At the sewer farm locations there are only faint furrows and desert vegetation today. North of Canal Camp a well and several foundations from the camp water system remain (Figure 4.111).

The relocation center landfill, located west of Butte Camp, consists of a large open pit and a partially-filled trench (Figure 4.112 and 4.113). Present are abundant ceramics and glass, marbles, glass beads, trash cans, enamelware pitchers, and other items (Figures 4.114 and 4.115). Some digging at the landfill is evident, but none of the excavations

Figure 4.112. Landfill at the Gila River Relocation Center.

Figure 4.113. Landfill at the Gila River Relocation Center.

Figure 4.114. Artifacts at the Gila River Relocation Center landfill.

Figure 4.115. Artifacts at the Gila River Relocation Center landfill.

Figure 4.116. Typical glass artifacts from the Gila River Relocation Center landfill.

Figure 4.117. Typical ceramics from the Gila River Relocation Center landfill.

Figure 4.118. Flattened cans at the Gila River Relocation Center landfill.

Figure 4.119. Relocation center display at the Gila River Indian Reservation Cultural Center.

Figure 4.120. Relocation center display outside the Gila River Indian Reservation Cultural Center.

appear to be very recent. In 1995 a small collection of artifacts picked up at the landfill 25 years earlier was given to the senior author. It includes 16 complete bottles, a small "Christian Dior" perfume bottle, American and Japanese ceramic fragments, and a glass marble (Figures 4.116 and 4.117). Many similar items remain on the surface at the landfill today. South and east of the landfill there are numerous small trash piles likely similar to those investigated (and now gone) along the east and south sides of Butte Camp. There is also a large pile of flattened tin cans that were apparently processed for recycling but discarded when the relocation center was closed (Figure 4.118).

Interpretation
The Canal and Butte Camp sites are located on the Gila River Indian Reservation. The sites are treated as sacred sites by the tribe (Cohen 1994) and public access is restricted. The perimeters of both camps are posted with "no trespassing" signs. A permit must be obtained from the Gila River Indian tribe to visit the sites. A minimum fee of $100

is charged for the permit, but is normally waived for former evacuees and their immediate family members. Visitors without a permit are subject to arrest and a tribal court hearing.

At Gila River Indian Reservation Cultural Center, located 4 miles north of the camps along Interstate 10 (Exit 175), there is an exhibit and outdoor display about the relocation center prepared by the Arizona Chapter of the Japanese American Citizens League. Located inside the Cultural Center the exhibit includes text, maps, historical photographs, and artifacts from the camps (Figure 4.119). The outdoor display includes information similar to that on memorial markers present at each of the two camps (Figure 4.120).

Three years were spent getting permission from the Gila River Indian tribe to place the memorial markers at the camps. One of the conditions for their approval was that the Japanese American community never ask for National Landmark or any other official designation

Figure 4.121. Memorial marker at Canal Camp.

Figure 4.122. Memorial marker at Butte Camp.

Figure 4.123. Memorial marker at Butte Camp listing the names of Japanese Americans from the Gila River Relocation Center killed in World War II.

(Joe Allman, personal communication, 1997). Any such designation is seen by the tribe as a threat to their sovereignty. In fact, in 1978 a National Register of Historic Places nomination was prepared by the Arizona State Parks Board, however the nomination was withdrawn when it was learned that there would be no support from the tribe.

The memorial marker at Canal Camp, located near the foundation of the administration building and a flagpole base, includes a map and historical photograph of the camp and some text explaining the history (Figure 4.121). At Butte Camp two markers were placed at the servicemen's honor roll monument. One provides historical information, similar to that at Canal Camp, and the other lists those from the relocation center who were killed in World War II (Figure 4.122 and 4.123). The plaques were dedicated in 1995, during ceremonies held during the 50th Anniversary Gila River Relocation Center Reunion (Figure 4.124).

Figure 4.124. Dedication ceremony at Butte Camp (1995).

Chapter 5

Granada Relocation Center

The Granada Relocation Center was located in southeastern Colorado 140 miles east of Pueblo. The relocation center site is 16 miles east of the town of Lamar and 15 miles west of the Kansas border. The relocation center's common name was derived from the small town of Granada, less than a mile away. However, the postal designation was Amache, after a Cheyenne woman who was married to John W. Prowers, a nineteenth century rancher for whom the county is named.

Averaging about 3,600 feet in elevation, the relocation center is on a wind-swept prairie that slopes gently from south to north toward the Arkansas River, 2½ miles north. Cottonwoods grow along the river, but without irrigation, the land is fairly arid, with wild grasses, sagebrush, and prickly pear cactus common.

The 10,500 acres of the relocation center reserve had been 18 privately owned farms and ranches, acquired by the WRA through purchase or condemnation (Figure 5.1). The largest parcels included the former company town of Koen, owned by the American Crystal Sugar Company, and the XY Ranch, founded by Fred Harvey in 1889 (Figure 5.2). For the planned agricultural projects, the WRA also purchased water rights to parts of the Lamar, Manvel, and XY canals, which flowed through the reserve and fed existing irrigation ditches. The Wolf Creek drainage flows northeast to the river just west of the developed part of the relocation center, but the creek bed is currently dry most of the year.

Construction of the relocation center began June 12, 1942, with a crew of up to 1,000 hired workers and 50 evacuee volunteers; the general contractor was Lambie, Moss, Little, and James of Amarillo, Texas. The center was in operation by the end of August 1942, and reached the maximum population of 7,318 by October. Although Granada had the smallest population of the ten relocation centers, it was the tenth largest city in Colorado when it was occupied. Evacuees were from the

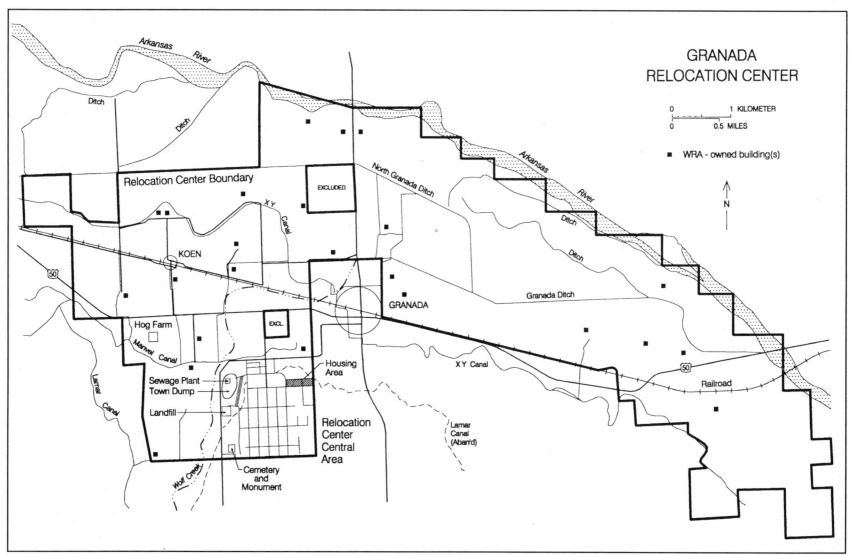

Figure 5.1. Granada Relocation Center.

Figure 5.2. XY Ranch lands today.

Merced and Santa Anita assembly centers. There were over 560 buildings, including a few composed of sections of former Civilian Conservation Corps buildings transported to the site (Simmons and Simmons 1993).

The central or developed portion of the relocation center was located on a low bluff overlooking the flood plain and farmlands, which extended to the north and east all the way to the Arkansas River. Like most of the relocation centers, buildings and streets were laid out on a north-south grid within an area about one mile square (Figure 5.3). East-west roads were consecutively numbered from 1st on the north to 12th Street on the south. North-south roads extended from "D" Street on the west to "L" Street on the east (I and J were not used). Shorter roads at a slight angle to the grid in the coal storage area were designated "A" and "B" Streets; "C" Street ran adjacent and parallel to A and B Streets before continuing due south next to the residential area.

The entire developed area was surrounded by a four-strand barbed wire fence, with six watch towers along the perimeter. Equipped with searchlights and staffed by military police guards as were the guard towers at other relocation centers, the six at Granada were unique in their octagonal lookout enclosures (Figure 5.4). The only gate in the perimeter fence was at "G" Street, near the center of the north side, approximately one-half mile south of U.S. Highway 50. On the east side of the entrance was the Military Police compound, which included an administration building with a flagpole out front, a guardhouse, four barracks buildings, an officers quarters building, a mess hall, two recreation buildings, a dispensary, a post exchange, a garage, storage house, and a tool house. In the later stages of the center's operation when the military police detachment was greatly reduced in number, the WRA used some of the buildings in this area for staff housing and offices (Simmons and Simmons 1993).

A visitor center was located south of the Military Police compound at the southeast corner of 4th and "G" Streets. The motor pool area, which included an office, storage building, gas station, and one other building, was just to the south of the visitor center. Farther to the east was the hospital complex, with 17 buildings including an administration building, mess hall, doctors' and nurses' quarters, wards, storehouse, laundry, and heating plant.

On the west side of the entrance were the administration and warehouse areas. The administration area included several office buildings, a warehouse, a garage, a shop, a post office, a store, and a recreation building. A staff housing area, to the southwest of the administration area, included a mess hall, four dormitories, and ten staff apartment buildings (Figure 5.5). The center's water reservoir, a pump station, a well house, and the fire station were located east of the staff housing area, on the west side of "G" Street. The warehouse area (Figure 5.6), in the northwest corner of the developed area,

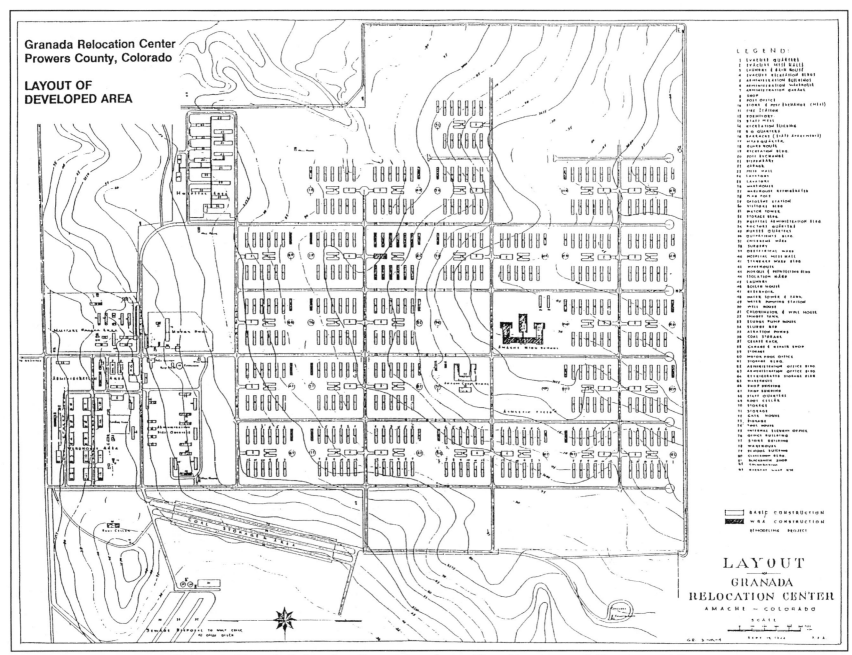

Figure 5.3. Granada Relocation Center central area (from Simmons and Simmons 1993).

included fifteen large warehouses, a butcher shop, two latrines, a storage building, and a lumber yard.

Domestic water was supplied by four 800-foot-deep wells and stored in a 200,000-gallon concrete reservoir located south of the staff housing area. To provide water pressure, water was then pumped to a 72-foot-high 25,000-gallon water tower in the southeast corner of Block 12K, in the evacuee residential area.

The evacuee residences were south of 6th street, and separated from the administration areas by more barbed wire fencing (Figure 5.7). There were 30 residential blocks, designated by a number and letter combination (such as 6B or 11H) which reflected the street intersection at the block's northwest corner. The WRA blueprint depicts only every other east-west street, suggesting some of these street intersections were only hypothetical, but given that the entire area was cleared before construction began, it seems likely these named streets could also have been used as thoroughfares, even if they weren't surfaced roads.

Figure 5.4. Watch tower at Granada (Joe McClelland photograph, Bancroft Library, University of California, Berkeley).

Figure 5.5. Staff housing area at Granada (Joe McClelland photograph, Bancroft Library, University of California, Berkeley).

Figure 5.6. Warehouse area at Granada (Joe McClelland photograph, Bancroft Library, University of California, Berkeley).

105

Figure 5.7. Evacuee residential area at Granada (Joe McClelland photograph, Bancroft Library, University of California, Berkeley).

Each block was laid out according to standard plans, with 12 barracks each measuring 20 feet by 120 feet, a mess hall, a combination laundry, bath, and latrine building, and a recreation building. Construction of the evacuee buildings at Granada differed from the other relocation centers. Instead of post-and-pier foundations, barracks had slab foundations, or concrete perimeter foundations with brick floors (Figure 5.8; DeWitt 1943). The evacuee buildings also had fibre board or asbestos shingle siding, rather than the tarpaper common at most of the other relocation centers.

Twenty-nine of the residential blocks were used for housing; the buildings in one of the blocks, 8H, were used for classrooms. A 1943 WRA blueprint indicates ten addition residential blocks were planned but never built (Figure 5.9). Two silk screening shops, the Red Cross, the YMCA, a town hall, five churches, a recreation office, scouts, and other groups were housed in recreation buildings (Figures 5.10 and

Figure 5.8. Preparing barracks foundation at Granada (Tom Parker photograph, Bancroft Library, University of California, Berkeley).

5.11). The silk screen shop produced color posters under contract to the U.S. Navy (Simmons and Simmons 1993).

Several blocks in the residential area were reserved for special uses, and therefore had different configurations of buildings, or were left undeveloped. The high school, in Block 10G, was completed in early 1943 of wood frame construction on cinder block and concrete foundations. In plan, the high school complex was shaped like an "E," with the main section over 300 feet long and 40 feet wide, and the two wings at either end approximately 180 feet by a maximum of 90 feet. The auditorium/gymnasium building, 68 by 144 feet in size, was located between the classroom wings, and was connected to the main section by a covered arcade (Figures 5.12 and 5.13). Locker rooms and

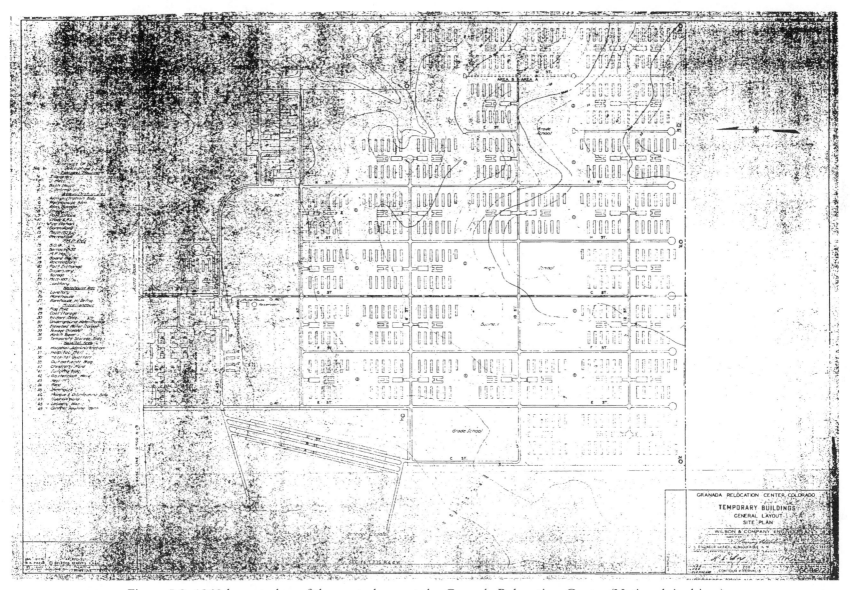

Figure 5.9. 1942 layout plan of the central area at the Granada Relocation Center (National Archives).

Figure 5.10. Recreation hall in Block 10H at Granada used as a church (Tom Parker photograph, Bancroft Library, University of California, Berkeley).

a boiler room were located in the auditorium basement (Simmons and Simmons 1993). The high school was the most expensive building constructed in Prowers County up to that time, arousing the envy and ire of some local residents already resentful that private land had been condemned for the center. Politicians stopped construction of an elementary school, so that the existing barracks in Block 8H continued to be used (Simmons and Simmons 1993). Immediately west of the high school, Block 10F remained open as an athletic field, while Block 9G, to the north, was also vacant.

Figure 5.11. Boy Scout headquarters at Granada (Joe McClelland photograph, Bancroft Library, University of California, Berkeley).

Figure 5.12. South entrance to Granada High School (Joe McClelland photograph, Bancroft Library, University of California, Berkeley).

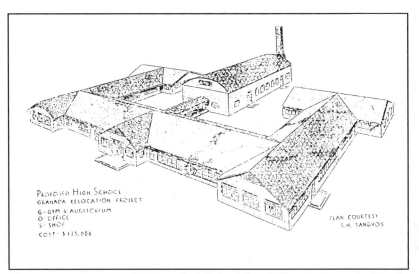

Figure 5.13. Proposed Granada High School (from *Granada Pioneer* 11/26/42).

Figure 5.14. Evacuee barracks at Granada, view from water tower (Joe McClelland photograph, Bancroft Library, University of California, Berkeley).

Figure 5.15. Evacuee barracks at Granada (Joe McClelland photograph, Bancroft Library, University of California, Berkeley).

109

Figure 5.16. Evacuee barracks and outhouses at Granada (Joe McClelland photograph, Bancroft Library, University of California, Berkeley).

Figure 5.17. Coal storage area at Granada (Joe McClelland photograph, Bancroft Library, University of California, Berkeley).

Block 9F, northwest of the high school, contained the co-op store, a warehouse, the internal security office, and another office building. The U-shaped co-op store in Block 9F, constructed in 1943, was the second largest building at the center, with a 40 foot by 100 foot main section and two 40 foot by 60 foot wings. The co-op contained a dry goods store, variety store, shoe store, canteen, beauty shop, barber shop, shoe repair shop, watch repair shop, cleaning and pressing agency, a radio repair shop, an optometry dispensary, and a newspaper department (Simmons and Simmons 1993).

Historical photographs show that evacuees landscaped the barren surroundings with gardens, including transplanted trees (Figure 5.14 and 5.15). An unusual feature of the Granada center that also appears in the historical photographs is the presence of what look like small outhouses between the barracks area and the perimeter fence (Figure

5.16). These may be the privies used during the fall of 1943 when the evacuees arrived before the utilities were completed (Simmons and Simmons 1993). Joe Norikane recounts having to drive a water truck from latrine to latrine to flush the toilets (Personal communication, 1999).

More fencing enclosed the area west of the residential area, which included the cemetery, coal storage areas (Figure 5.17), root cellars, the landfill, and the sewage treatment plant. The sewage treatment plant included an "Imhoff" tank, a pump house, a sludge bed, and aeration ponds. Treated effluent was discharged towards Wolf Creek via an open ditch.

In spite of its small population, Granada had one of the largest and most diversified agricultural enterprises of the ten relocation centers.

Figure 5.18. Irrigating lettuce field at Granada (Joe McClelland photograph, Bancroft Library, University of California, Berkeley).

The farm program included the raising of vegetable crops, feed crops, beef and dairy cattle, poultry, and hogs (Figures 5.18-5.23). Even the high school had a 500-acre farm, operated by vocational agriculture students (*Granada Pioneer* 5/19/43). Granada had an advantage over other centers in that its fields and canals were already in place, needing only minor repairs. Existing agricultural facilities were incorporated into the center's farm program: for example, the relocation center's dairy made use of an existing dairy farm, and the hotel at Koen was used as a mess hall for farm workers. A blacksmith shop located at Koen also utilized an existing facility (Figure 5.24). Expedient trench silos were used to store corn, celery, and other foods (Figure 5.25).

Fields and pastures, located to the north and east of the central developed area of the relocation center, extended to the Arkansas River and almost surrounded the town of Granada. Water for the fields was supplied by canals. Official WRA reports indicate that in 1943, 469 acres were farmed at Granada; in 1944, there were 505 acres

Figure 5.19. Potato harvest at Granada (Joe McClelland photograph, Bancroft Library, University of California, Berkeley).

of vegetables and 2,185 acres of field crops. A May 1943 WRA map produced at the relocation center, however, gives somewhat higher figures, with 540 acres of vegetables, 1,650 acres of grain, 515 acres of alfalfa, 2,895 acres of pasture, 340 fallow, and 855 wasteland (Figure 5.26). Some 2,380 acres of the relocation center holdings, mostly lands northwest of the town of Granada, are listed as licensed acres, probably indicating the areas were leased back to local farmers.

WRA blueprints indicate the hog farm and at least one chicken farm were located northwest of the central area. Cattle ranch facilities may have been at the east end of the reserve, to make use of existing XY Ranch buildings. All agricultural activities likely used existing buildings, with new additions and repairs as needed. In 1944 the relocation center raised 456 cattle, 1,017 hogs, 4,712 chickens, and 2,210 egg chickens (WRA 1944).

Figure 5.20. Cattle herd at Granada (Joe McClelland photograph, Bancroft Library, University of California, Berkeley).

Figure 5.21. Milking shed at dairy farm at Granada (Tom Parker photograph, Bancroft Library, University of California, Berkeley).

Figure 5.22. Chicken farm at Granada (Joe McClelland photograph, Bancroft Library, University of California, Berkeley).

Figure 5.23. Hog farm at Granada (Joe McClelland photograph, Bancroft Library, University of California, Berkeley).

Figure 5.24. Evacuee-run blacksmith shop at Koen (Joe McClelland photograph, Bancroft Library, University of California, Berkeley).

Figure 5.25. Constructing a trench silo at Granada (Joe McClelland photograph, Bancroft Library, University of California, Berkeley).

The military police unit left the relocation center in mid-September 1945 and the Granada Relocation Center officially closed on October 15, 1945, when the last group of eighty-five evacuees departed (Simmons and Simmons 1993). The central area was sold to the town of Granada for $2,500. Through 1946 and 1947 buildings were dismantled and sold, some going to school districts in the area, some going to the town, and some hospital buildings going to the University of Denver. Other lands of the relocation center reserve were leased and then sold to local farmers, with the original buildings intact.

Central (Fenced) Area

Today, the site of the Granada Relocation Center is remarkably intact, compared to many of the other relocation center sites. The central area is presently owned by the town of Granada, and one of the relocation center wells is used as the water source for the town. The only standing structures remaining from the relocation center use are a poured concrete room which was part of the co-op store, a small brick building at the cemetery, and the water reservoir and associated pump and well houses. However, traces of the whole central area of the relocation center are present – slab and footer foundations for most of the buildings remain, underground utilities appear to be intact (Figure 5.27), and roads still delineate the original blocks (Figure 5.28). Many of these roads, surfaced with a light tan gravel, are still driveable. Chinese elms and cottonwoods planted by the evacuees still survive and are the dominant vegetation, showing up in orderly rectangles on the USGS topographic map on the otherwise treeless prairie. Even most of the original security perimeter fence around the central area is still in place.

113

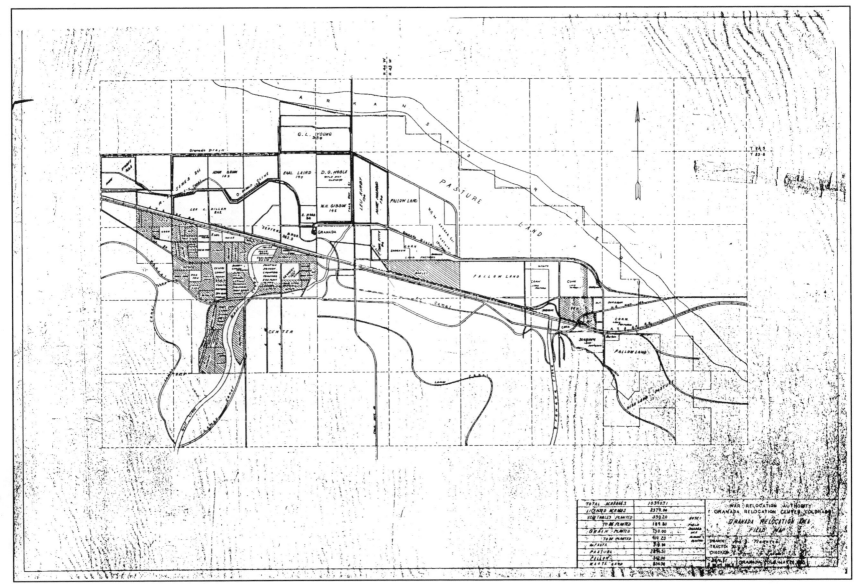

Figure 5.26. Farm fields at the Granada Relocation Center (National Archives).

Figure 5.27. Manhole in Block 10E at Granada.

Figure 5.28. Relocation center road at Granada today.

There appear to have been only four major disturbances to the site since the buildings were removed in the 1940s: (1) a housing complex built where the hospital had been; (2) the present town landfill north of the relocation center landfill in the sewage treatment plant area; (3) a cylindrical metal water tank in Block 11K, added in the late 1960s; and (4) a recent well in Block 11F.

Hospital, Administration, and Warehouse Areas
There are modern houses in the hospital area, in the northeast part of the central area (Figure 5.29). According to Simmons and Simmons (1993), existing foundations were cleared in 1968 and the "Vista Nueva" housing complex was constructed for migrant farm workers. Originally built by a group of growers, the project is now owned by the Colorado Rural Housing Development Corporation; because of a decreased need for migrant laborers, the buildings are up for sale for removal from the site (Simmons and Simmons 1993). North of the housing area the concrete foundations of the hospital laundry and the boiler house are still present (Figures 5.30 and 5.31).

In the administration area there are foundations, a few low sandstone and concrete retaining walls, and what may have been decorative planters (Figure 5.32). In the staff housing area the foundations of the four dormitories and the mess hall remain. There is no evidence of the staff apartments other than four large sandstone rock and concrete boxes adjacent to roads where the apartment buildings would have been located (Figure 5.33). These measure about 10 feet by 15 feet by 2 feet high and are in poor condition; the structures may have been decorative planters for the apartment buildings.

Some of the water system features south of the administration area are still standing, including the concrete reservoir, which is covered with wood and rolled roofing (Figure 5.34), a concrete block well house (Figure 5.35), and a pump house with partial concrete walls (Figure 5.36). Apparently the reservoir and well house are still used; the pump house, which once pumped water to the relocation center water tower, is no longer necessary, since gravity provides enough pressure for the

Figure 5.29. Housing complex within the former hospital area at Granada.

Figure 5.30. Foundation of hospital laundry building at Granada.

Figure 5.31. Foundation of hospital boiler house at Granada.

Figure 5.32. Foundation in the administration area at Granada.

Figure 5.33. Remnants of a rock and concrete feature in the staff housing area at Granada.

Figure 5.34. Water reservoir at Granada today.

Figure 5.35. Well house used by the town of Granada.

Figure 5.36. Ruins of pump house at Granada.

Figure 5.37. Foundation blocks of water tower at Granada.

water to reach town. Along the southern perimeter of the evacuee residential area the foundation blocks of the water tower are intact (Figure 5.37).

Near the water reservoir the fire station foundation is still present. Most of the warehouse foundations have been removed. Only two concrete slab foundations (Figure 5.38) and two other partial foundations remain. Some small pieces of rubble have been left around trees. In the motor pool area there are three foundations.

Residential Area

The slab foundations of most of the mess halls and communal bathroom and laundry buildings are still in place (Figures 5.39-5.41). Foundations for barracks, too, are unusually intact. Although barracks at other relocation centers rested on concrete blocks, at Granada barracks have concrete perimeter foundations, some rising about two feet above the ground surface(Figure 5.42), or complete concrete slabs (Blocks 10E, 11E, 11H, 12H, and 12K; Figure 5.43). Bolts to attach

the wooden portion of the structure project from the foundations. At least one foundation retains a brick and concrete support for a coal-burning heater (Figure 5.44). The foundations are overgrown and distorted by trees and brush, and some of those that were not present may have been buried by sheet wash silt. Others, however, are completely missing: according to Simmons and Simmons (1993), foundations along the western edge of the residential area were reportedly broken up and used as rip-rap in area canals.

In the high school area the concrete block foundations have been removed, probably for reuse, but there are several small entry slabs and a larger L-shaped patio-like slab that once wrapped around one of the corners of the school building (Figures 5.45 and 5.46). Remains of a baseball backstop were observed in the athletic field to the west of the school. Foundation remains and a small concrete vault similar to one remaining at the Heart Mountain Relocation Center are at the co-op store location (Figures 5.47 and 5.48). The vault measures about 12 feet square by 9 feet high.

Archaeological evidence of evacuee improvements, other than the relict trees, is rare. Concrete "stones" near one mess hall slab were probably part of a decorative garden (Figure 5.49). No inscriptions or graffiti were observed in any of the concrete slabs or footings.

Western Area

The fenced western portion of the central area encompasses the landfill, sewage treatment plant, coal storage area, root cellar, and the cemetery. Today the dump for the town of Granada is where the buildings of the sewage treatment plant were located.

The relocation center landfill has no apparent vandalism. Abundant artifacts include numerous glass bottles and ceramics, but not many Japanese ceramics (Figures 5.50 and 5.51). Adjacent to the landfill there is a large can and ceramic dump that likely dates to the abandon-

Figure 5.38. Concrete slab foundation of a warehouse at Granada.

Figure 5.39. Concrete slab foundation of mess hall in Block 9L at Granada.

Figure 5.40. Concrete slab foundation of bathroom/laundry building in Block 11K at Granada.

Figure 5.41. Detail of concrete bathroom slab in Block 10E at Granada.

Figure 5.42. Concrete perimeter barracks foundation in Block 12F.

Figure 5.43. Concrete slab barracks foundation in Block 11H.

ment of the center (Figure 5.52). The ponds and a few concrete walls from the sewage disposal system are still present in the northwest portion of the center (Figure 5.53). No evidence of the coal storage area was observed, but the root cellar is indicated by a slight depression, which even shows up on the USGS topographic map.

The WRA blueprint indicates that the original access to the cemetery was via a curving road approaching from the north, but the cemetery is now reached by an east-west road from the southwest corner of the evacuee housing area. Within a large fenced area at the cemetery there is a recent memorial monument, a small building, and a smaller fenced area with nine marked burials (Figures 5.54 and 5.55). The current grave markers are all of the same design and were apparently added in recent years, including one marker bearing the inscription "Evacuees Unknown."

The small building at the cemetery has a concrete foundation, brick walls, and a wood frame and corrugated metal roof. It is located where a "columbarium" is depicted on the September 1944 WRA map, just west of the grave sites. The building was apparently constructed by evacuees to store cremated remains; shortly before the camp was closed evacuees placed a polished granite slab inside to honor those who died at Granada. The slab is inscribed with Japanese text and the date September 1945 in English (Figure 5.56). The Japanese text reads "Memorial tower established in Showa 20 (1945) by the Japanese at Amache Relocation Center." The slab is chipped in several areas where rifle slugs have struck the surface.

Security Features

The foundation blocks of all six perimeter watch towers are intact (Figures 5.57 and 5.58). Each consists of four square blocks of poured concrete forming a square about 8 feet on a side; each block has metal straps to attach a support post for the tower. In the center of the

Figure 5.44. Brick and concrete pad for coal heater in Block 7E.

Figure 5.45. Concrete entries at the high school location.

Figure 5.46. Concrete patio at the high school location.

Figure 5.47. Concrete building at the co-op location.

Figure 5.49. Decorative landscaping at the Block 12F mess hall location.

Figure 5.48. Foundation at the co-op location.

square is a fifth piece of poured concrete, oblong instead of square, with straps to attach a ladder.

Much of the existing perimeter barbed wire fence around the central area is likely original, although it may have been repaired over the years. The original entrance gate area has been blocked off (Figure 5.59), and the current entrance to the site is via "E" Street, which provides access to the town dump. The fence that separated the evacuee residence area from the administration area has been removed.

In the military police compound, all of the foundations for the buildings marked on the WRA blueprints are still present, although some have been damaged by trees (Figure 5.60). The interior roads and driveways in the compound are discernible but overgrown with vegetation.

Figure 5.50. Granada Relocation Center landfill.

Figure 5.51. Ceramics at the Granada Relocation Center landfill.

Figure 5.52. Can and ceramic dump at the Granada Relocation Center landfill.

Figure 5.53. Remains at the Granada Relocation Center sewage treatment plant.

Figure 5.55. Monument and brick building at the Granada Relocation Center cemetery.

Figure 5.54. Graves at the Granada Relocation Center cemetery.

Figure 5.56. 1945 monument inside small building at the Granada Relocation Center cemetery.

Figure 5.57. Southwest corner watch tower foundation blocks.

Figure 5.59. Original relocation center entrance today.

Figure 5.58. Southeast corner watch tower foundation blocks.

Outlying Area

The locations of the relocation center hog and chicken farms are now farm fields. Numerous other outlying buildings noted on WRA blueprints as WRA-owned are still present, and most are currently in use (Figure 5.61). None appear to have been built by the WRA; all are likely pre-existing buildings taken over when the WRA purchased the land. Except for the Lamar Canal, the fields and canals used by evacuees are still in use.

Some building locations now have mobile homes, which may be making use of old foundations or utilities. An old rock building and other ruins remain at the Koen townsite, and there is a rock house ruin just east of town in the same location as one of the WRA buildings depicted on the map. At the XY Ranch, there are two warehouses and two mobile homes. Several relocated barracks from the relocation center are still in the surrounding area (Figure 5.62).

Figure 5.60. Foundation remains in the military police compound at Granada.

Figure 5.61. Farm at the location of formerly WRA-owned buildings.

Figure 5.62. Relocated barracks east of the town of Granada.

Figure 5.63. Sign along U.S. Highway 50 in 1994.

Interpretation

The Granada Relocation Center is marked on a large wall map at the State of Colorado Welcome Center in Lamar and it is mentioned in several tourist brochures available at the Welcome Center. The relocation center itself is 16 miles east of Lamar, one-half mile south of U.S. Highway 50. In 1994, the turnoff to the site was indicated by a small wood sign nailed to a tree (Figure 5.63).

The central area of the relocation center is completely fenced and is currently used for cattle grazing. In addition, the town of Granada operates a dump in the northwest corner of the parcel. Access into the site and to the memorial at the relocation center cemetery is through the dump entrance, which limits visiting to hours when the dump is open. Inside the fenced area nearly all of the relocation center roads

Figure 5.64. Monument placed at the Granada Relocation Center Cemetery in 1983.

Figure 5.65. Scale model of the Granada Relocation Center built by Granada High School students Renee Bochatey, Mike Bridge, Greg Grasmick, Tommy Grasmick, Tonya Malone, Melissa Medina, and Brett Schnabel.

are passable. Additional signs direct visitors to the relocation center cemetery, where there are marked graves, and the brick structure with the granite slab monument, described above.

A 10-foot-tall monument, with "Amache Remembered" inscribed at the top, was placed at the cemetery by the Denver Central Optimists Club in 1983 (Figure 5.64). The text says in English that the monument is "dedicated to the 31 patriotic Japanese Americans who volunteered from Amache and dutifully gave their lives in World War II, to the approximately 7000 persons who were relocated at Amache, and to the 120 who died there during this period of relocation, August 27, 1942, October 15, 1945." On the sides of the monument are the names of the 31 soldiers.

At nearby Granada High School, students under the direction of teacher John Hopper have researched the relocation center, contacted former evacuees for information, and constructed a scale model

(Figure 5.65). The relocation center site was listed on the National Register of Historic Places in 1994; the nomination form, prepared by Simmons and Simmons (1993), summarizes the history of the relocation centers and provides many details about the camp layout and operations, and includes stories garnered from the local press about how the center was perceived by local residents.

In 1994 the state of Colorado provided funds to improve access and refurbish some of the site, and in 1998 the Denver Optimist Club received a grant from the Civil Liberties Public Education Fund to develop the site. Plans call for installation of interpretive signs, development of a walking/driving tour, and the construction of gravel paths, one through a typical barracks block and one at the cemetery.

Chapter 6

Heart Mountain Relocation Center

The Heart Mountain Relocation Center was located in Park County, in northwest Wyoming, 12 miles northwest of the town of Cody. Situated on terraces of the Shoshone River, the relocation center lies at 4700 ft elevation, within open sagebrush desert. Heart Mountain, a detached limestone fault block rising to 8123 ft elevation 8 miles to the west, forms a dramatic backdrop to the relocation center.

The relocation center reserve encompassed 46,000 acres (Figure 6.1). The adjacent Vocation railroad siding and existing Bureau of Reclamation irrigation developments likely influenced the location choice; construction was begun June 15, 1942, with a crew of 2,000 workers. The first evacuees, from California, Oregon, and Washington, arrived August 11, 1942, and the center was in operation until November 10, 1945. With a maximum population of 10,767, the center was the third largest city in Wyoming. Local residents recall that it was one of only a few communities in the state to have electricity.

The Heart Mountain Relocation Center was a major part of the largest single draft resistence movement in U.S. history. To protest the unconstitutional confinement of their families, 315 Japanese Americans from all ten relocation centers were imprisoned for resisting induction into the military. Heart Mountain had the highest rate of resistance, with a total of 85 men imprisoned for draft law violations. The Heart Mountain total included seven leaders of the Heart Mountain Fair Play Committee who were convicted for conspiring to violate the Selective Service Act and for counseling other draft-age Nisei to resist military induction. In spite of substantial draft resistance at Heart Mountain, 700 men reported for their selective service physicals; of these, 385 were inducted, of whom eleven were killed and fifty-two wounded in battle.

The central area of the relocation center covered two terraces of the Shoshone River, which flows northeasterly along the eastern boundary of the reserve. The administration and residential areas were on the

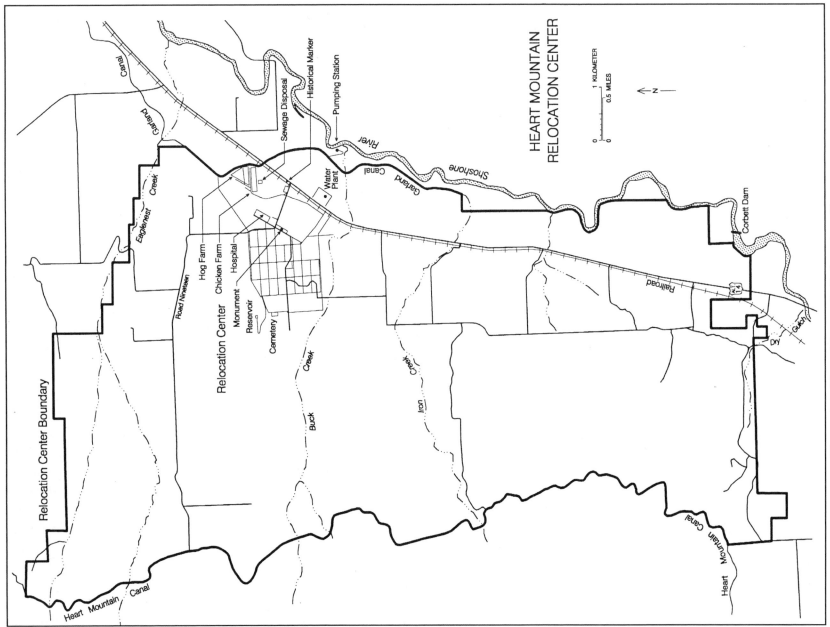

Figure 6.1. Heart Mountain Relocation Center.

Figure 6.2. Oblique aerial view of the Heart Mountain Relocation Center (WRA photograph, National Archives).

upper terrace (Figures 6.2 and 6.3). Support facilities and the hog and chicken farms were on the lower terrace. All were within the fenced area, guarded by nine watch towers. There was a sentry post at the main entrance and gate houses on the north, west, and south sides of the central area.

The hospital complex, on the upper terrace at the far eastern edge of the central area, included 17 buildings with connecting covered walkways (Figure 6.4). Two of the buildings, a hostel and a garage, were former Civilian Conservation Corps (CCC) buildings. The administration and staff housing area, just southwest of the hospital complex, included eight office buildings, a fire station, a store, the post office, a garage, a storage building, 15 apartment and dormitory buildings, a recreation building, and a mess hall. Buildings of both the hospital complex and the administration area were laid out adjacent to Central Avenue, which ran southwest-northeast, roughly following the contour of the terrace.

The residential area, laid out on a north-south grid, was divided into 30 blocks, with 20 actually used for barracks. All but Block 7 were twice the size of blocks at the other relocation centers, with each block having 24 barracks, instead of the usual 12, and two mess halls, two recreation halls, and two toilet/laundry buildings. In all, there were 468 20-by-120-ft barracks. Blocks 5 and 20 were open areas, labeled "play areas" on WRA blueprints. Blocks 3, 4, 10, 11, 18, and 19, along the interior of the west side of the fenced area, also were never used for barracks. Victory gardens were located in Blocks 10 and 11, and the center's cemetery was located west of Block 19. A large pit was dug for use as swimming pool east of the residential area, on the lower terrace near a canal that ran through the center.

A high school, completed by the evacuees May 27, 1943, was constructed in Blocks 13 and 16. It included a large building with several wings and three smaller buildings. At least one of the smaller buildings was moved to the relocation center from a nearby CCC camp (Figure 6.5).

On the lower terrace, next to the railroad, were the warehouse and motor pool area, with 60 buildings (Figure 6.6). Fifteen of the buildings were from a nearby CCC camp, and one was formerly a Works Progress Administration (WPA) building. Nearby to the northeast were three root cellars, a tool shed, and a relocated WPA shelter. The military police area was located at the entrance from State Highway 11 (now U.S. Highway Alt. 14). The WRA map indicates there were 19 buildings there, including a visitor building recycled from the CCC camp. Later, the military police contingent was reduced, and four buildings were relocated to the administration and staff housing area.

Also on the lower terrace, in the northeast portion of the camp, were the hog and chicken farms and the sewage disposal plant. At the hog farm, the WRA blueprint lists 13 hog sheds, loading chutes, and other facilities. At the chicken farm there were at least 23 chicken houses, a warehouse, a granary, a grain bin, some privies, and a lunch shelter. All

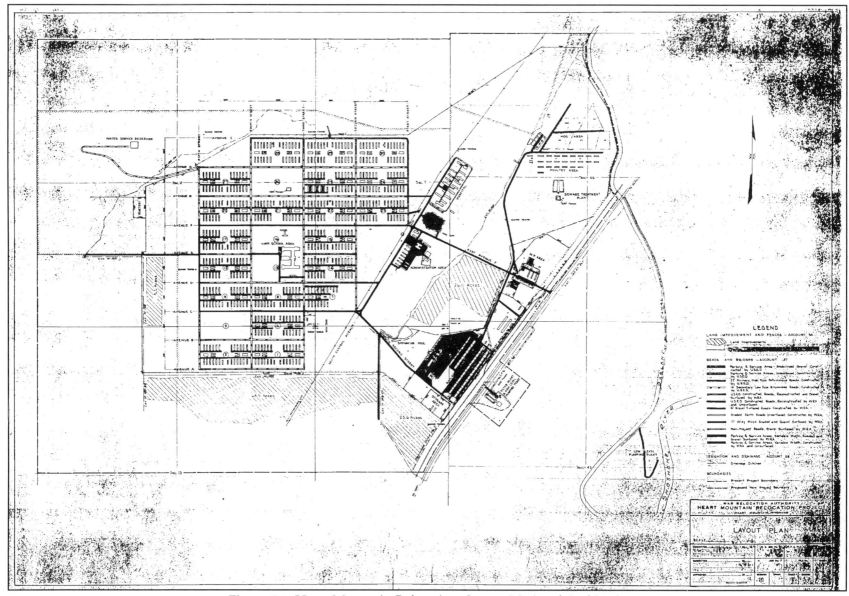

Figure 6.3. Heart Mountain Relocation Center (National Archives).

Figure 6.4. Heart Mountain Hospital (Hikaru Iwasaki photograph, Bancroft Library, University of California, Berkeley).

Figure 6.6. Evacuees arriving through the warehouse area (Tom Parker photograph, Bancroft Library, University of California, Berkeley).

Figure 6.5. Reassembling a CCC building for use as a school building (Tom Parker photograph, Bancroft Library, University of California, Berkeley).

Figure 6.7. Imhoff tank under construction at the sewage disposal plant; note size of structure in relation to workers (WRA photograph, National Archives).

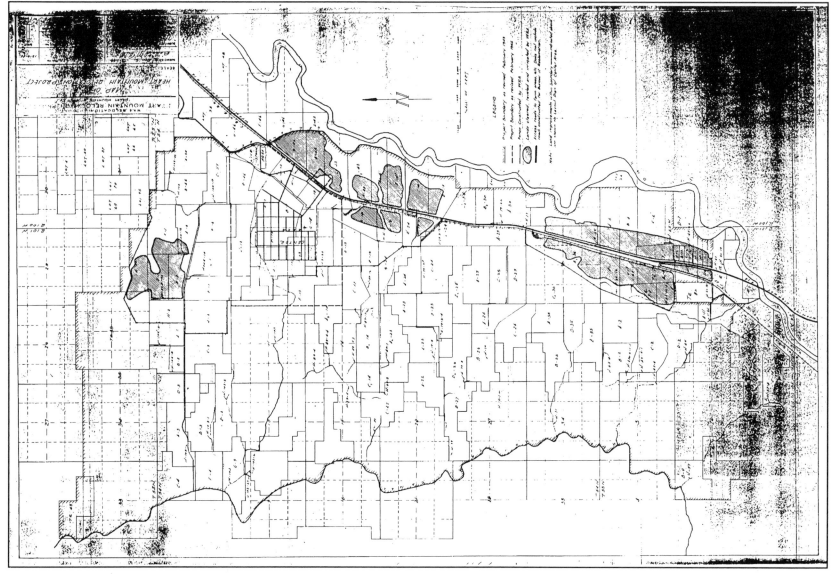

Figure 6.8. Farm fields at the Heart Mountain Relocation Center (National Archives).

Figure 6.9. Farm field at Heart Mountain (Hikaru Iwasaki photograph, Bancroft Library, University of California, Berkeley).

Figure 6.10. Transporting barracks from Heart Mountain (Big Horn Basin Project Photography Collection, John Taggart Hinckley Library, Northwest College).

of the sizable buildings were from a CCC camp. The sewage disposal plant included sludge beds, a pump house, a chlorination house, and a large buried "Imhoff" tank (Figure 6.7).

Water for domestic use was pumped from the river (at the "low-level pumping plant") to a filter plant and pumping station (the "high-level pumping plant") across the highway from the warehouse area. Water was then pumped to a concrete reservoir on a low ridge northwest of the residential area.

Water for farming came from canals, most already in place from the Bureau of Reclamation's (BOR) Heart Mountain Reclamation Project. Evacuees, however, did construct 1 mile of canal, and used 850 tons of bentonite to waterproof some of the existing canal sections that leaked (Mackey 1998). A little over 1,000 acres were cleared for farming. Fields were located adjacent to the south and east of the central area, including across (east of) the highway. Other fields were located to the north and along both sides of the highway from the central area to 3½ miles south (Figures 6.8 and 6.9).

After the relocation center was closed, buildings and equipment were auctioned off and farmers moved in to homestead the area (Figure 6.10). The farmers benefitted from the canal construction and repair and the land clearing accomplished by the evacuees. The BOR retained buildings in the hospital and staff housing area for offices, storage, and maintenance shops. Subsequently, the local Irrigation District used the buildings until 1980 (Larson et al. 1995).

There have been several recent studies of the relocation center, which provide information on the past history and current condition. In 1983 Michael Gorman of the Wyoming Recreation Commission reviewed the history of the camp and completed a National Register nomination for the hospital complex, which is located on BOR land. The parcel was listed on the National Register of Historic Places in 1985. In 1986 real estate appraiser George Page developed salvage estimates for two of the wood frame buildings in the staff housing area. His assessment provides information about construction details and the condition of the buildings at that time, which suffered from neglect and vandalism (Page 1986).

For a pipeline project, Welch et al. (1988) recorded features in the warehouse area, and noted extensive disturbance from fields and other agricultural activities. Additional features and artifacts of the hospital and administration complexes were recorded as part of a cultural resources inventory by Penny et al. (1990), who recommended that the National Register district be expanded to include the entire BOR parcel. Rose (1992) prepared a condition assessment of the four standing buildings for the BOR, and Larson et al. (1995) presented a paper at the Society for Historical Archaeology meetings which outlined the history of the center and its research potential.

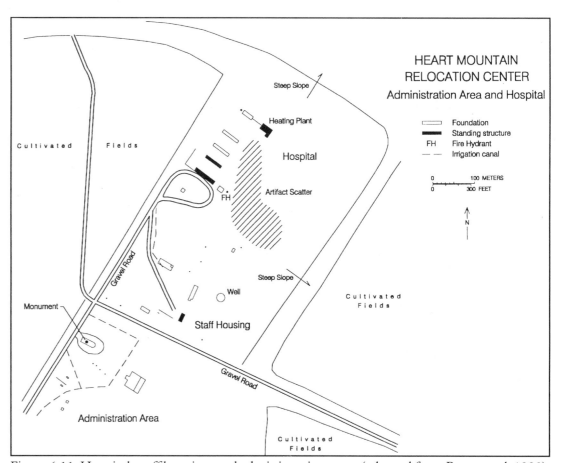

Figure 6.11. Hospital, staff housing, and administration areas (adapted from Penny et al. 1990).

Central (Fenced) Area

Most of the land at the Heart Mountain relocation center is currently under cultivation. However, three areas have intact features: the administration and hospital complexes, on Bureau of Reclamation land; the warehouse and root cellar areas on private land; and a portion of the high school, also on private land. Each area is discussed in more detail below. There are a total of six standing buildings, three at the hospital complex, one within the adjacent staff housing area, one small room or vault at the high school, and a root cellar in the warehouse area.

Hospital, Staff Housing, and Administration Areas

The hospital and administration areas are located on public land administered by the BOR, which retains a 71-acre parcel. The three buildings still standing in the hospital area include the boiler house

136

Figure 6.13. Interior of hospital boiler house.

Figure 6.12. Hospital boiler house at Heart Mountain.

with its large smokestack, a warehouse, and a mess hall (Figure 6.11). All three buildings are abandoned, and windows and doors are broken or missing. All are of similar construction: foundations are poured concrete, walls and roofs are wood frame sheathed with boards and covered with asphalt shingles on the sides and rolled roofing on top.

The boiler house measures 50 by 90 foot in plan; the clay brick chimney tapers from a 8½-feet-wide base and reaches over 75 feet in height (Figures 6.12 and 6.13). The warehouse (called a personnel housing unit in Penny et al. 1990 and Rose 1992) is 24 by 120 foot in plan (Figure 6.14); the mess hall (called a ward in Penny et al. 1990) is 40 by 180 ft (Figure 6.15). Designations used in this report are based on those listed on the WRA blueprints. For more detailed descriptions the reader is referred to Rose (1992).

In addition to the buildings there are numerous other features present, including power poles, a loading dock, a fire hydrant, a manhole, and two 20-by-120-foot concrete slabs (Figures 6.16 and 6.17). The WRA

Figure 6.14. Hospital warehouse at Heart Mountain.

Figure 6.15. Hospital mess hall at Heart Mountain.

blueprint suggests the slabs, north of the standing warehouse, are foundations of an additional warehouse and the morgue. A smaller slab north of the morgue slab is 36 feet by 87 feet; this foundation, connected to the boiler house with a concrete sidewalk, is in the location of the hospital laundry on the WRA blueprints (Figure 6.18). It appears to have been converted to a service station after the relocation center use, and there is a concrete gasoline pump island adjacent (Figure 6.19). East of the hospital along the edge of the terrace there is some relocation center building debris, as well as several post-relocation-center trash dumps.

The staff housing area adjacent to the hospital complex still has one of its original buildings, used by the Heart Mountain Extension Club from 1953 to 1985. The building, 24 feet by 50 feet, is actually only half a building (Page 1986). Walls are wood frame with cement/asbestos fiber shingles, the roof has asphalt shingles (Figure 6.20). Other features present in the staff housing area include two concrete slab foundations, one 26 by 80 feet and one 26 by 125 feet, a

7-foot-square concrete cellar (Figure 6.21), and possible concrete perimeter foundation remnants of two other buildings. There are four manholes in place, two power poles still standing, and a sign post that may have been a street sign during the relocation center use. A stone and concrete barbeque in the area was probably constructed and used by the Main family, according to Larson et al. (1995:6); noted inscribed in the mortar were the names "Becky," "Pop," "CEI," "Momy," "MARG," "Sally 1944," "LAW 50," and "1944" (Penny et al. 1990).

There is a memorial at the former administration area where the Honor Roll was constructed in front of Administration Building No. 1 (as listed on WRA blueprints) during the relocation center occupation. The Honor Roll consists of a large wooden sign within a raised rock and concrete planter and an original flag pole (Figure 6.22). No text remains on the Honor Roll, but the sign once included the names of Japanese American servicemen from Heart Mountain.

Figure 6.16. Fire hydrant in hospital area.

Figure 6.17. Concrete slab in hospital area.

Figure 6.18. Concrete slab of hospital laundry building.

Figure 6.19. Gasoline pump island in hospital area.

Figure 6.20. Building in staff housing area.

Figure 6.21. Basement in staff housing area.

Figure 6.22. Honor Roll in administration area.

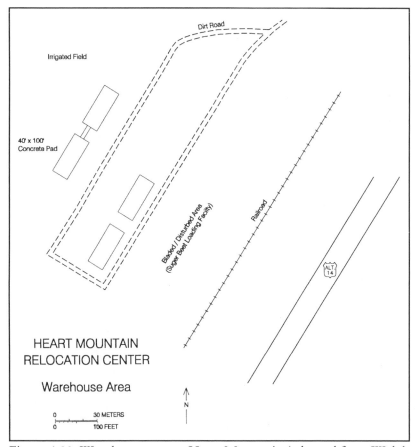

Figure 6.23. Warehouse area at Heart Mountain (adapted from Welch et al. 1988).

Figure 6.24. Root cellar at Heart Mountain.

Figure 6.25. Detail of root cellar vents.

South and east of the Honor Roll there are concrete slabs, footings, building debris, a manhole, and other traces of former buildings. Slabs include two measuring 14 feet by 14 feet, two measuring 14 feet by 21 feet, and one 125 feet by 125 feet in size. The larger slab was the foundation of Administration Building No. 5, according to the WRA blueprints; the smaller ones do not conform to buildings on the blueprints, but may have been patios for staff apartments.

Warehouse Area

In the warehouse area there are four 40 by 100 foot slabs, two connected with a 9-foot-ramp (Figure 6.23; Welch et al. 1988). One of the slabs has a mobile home on it. A dilapidated root cellar northeast of the warehouse area is still present (Figures 6.24 and 6.25). Construction of the root cellar, however, may pre-date the relocation center (John Collins, local resident, personal communication, 1994).

140

Figure 6.26. Residential area, Heart Mountain Relocation Center (Tom Parker photograph, Bancroft Library, University of California, Berkeley).

Figure 6.27. Residential area at Heart Mountain today.

Other Areas

Cultivated fields now cover all of the former evacuee barracks area (Figures 6.26 and 6.27). However, a portion of the former high school location has been left uncultivated. Within this area there is small concrete building that might have been a vault (Figure 6.28). The cemetery location is also now farm land. The burials were removed when the center was closed; seven were re-buried in the cemetery at Powell, Wyoming (Inouye 1997).

On the lower terrace the locations of the hog farm, sewage treatment plant, and military police compound are now fields. The sewage disposal plant, a massive underground tank, likely remains buried. The swimming pool, which was likely never lined with concrete, is still evident as a depression, though silted in and overgrown with vegetation (Figure 6.29 and 6.30).

Security Features

No guard tower remains were relocated, probably because of the extensive disturbance caused by agriculture. However, in the warehouse area there are portions of the original perimeter fence (Figure 6.31). These remnants are of more substantial construction then those evident in any other relocation center except Tule Lake, and contrast with the typical 5-strand barbed wire depicted in early fence photographs. The warehouse fence may have been upgraded sometime during the relocation center occupation: the hospital and administration areas were the scene of some of the work stoppages and protests revolving around unfair working conditions and discrimination (Larson et al. 1995:6), and the warehouse area may have been seen as a potential target of protest activity.

Figure 6.28. Concrete structure at the location of the Heart Mountain Relocation Center high school.

Figure 6.30. Remains of swimming pool diving board.

Figure 6.29. Swimming pool at Heart Mountain today.

Figure 6.31. Remnants of the perimeter security fence southeast of the warehouse area.

Figure 6.32. Remains of the low-level pumping plant.

Figure 6.33. Concrete reservoir at Heart Mountain.

Outlying Area

The relocation center landfill could not be relocated even after searching the area depicted on WRA blueprints. Since this area is now farm fields the dump may be buried, or it may have been located elsewhere. There is a large dump just west of the relocation center site, but it appears to contain only post-relocation center material.

Foundations of the "low-level pumping plant" which pumped water to the filter plant remain on the bank of the Shoshone River. A 20-foot-by-45-foot foundation is located in an area overgrown with vegetation (Figure 6.32). The area just east of the highway from the relocation center where the water plant and "high-level pumping plant" were located is now two separate farms. It is not known if any buildings or foundations from the relocation center use remain.

The concrete water reservoir is still on the ridge northwest of the evacuee barracks area. About 120 feet by 150 feet in size, it apparently originally had a wood and shingle roof (Figure 6.33). There is a small trash dump nearby consisting mostly of cans. The dump probably post-dates the relocation center use, since cans were generally recycled during the war. The dump contains a 1959 Wyoming automobile licence plate, also suggesting later deposition. All of the canals and fields used by the relocation center are still being used. Rock and concrete work along the Heart Mountain Canal, noted on WRA blueprints as done by the evacuees, is still evident in numerous spots, especially at bridges and head gates.

Interpretation

In 1995 the Buffalo Bill Historical Center in the town of Cody had a temporary exhibit on the Heart Mountain Relocation Center. Located in a well-traveled area of the museum, the display included text, photographs, examples of the relocation center newspaper, the

Figure 6.34. Historical marker placed along U.S. Highway Alt. 14 by the American Legion.

mimeograph machine that printed the newspaper, a Wyoming state flag used by the relocation center Girl Scout troop, a child's diary, and other artifacts.

Fifteen miles north of Cody along U.S. Highway Alt. 14, there is a historical monument placed by the American Legion and a directional sign to the relocation center memorial park. The American Legion marker, erected in 1963, mentions the state-of-the-art sewage system, excellent schools, and other amenities that were available to the evacuees (Figures 6.34 and 6.35).

The original Honor Roll, which was inscribed with the names of soldiers from the relocation center, is the central piece of the Heart Mountain Memorial Park (Figures 6.36-6.40). The park was initiated by the Heart Mountain Relocation Center Memorial Association, formed by homesteaders after World War II. The park includes plaques, a sidewalk, and a graveled parking area surrounded by large

Figure 6.35. Detail of marker placed by the American Legion.

rocks. Also there is a concrete slab that once supported a brick chimney with a plaque noting it was moved from Block 23. To the north are the three standing hospital buildings and the staff residence. The Heart

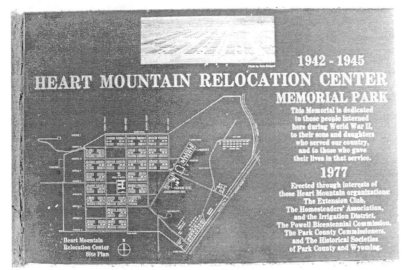

Figure 6.36. Detail of historical marker at memorial park.

Figure 6.37. Detail of historical marker at memorial park.

Figure 6.38 Detail of historical marker at memorial park.

Figure 6.39. Detail of historical marker at memorial park.

Figure 6.40. Heart Mountain Memorial Park.

Figure 6.41. Barracks building later moved to the Japanese American National Museum in Los Angeles.

Figure 6.42. Recycled barracks along State Highway 120 north of Cody, Wyoming.

Figure 6.43. Crown Hill Cemetery, Powell, Wyoming.

Mountain Foundation has obtained an option on 50 acres of land adjacent to the remaining relocation center buildings and is currently raising donations for its purchase. In addition, the Foundation has recently received a grant to construct a Learning Center and a replica of the original Honor Roll.

There are several fine examples of former barracks in the surrounding area. One was donated to the Japanese American National Museum in Los Angeles (Figure 6.41). It was dismantled, trucked, and reassembled there. Another good example of a recycled barracks is on a farm just north of Cody on State Highway 120. It appears to be unused at present (Figure 6.42).

Also at the Japanese American National Museum in Los Angeles is a 55-gallon barrel full of small stones, each one carefully inscribed with a Japanese character. The barrel had been uncovered near the former relocation center cemetery by local landowners Les and Nora Bovee, who donated them to the museum in 1994. It has been theorized that the stones may have been Buddhist *sutras* to memorialize the dead, but the museum is still seeking more information about them (*JANM Quarterly* Summer 1994).

The burials at the relocation center cemetery were moved to the Crown Hill Cemetery in the town of Powell, 11 miles northeast of Heart Mountain. The cemetery is located on the eastern edge of Powell on the south side of Lane 7 (Cemetery Road). Section 13 of the cemetery contains five headstones with Japanese surnames. Three of the headstones are large river-worn cobbles set in concrete (Figure 6.43). The inscriptions on one face of each cobble are English and those on the other face are Japanese. The inscribed dates indicate these people died in November and December 1942 (Figures 6.44-6.46). The other two headstones noted at the cemetery are typical western designs and include 1945 and 1946 dates (Figures 6.47 and 6.48).

Figure 6.44. Headstone at Crown Hill Cemetery.

Figure 6.45 Headstone at Crown Hill Cemetery.

147

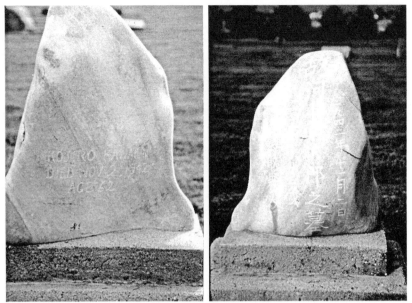

Figure 6.46 Headstone at Crown Hill Cemetery.

Figure 6.48. Headstone at Crown Hill Cemetery.

Figure 6.47 Headstone at Crown Hill Cemetery.

148

Chapter 7

Jerome Relocation Center

The Jerome Relocation Center was located in Chicot and Drew Counties, Arkansas, 18 miles south of McGehee and 120 miles southeast of Little Rock. It was one of two relocation centers in Arkansas – 27 miles north was the Rohwer Relocation Center. The relocation center was named after the town of Jerome, which was located one-half mile south. However, the official post office designation for the center was Denson.

The relocation center site is located in the Mississippi River delta region about 12 miles west of the river. At an elevation of 130 feet, the area is laced with cut-off meanders and bayous. Big and Crooked Bayous flow from north to south in the central and eastern part of the former relocation center reserve. Today the forests that once covered the area are now mostly gone, replaced by rice and soybean fields and fish farms.

The relocation center reserve encompassed 10,000 acres of tax-delinquent lands purchased through a trust agreement in the late 1930s by the Farm Security Administration (Figure 7.1). Plans had been to develop the lands by clearing trees and draining swampy areas so that they could provide subsistence for low-income farm families (Bearden 1989).

The roughly 500-acre central area of the relocation center was on the western edge of the reserve along U.S. Highway 165. Construction by A.J. Rife Construction Company of Dallas, Texas, began July 15, 1942, and the center was ready for use on October 6, 1942. The maximum population, reached in November 1942, was 8,497. Internees were from California and Hawaii. Jerome was the last of the relocation centers to open and, in June 1944, the first to close.

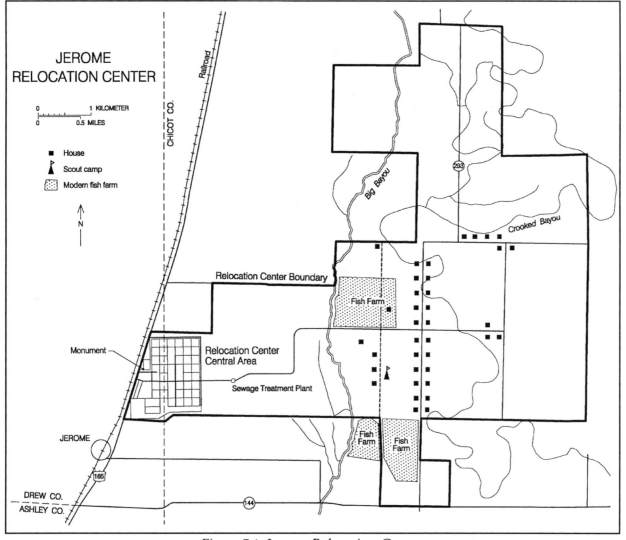

Figure 7.1. Jerome Relocation Center.

moved out through the WRA leave process. Jerome was chosen for closure for three reasons: it was the least developed of the relocation centers, it had one of the smallest populations, and the nearby Rohwer Relocation Center could absorb most of the Jerome residents reducing the amount of transportation needed.

While across the country there were several instances of military police shooting relocation center residents, Jerome was the site of the only known shooting of evacuees by a local civilian. A tenant farmer on horseback on his way home from deer hunting came across three Japanese Americans on a work detail in the woods. Thinking the Japanese Americans were trying to escape, he fired one round of buckshot, wounding two of them. Referring to the fact that a Caucasian engineer supervisor was present, the farmer explained he thought the supervisor was trying to aid the escape (*Denison Tribune Communiqué* 11/17/42).

The closure of the Jerome Relocation Center was cited as a sign of the WRA's success in placing Japanese Americans in jobs and homes outside of the West Coast restricted zone. The overall population of the ten relocation centers declined in 1944 as over 18,000 evacuees

The relocation center was divided into 50 blocks surrounded by a barbed wire fence (Figures 7.2 and 7.3), a patrol road, and seven watch towers (Figure 7.4). The only entrances were from the main highway on the west and on the backside (east) of the central area. Only the

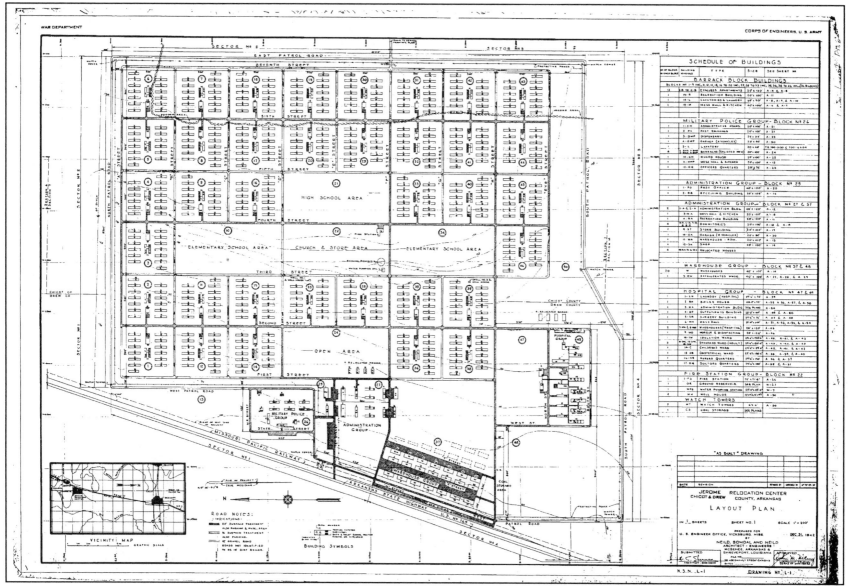

Figure 7.2. Jerome Relocation Center central area (National Archives).

Warehouse Area

Watch Tower
Military Police Compound

Administration Area

Relocated Houses

Residential Area

Auditorium

Figure 7.3. Panorama view of the Jerome Relocation Center from the southwest

Figure 7.4. Jerome watch tower (Charles E. Mace photograph, Bancroft Library, University of California, Berkeley).

Figure 7.5. Military police compound at Jerome (Charles E. Mace photograph, Bancroft Library, University of California, Berkeley).

Figure 7.6. Typical Jerome street scene (Hikaru Iwasaki photograph, Bancroft Library, University of California, Berkeley).

Residential Area — Watch Tower — Relocated Barns — Hospital Boiler House — Hospital — Morgue

(Hikaru Iwasaki photograph, Bancroft Library, University of California, Berkeley).

Figure 7.7. Barracks, Block 44, Jerome Relocation Center (Charles E. Mace photograph, Bancroft Library, University of California, Berkeley).

Figure 7.8. Young children at Jerome (Gretchen Van Tassel photograph, Bancroft Library, University of California, Berkeley).

Figure 7.9. Multi-purpose auditorium at Jerome (Hikaru Iwasaki photograph, Bancroft Library, University of California, Berkeley).

residential blocks were consistent in size, but all of the blocks were on a north-south grid, except for the warehouse block which was aligned with the adjacent Missouri Pacific railroad.

There were over 610 buildings at the center. The military police compound (designated Block 26), located north of the main entrance, included 12 buildings (Figure 7.5). The administration area (Blocks 24, 25 and 37) had 18 buildings; four of these, listed on the WRA blueprints as "relocated houses," were likely used for staff housing. The warehouse area (Block 37) had 21 buildings, and the hospital (Blocks 47 and 49) had 16 buildings. Block 50, east of the hospital, had four "relocated barns." Block 48, south of the warehouses, was used for coal storage.

The 36 residential blocks were located east of the military police and administration areas (Figures 7.6-7.8). They lay within a rectangle six blocks east-west by eight blocks north-south. The easternmost row was noted as "wooded." Each residential block had twelve 20 foot by 120 foot barracks, a recreation building, a mess hall, and a combined bathroom and laundry building. Well houses were located in Blocks 23 and 39.

Three blocks (10, 21, 22, and 34) were set aside for a high school and elementary schools. However, it appears that no school buildings were ever built in these areas. Instead, one or more residential blocks were likely used for schools. The caption of a June 1944 photograph of a general-purpose auditorium indicates it was only recently completed (Figure 7.9). On WRA blueprints Block 22 is labeled as the "church and store area," but the buildings listed there include only a fire house, a pumping station, and a water storage tank.

The sewage treatment plant was located about one-half mile east of the residential area. A 1943 WRA blueprint shows a cemetery just inside the perimeter fence in the southwest corner of the relocation center,

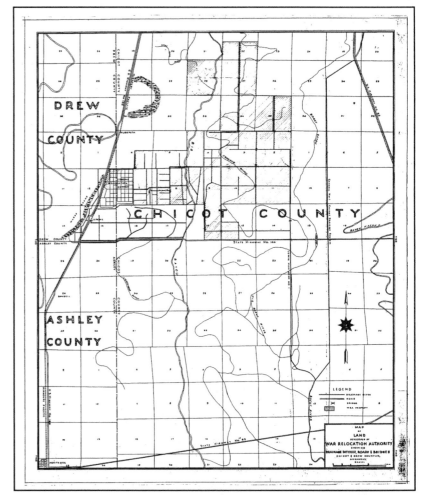

Figure 7.10. Evacuee-constructed ditches at the Jerome Relocation Center (National Archives).

but reportedly the cemetery was never used.

Outside the fenced central area the evacuees cleared land for farming, dug ditches, and built bridges (Figures 7.10 and 7.11). Many of the trees cleared were put to use: between July 1943 and February 1944,

154

Figure 7.11. Drainage Ditch No. 1 at Jerome (Charles R. Lynn photograph, Bancroft Library, University of California, Berkeley).

Figure 7.12. Sawmill at the Jerome Relocation Center (Tom Parker photograph, Bancroft Library, University of California, Berkeley).

Figure 7.13. Cabbage harvest at Jerome (Gretchen Van Tassel photograph, Bancroft Library, University of California, Berkeley).

Jerome produced over 280,000 board feet of lumber and over 6,000 cords of firewood (Figure 7.12).

The Jerome and Rohwer relocation centers grew 85 percent of their own vegetables (Figure 7.13; Bearden 1989). In 1943, 630 acres were put under cultivation at Jerome. In 1944, 718 acres were under cultivation, 200 additional acres were cleared but not farmed, and several hundred more acres were partially cleared (*Denson Tribune Communiqué* 2/22/44).

Over 1,200 hogs were raised by the evacuees for consumption at the center. The hog farm location is not known, but it likely utilized an existing farm within the relocation center reserve. A map in the *Denson Tribune Communiqué* (3/9/43) shows 37 houses within the reserve, most east of Big Bayou along a north-south road(now State Highway 293).

Four miles east of the residential area the evacuees built a 45-acre scout campsite. Three five-room buildings near the camp site were used as a scout headquarters and field houses.

After the relocation center was closed in 1944 it was converted into a Prisoner of War camp for Germans, although the POWs were confined to the central area and did not work the surrounding fields. All of Block 1 was occupied by a German general captured at the Battle of the Bulge and his orderlies. Another block was isolated from the rest of the camp to house SS troops. Two German POWs who escaped later turned themselves in (John Ellington, personal communication, 1994).

Central Area

Currently the former administration and barracks area is delimited by U.S. Highway 165 on the west and rows of windbreak trees on the north and south. The central portion is owned by John Ellington; the area that once housed over 8,000 people is now occupied and farmed by one extended family. John Ellington lived on a farm east of the relocation center in the 1940s and has lived in the vicinity since 1932. He met numerous Japanese Americans when they were working on surrounding farms and also when he visited the center.

There are currently several residences and farm buildings in the central area (Figure 7.14). Remains from the relocation center include a large brick smokestack, a concrete water reservoir, two "relocated houses," and several concrete slab foundations. Only an occasional artifact possibly associated with the relocation center was seen in the central area. These include fragments of clear and amber glass, hotel ware ceramics, concrete, and bricks.

The relocated houses (Figure 7.15) were originally built by the Farm Security Administration and moved to the relocation center by the WRA (John Ellington, personal communication, 1994). Near one there is a fire hydrant with a 1942 date (Figure 7.16).

The most salient feature remaining at the site is the 100-foot-tall yellow brick hospital boiler house smokestack (Figures 7.17 and 7.18). The smokestack is in poor condition; a portion of the top has already fallen.

The massive concrete reservoir, located in what once was the central area, now stands unused amongst the farm fields (Figures 7.19 and 7.20). Nearby, concrete pads and machinery from the two deep wells that supplied the relocation center also remain (Figure 7.21). According to John Ellington's son, a previous owner had cleared the immediate area, dug ditches, and reused the deep water wells in an attempt to grow rice.

Several of the concrete slabs for buildings in the administration area are still in existence and serve as foundations for farm buildings. Seven concrete slabs and asphalt paving in the warehouse area are used as foundations for grain silos and to store farm equipment (Figure 7.22).

Most of the residential area has been cleared and leveled and is under cultivation for rice and soybeans (Figure 7.23). But some of the raised gravel roads are still used (Figure 7.24). There are no variations in soil or vegetative growth to indicate the original slab or pier foundations in the fields, and it is not known if they lie buried or were removed. Within the central area a low-lying flooded area (possibly a recent borrow pit) had abundant concrete debris, likely from relocation center building foundations, along its banks.

Figure 7.14. Site of the Jerome Relocation Center today.

Figure 7.15. "Relocated House" at Jerome today.

Figure 7.16. 1942 fire hydrant at Jerome.

Figure 7.17. Hospital boiler house and smokestack (Tom Parker photograph, Bancroft Library, University of California, Berkeley).

Figure 7.18. Smokestack at Jerome today.

157

Figure 7.19. Water reservoir under construction (Tom Parker photograph, Bancroft Library, University of California, Berkeley).

Figure 7.20. Water reservoir at Jerome today.

Figure 7.21. Deep water well at Jerome today.

Figure 7.22. Warehouse area at Jerome today.

Figure 7.23. Residential area at Jerome today.

Figure 7.24. Relocation center road today.

Figure 7.25. Watch tower foundation blocks.

Security Features

Along the southern perimeter of the former residential area there are a few concrete fragments and foundation blocks from a watch tower, obviously displaced (Figure 7.25). The perimeter fence is gone and no other watch tower foundations were seen.

Outlying Area

One-half mile east of the relocation center residential area is the sewage treatment plant. It is in good condition and much of its associated machinery, such as pumps and other equipment, still remain. One interesting feature of the plant was the innovative use of filter rock, much of which is still present (Figures 7.26-7.28).

No other outlying features definitely associated with the relocation center were identified. West of the relocation center and U.S. Highway 165 are the Jerome railroad siding and the old highway (Figure 7.29). When the relocation center was in use, the highway was on the west side of the railroad. The present highway, east of the railroad, was constructed through the western edge of the central area, where H Street, the boundary fence, and the west patrol road were once located.

Most of the surrounding countryside, including the scout camp, is now irrigated fields or fish farms. Little remains of the forest that covered most of the area in the 1940s. Currently-used ditches follow the 1940s alignments. All are unlined, and have steel pipe control gates and valves (Figure 7.30).

Interpretation

The relocation center site is commemorated by a 10-foot-tall granite boulder monument along the east side of U.S. Highway 165 (Figure 7.31). In 1992, John Ellington gave his permission for construction of the monument and also indicated that he would not remove the hospital boiler house smokestack, now a local landmark. However, the smokestack is in need of stabilization, since it has begun to deteriorate. Although the relocated center site is on private land, the Ellingtons have allowed visitors to see the remaining features, and are a wealth of information.

Figure 7.26. Sewage treatment plant under construction (Tom Parker photograph, Bancroft Library, University of California, Berkeley).

Figure 7.27. Sewage treatment plant at Jerome today.

Figure 7.28. Equipment at the Jerome sewage treatment plant today.

Figure 7.29. Old highway west of Jerome.

Figure 7.30. Typical ditch at Jerome.

Figure 7.31. Historical monument at Jerome.

Chapter 8

Manzanar Relocation Center

The Manzanar Relocation Center was in east-central California, in southern Owens Valley. Located for the most part on the west side of U.S. Highway 395, it is 220 miles north of Los Angeles and 250 miles south of Reno, between the towns of Lone Pine and Independence. The central portion of the relocation center site is now a National Historic Site administered by the National Park Service. Outlying portions of the relocation center are on city of Los Angeles land administered by the Department of Water and Power and public land administered by the Bureau of Land Management.

On the western edge of the Basin and Range province, the topography of the area is dramatic, with the steep Sierra Nevada to the west and the White-Inyo Range to the east. Mount Williamson, the second highest peak in the Sierra Nevada at 14,375 feet, is 10 miles southwest. The National Historic Site itself is located where the coalesced alluvial fans of the Sierra meet the valley floor at 3900 feet elevation.

Figure 8.1. Manzanar with Mount Williamson in the background (Dorothea Lange photograph, National Archives).

Figure 8.2. Confiscated evacuee automobiles (Clem Albers photograph, Bancroft Library, University of California, Berkeley).

The Owens Valley is in the rainshadow formed by the Sierra Nevada. Independence has a mean annual precipitation of just under 5 inches and Lone Pine approximately 6 inches. However, the valley is well-watered by Sierran streams and the relocation center site is located between two perennial streams which flow east from the Sierra Nevada, Shepherd Creek on the north and George Creek on the south. The stream flow of Bairs Creek, which crosses the southwest corner of the relocation center central area, is intermittent.

Summers are hot and winters cold, and the natural vegetation in the vicinity is desert scrub (for example, rabbitbrush and sagebrush). Non-native trees, mostly black locust, cottonwood, tamarisk, and fruit trees from abandoned ranches, farms, and the relocation center, form a band across the site.

Figure 8.3. Evacuees arriving at Manzanar (WRA photograph, National Archives).

The Manzanar Relocation Center, established as the Owens Valley Reception Center, was first run by the U.S. Army's Wartime Civilian Control Administration (WCCA). It later became the first relocation center to be operated by the War Relocation Authority (WRA). The center was located at the former farm and orchard community of Manzanar. Founded in 1910, the town was abandoned when the city of Los Angeles purchased the land in the late 1920s for its water rights. The Los Angeles aqueduct, which carries Owens Valley water to Los Angeles, is a mile east of Manzanar.

Begun in March of 1942, the relocation center was built by Los Angeles contractor Griffith and Company. Construction proceeded 10 hours a day 7 days a week; major construction was completed within six weeks. On March 21 the first 82 Japanese Americans made the 220-mile trip by bus from Los Angeles. More volunteers soon followed to help build the relocation center: over the next few days 146 more

Japanese Americans arrived in 140 cars and trucks under military escort (Figure 8.2). Another 500 Japanese Americans, mostly older men, arrived from Los Angeles by train. By mid April, up to 1,000 Japanese Americans were arriving at Manzanar a day and by mid May Manzanar had a population of over 7,000 (Figure 8.3). By July Manzanar's population was nearly 10,000. Over 90 percent of the evacuees were from the Los Angeles area; others were from Stockton, California, and Bainbridge Island, Washington.

The central developed portion of the relocation center covers an area of approximately 540 acres (Figure 8.4). Eight watchtowers were completed on the perimeter by August 1942, and a five-strand barbed wire fence around the central area was completed by the end of the year. A military police compound with 13 buildings was located beyond the southeast quarter of the relocation center central area, south of Bairs Creek and west of U.S. Highway 395.

Paved or oiled roads divided the central portion of the relocation center into 67 blocks, including 36 residential blocks, two staff housing blocks, an administrative block, two warehouse blocks, a garage block, and a hospital block (Figure 8.5). The 24 remaining blocks, located throughout the center, served as firebreaks. East-west roads were designated by numbers starting with 1st street at the relocation center entrance and proceeding north. The one road south of 1st Street was named Manzanar Street. North-south roads were designated by letters, starting with "A" street on the east and ending with "I" Street on the west. The evacuee residential blocks were designated 1 through 36; none of the other blocks were designated by number. The relocation center was aligned with U.S. Highway 395, rather than true north.

After initial construction, all additional buildings at Manzanar were completed using paid evacuee labor. Major undertakings included construction of 18 residential buildings for staff personnel; construc-

tion of an auditorium (Figure 8.6); and the construction of chicken and hog farms. Other new construction included a laundry in the staff housing area, a sentry post and police post at the relocation center entrance, an entry post at the military police compound, and a residence for the chief medical officer and appointed nurses at the hospital. In the warehouse area a root cellar, two latrines, and a garage were constructed. Also built by evacuees were a garbage can washing rack and incinerator near the hospital, a dehydration plant, Judo and Kendo buildings, a lath house, three orphanage buildings, and two outdoor theaters.

The administration block was at the relocation center entrance on the south side of 1st Street. It included nine buildings: an L-shaped office building, a town hall, a post office, a mess hall, and five staff apartment buildings. To the south of the administration block there was additional staff housing consisting of 14 apartment buildings, three dormitories, and a laundry.

West of the administration block was a garage block, a fire break, and two warehouse blocks. Buildings in the garage block included two automotive repair shops, a refrigerated warehouse, and eight other warehouses. The warehouse blocks had 29 warehouses and two latrines. A motor pool, including a service station, gasoline pump, the motor pool office, and a small unnamed structure, was south of the garage block. Four garages and a latrine were located southwest of the warehouse blocks.

Factories were located on the south side of the relocation center between the warehouse blocks and the perimeter security fence. The WRA intended the primary work at Manzanar to be industrial rather than agricultural. However, complaints from labor unions over unfair competition soon forced the WRA to limit industrial production to items slated for internal use. The chief industrial projects at Manzanar included a garment factory, a mattress factory, a food processing unit,

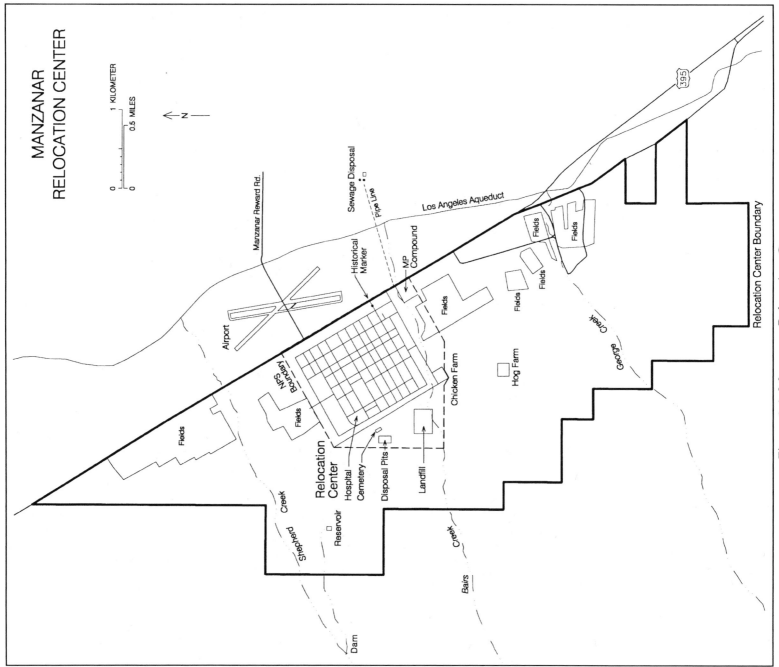

MANZANAR RELOCATION CENTER

1 KILOMETER

0.5 MILES

N

Manzanar Reward Rd.

Airport

Historical Marker

Sewage Disposal

Pipe Line

MP Compound

Los Angeles Aqueduct

Fields

Fields

Fields

Fields

Fields

NPS Boundary

Fields

Relocation Center

Hospital

Cemetery

Disposal Pits

Landfill

Chicken Farm

Hog Farm

George Creek

Reservoir

Shepherd Creek

Bairs Creek

Dam

Relocation Center Boundary

395

Figure 8.4. Manzanar Relocation Center.

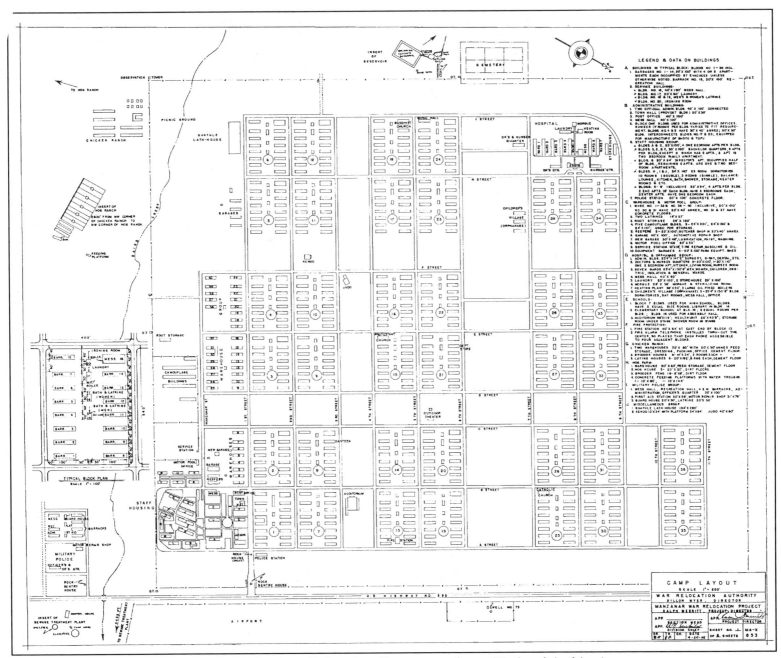

Figure 8.5. Manzanar Relocation Center central area (National Archives).

Figure 8.6. Auditorium under construction (WRA photograph, National Archives).

Figure 8.7. Camouflage net factory at Manzanar (WRA photograph, National Archives).

and a short-lived camouflage net factory. Other smaller-scale industries included a furniture shop, an alterations shop, a typewriter repair shop, a sign shop, and a domestic sewing machine repair shop.

The garment factory, the first industrial project to get underway at Manzanar, was started in May 1942 in the Block 2 ironing room by ten women with a borrowed portable sewing machine. The factory was later relocated to two warehouses, where 38 industrial machines replaced borrowed domestic machines.

The camouflage net factory was run by the Southern California Glass Company under contract with the U.S. Army. The camouflage net factory included three buildings 300 feet by 24 feet by 18 feet tall for net garnishing, a 24-foot-by-100 foot enclosed shed with an attached 60-foot-by-100-foot open shed for net cutting, and a 24-foot-by-150-foot shed for storage. Two of the net garnishing buildings had 12 foot

by 20 foot additions. Net production began in June 1942 (Figure 8.7). The net factory was a major source of conflict within the relocation center, because its employees received higher wages than all other Manzanar workers and only U.S. citizens could work there.

The easternmost building of the camouflage net factory complex (the 24-foot-by-150-foot storage shed) was remodeled by the WRA for use as a mattress factory. The factory was destroyed by a fire in 1943. During its operation the factory employed a crew of 19, and produced 4,020 mattresses. The dehydration plant was a 24-foot-by-100-foot building. West of the factories there was a 26-foot-by-100-foot root storage building.

The relocation center hospital was in the northwest corner of the central area, west of evacuee residential blocks 29 and 34. It included

Figure 8.8. Manzanar Children's Village (Dorothea Lange photograph, Bancroft Library, University of California, Berkeley).

an administration building, a doctors' quarters, a nurses' quarters, seven wards, a mess hall, a laundry, a heating plant, and a morgue, all connected by covered wooden walkways. An apartment building for Caucasian hospital staff was built using evacuee labor in a firebreak south of the hospital.

All Japanese American orphans in the restricted zone, even half-Japanese babies living in Caucasian foster homes, were sent to Manzanar. An orphanage, called Children's Village, was located near the hospital in the firebreak east of Block 29. Since the barracks provided for the evacuees were unsuitable for young children, three new one-story buildings with running water, baths, and toilets were completed in June 1942 by the evacuees. One building contained an office, superintendent's apartment, a recreation room, a kitchen, and a dining room. Another was divided into three wards: a nursery, a

small children's dormitory, and a girls' dormitory. The third building was also partitioned to form three sections: a dormitory for small boys, another for older boys, and a storeroom. Over 100 children would eventually be housed at the Children's Village (Figure 8.8).

Each of the 36 evacuee residential blocks contained fourteen 20-foot-by-100-foot barracks, a mess hall, a recreation hall, two communal bathhouses, a laundry room, an ironing room, and a heating oil storage tank. The only exception was at Block 33, which lacked a recreation building. All of the buildings were constructed of wood frame, board, and tarpaper. Foundations for the barracks, mess halls, and community buildings were concrete footing blocks set at 10 foot intervals (post and pier). Foundations of the bathhouses, laundry rooms, and ironing rooms were concrete slabs.

Although the barracks buildings and block layout were standardized, the evacuees personalized their surroundings by adding sidewalks, entries, rock-lined pathways, gardens, and small ponds (Figure 8.9). Some evacuees hand-dug basements under their barracks. Many of the residential blocks also had large community pond and garden complexes. Nearly every residential block also had its own volleyball court, a majority had basketball courts, and some had playground equipment.

The barracks and recreation buildings were also used for churches, a general store, a sporting goods store, a canteen, gift shops, a beauty parlor, a barber shop, a dressmaking shop, a shoe repair shop, a watch repair shop, a flower shop, a mail order counter, a laundry, and after April 1943 a photography studio. Block 1, at the relocation center entrance, was used for community offices and bachelors' apartments. The laundry and ironing buildings were interconnected and used for the manufacture of shoyu and tofu. All of Block 7 and the mess hall, ironing room, and one barracks of Block 2 were used for a high school. An auditorium was built by the evacuees in the fire break

Figure 8.9. Barracks landscaping (WRA photograph, National Archives).

Figure 8.10. Pleasure Park (Ansel Adams photograph, Library of Congress).

north of the high school. Block 16, in the central portion of the residential area, was used for elementary schools and a community center. A fire station was in a specially built building on the east side of Block 13.

Major developed recreation areas included a picnic area with walkways, bridges, open-air fireplaces, and a nine-hole golf course at Bairs Creek and several other community parks. Rose Park (later renamed Pleasure Park and then Merritt Park in honor of the relocation center director) was located in the firebreak between Blocks 33 and 23. It was begun in the fall of 1942 with domestic rose buds grafted to native root stock. Eventually, it included over 100 species of flowers, two small lakes, a waterfall, a bridge, a Japanese tea house, a Dutch oven, and pine trees (Figure 8.10). Cherry Park, south of the Children's Village, was begun when a nursery wholesaler donated 1,000 cherry and wisteria trees.

Holes were dug at the park for swimming pools, but due to water shortages and LADWP concerns over contamination to the Los Angeles Aqueduct, they were instead seeded with grass. North Park was located between Block 32 and the perimeter security fence. It included two rock fireplaces in a grove of large cottonwoods that remained from an old ranch. Two parks were located outside the perimeter security fence, ¼ mile and 1 mile south of the residential area. The "South Parks" opened in early 1943 under a permit system, as restrictions were relaxed and the evacuees were allowed to leave the central area.

Sports facilities included football fields and baseball diamonds in many of the firebreaks. A judo building was constructed in the firebreak between Blocks 10 and 16 and a raised wooden platform for kendo was built in the firebreak between Blocks 10 and 11. Outdoor theaters were located in the southwest corner of the relocation center and in the firebreak between Blocks 20 and 21.

Figure 8.11. Victory gardens in a firebreak at Manzanar (Dorothea Lange photograph, Bancroft Library, University of California, Berkeley).

Within several firebreaks and the cleared area between the evacuee housing and the perimeter security fence there were victory gardens divided off into individual plots of varying sizes (Figure 8.11). Evacuees also coaxed thousands of dollars worth of fruit from the hundreds of apple and pear trees that had been neglected since the town of Manzanar was abandoned. Some Manzanar evacuees conducted experiments supported by the California Institute of

Figure 8.12. Lath house with seedling guayule plants (Dorothea Lange photograph, Bancroft Library, University of California, Berkeley).

Technology on extracting rubber, needed for the war effort, from guayule, a small woody shrub native to the southwestern United States (Figure 8.12). Other rare plants were also cultivated to help offset war-related shortages.

Large-scale farming took place outside the fenced central area (Figures 8.13-8.15). As early as April 1942 evacuees cleared a 120-acre field south of the residential area, reconditioned eight miles of old ditch, and dug two miles of new canal. In 1943, an additional 320 acres were cleared for farming, and a new system of lined ditches and pipelines

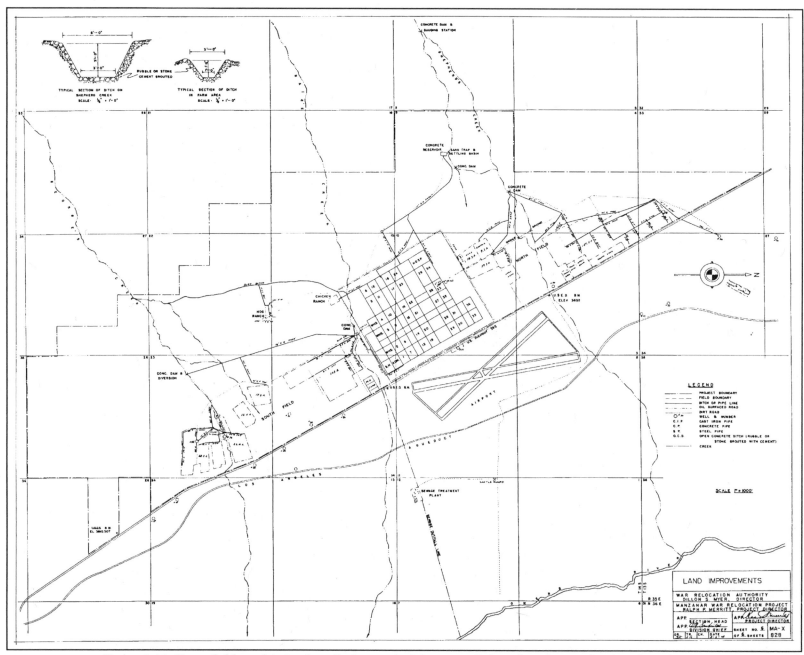

Figure 8.13. Farm fields and irrigation ditches at the Manzanar Relocation Center (National Archives).

Figure 8.14. 1944 aerial photograph showing relocation center farm fields north and south of the developed area at Manzanar, north to right (Los Angeles Department of Water and Power).

LADWP delayed clearance due to concerns that the daily washing of the hog pens would contaminate the city's water supply. The hog farm, ½ mile south of the relocation center, included six pens with concrete feeding floors and a feed storage building. In December 1943, 199 cows were purchased to start a meat herd. However, the high cost of feed prohibited maintaining the herd in peak condition, so the entire cattle project was disbanded within a year.

Initially sewage was treated in a 100-foot-by-20-foot-by-6-foot-deep septic tank. But, by the end of August 1942, a sewage treatment plant was completed 1½ miles east of the relocation center. The 1.25 million gallon a day capacity sewage treatment plant included a control room, a clarifier, a digester, a chlorination tank, and four settling ponds. The settling ponds were apparently never used: LADWP was concerned that the ponds would provide a breeding place for ducks that would then contaminate the aqueduct. Instead the liquid sewage was chlorinated and allowed to flow via an open ditch into the Owens River.

A cemetery for the relocation center was located just outside the fenced central area on the western perimeter. A commemorative

was constructed. Dams were built on Shepherd and George Creeks and to supplement the stream diversions old wells were reconditioned and used.

An evacuee-constructed chicken farm was completed December 31, 1943. Located just outside the southwest corner of the fenced central area, it included a combination office, egg and feed storage, and slaughter house, 48 hen houses, 16 brooder houses, and an incinerator. The hog farm was not completed until April 30, 1944, because

Figure 8.15. Relocation center farm field (Dorothea Lange photograph, Bancroft Library, University of California, Berkeley).

monument was built in the cemetery in August 1943. Over 135 people died at Manzanar during operation of the relocation center, but only 15 were buried in the cemetery. After the relocation center closed, all but six of the burials were moved to other cemeteries (Merritt 1946).

On November 21, Manzanar was the sixth relocation center to close. Salvage of the relocation center's buildings and materials was administered by the War Assets Administration. By December 1946, except for a few buildings in the administration and staff housing area, Manzanar was completely dismantled. The remaining buildings were used for a Veterans Housing Project. Records show 126 veterans and other people living there in August, 1948. But the veterans resided at Manzanar for only a couple of years and the building were removed. Inyo County purchased the relocation center auditorium after the

center closed and leased it to the Independence Veterans of Foreign Wars, who used it as a meeting hall and community theater until 1951. It was then used by the Inyo County Road Department until purchased by the National Park Service in 1996.

Manzanar was the site of one of the most serious civil disturbances to occur at the relocation centers, the "Manzanar Riot" or "Manzanar Revolt." The revolt erupted in December 1942 following months of tension and gang activity between Japanese American Citizens League (JACL) supporters of the administration and a large group of Issei and Kibei. Many of the evacuees did not regard the young JACL leaders, whom the administration relied upon, as representatives. Aliens were excluded from positions of importance in the relocation center administration, and from the better-paying jobs. Public meetings turned into shouting sessions; there were beatings, and death threats against the pro-administration Nisei were common. Recycling and garbage collection trucks with Kibei crews flying Black Dragon flags tried to stop work at the camouflage net factory, threatened workers, and even attempted to run people over. A fire was set in late November at the co-op store, which was seen as a symbol of JACL collusion.

On December 6 a JACL leader was beaten by six masked men. Harry Ueno, the leader of the Kitchen Workers Union, was arrested for the beating and removed from the center. Soon afterward, 3,000 to 4,000 evacuees held a meeting, marched to the administration area, and selected a committee of five to negotiate with the administration. In exchange for a promise of no more demonstrations, the center director agreed to bring Ueno back to the relocation center jail.

However, when Ueno was returned the crowd formed again. Fearing the worst, the director called in the military police. The crowd sang patriotic Japanese songs, taunted the soldiers, and even threw rocks at the military police, who then used tear gas to break up the crowd. When a truck was pushed toward the jail, the military police fired into the crowd. A 17-year-old boy was killed instantly. A 21-year-old man, shot through the stomach, died in the hospital several days later. Nine other evacuees were wounded, one evacuee was treated for exposure to tear gas, and a military police corporal was wounded by a ricocheting bullet.

The committee of five was immediately arrested. Mess hall bells rang as the military police, augmented by local National Guard volunteers, patrolled the streets inside the relocation center trying to restore order. Several times during the night tear gas was used to break up crowds and impromptu meetings at mess halls. Gangs armed with knives and other weapons searched for individuals on a well-publicized death list. Sixty-five people, including the JACL leader who had been beaten, were housed in the military police compound for their own protection. Three days later they were transferred to a former CCC camp in Death Valley where they would live for the next 2½ months.

In the following days 15 "troublemakers" were removed from the relocation center and held in local jails. In January they were sent to Department of Justice camps if they were aliens or to the WRA isolation center at Moab if they were citizens. The breadth of the revolt at Manzanar is evident in that only two of the 16 arrested and removed from the relocation center were from the same residential block (Ueno and another were from Block 22). And, there was widespread support for the "troublemakers": most work in the relocation center stopped for several weeks. Oil delivery and kitchen crews kept working, but all other work was suspended by the administration until after Christmas, since evacuees refused to show up. The camouflage net factory never reopened.

Figure 8.16. 1993 oblique areal view of the central area of the Manzanar Relocation Center.

Central Fenced Area

All of the relocation center features at Manzanar have been recorded in detail, as part of studies undertaken for the General Management Plan for the National Historic Site (Burton 1996). The following descriptions are condensed from that report. Only three of the over 800 buildings originally at the relocation center remain. However, there is abundant evidence of relocation center features, including walls, foundations, sidewalks, steps, manholes, sewer and water lines, landscaping features, ditches, and trash concentrations. Much of the relocation center road grid remains, but many of the roads in the western third are buried by alluvium or overgrown with vegetation (Figure 8.16). Other roads are cut by gullies and major portions of two roads (1st and 7th Streets) have been destroyed by gully erosion. By far the most prevalent artifact types at the site are window and bottle glass fragments and wire nails. However, a tremendous variety of artifacts dating to the relocation center use are scattered across the central area.

Figure 8.17. Entrance to the Manzanar Relocation Center today.

Figure 8.18. Military police sentry post at the Manzanar Relocation Center today.

Figure 8.19. Internal police post at the Manzanar Relocation Center today.

Figure 8.20. Concrete slab foundation of the Manzanar police station.

Figure 8.21. Sidewalk at the location of the Manzanar administration building.

Figure 8.22. Traffic circle in the administration area at Manzanar.

Figure 8.23. Inscription in the concrete top of the traffic circle.

Figure 8.24. Small concrete slab in the administration area at Manzanar.

Figure 8.25. Patio and walls at the Manzanar Relocation Center director's residence.

Entrance and Administrative Areas

Two paved roads run east-west from U.S. Highway 395 into the relocation center. Between these roads are two evacuee-constructed buildings, a sentry post and a police post, and a low rock-encircled earthen mound with wooden posts remaining from the relocation center entrance sign (Figure 8.17). There are rock alignments along the outside edges of the roads and rock-outlined parking spaces along the north road between the sentry post and the police post.

The sentry post is a 13-foot-by-14-foot one-room rock and concrete building (Figure 8.18). Across the road north and south of the sentry post along the perimeter there are short sections of rock and concrete walls. There is a decorative concrete tree stump on each side of the sentry post. Moved to a house in the nearby town of Independence in the 1955, the two stumps were returned in 1999. Located west of the sentry post, the police post is an 8-foot-by-10-foot one-room rock and concrete building (Figure 8.19). The sentry post and police post both have pagoda-style wood shake roofs and simulated wood concrete lintels over the doors and windows. North of the police post is the 20-foot-by-100-foot concrete slab of the police station (Figure 8.20).

Southwest of the entrance the administration office building location is outlined by an L-shaped rock alignment. Within the rock alignment there are four concrete footing blocks and a small concrete foundation that apparently once held a safe. On the building exterior on the north side there are two circular planters and a sidewalk incorporating a diamond-shaped planter with a metal flagpole base (Figure 8.21).

Southwest of the administration building there is a 30-foot-diameter rock and concrete planter within a traffic circle (Figure 8.22). It has many inscriptions listing Japanese American names, hometowns, and dates (Figure 8.23). A 40-inch-by-60- inch concrete slab located west of the traffic circle is divided into six panels; two are inscribed with the name "Kubota" and one has a "4/1/42" date (Figure 8.24). Remains at the staff mess hall consist of concrete footing blocks and a concrete slab with a few inscribed Japanese characters. The only remains at the town hall building and the post office are landscaping features: both have rock alignments at their north end and the town hall building has a concrete sidewalk.

The most prominent feature remaining in the staff housing area is a concrete slab patio and 3-foot to 6-foot-high wall of granite boulders and concrete at the director's residence (Figure 8.25). Also at the director's residence there are three concrete entryways, a small slab for a water heater, some concrete footing blocks, and a rock-outlined asphalt parking area. Remains of the staff apartment and dormitory buildings include concrete walkways and steps (Figure 8.26), small concrete slabs for water heaters (Figure 8.27), and a few concrete footing blocks. At one building location there is a concrete and rock pedestal, 30 inches high with a simulated wood grain top, that may have once held a sign (Figure 8.28). At another building location there is a 2½-feet-to-5-feet high concrete and rock wall enclosing a concrete slab patio (Figure 8.29). Remains of the evacuee-built laundry room in the staff housing area consist of a 16-foot-by-20-foot concrete slab with a central floor drain.

Other remains in the administration and staff housing areas include a concrete slab and brick-lined pit (possibly a barbecue), a clothesline pole base, rock alignments bordering roads, parking areas, and buildings, remnants of asphalt roads and parking areas and gravel walkways, intact manholes, concrete and rock ditches, and storm drains. Remains of a staff victory garden are located between the staff housing area and the perimeter fence.

West of the administration and staff housing area are the foundations of the service station and gasoline pump (Figure 8.30). Nearby, the motor pool office location is indicated by concrete stoops on the north and west sides of an apparent 20-foot-by-50-foot building pad

Figure 8.26. Concrete steps to building in the administration and staff area.

Figure 8.27. Concrete slab for water heater at a staff apartment.

Figure 8.28. Rock and concrete pedestal for a sign in the administration and staff area.

Figure 8.29. Rock and concrete wall at staff apartment.

Figure 8.30. Concrete island from gasoline pump.

Figure 8.31. Concrete slab foundation of automotive service garage.

Figure 8.32. Concrete slab foundation of building at the camouflage net factory.

Figure 8.33. Barrel hoops near the camouflage net factory.

Figure 8.34. Concrete slab foundation of the hospital laundry.

and a surrounding rock alignment. An inscription and a hand and a foot print are on the west entry slab. A pipe flush to the ground centered between two tall poles is likely the remains of an entrance gate to the motor pool parking area.

Remains in the garage block include the automotive repair shop foundation and the automotive service garage foundation (Figure 8.31). Two parallel 20-foot-by-100-foot foundations are from the refrigerated warehouse. Both are perimeter foundations into which a concrete slab was later poured. The refrigeration equipment was apparently at the north end of each slab, where there is a waste pipe, two other pipes, a floor drain, and a remnant dividing wall. In the south-central portion of the block there is a 6-foot-by-10-foot concrete slab with the center portion broken out. Its central location suggests it may have been a latrine. Other features include three concentrations of rocks and boulders, two manholes, and a few concrete footing blocks at the locations of two other buildings.

Remains in the two warehouse blocks include a 20-foot-by-100-foot concrete floor of five contiguous 20-foot-by-20-foot slabs. There is a mostly buried concrete driveway on the south end. One or more concrete footing blocks remain at nineteen of the other warehouses. Two latrine concrete slabs, one in each warehouse block, are 16 feet by 27 feet, divided into two rooms. Other features noted in the warehouse blocks include three asphalt driveways, some indistinct rock alignments, and two manholes. Southwest of the warehouses, where there were additional garages, there are three 20-foot-by-100-foot structure pads, each indicated by a leveled area with concrete footing blocks along one side, and one mostly buried 20-foot-by-100-foot concrete slab.

Factory Area

At the camouflage net factory location there are four parallel concrete slab foundations. Three measure 24 feet by 300 feet (Figure 8.32). One has numerous rust stains from steel drums on its north end. Another has an attached concrete slab 2 foot by 3 foot with an incomplete inscription reading: "MAR. 30TH 194..." The westernmost net factory foundation is a 24-foot-by-100-foot concrete slab. Southwest of the net factory foundations there are two small U-shaped concrete foundations, possibly tank supports, and a pile of hotel ware ceramic fragments. Southeast of the net factory, just outside the perimeter security fence, there is a roughly 1 acre area that includes hundreds of barrel hoops (Figure 8.33), several large piles of brown and clear glass jug fragments, and other trash that may be related to the factory operation or demolition.

To the west of the net factory foundations was the garment factory location, now indicated by a dirt mound and remnants of a concrete border, possibly from a perimeter foundation. Remains of the root storage building consist of a dirt mound, a small depression, and some sinkholes, possibly indicating an infilled trench or pit. East of the net factory foundations, the mattress factory location is indicated by rock and concrete alignments at its north end. A dirt road now runs the length of the building site.

Hospital

In the main hospital area, some concrete footing blocks remain at the administration building, doctors' quarters, nurses' quarters, mess hall, wards, and storerooms. Across the road in the firebreak south of the hospital, at the location of the evacuee-built Caucasian hospital staff quarters, there is an 18-foot-by-4-foot sidewalk and entry, a 7-foot-square concrete slab entry, and a 5-foot-by-8-foot concrete slab entry.

Other buildings at the hospital had concrete slab foundations, still visible at the hospital laundry, heating plant, and morgue (Figures 8.34-8.36). A 90-foot-long sidewalk attached to the morgue leads toward the hospital laundry room. It has six inscriptions, including one in Japanese. North of the morgue, the garbage can washing rack

Figure 8.35. Foundation of the hospital heating plant.

Figure 8.37. Foundation of the garbage can washing rack.

Figure 8.38. Pulled manhole at hospital.

Figure 8.40. Steps at hospital ward.

Figure 8.36. Foundation of the morgue.

Figure 8.39. Concrete bench incorporated into retaining wall at the hospital.

Figure 8.41. Rock and concrete retaining wall at the hospital laundry.

178

Figure 8.42. Remains of pond and garden complex at the Manzanar hospital.

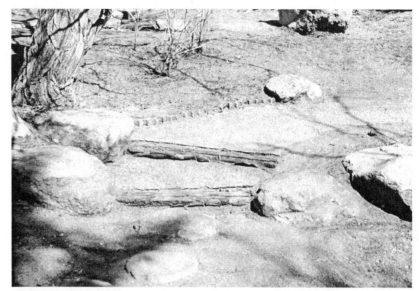

Figure 8.43. Stepping stones, wood steps, and concrete path at the hospital pond and garden complex.

foundation consists of a 20-foot-by-35-foot concrete slab with two concrete rings to support garbage cans, a drainage trough, and a large grease trap (Figure 8.37). Other features in the hospital area include three intact manholes, a destroyed manhole, and a pulled manhole that was once embellished to look like a tree stump (Figure 8.38). Within the perimeter of the central portion of the relocation center, just west of the morgue, is a 3-acre area that includes a landfill used by the hospital, and other dumps and scattered trash from later use of the relocation center (ca. 1946-1949). The landfill has been recently capped by the National Park Service to discourage digging by relic collectors.

The most significant remains at the hospital are landscaping features built by the evacuees. These include rock and concrete retaining walls, an elaborate garden complex, rock alignments along the road east of the hospital, rock circles around trees, and a rock circle and a few rock

Figure 8.44. Barracks footing blocks at Manzanar.

clusters in the administration building area. A 3-foot-high rock and concrete retaining wall located between the administration building and the hospital wards incorporates a concrete bench with a simulated wood finish and curving rock and concrete steps to each of the wards (Figures 8.39 and 8.40). The retaining wall is partially buried and has been cut in two areas by gullies and two stairways have been destroyed. The laundry slab is enclosed on three sides by a 1½-foot-high rock and concrete retaining wall; there is a cobblestone entryway with steps centered on the east side and a concrete entry ramp on the south end (Figure 8.41). The garden complex, located on the east side of the doctors' quarters location, includes a large concrete-lined pond and other landscaping features (Figures 8.42 and 8.43; Table 8.1).

Evacuee Residential Area
Within the evacuee area little evidence remains of the barracks themselves. Concrete footing blocks are at some of the barracks locations (Figure 8.44), as are some of the pipes of the water faucets that were on the exterior of every other barracks. Concrete or rock overflow basins are present at many of the water faucets, including one in Block 19 inscribed with "June 6, 1943" and one in Block 11 inscribed with "1944" (Figures 8.45 and 8.46). At some of the barracks locations there are shallow depressions likely from infilled basements.

Nearly all of the concrete slab foundations for the latrines, laundry rooms, and ironing rooms are intact. However, some are buried by sheet wash, and in Block 1 all of the slabs have been broken up and piled and in Block 7 they have been removed. The laundry room slabs measure 20 feet by 50 feet. The ironing room slabs are 20 feet by 28 feet. The latrines consisted of two separate (men's and women's) 20-foot-by-30-foot buildings. The women's has holes for 10 toilet fixtures, the men's has eight; each had a single shower stall and a single hot water heater (Figure 8.47).

Manholes remain in many of the blocks (Figure 8.48), but water and

Figure 8.45. Exterior faucet in the evacuee barracks area at Manzanar.

Figure 8.46. Exterior faucet in the evacuee barracks area at Manzanar.

Figure 8.47. Overhead view of a concrete slab foundation of a men's latrine.

Figure 8.48. Manhole and cover.

Figure 8.49. Fire hydrant.

Figure 8.50. Concrete stoop with embedded pipe fragments.

Figure 8.51. Simulated wood concrete stoop.

Figure 8.52. Concrete stoop with address formed by embedded stones.

Figure 8.53. Handprints in concrete.

Figure 8.54. Rock alignments at barracks entry.

Figure 8.55. Partially exposed concrete-lined wading pool.

Figure 8.56. Wood arbor.

Figure 8.57. Wood clothesline pole.

182

sewer lines appear to have been removed from some blocks. Only two fire hydrants remain, both are near the auditorium. One is surrounded by a circle of rocks (Figure 8.49). Lettering on the hydrants indicate they were made by Pacific States of Provo, Utah.

Evidence of hundreds of evacuee landscaping improvements are still present, and together they comprise some of the most significant features at the relocation center site. These include concrete, rock, cobblestone, and asphalt sidewalks, walkways, and entries. Some entries were decorated, such as a concrete stoop with imbedded glazed pipe fragments at Barracks 8, Block 3, a simulated-wood concrete stoop at Barracks 2, Block 9, and an incised and painted concrete stoop on the south side of Barracks 13, Block 22 (Figures 8.50 and 8.51). Some include addresses, "9=6=1" (Block 9) and "15-13-4" (Block 15), names, or dates, "Shintani May 21, 1944" (Block 11) and "May 8, 1942" (Block 34) (Figure 8.52). A small concrete slab on the south side of Barracks 11, Block 18, has two deliberate handprints (Figure 8.53). Photographs at the Eastern California Museum indicate that more inscriptions were once within the central area.

Other landscaping features and improvements include rock alignments along roads, around trees, and at barracks entries (Figure 8.54), a rock and concrete fountain, a concrete-lined wading pool (Figure 8.55), an arbor (Figure 8.56), clothesline posts (Figure 8.57), low fences and walls, and wooden borders and edging. The most elaborate evacuee improvements were gardens, many with ponds, waterfalls, walkways, and bridges (Figures 8.58-8.62; Table 8.1).

There are still slabs from the relocation center fire department in the east-central portion of Block 13 with various levels and types of concrete indicating more than one building episode (Figure 8.63). The entry ramp has a few shoe imprints and several inscriptions (Figure 8.64). There are two storm drains constructed of concrete and rock along the road east of Barracks 1, Block 1. A 40-foot-by-100-foot concrete slab (possibly a patio) covers the entire area between Barracks 13 and 14 in Block 13.

Other Areas and Features

The auditorium, constructed by the evacuees, is a 12,500-square-foot wood frame building with horizontal siding on the north, east, and south sides and vertical siding on the west side (Figure 8.65). It consists of a central 82-foot-by-125-foot structure (auditorium) with a low-pitched gambrel roof, with a two-story extension on the west side (entry and projection booth) and a one-story wing along the north side (dressing and rest rooms). A similar wing along the south side of the building was removed prior to the early 1950s; the "cornerstones" from this wing were dumped in Block 13 (Figure 8.66). The building has been further modified for use as a vehicle maintenance facility by the Inyo County Road Department. The auditorium wood floor was replaced by a concrete slab and the stage at the east end of the auditorium was removed and replaced by a large truck door.

South of the auditorium was Block 7, used as the relocation center high school, but because the northern one-third of the block was within the fenced Inyo County Maintenance Yard, it has been very disturbed. The concrete slabs for the men's latrine, the women's latrine, the laundry room, and the ironing room have been removed; all that remains of them is a small pile of concrete rubble. Barracks remains consist of two concrete footing blocks, eight upright water faucet pipes, and a few evacuee-constructed rock alignments. Recently a septic system for the auditorium was put in Block 7 by the National Park Service.

Little remains at the elementary school, which made use of the buildings in Block 16, other than the concrete slabs of the toilets, laundry, and ironing room, some rock alignments, and a few other disturbed landscaping features.

Figure 8.58. Rock work at Block 9 pond and garden complex.

Figure 8.59. Block 22 pond and garden complex.

Figure 8.60. Concrete bridge at Block 22 pond and garden complex.

Figure 8.61. Block 34 pond.

Table 8.1. Representative ponds and gardens at Manzanar.

Block	Description
Hospital	An elaborate garden complex, located on the east side of the doctors' quarters, includes a large concrete-lined pond, a stream, dispersed boulders for seating, two winding concrete walkways, boulder stepping stones, wood-reinforced pathway steps, rock borders, and other landscape features.
2	A small concrete-lined pond at the southeast corner of Barracks 2.
6	A rock garden, with some live and dead bamboo, covered with debris and leaf litter located between Barracks 14 and the mess hall.
9	An elaborate garden complex located between Barracks 14 and the mess hall, includes a large landscaped mound, boulders, a stream, rock alignments, and a buried pond. A concrete stoop for the mess hall has a simulated wood pattern and color. Another concrete stoop, on the east side of Barracks 2, has the same pattern and color.
10	An elaborate garden complex located between Barracks 12 and 13 with a concrete-lined pond, earthen mound, bench, and rock alignments.
12	An elaborate garden complex located between Barracks 14 and the mess hall, with a large concrete-lined pond, a stream with waterfalls, an island, a sidewalk, and rock alignments.
15	A small garden at the south and southeast end of Barracks 8, with concrete sidewalks, a concrete stoop, rock alignments, and a 3-foot-high upright automobile driveline used as a decorative element.

Block	Description
22	An elaborate garden complex located between Barracks 14 and the mess hall, includes a concrete-lined pond, a concrete sidewalk, a bridge, a waterfall, an island, and rock alignments. Inscribed in the concrete top of the bridge is "AUG. 9, 42" and in the north end of the pond the date "8-7 1942" is formed with small stones imbedded in concrete.
24	A small concrete-lined pond located between Barracks 5 and 6, with a concrete and rock channel leading away from it at the southwest corner of the mess hall.
24	A small concrete-lined pond, concrete slabs, a walkway, and rock alignments located between Barracks 8 and 9.
34	An elaborate garden complex located between Barracks 14 and the mess hall, includes a rocky mound, a concrete-lined pond, a stream, a bridge, rock alignments, and a collapsed barbed wire fence. The rocks used in the garden are metavolcanic, rather than the more commonly used local granite boulders and cobbles.
35	Rock alignments, cobblestone and concrete stoops, two 3-foot high circular planters, and a small concrete bridge along the west and north sides of Barracks 8.
36	A concrete-lined pond, a possible rock and concrete fountain, and a rock-lined concrete bridge with the inscription "36-12" located at the north end of Barracks 12.
36	A small garden with a cholla, a beavertail, and a barrel cactus located northeast of Barracks 14.

Figure 8.63. Concrete slab foundation of the Manzanar fire station.

At the Children's Village, the three building locations are marked by some of the original foundation blocks. Gully erosion has destroyed the original road to the north of the Children's Village; a replacement dirt road now crosses the building locations.

Remains of sports and recreation facilities can be found within the evacuee residential area. A basketball post is at Block 3. There are decorative rock alignments, concrete slabs, concrete stoops, and elaborate rock-lined cobble and concrete walkways at the location of the evacuee-built judo house south of Block 16 (Figure 8.67). Remains of baseball and softball fields in the firebreak between Blocks 19 and 25 include lumber fragments and downed chicken wire, mostly buried by drifting sand, where the backstops used to be, and a low earthen mound at the baseball field's pitcher's mound. There is a wood home plate in the firebreak between Blocks 30 and 35 (Figure 8.68).

Figure 8.62. Block 12 pond and garden complex.

Figure 8.64. Inscriptions at the Manzanar fire station.

The firebreak west of the auditorium includes evidence of three tennis courts. There is a simple rock alignment remaining at one, remnants of concrete and rock net supports and an area of discolored soil (possibly from a clay court) at another, and a partial concrete border at the third one. The concrete border, roughly the size of a standard tennis court, has been badly damaged by a recent ditch.

The eastern one-third (firebreak) of Block 34 was used as a lavishly landscaped park, variously named Rose, Pleasure, and Merritt. This area has been heavily disturbed with most landscaping elements destroyed. At both the southwest and southeast corners of the park at the road there is a large elongated boulder cemented upright on a low flat boulder (Figure 8.69). Scattered rocks at both locations are probably the remains of associated rock alignments. Remains at a former teahouse location in the southwest portion of the park consist of a raised rectangular area enclosed by a rock border (Figure 8.70). To the north there are scattered rocks and a large depression. Further to the north there is another smaller depression and a small area of concrete and rock work. Apparently mostly buried, the feature may have been a concrete-lined pond or possibly the remains of a Dutch oven shown in this area on WRA blueprints. Between this feature and the teahouse location there are the disturbed remains of a large rock garden and a possible fountain.

Two large barbecue grills (Figure 8.71), constructed of concrete and stone, are in the central portion of the northern perimeter in an area used by the evacuees as a park (North Park). One is inscribed with "Ray Kobote, August 1943." Another grill, of much less substantial construction, is located in the perimeter southwest of Block 4. It consists of a crude, low U-shaped grill-like feature made of cement and concrete blocks.

In the southwest corner of the central area, west of the lath house location, there are several depressions, concrete rubble, and a portion of concrete wall at the location of the first relocation center outdoor theater. No remains associated with the nearby golf course and developed picnic area on Bairs Creek were located. Two concentrations of concrete steps and other rubble along the edge of Bairs Creek appear to be from dismantled buildings in the administration area.

There are still remnants of the evacuee and staff victory gardens in the firebreaks and around the perimeter of the residential area. Sections of pipe and ditches (both earthen and concrete-lined), some including lumber, fencing, and culverts, remain from the irrigation systems (Figure 8.72). The irrigation system that diverted water from Bairs Creek to the staff victory garden is largely intact, though no longer in use. It includes a dam, a concrete pipeline, earthen ditches, and a settling basin. Inscribed within the concrete cap wall of the dam is the date "1942." Along the ditch there are a low U-shaped concrete water diversion structures, one has several inscriptions, including names, initials, four 1943 dates (Figure 8.73), and a fallacious 1940 date.

Figure 8.65. Manzanar auditorium in 1994.

Figure 8.66. Auditorium cornerstone.

Figure 8.67. Remains of the Manzanar judo house.

Figure 8.68. Baseball home plate in firebreak at Manzanar.

Figure 8.69. Tour examines rock work at Merritt (Pleasure) Park.

Figure 8.70. Teahouse location at Merritt (Pleasure) Park.

Figure 8.71. Barbeque grills at Manzanar North Park.

Figure 8.72. Concrete and rock irrigation ditch for victory gardens.

Figure 8.73. Inscription in a diversion box of the staff victory garden irrigation system.

Figure 8.74. Pear trees near the Manzanar Children's Village.

Figure 8.75. Watch tower foundation blocks.

Many of the fruit trees planted by the earlier town residents and cared for by the evacuees still remain. The best examples are east of the Children's Village and northeast of Merritt Park (Figure 8.74).

There are no remains apparent at the guayule lath house that was southwest of Block 6. But nearby there are several features likely associated with the lath house, including a large rectangular area enclosed by tamarisk and a barbed wire fence, two shallow rectangular depressions possibly from gardens, and an 11-foot-square concrete slab with the inscription "12.30.42." Nearby are concentrations of sanitary seal cans with punched bottoms which were probably used for seedlings.

Other features in the perimeter of the central area include a capped well, a fuel oil storage tank area, and numerous small artifact concentrations. Most of the latter were probably deposited as the relocation center was abandoned. Also present are three building foundations; although two are depicted on the WRA blueprints, their functions are unknown. One has the inscription "1944." They may have served as storage for the victory gardens or outlying farms.

Security Features
As discussed above the sentry post and police post both remain at the relocation center entrance, as does the foundation of the police station, where the shootings of the "Manzanar Riot" occurred.

Remains of seven of the eight watch towers around the fenced perimeter are present. Nothing remains of the tower in the northeast corner of the relocation center; the location is now within a graded road. Although two other towers were located within the same road, pulled footings were found near their original locations. The pulled footings varied from 3 feet to 4 feet in total length, and a maximum of 2 feet in diameter. At the five remaining watch tower locations,

Figure 8.76. Inscription near the southwest watch tower.

Figure 8.78. Concrete slab foundation in the Manzanar military police compound.

Figure 8.77. Original section of the perimeter security fence along U.S. Highway 395.

foundations visible above ground consist of four 1½-foot-by-1½-foot concrete footing blocks with steel straps, spaced 11 feet apart (Figure 8.75).

Near the watch tower footing blocks in the southwest corner of the central area there is a rock and concrete penstock inscribed with a first name, initials, a date, and the epithet "JAP CAMP" (Figure 8.76). In addition, "Summers 1942" is formed by pebbles that were pressed into the wet concrete of the penstock. Charlie Summers was the local contractor that built the relocation center watch towers. Not much remains at the three gate house locations, once located at roads to the outlying farm fields and the relocation center landfill. At the gate house on the north perimeter there is a small rock concentration, and at the gate house on the west perimeter, there are some rocks and asphalt. There are no apparent remains of the gate house on the south side of the relocation center.

Figure 8.79. Monument at the Manzanar Relocation Center cemetery.

Portions of the existing barbed wire fences on the west, north, and possibly east sides of the central area appear to be from the relocation center (Figure 8.77). These fence sections are constructed of either 4-inch by 4-inch or 4-inch by 6-inch wooden posts (both nominal and actual), placed approximately 16 feet apart. These posts are distinguished from those in typical range fences in the area by their material, height (extending over 5 feet high), and patterns of nail holes. Nail holes indicate these posts originally held five wire strands at about 12-inch intervals starting at 12 inches above the ground. The top and bottom strands have been removed.

At the military police compound the locations of all 13 known buildings, except the evacuee-constructed entry post, can be discerned. Barracks locations are defined by level areas, some with a few concrete footing blocks. The officers' quarters location has a rock-lined walkway and a small yard. The guard house (military personnel jail), latrine, and first aid buildings are evident by concentrations of wire nails, concrete chunks, and other structural debris. Most of the sizable rocks at the site have traces of white paint on them. At the location of the military police motor repair shop there is a terraced area with six large concrete foundation blocks with embedded iron bars. Artifacts in the vicinity include a small electric motor core, over 25 metal bushings, and an electrical porcelain knob. A 20-foot-by-25-foot concrete slab east of the motor repair shop location is inscribed with three sets of initials (Figure 8.78). No building is shown on WRA blueprints at this location, however the slab is visible on a 1944 aerial photograph. Another enigmatic feature, located south of the barracks area, is a 1-foot-wide concrete perimeter foundation, outlining an area 7½ feet by 9½ feet in size.

Outlying Area

There are features remaining from virtually all of the relocation center developments outside the central fenced area. This includes the cemetery, farm fields and ditches, the chicken and hog farms, the water supply system, the sewage disposal system, and other features.

Cemetery

The relocation cemetery is located on the west side of the central fenced portion of the relocation center. At the cemetery there is a large concrete obelisk with Japanese inscriptions on two sides (Figure 8.79). The inscription on the front (east) side translates as "Monument to console the souls of the dead" and the inscription on the back (west) side translates as "Erected by the Manzanar Japanese August 1943." Around the monument there is a concrete slab and nine concrete posts shaped and stained to resemble wood. Within the fenced cemetery area there are 14 rock-outlined grave plots (Figures 8.80 and 8.81); three have cut stone markers with inscriptions and four have wood posts. Also within the fenced cemetery area there are numerous concrete foundations for wood fence posts, several with inscriptions. These remain from a fence constructed by the Manzanar Committee in the 1970s. Across a dirt road north of the fenced cemetery enclosure there are three rock-outlined pet graves (Figure 8.82).

Farm Fields and Irrigation Ditches

The only relocation center farm fields currently in use are the northernmost fields along the west side of U.S. Highway 395. All of the other fields and ditches of the relocation center farms lie abandoned.

Outside of the cultivated fields the ditches that brought irrigation water to the north fields are in good condition and easy to follow (Figure 8.83). There are numerous inscriptions in the concrete of the ditches, including names, initials, dates, Japanese characters, expressions of love, and a geometric design (Figure 8.84). A dam on Shepherd Creek, measuring approximately 46 feet across, was built for the early twentieth century town of Manzanar. Evacuees raised the height of the dam by adding 18 inches of concrete wall, and inscribed

two sets of initials on top.

North and northeast of the northernmost farm fields there are two wells located on opposite sides of U.S. Highway 395, that were connected by a 2,750-foot-long concrete pipeline, now partially destroyed. An upturned concrete support near one of the wells is inscribed with "FINISHED BY TOM FUJISAKI & CREW MAR. 23, 1944" (Figure 8.85). Parts of two bridges over Shepherd Creek built by the evacuees to access the north fields are still in use.

Just south of the central area there are many remnants of the irrigation system that watered the southern farm fields, including concrete-lined and dirt ditches, concrete diversion boxes with wooden gates, a concrete pipeline, a 45-foot-long dam across George Creek, wells, and other features (Figures 8.86-8.88). The pipeline alignment appears as a raised berm for most of its length. Concrete piers were used to support the pipeline where it crossed washes and low spots. The top of two of these supports, on the south side of a small wash, each have a Japanese poem inscribed on them (Figure 8.89). The concrete ditches and diversion boxes include inscribed names, initials, dates, military slogans, and the greatest concentration of Japanese language inscriptions at the relocation center (Figure 8.90 and 8.91).

At George Creek, 1 mile south of the central area just west of U.S. Highway 395, there is a dam, a bridge, two wells, concrete-lined ditches and concrete pipelines, and various water control features (Figure 8.92). Inscriptions in the irrigation ditches include dates and Japanese characters translated as family names. There is an upright boulder with two smaller cemented rocks as decorative elements at each corner of the 10-foot-by-16-foot bridge (Figure 8.93). Six inscriptions in the concrete of the retaining walls at the bridge and a nearby pipe support include names, dates, Japanese characters translated as "Built by E Group in March 1944," and two place names, both "TUCSON," one dated "3/6/44."

Figure 8.80. First grave at the Manzanar Relocation Center cemetery.

Figure 8.81. Grave at the Manzanar Relocation Center cemetery.

Figure 8.82. Pet cemetery at Manzanar.

Figure 8.83. Concrete-lined irrigation ditch near Shepherd Creek.

Figure 8.84. Inscription in the Manzanar North Fields irrigation ditch.

Figure 8.85. Inscription at well north of the Manzanar North Fields.

Figure 8.86. Wood control gate on one of the South Fields irrigation ditches.

Figure 8.87. Irrigation ditch for the Manzanar South Fields.

Figure 8.88. Irrigation ditch for the Manzanar South Fields.

Figure 8.89. Japanese poem inscribed on pipeline support.

Figure 8.90. Inscription on South Fields irrigation ditch.

Figure 8.91. Inscription on South Fields irrigation ditch.

Figure 8.92. Dam and retaining walls on George Creek.

Figure 8.93. Bridge over George Creek.

Figure 8.94. Oblique aerial view of the Manzanar chicken farm today.

Figure 8.95. Foundation of the slaughterhouse/office at the Manzanar chicken farm.

Figure 8.96. Incinerator at the Manzanar chicken farm.

Figure 8.97. Inscription at the Manzanar chicken farm.

Chicken and Hog Farms

The relocation center chicken farm was located just outside the southwest corner of the fenced central portion of the relocation center. Remains include numerous concrete slab foundations of the office and processing plant and coops, rock and concrete retaining walls, rock alignments, and an ornate 6-foot-high incinerator made of rock and concrete (Figures 8.94-8.96). Rows of black locust trees enclose the site, and within the site there are many more black locust trees and one Arizona cypress. Sheet wash has buried portions of some slabs and some features are overgrown by brush and weeds. Inscriptions in the concrete include mostly names and Japanese characters (Figure 8.97). Artifacts at the chicken farm include window glass fragments, bottle glass fragments, hotel ware ceramic fragments, wire nails, cans, pieces of lumber, bricks, clay sewer pipe fragments, and electrical porcelain knobs.

The relocation center hog farm, located ½ mile south of the residential area, includes several concrete slabs, some with feed troughs (Figure 8.98), a rectangular pen area defined by alignments of black locust trees, other related structures and features, scattered artifacts, and a 1,150-foot-long access road and pipeline. A concrete weir box and section of concrete-lined ditch where water was diverted from a dirt ditch has a partial 1940s date and a group of damaged Japanese inscriptions translated as seven family names and "Group B."

Water System and Reservoir

A dam on Shepherd Creek, 1½ miles northwest of the central area, diverted water into an earthen ditch to the relocation center reservoir and settling basin, ½ mile northwest of the central area.

The concrete reservoir consists of a 120-foot-by-180-foot concrete-lined pool (Figure 8.99). To raise the water level a low stone and concrete wall was added by an evacuee work crew in February 1943. Several inscriptions were made in the wet concrete of the low cap wall.

These include Japanese characters, names and dates, and the notation "STONE WALL BY EMERGENCY CREW 2/25/43" made of embedded pebbles. A large boulder along a dirt road on the west side of the reservoir was plastered with a thin layer of cement and inscribed while wet with the Japanese characters for "peace" (Figure 8.100).

A concrete-lined settling basin, approximately 75 foot by 80 foot, is located adjacent to the reservoir (Figure 8.101). On the east end there is a concrete wall with an opening to the reservoir and a spillway for bypassing the reservoir. Several areas along the wall have bottle caps pressed into the concrete and three groups of inscriptions were made while the concrete was wet. All Japanese characters, they have been translated as "the army of the emperor occupied territory, 2/17/43, to Manzanar," "banzai, the Great Japanese Empire, Manzanar Black Dragon Group headquarters," and "beat Great Britain and the USA" (Figures 8.102 and 8.103). During the relocation center occupation the inscriptions would have been under water most of the time.

A concrete- and rock-lined ditch directed water from a sand trap to the settling basin. Numerous inscriptions were made on top of the ditch wall and sand trap while the concrete was wet. Included are names, dates, Japanese characters, and the notation "CONSTRUCTED BY CHODO & INC. NOV. 9 43" (Figures 8.104-8.106).

A concrete slab approximately 7 foot by 10 foot at the northwest corner of the reservoir was the foundation of a chlorination shed. A storeroom shown on WRA blueprints is indicated by wire nails, window glass, roofing, and scattered fragments of drywall and wood.

Below the reservoir, nearly 3 miles of open concrete- and rock-lined ditches and buried concrete pipelines, several concrete weir boxes, the ten-sided 30-foot-diameter concrete slab foundation of the chlorination tank (Figure 8.107), and other water system features remain. All of the ditches are easy to follow, although many sections are damaged

Figure 8.98. Manzanar hog farm today.

or silted in. The largest ditch segment, which originally held a steel pipeline, ran from the relocation center reservoir to the chlorination tank. All of the pipe has been removed.

Other ditches carried part of the water from the main pipe alignment to irrigate victory gardens within the central area of the relocation center. The ditches average 3 foot wide at the top and 1 foot wide at the bottom and are 1½ feet deep. Segments of concrete pipe were used to span washes. On the west side of the chlorination tank foundation there is a concrete-lined ditch inscribed with names, dates, and Japanese characters.

Sewage Treatment Plant

The sewage treatment plant, located about 1 mile southeast of the relocation center residential area, was connected to the relocation center via a 4,600-foot-long sewerline. Manholes were spaced along the pipeline at 100 foot to 300 foot intervals, but many of the manholes have been destroyed.

Evidence of all of the sewage treatment plant structures remain (Figures 8.108 and 8.109). The control room remains consist of the 3-foot- high raised concrete slab foundation of a three-room structure measuring 30 feet east-west by 60 feet north-south. There are remnants of a decorative rock alignment on the north side of the foundation. North of the control room foundation, there is a series of concrete tanks of various proportions connected by 18-inch-diameter concrete pipe which totals about 220 feet in length.

The digester is an enclosed tank 42½ feet in diameter and 19½ feet high. The clarifier is a partially buried, round open-topped tank approximately 65 feet in diameter, with an interior depth of about 11 feet. One side of the tank is broken out, and all equipment has been removed. The chlorine tank is a rectangular concrete box measuring 36½ feet by 16½ feet, and extending 4 feet above the ground surface. Other remains at the sewage treatment plant include a concrete enclosure for a small pump, possible light fixture foundations, four rectangular settling ponds grouped together to form a larger 100-foot-by-200-foot rectangle, and an earthen ditch that carried treated sewage towards the Owens River.

Landfill and Disposal Pits

The relocation center landfill covers 18 acres north of Bairs Creek about 1,000 feet west of the fenced central portion of the relocation center. The landfill consists of scattered trash and buried trash-filled trenches. There appears to have been at least five trenches, up to 400 feet long and 6 feet deep. Thousands of artifacts have been exposed by

Figure 8.99. Oblique aerial view of the Manzanar water reservoir today.

Figure 8.100. Boulder inscribed with Japanese characters for "peace."

Figure 8.101. Setting basin at the Manzanar water reservoir.

Figure 8.103. Japanese inscriptions at the setting basin translated as "banzai, the Great Japanese Empire," and "Manzanar Black Dragon Group headquarters."

Figure 8.102. Japanese inscription at the setting basin translated as "beat Great Britain and the USA."

Figure 8.104. Inscription at the sand trap.

Figure 8.105. Inscription at the sand trap.

Figure 8.106. Inscription at the sand trap.

Figure 8.107. Concrete slab foundation of the chlorination tank.

Figure 8.108. Control room and digester at the Manzanar sewage treatment plant.

Figure 8.109. Clarifier at the Manzanar sewage treatment plant.

plates, dishes, platters, and cups. The landfill was capped by the National Park Service in 1998 to deter digging by collectors.

A 2½-acre area west of the relocation center cemetery was used for trash disposal when the relocation center closed. One area was used exclusively for the disposal of government-issued hotel ware ceramics (Figure 8.112), other areas were used for the disposal of large debris, such as vehicles, vehicle parts, concrete, and other items. Portions of at least ten partially buried vehicles are visible (Figure 8.113).

Other Features

Remains at the evacuee parks south of the central area include two concrete ovens. One, 4 feet by 6 feet, is within a small, now roofless, one-room concrete and rock structure about ¼ mile south of the central area (Figure 8.114). The oven, proportionally too large for the structure, was built by evacuees. The building itself is from a historical ranch that was in use from around the turn of the century until the mid-1930s. The other oven, of concrete and rock, was built by the

relic collectors at the two easternmost trenches (Figure 8.110). These include Japanese and government-issued ceramic fragments and dozens of intact bottles (mostly clear, with a wide variety of different shapes and sizes), some with readable paper labels (Figure 8.111). Also present in lesser amounts are sanitary seal cans, trash can lids, barbed wire, automobile parts, cast iron fragments, screws, wire nails, and oil drums. A separate deposit, cut by a recent gully, contains roofing materials, drywall, and thousands of fragments of government-issued

Figure 8.110. Manzanar Relocation Center landfill in 1994.

Figure 8.111. Typical artifacts at the Manzanar Relocation Center landfill.

Figure 8.112. Ceramic disposal pit at the Manzanar Relocation Center.

Figure 8.113. Partially-buried evacuee automobile west of the Manzanar cemetery.

Figure 8.114. Evacuee-built oven ¼ mile south of the central area.

Figure 8.115. Inscription in the clapboard of the Lone Pine train station.

Figure 8.116. Oblique aerial view of the Manzanar airport today.

Figure 8.117. Barracks buildings at the Willow Motel in Lone Pine.

Figure 8.118. Sign along U.S. Highway 395.

evacuees within a two-room adobe-mortared rock building at an abandoned ranch 1 mile south of the central area. It is 5 feet by 7 feet in size with a 6-foot-high chimney.

There are some inscriptions carved into the clapboard siding of the Lone Pine train station (Figure 8.115). Six evacuees worked at the train station unloading materials destined for the relocation center. Only two of six known inscriptions (Garrett and Larson 1977) remain at the station; others were stolen by removing the clapboard sometime in 1992, just after the depot was no longer watched by a caretaker. The removed inscriptions were later donated anonymously to the Eastern California Museum (Bill Michael, personal communication, 1999).

A World War II-era airport was located just across U.S. Highway 395 from the relocation center central area. Built for the Army in 1941 for bomber pilot training, testing experimental aircraft, and aircraft emergencies, it apparently was never used by the relocation center. There are many features remaining at the airport including a power-house, a hangar foundation, a storage building foundation, an aircraft parking area, a wind-T support, two 5,000-foot-long asphalt-paved runways forming an X, a taxiway, and a small trash dump (Figure 8.116).

At least fourteen relocation center buildings are still in the nearby towns of Independence and Lone Pine where they were moved after Manzanar closed. The condition of the moved structures is highly variable, but many still retain substantial architectural integrity. They include barracks, staff apartments, and the missing south wing of the auditorium (now the Lone Pine American Legion Hall). The Willow Motel in Lone Pine is made of three barracks buildings (Figure 8.117). Also in Independence are the decorative concrete gate posts originally at the relocation center entrance.

Interpretation

Manzanar is a registered State of California Historic Site, and is listed on the National Register of Historic Places as a National Historic Landmark. In 1992 Congress designated Manzanar a National Historic Site, and the National Park Service maintains a temporary office in Independence. Plans call for the restoration of the relocation center auditorium as an interpretive center, and the reconstruction of a watch tower and one or more barracks. Driving and walking tours will tell the story of the relocation center while directing visitors to various features.

Along U.S. Highway 395 a sign points out the relocation center and there are turning bays for entering the site at the original entrance (Figure 8.118). At the entrance a State of California Historic Site marker has been added on to front (east) facade of the military police sentry post (Figure 8.119 and 8.120). On the back side of the sentry post there is a National Park Service information display. To the north of the sentry post there is a large granite boulder with a brass National

Figure 8.119. Historical marker at the military police sentry post.

Figure 8.120. Detail of the historical marker at the sentry post.

Figure 8.121. National Historic Landmark plaque at Manzanar.

Historic Landmark plaque (Figure 8.121); to the south there is a free-standing Blue Star Memorial Highway marker (Figure 8.122).

One mile west of the entrance, the relocation center cemetery with its large memorial tower is the focus of the annual Manzanar Pilgrimage held the last Saturday of April (Figures 8.123 and 8.124). On the cemetery monument and graves visitors have placed assorted artifacts, most apparently from the nearby ceramic disposal pit, but the offerings also include historical artifacts from other areas, flowers, coins, and origami. There is a large graded parking lot adjacent to the cemetery. The current fence around the cemetery is a replica of the original fence built by the evacuees.

The Eastern California Museum in Independence has an extensive display about the Manzanar Relocation Center, including artifacts and photographs (Figure 8.125). The museum maintains a comprehensive archive that includes World War II-era home movies taken at Manzanar. The museum also has the partial remains of a salvaged watch tower.

Figure 8.122. Blue Star Memorial Highway marker.

Figure 8.123. Manzanar pilgrimage.

Figure 8.124. Manzanar pilgrimage.

Figure 8.125 Manzanar display at the Eastern California Museum in Independence.

Chapter 9

Minidoka Relocation Center

The Minidoka Relocation Center was located in Jerome County, Idaho, 15 miles east of Jerome and 15 miles northeast of Twin Falls. The relocation center was also known as Hunt, after the official Post Office designation for the area, since there was already a town of Minidoka in Idaho, 50 miles east.

The relocation center lies within the Snake River Plain at an elevation of 4000 feet. The natural vegetation of this high desert area is dominated by sagebrush and other shrubs. Dominant geological features of the area are thin basaltic lava flows and cinder cones overlying thick rhyolite ash. The most notable topographic feature at the site is the wide meandering man-made North Side Canal (Figure 9.1). For the most part, the canal formed the southern boundary of the 33,000-acre relocation center reserve (Figure 9.2).

Five miles of barbed wire fencing and eight watch towers surrounded the administrative and residential portions of the relocation center,

Figure 9.1. North Side Canal (Francis Stewart photograph, Bancroft Library, University of California, Berkeley).

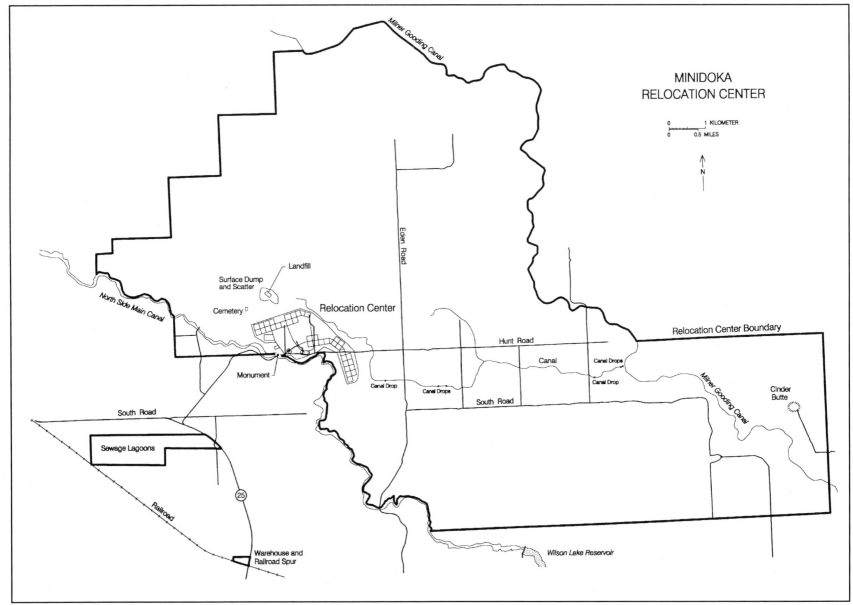

Figure 9.2. Minidoka Relocation Center.

Figure 9.3. Residents of Block 34 (from *Minidoka Interlude* 1943).

which was located on 950 acres in the west-central portion of the reserve. Built by the Morrison-Knudsen Company, construction began June 5, 1942, and the relocation center was in operation from August 10, 1942 to October 28, 1945. The maximum population was 9,397; evacuees were from Oregon, Washington, and Alaska (Figure 9.3). In early 1943, all of the Bainbridge Island (Washington) residents interned at the Manzanar Relocation Center under the authority of the first Civilian Exclusion Order were moved to Minidoka. The transfer was at their own request, not only to be closer to their original home, but also because they were often at odds with their new neighbors from Terminal Island in Los Angeles.

There were over 600 buildings at the relocation center. Minidoka had an unusual layout due to the uneven terrain. At the other relocation centers, the barracks were all within a single large rectangular area subdivided into blocks, aligned on a single grid system. At Minidoka, the barracks blocks are in four separate groups following the arc of the North Side Canal, so that the block grids vary from the standard north-south orientation. Administration areas of the relocation center also were geographically separate, with their grids laid out at slightly different angles (Figures 9.4-9.6). There were 31 buildings in the administration and staff housing area, 19 buildings in a warehouse and motor pool area, 17 buildings at the hospital, and 15 buildings at the military police compound. Another unusual feature of the Minidoka layout is that although the residential blocks were numbered up to 44 not all numbers were used. Several blocks (for example, 9 and 11) never existed.

Each of the 35 residential blocks had 12 barracks, a mess hall, a recreation hall, and a central H-shaped building with bathrooms, showers, and a laundry. Also within the residential areas were four general stores, two dry-goods stores, two barber shops, a beauty shop, two mail-order stores, two dry cleaning stores, two watch repair stores, two radio repair shops, a check-cashing service, two elementary schools, a health clinic, and two fire stations. A civic center, high school, and the evacuee-run community offices were centrally located in Block 23. In the vacant area between administrative areas and residential blocks were wells, a well house, and a sewage disposal plant.

A gym was built by the evacuees adjacent to Block 23, and evacuees pursued outdoor sports as well. They constructed nine baseball diamonds, and in the winter water was diverted into a natural depression southeast of Block 44 for ice skating (Jim Kubota, personal communication, 1995). Swimming in the North Side Canal was common in the summer, however after a drowning accident, two swimming pools were constructed by the evacuees (Figure 9.7).

Evacuees constructed an irrigation canal to the relocation center from the Milner-Gooding Canal 5 miles east. Because of the topography the North Side canal could not used by the relocation center for irrigation without a costly pumping plant. Both the Milner-Gooding and North Side Canals had their takeout from the Snake River at Milner Dam 20 miles to the southeast. A total of 350 acres were cleared and farmed by the evacuees the first year. In 1943, 420 acres were under cultivation and in 1944 about 740 acres were planted. A variety of garden

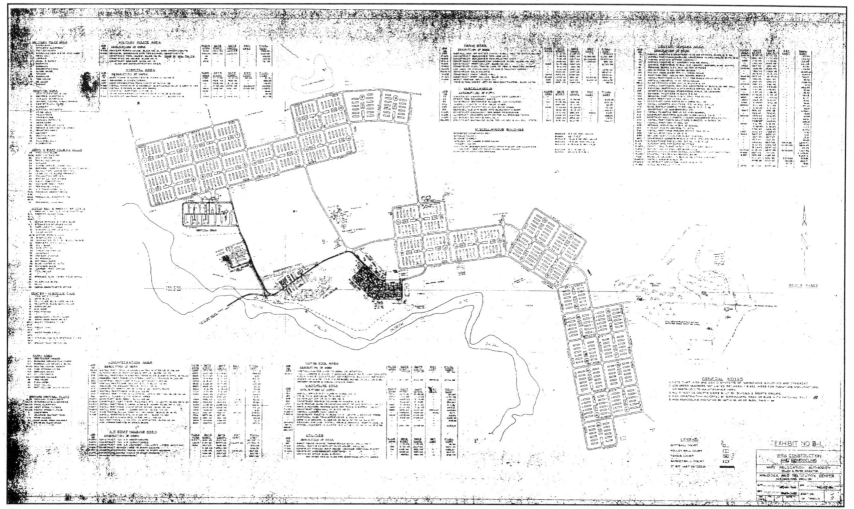

Figure 9.4. Minidoka Relocation Center (National Archives).

vegetables were grown in the fields, located mostly north and east of the fenced residential areas (Figure 9.8). Just outside the east side of the fenced residential area was a farm mess hall, a hog and chicken farm, and a landscaped park and picnic grounds watered with water initially hand-carried from a nearby canal.

A small cemetery was northwest of the central fenced portion of the relocation center (Yamaguchi 1989:41). When the relocation center was closed all of the bodies were exhumed and re-buried elsewhere. Some metal coffins remained and have been used for such things as feed and watering troughs.

206

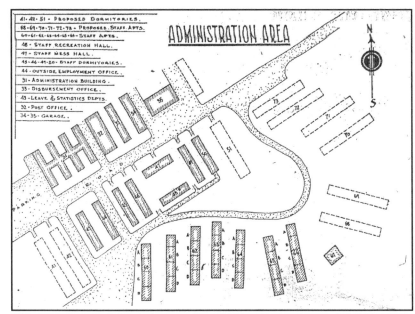

Figure 9.5. Administration and staff housing area at the Minidoka Relocation Center (from *Minidoka Irrigator* 9/25/43)

Sewage lagoons were located about 2 miles southwest of the residential areas, on the other side of the North Side Canal. Also south of the canal, according to the WRA blueprints, was a warehouse at a railroad spur that served the relocation center.

After the relocation center was closed, the area was divided into small farms. Forty-three of these small farms were allotted in 1947 to World War II veterans, whose names were drawn in a lottery. In 1949 another 46 small farms were allotted. Each veteran also received two barracks. The first group of veterans lived in Block 30 of the relocation center until they could move their barracks to their own farms. The veterans and their families had to share the block's common bathroom and "some of the wives were upset to have to use community shower facilities" (Smith 1987), probably echoing the sentiments of the first, involuntary inhabitants.

Figure 9.6. Oblique aerial view of the Minidoka Relocation Center (from *Minidoka Interlude* 1943).

Central (Fenced) Area
About 93 acres of the central area of the former relocation center are currently public land, managed by the Bureau of Reclamation. The parcel includes the original entrance and the former administration,

Figure 9.7. Swimming pool located south of warehouses (WRA photograph, Bancroft Library, University of California, Berkeley).

staff housing, warehouse, and motor pool areas. At the entrance there are standing basalt and concrete walls of a guard house and waiting room, a small area across the road from the guard house that once was an ornamental garden, and historical markers (Figures 9.9-9.13). The waiting room has a large stone fireplace integral with the building's stone walls.

In the administration and staff housing area there is a large concrete slab, footing blocks and small concrete slabs at other building locations, rock alignments, manholes, numerous rock-lined gravel pathways overgrown with grass, and a few remaining hard-pressed trees (Figures 9.14 and 9.15).

The warehouse and motor pool areas include a root cellar, which is abandoned and in danger of collapsing (Figures 9.16 and 9.17), as well as 14 concrete slabs from warehouse buildings. Two of the slabs have had relocated staff apartments placed on them and one still has half of its original building still intact (Figures 9.18 and 9.19). Other remains include a building slab and concrete island for gasoline pumps at the service station location (Figure 9.20), a large fat trap south of the warehouses, and scattered debris. Just southeast of the warehouse area there is a large depression from one of the relocation center swimming pools and several small trash dumps.

With a few exceptions, beyond the Bureau of Reclamation lands little remains of the relocation center. Most of the central area is now cultivated fields of alfalfa, potatoes, and other crops. Concrete rubble from cleared building foundations has been pushed to the perimeter of many fields. The relocation center water wells appear to be still in use and the foundations of the two water towers still remain. The sewage disposal plant location is now within a cultivated field, but several large foundations still remain.

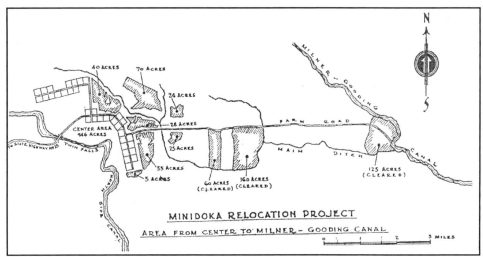

Figure 9.8. Farm fields at Minidoka (from *Minidoka Irrigator* 7/21/44).

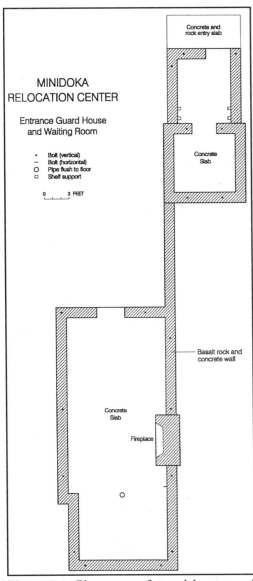

Figure 9.9. Plan map of guard house and waiting room at Minidoka.

Figure 9.10. Guard house today.

Figure 9.11. Chimney in waiting room.

Figure 9.12. Guard house and waiting room.

Figure 9.13. Remains of ornamental garden at the relocation center entrance.

Many of the farm houses in the area appear to be recycled barracks or other relocation center buildings, but most have undergone extensive remodeling, with new siding and additions. Firehouse No. 1, now used as a garage, is still in its original location.

Security Features

Of the security features at Minidoka only a portion of the barbed wire fence along the North Side Canal remains (Yamaguchi 1989:69). An unusual feature on the western edge of the residential area near the perimeter fence location may have been security-related. It consists of a 10-foot-square concrete base on a low rise that, according to local residents, supported a searchlight used by the military police (Figure 9.21).

Outlying Area

The relocation center landfill, on BLM land north of the former residential area, consists of a large partially filled pit. Remains there include abundant Japanese ceramics, a "Coke" bottle fragment from

Figure 9.14. Concrete slab in the administration area.

Figure 9.16. Root cellar under construction (from *Minidoka Interlude* 1943).

Figure 9.15. Manhole in the administration area.

Figure 9.17. Root cellar at Minidoka today.

Figure 9.18. Relocated staff apartment on a warehouse slab.

Figure 9.19. Motor and tire repair shop (half of original building).

Fresno, California, numerous smashed trash cans, and many other items (Figures 9.20 and 9.21). Also present in the landfill vicinity is material apparently deposited after the abandonment of the relocation center, including building debris from field clearing, recently dumped trash, and a stripped vehicle. Some digging in the landfill by artifact collectors was apparent.

The fields and canals made by the evacuees are still in use today. Basalt boulder and concrete "drops" constructed by the evacuees on the canal that supplied the relocation center farm fields are still in excellent condition (Figures 9.22 and 9.23). The hog and chicken farms are now cultivated fields. There is a concrete slab remaining at the location of the farm workers' mess hall.

To the south of the relocation center, at the crossing of State Highway 25 and the Idaho Short Line Railroad, is the railroad siding and warehouse area depicted on WRA blueprints. The warehouse is gone and the area is overgrown with

vegetation and covered with abundant 1950s and 1960s trash. However, the grade of the railroad spur and a leveled loading area are still apparent. Coal destined for the relocation center was apparently off-loaded onto trucks here, since copious amounts of coal residue cover the area

Figure 9.20. Concrete island from gasoline pumps.

Figure 9.21. Concrete slab reportedly for a searchlight.

Figure 9.22. Minidoka Relocation Center landfill.

Figure 9.24. Canal drop under construction (from *Minidoka Interlude* 1943).

Figure 9.23. Japanese ceramics at the Minidoka Relocation Center landfill.

Figure 9.25. One of seven canal drops at the Minidoka Relocation Center today.

Figure 9.26. Former Minidoka mess hall, now the VFW hall in Jerome, Idaho.

Interpretation

In Jerome, the County Historical Museum has a small but apparently very popular display on the relocation center. One of the volunteers there lamented that "people are more interested in [the relocation center] than the rest of the exhibits." Also of interest, the Veterans of Foreign Wars (VFW) building adjacent to the Museum was a mess hall moved from the relocation center (Figure 9.26).

East of Jerome on State Highway 25 at the turnoff to the relocation center site there is a large state historical marker (Figure 9.27). Within the relocation center itself, at the stone guard house and waiting room at the Hunt Bridge, there is a small parking area, paths, and interpretative signs about the internment (Figures 9.28-9.30). Also commemorated here are the Japanese Americans from the relocation center who died serving in the military during World War II. Nearly 1,000 from Minidoka served in the army; Minidoka had the largest casualty list of the ten relocation centers.

Figure 9.27. Historical markers at intersection of Hunt Road and State Highway 25.

Figure 9.28. Historical markers at the guard house and waiting room.

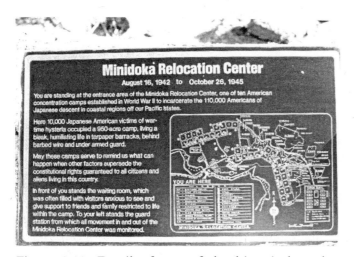

Figure 9.29. Detail of one of the historical markers located at the entrance.

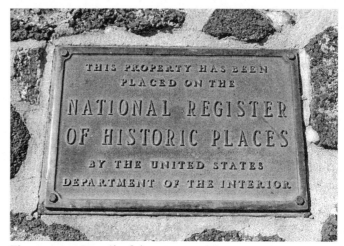

Figure 9.30. Detail of the National Register plaque at the entrance.

A public ceremony was held at the site in 1979 when it was added to National Register of Historic Places (Conley 1982:198). The parking lot, paths, and interpretative signs were completed a few years after the ceremony (Turner 1989).

Recently, the Jerome County Historical Society has acquired two original Minidoka barracks and moved them to their in-progress

"Idaho Farm and Ranch Museum" located north of Twin Falls at the junction of Interstate 84 and U.S. Highway 93. One of the barracks will be used to interpret the relocation center and the other will be renovated for other uses (Figure 9.31).

Figure 9.31. Partially restored barracks from Minidoka at the Idaho Farm and Ranch Museum.

Chapter 10

Poston Relocation Center

The Poston or Colorado River Relocation Center was located in La Paz County, Arizona, 12 miles south of the town of Parker. Poston was named after Charles Debrille Poston, the first Superintendent for Indian Affairs in Arizona. Poston was directly responsible for the establishment, in 1865, of the Colorado River Reservation, where the center is located (Figure 10.1). La Paz County is a fairly recent political entity; during World War II the Poston area was part of Yuma County.

The Colorado River is about 2½ miles west of the relocation center; this section of the Colorado River Valley from the relocation center vicinity north to Parker Dam is known as Parker Valley. At only 320 feet elevation, the area lies within the lower Sonoran desert. Summers are hot, and, because of the proximity of the river, humid; in the winter days are cool and nights cold.

The Colorado River Indian Reservation Tribal Council opposed the use of their land for a relocation center, on the grounds that they did not want to participate in inflicting the same type of injustice as they had suffered. However, the tribe was overruled by the Army and the Bureau of Indian Affairs (BIA). In a verbal agreement the WRA turned over administration of the center to the BIA. The BIA considered the relocation center an opportunity to develop farm land on the reservation with the benefit of military funds and a large labor pool. The WRA did not take full control of the Poston Relocation Center until December 1943.

The Poston Relocation Center consisted of three separate cantonments at three-mile intervals. Known officially as Poston I, II, and III, the evacuees nicknamed them Roasten, Toasten, and Dustin. Construction on Poston I began March 27, 1942, with the contractor Del Webb, later of Sun City fame. Del Webb had a large work force already mobilized for military contracts, and built Luke Air Force Base near Phoenix in March 1941. However, the relocation center was Del

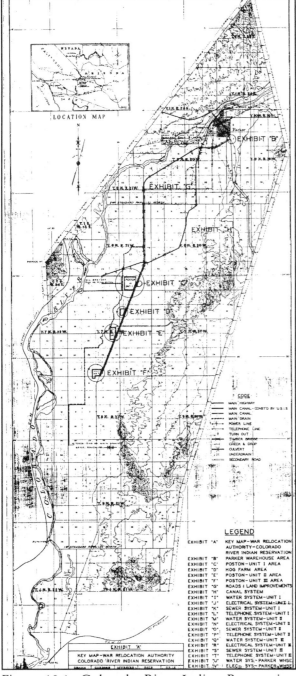

Figure 10.1. Colorado River Indian Reservation (National Archives).

Webb's biggest challenge up to that time. Webb had a construction job in progress at Blythe, and when he got the contract to build the camps he diverted his crew to Parker. With equipment brought up from Blythe, the initial ground clearing was done in one day (Figure 10.2).

Using 5,000 workers on a double work shift, Poston I was completed in less than three weeks (Figures 10.3-10.5). The pine specified for construction was in short supply, so heart redwood was substituted. When the redwood shrunk much more than expected, millions of feet of thin wood strips had to be ordered to fill the cracks (Finnerty 1991). Because of the heat in Arizona, the standard tarpaper barracks construction was modified so that the buildings had double roofs. A new contract was awarded to Webb to build Poston II and III within 120 days (Finnerty 1991). Guard towers were not constructed at Poston, as they were at the other relocation centers; here they were considered unnecessary because of the isolated location, in the desert at the end of a road.

The relocation center began operation May 8, 1942, with the arrival of 11 Japanese-American volunteers. Within days there were 250 more volunteers, who cleaned up and prepared the barracks for the arrival of over 7000 evacuees over the next three weeks (Leighton 1945). The maximum population for all three cantonments was 17,814, reached in September 1942. Poston was the largest relocation center in the country, and the third largest city in Arizona. Evacuees were from the Mayer, Salinas, Santa Anita, and Pinedale assembly centers.

By the fall of 1942 heating stoves had not yet been installed, so barracks and offices were unheated, and extremely cold without wallboard or insulation. Evacuees huddled around makeshift bonfires within each block for warmth. In addition, promised clothing and clothing allowances had not been delivered, and salaries had not been paid since September. Adding insult to injury, government resources

Figure 10.2. Poston site partially cleared (Clem Albers photograph, Bancroft Library, University of California, Berkeley).

Figure 10.4. Unloading lumber at the Poston site (Fred Clark photograph, Bancroft Library, University of California, Berkeley).

Figure 10.3. Rolls of roofing paper at the Poston site (Clem Albers photograph, Bancroft Library, University of California, Berkeley).

Figure 10.5. Construction underway at Poston I (Fred Clark photograph, Bancroft Library, University of California, Berkeley).

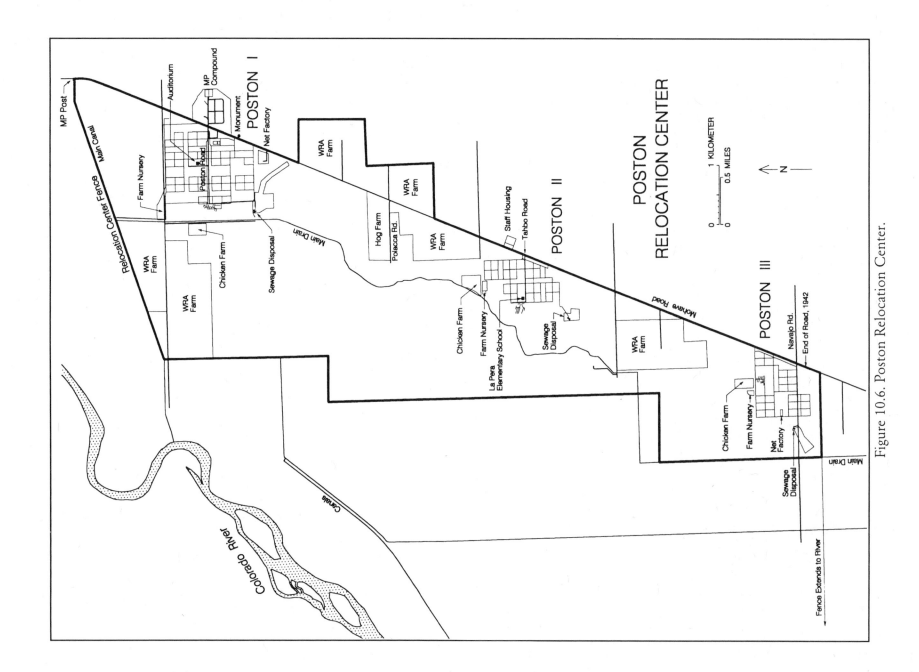

Figure 10.6. Poston Relocation Center.

were spent to fence in the evacuees rather than to remedy these problems or to construct chicken and hog farms that could alleviate food shortages. Further, the administration was seen as curtailing the power of the evacuees' representative council, misappropriating supplies meant for evacuees, and fomenting paranoia by soliciting information about troublemakers.

Given the discontent, all that was needed was a spark for the center to come close to open revolt. In November 1942 a suspected informer was beaten and administration officials arrested two Kibei men. Demanding that the arrested men be released, workers went on strike on November 19, and the police station was picketed. The unity of the strikers wavered, however, when many found the use of Japanese national symbols by some demonstrators (flags and music) too anti-American. The assistant director, in charge during the director's absence, resisted recommendations from some of his staff to call in the military to break the strike, and negotiated with the leaders of the protest. The strike ended peacefully on November 24, when a compromise settlement was reached by the director and members of the evacuees' Emergency Executive Council. One suspect was released for lack of evidence, the other was released on his own recognizance and the case was turned over to the U.S. Attorney, who later declined to prosecute the case.

Most of the administration staff who had advocated a hard-line stance against the strikers soon left (Leighton 1945). Tensions slowly abated, and the evacuees and staff gradually returned to their routines as conditions improved. The last evacuees left Poston November 28, 1945. A few Hopi Indian families moved in before the last Japanese Americans left to keep the farms going. After the relocation center was closed, the barracks and other buildings were sold, moved, and reused, and fields were converted to Reservation use.

The three separate camps, Poston I, II, and III, were laid out from north to south at about 3-mile intervals along what is now known as Mohave Road, which at the time ended at the south end of the project at Poston III (Figure 10.6). The three camps were surrounded by a single fence. Although the fence excluded Mohave Road, traffic was controlled by a military police post about 1 mile north of Poston I. All three camps were bounded on the east by Mohave Road and on the west by the "main drain" canal.

There was a gate house at the Poston I entrance off Mohave Road at 7th Street; Poston II and III did not have gate houses. In all three camps, numbered streets ran east-west, lettered streets ran north-south. The only named streets were in the staff housing area east of the main road at Poston I: Military Street and Indian Street ran east-west, Sollier and Skidmore Avenues ran north-south.

Poston I, the largest of the three units, was the farthest north. It included administration offices, three staff housing areas, warehouses, 36 residential blocks for evacuees, and the hospital and military police compound for the entire center (Figure 10.7).

The evacuee residential blocks at Poston I were laid out both north and south of a fire break between 6th and 7th Streets (the firebreak is the location of the present Poston Road). The blocks were generally grouped by fours, separated by fire breaks. Each block contained fourteen 20-by-100-foot barracks, a mess hall, a recreation building, a men's latrine, a women's latrine, a laundry, an ironing building, and a fuel oil shed. Recreation halls were used for various purposes, including a sewing school, churches, service organizations, beauty and barber shops, and internal police offices.

Internees added their own improvements to the residential area, such as ponds, gardens, and trees and other vegetation to cut down on the dust and heat (Figures 10.8 and 10.9). Ditches ran east-west and north-south through the fire breaks, and three swimming pools were

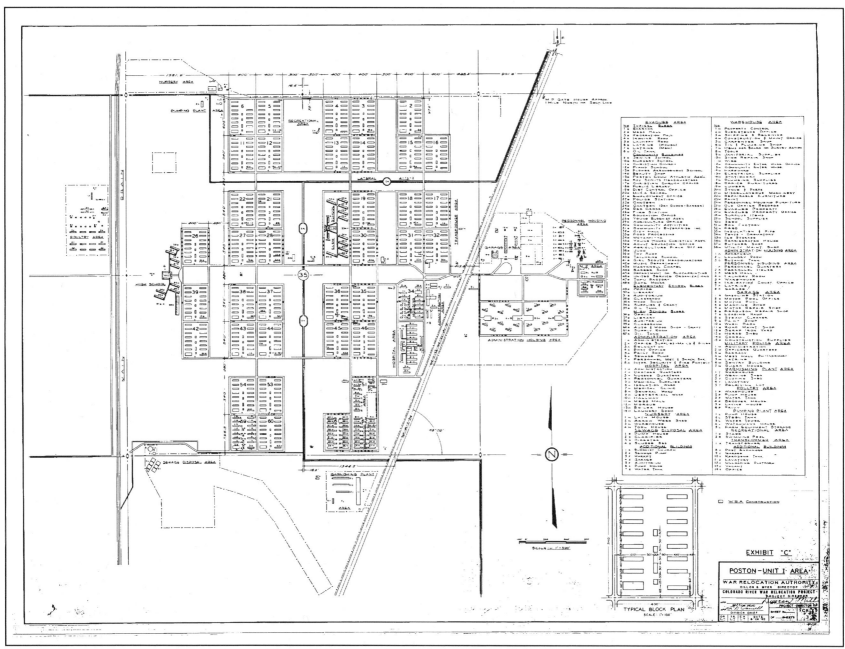

Figure 10.7. Poston I central area (National Archives).

Figure 10.8. Poston I (WRA photograph, National Archives).

Figure 10.9. Pond at Poston I (Francis Stewart photograph, Bancroft Library, University of California, Berkeley).

constructed along the ditches. A fire station was located east of Block 30. The mess hall in Block 32 was used for an agricultural office. Evacuees constructed a large stage in the firebreak west of Block 4 (Figure 10.10), and canteens were located east of Block 28 and west of Block 34.

Since no arrangements had been made for schools, evacuees built their own classrooms and school auditoriums. The elementary school at Poston I was located west of Blocks 19 and 30, and included an office, library, auditorium, 10 classroom buildings, and covered walkways. The high school, located west of the evacuee residential area, included an office, library, auditorium, auto and wood shop, and eight classroom buildings. Sufficient lumber was not available, so walls were constructed of adobe, a material foreign to most evacuees (Figures 10.11-10.15). Many evacuees considered the material inferior and too labor-intensive. The difficult work was exacerbated by the 115-degree temperatures, and the fact that the adobe ruined their clothes (Leighton 1945). The elementary school auditorium and classroom buildings, although now abandoned, still stand.

Next to the residential area in the northwest corner of the fenced area was the domestic water pumping plant, which included a pump house, steel tank, watchman's house, and a farm equipment storage building (evacuee-built).

Figure 10.10. Kabuki theater at Poston I (WRA photograph, University of Arizona Library, Special Collections).

The Poston I administration area, to the left of the entrance south of 7th Street, had seven buildings. A staff housing area was located just to the west in Block 34, and had eight apartment buildings, eight small houses, a mess hall, and two offices. South of the administration area was the warehouse area (Blocks 51, 61, 62), with 42 buildings, plus an evacuee-built ice storage and a butcher shop, maintenance shops, a box factory, and a crematory. Burial services were under contract to a Yuma firm that started construction of a crematory next to the hospital. However, the evacuees forced the crematory to be moved to the warehouse area, as the hospital location was thought to be bad for morale (Bailey 1971:97-98).

The hospital, with 17 buildings with connecting walkways, was south of the staff housing and west of the warehouse area. At the far south end of Poston I, south of the warehouses, was the camouflage net factory, with a warehouse, weaving shed, cutting shed, office, and latrine. Just to the west of the net factory was an evacuee-built tofu factory.

East of Mohave Road at Poston I were other facilities, outside the main security fence. An administration office and market/snack bar were located at the corner of Mohave Road and 7th Street (now Poston Road). Farther east was the military police compound with 12 buildings, a pump house, and a water tank. Two staff housing areas and a shop/garage area were built between the snack bar and the military police compound using evacuee labor. In the staff housing areas there were 11 houses, 20 apartments, six warehouses, an office, a latrine, four laundries, and eight other small buildings. In the garage and motor pool area there were 11 buildings including an office, gasoline station, machine shop (Figure 10.16), repair shops, paint shop, horse shed, and corral.

Ancillary facilities at Poston I were located within the fence, near the evacuee residential area. To the west of the barracks was a chicken farm, with a warehouse, pump house, water tank, four brooder houses, 12 laying houses, 14 small coops, and a privy built by evacuees. Northwest of the barracks was a farm nursery, with a lath house, arrow weed shed, warehouse, and tool shed, all of evacuee construction. The sewage treatment plant, which included a pump house, clarifier, digester, and sludge beds, was located just southwest of the barracks area.

Three and a half miles south of Poston I, Poston II included an administration area, staff housing, a garage area, warehouses, and a net factory, as well as evacuee residential blocks (Figures 10.17 and 10.18). The camp was bisected by a north-south canal, which fed a large swimming pool in the center of the camp. Block numbers were

Figure 10.11. Evacuee making adobe bricks (Francis Stewart photograph, Bancroft Library, University of California, Berkeley).

Figure 10.12. Drying adobe bricks (Francis Stewart photograph, Bancroft Library, University of California, Berkeley).

Figure 10.13. Adobe brick factory (Francis Stewart photograph, Bancroft Library, University of California, Berkeley).

Figure 10.14. Mixing mud for adobe bricks (Francis Stewart photograph, Bancroft Library, University of California, Berkeley).

Figure 10.15. Pouring foundation for school (Francis Stewart photograph, Bancroft Library, University of California, Berkeley).

Figure 10.16. Machine shop at Poston I (Francis Stewart photograph, Bancroft Library, University of California, Berkeley).

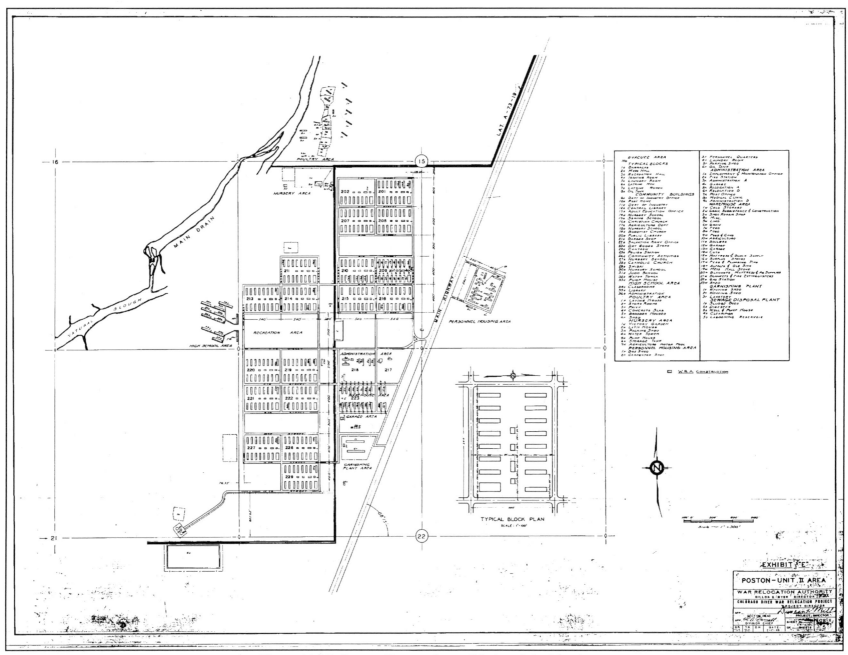

Figure 10.17. Poston II central area (National Archives).

Figure 10.18. Aerial view of Poston II under construction (Fred Clark photograph, Bancroft Library, University of California, Berkeley).

consecutive, beginning with 201 to distinguish the numbers from those of Poston I.

Staff housing at Poston II was located on the east side of Mohave Road, outside the fenced area. It included a carpentry shop, two houses, eight apartments, and two evacuee-built sheds. The entrance to Poston II was at 7th street. The administration area, located within the fence south of the entrance (Blocks 217 and 218) had ten buildings, including a cold storage building, a medical clinic, a fire station, five office buildings, a storage building, and a post office.

The warehouse area, south of the administration area in Block 223, included 20 buildings. The garage area, south of the warehouse area,

included a gasoline station and an evacuee-built shed. Farther south still was the net factory, with two weaving sheds and a latrine.

On either side of 7th street were the 18 evacuee residential blocks, in groups of three or four separated by fire breaks. One of the blocks served as the elementary school. The high school, west of the residential area, was constructed by the evacuees of adobe. It included an office, library, and 10 classroom buildings. The fire break to the east of the high school served as the recreation area and athletic fields.

A chicken farm, with 15 laying houses, two brooder houses, four storage buildings, two sheds, and a privy (all evacuee-built), was located north of the evacuee residences. A farm nursery was located northwest of Block 202; the nursery included a lath house, a victory garden, and a packing shed, all built by evacuees. Between the nursery and Block 202 were a pump house, water tower, and storage tank.

The sewage treatment plant for Poston II was located southwest of the residences. It included a pump house, clarifier, digester, sludge beds, and sewage lagoon.

Poston III, the farthest south of the three units, included an administration area, a garage area, and a net factory, as well as 18 evacuee residential blocks (Figure 10.19). Block numbers began with 301. The administration area, garage, and warehouses were located north of the entrance, in a triangular area formed by Mohave Road, 3rd Street, and "I" Street. The administration area, in Blocks 313 and 314, included a mess hall, staff quarters, a garage, three offices, a clinic, a fire station, and a firemen's dormitory. The garage area, in Block 301, included five warehouses, a gasoline station, and a garage. The warehouse area, in Block 302, included 15 warehouses and a privy.

The 18 residential blocks at Poston III were arranged in three groups of six blocks; one of the blocks (Block 324) was used as the elementary

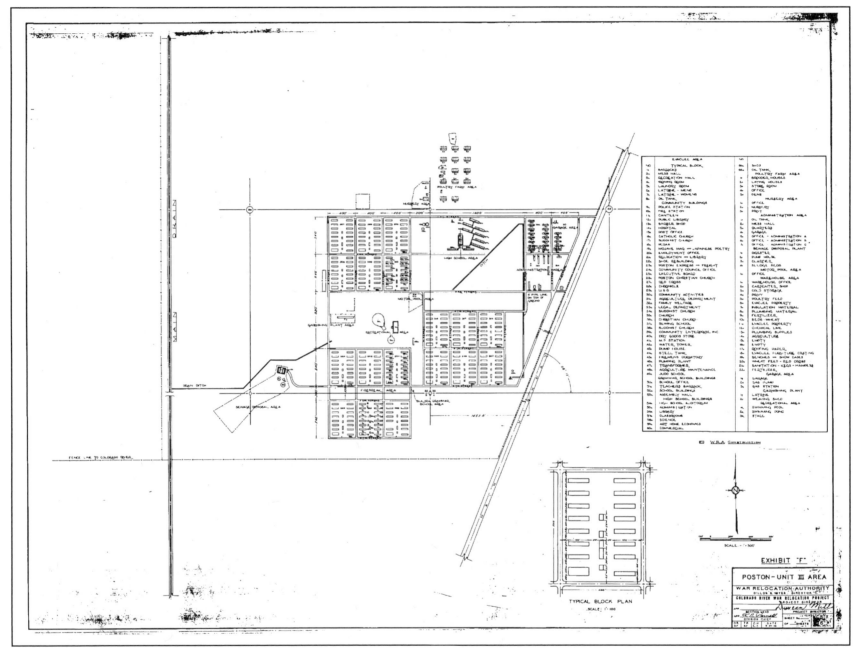

Figure 10.19. Poston III central area (National Archives).

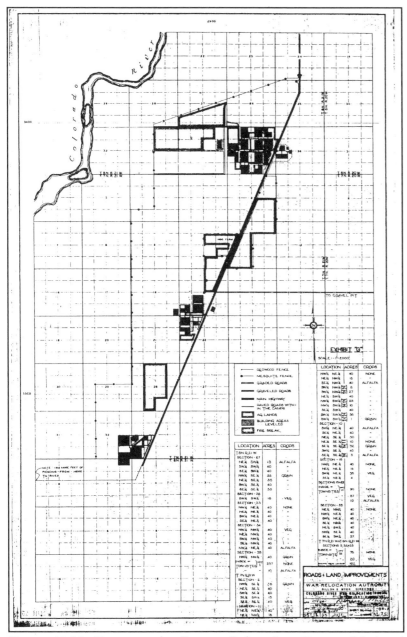

Figure 10.20. Farms at the Poston Relocation Center (National Archives).

Figure 10.21. Alfalfa field north of Poston (Clem Albers photograph, Bancroft Library, University of California, Berkeley).

school, and another (Block 310) for community services. The high school, constructed by the evacuees, was located in a large open space between the administrative area and the northernmost residential block. It included an office, library, auditorium, and seven classroom buildings, all of adobe. The west central open area, between the two westernmost residential blocks, included a net factory with a weaving shed and a latrine, a recreation area with two swimming pools and a stage, a motor pool, and a dry goods store.

The Poston III chicken farm was to the north of the high school, and included 11 laying houses, two brooder houses, a store room, and an office. Southwest of the chicken farm and northwest of the high school was the farm nursery, with an office, a nursery, and a privy, all evacuee-built. To the west of the southernmost residential area was the sewage treatment plant, which included a pump house, clarifier, digester, and sludge beds.

Figure 10.22. Main irrigation ditch at Poston (Clem Albers photograph, Bancroft Library, University of California, Berkeley).

Unlike most other relocation centers, at Poston the agricultural fields and developments were within the fenced security area (Figures 10.20-10.22). In 1943, 368 acres were cultivated; in 1944, over 1,400 acres of vegetables and 800 acres of field crops were under cultivation. In addition to the chicken farms at each of the three units mentioned above, there was a hog farm located between Poston I and II, with hogs subsisting mainly on center garbage. The hog farm contained 12 pens with sheds and feeding floors, six farrowing pens, and pasture. Facilities also included two small watchman's houses (8 foot by 10 foot, and 10 foot by 14 foot in size), a 20 foot by 100 ft warehouse, a 30 foot by 36 foot processing house, a motor house, cold storage, an 18½ by 33 foot slaughter house, a latrine, a water tank, a pump house, a garbage can washing station, and a fuel tank (Figure 10.23).

An additional warehouse for the relocation center area was built along the railroad outside of Parker. It included a railroad spur with unloading platforms, five warehouses, one refrigerated warehouse, fuel oil storage tanks, a substation, a water tank, a water tower, and a pump house (Figure 10.24).

Poston I

Most of the countryside around the three units that formed the Poston Relocation Center is covered by irrigated farm fields (Figures 10.25 and 10.26). The most prominent remains at the site today are those of the Poston I elementary school, where the adobe auditorium and nearby school buildings are still standing (Figures 10.27-10.31. At the southwest corner of the auditorium there is a dedication plaque that reads "POSTON ELEMENTARY SCHOOL UNIT I — JUNE 1943 AS + TF — BUILT BY THE JAPANESE RESIDENTS OF POSTON." Unfortunately the school buildings are now abandoned and currently in poor condition, and without stabilization will soon be damaged beyond repair.

A small housing area and trailer park is now across the road from the auditorium and school buildings to the west, in what used to be a firebreak containing a swimming pool. Beyond the elementary school all that remains of the evacuee area at Poston I are a few concrete slabs at the site of the high school, now a farm residence.

East of Mohave Road, the former garage area at Poston I is now used as a maintenance yard. A large building, the same location and shape as the machine shop on WRA blueprints, probably dates to the relocation center era (Figure 10.32). Portions of at least four other buildings in the garage area survive as well (Figure 10.33). To the south

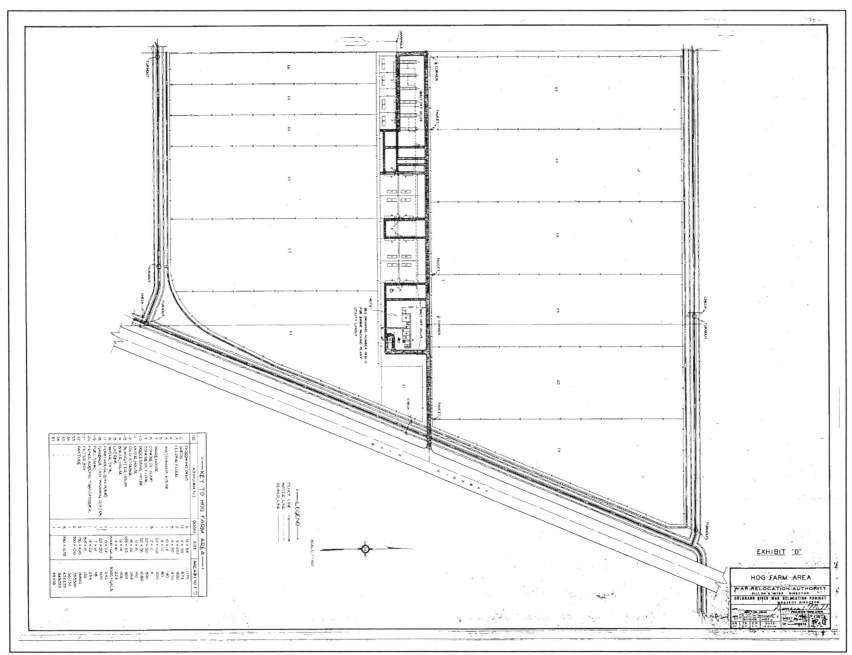

Figure 10.23. Poston Relocation Center hog farm (National Archives).

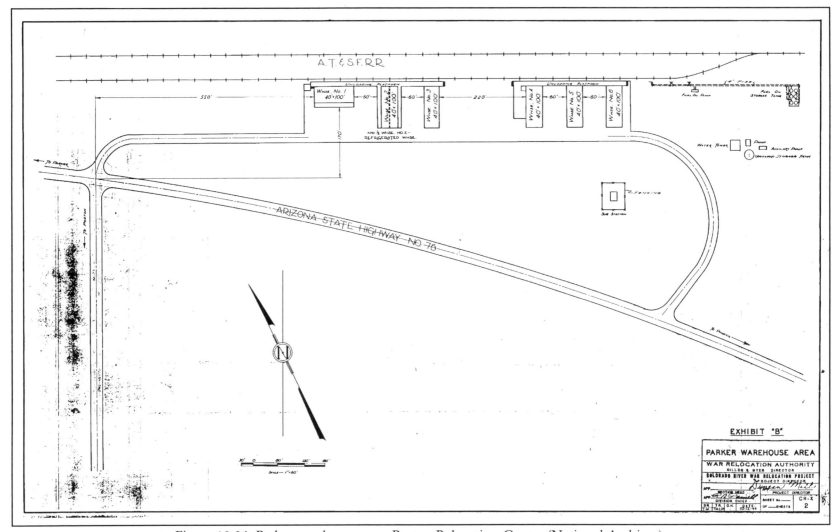

Figure 10.24. Parker warehouse area, Poston Relocation Center (National Archives).

of the garage area, the staff housing area is marked only by roads lined with large palm trees (Figure 10.34). Although the 1970 USGS map depicts the buildings, all are now gone, and there is a recent housing development on the land just to the south.

The sewage treatment plant for Poston I lies abandoned within farm fields about ¾ mile west of Mohave Road. It is in good condition and still has a lot of the associated pumps and other equipment not found at the other two Poston sewage treatment plants (Figures 10.35 and 10.36).

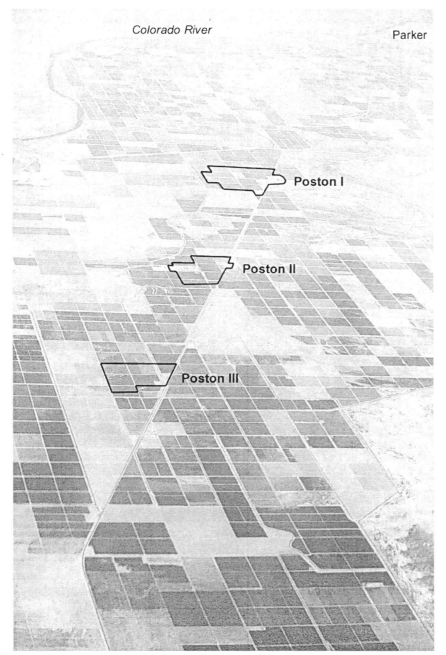

Figure 10.26. Barracks area at Poston I today.

Figure 10.25. Oblique aerial view of the Poston area today.

Figure 10.27. Poston I elementary school auditorium today.

Figure 10.28. Plaque at the Poston I elementary school auditorium.

Figure 10.30. Classroom building at the Poston I elementary school.

Figure 10.29. Interior of the Poston I elementary school auditorium.

Figure 10.31. Collapsed porch at the Poston I elementary school.

Figure 10.32. Poston I machine shop today.

Figure 10.34. Poston I staff housing area today.

Figure 10.33. Poston I garage area today.

Figure 10.35. Clarifier at the Poston I sewage treatment plant.

Figure 10.36. Top of digester at the Poston I sewage treatment plant.

Figure 10.37. Barracks area at Poston II today.

Poston II

Very little remains of the camp at Poston II. Most of the area is farm fields (Figure 10.37), and the La Pera Elementary School occupies what was once the recreation area. To the west of the elementary school, in what was the high school area, there is an auditorium, closed reportedly due to asbestos hazard (Figure 10.38). The auditorium itself is not likely a relocation center building since an auditorium is not shown on the July 1945 WRA blueprint of Poston II. However, there are a few inscriptions in a sidewalk at the auditorium, which indicate that some of the sidewalks there are remnants of the relocation center high school. The inscriptions include the numbers "221" and "229" (residential block numbers) and the initials "CK." Another inscription was found just north of Tahbo Road on the east side of the canal that ran through Poston II (Figure 10.39). On an overturned concrete block in the canal bank is the inscription "Y UMEDA 2-12-1943" (Figure 10.40).

About ¼ mile west of Mohave road there are two concrete slabs that may be foundations of relocation center buildings. One, now with a mobile home on it, is located along the canal that bisected Poston II in what would have been the warehouse area. Measuring roughly 20 ft by 100 ft in size, the slab is aligned north-south like the warehouses were. In the net factory area there is a 30 foot by 275 foot slab with 6½-foot-square footing blocks about 10 feet from each corner (Figure 10.41). This slab is aligned east-west like the net buildings were.

The most visible remains of Poston II are of the sewage treatment plant, on an unnamed dirt road about ½ mile west of Mohave Road (Figure 10.42 and 10.43). On the east side of the highway, the former staff housing area at Poston II now has churches, residences, and a relocation center hospital ward building moved from Poston I (Figure 10.44), according to local residents. The building, lacking its double roof but otherwise in fair condition and currently being remodeled, is located behind the Poston Community Baptist Church. According to Pastor Herb Schneider, the church wants to replace or rehabilitate the

Figure 10.38. School auditorium at the site of the Poston II elementary school.

Figure 10.40. Inscription in concrete block in ditch bank at Poston II.

Figure 10.39. Ditch through the center of Poston II.

Figure 10.41. Concrete slab foundation at the site of the Poston II camouflage net factory.

Figure 10.42. Poston II sewage treatment plant today.

Figure 10.43. Clarifier and overturned manholes at the Poston II sewage treatment plant.

structure. Another relocation center building at the church, a moved barracks, was recently torn down.

Poston III

The only intact remains of Poston III are those of the sewage treatment plant, located on the north side of Navajo Road about ¾ mile west of Mohave Road (Figure 10.45). All else are now farm fields under irrigation (Figure 10.46). Navajo Road follows the section line, which places it within the firebreak between 6th and 7th streets. Concrete rubble, perhaps from relocation center foundations, was noted along canals and berms in the Poston III area.

Security Features

No portion of the security fence, the sentry post north of Poston I, or

the gate house at Poston I remains. It appears that probably only one concrete foundation slab remain at the military police compound (Figure 10.47).

Outlying Area

The farm fields and irrigation ditches constructed by the evacuees are still in use and have been greatly expanded. The remains of the relocation center hog farm are located northwest of the intersection of Mohave and Polacca Roads (Figure 10.48). The portion of the hog farm closest to Mohave Road still has some intact slabs (Figure 10.49); most of those on the western end of the area have been up-rooted and piled. An inscription in the intact concrete slab foundation of the pump house reads "Div. of Soil 3/21/43" (Figure 10.50).

Along the railroad just east of the town of Parker are the remains of

Figure 10.44. Relocation center hospital building (from Poston I) at the site of the Poston II staff housing area.

Figure 10.46. Barracks area at Poston III today.

Figure 10.45 Poston III sewage treatment plant today.

Figure 10.47. Concrete slab foundation at the site of the Poston Relocation Center military police compound.

Figure 10.48. Site of the Poston Relocation Center hog farm today.

Figure 10.50. Inscription at the Poston Relocation Center hog farm.

Figure 10.49. Concrete slab foundation at the site of the Poston Relocation Center hog farm.

Figure 10.51. Site of the Poston Relocation Center Parker warehouse area today.

Figure 10.52. Hydrant at the site of the Parker warehouses.

Figure 10.54. Barracks moved to the town of Parker.

Figure 10.53. Concrete slab foundation for the fuel oil storage tanks at the Parker warehouse area.

Figure 10.55. Can lids used to patch knot holes in barracks floor.

Figure 10.56. Relocated barracks formerly used as Head Start School.

Figure 10.58. Monument and kiosk at Poston I.

Figure 10.57. Hospital building north of Poston I.

the relocation center warehouse complex. The western edge of the warehouse area is now occupied by a Chevrolet dealer, and there is little left of the warehouses or unloading platforms (Figure 10.51). However, four fire hydrants (Figure 10.52), which would have been located to the rear of the warehouses, are extant, as are several concrete slab foundations that likely date to the relocation center. One, measuring 25 feet by 38½ feet, held the fuel oil storage tanks, and has six 9½-foot-diameter stains from the storage tanks (Figure 10.53). A second slab foundation, 6 feet by 12 feet in size, was for the electrical substation, and a third slab, approximately 25½ feet in diameter, supported the water tank. Other slabs for pumps and the water tower are partially visible, partially covered by sediments.

Over 50 relocated buildings from the relocation center have been identified in the surrounding area and in the town of Parker (Raoul Roko, personal communication, 2000). Some still have their distinctive double roofs and other evidence of their former use: for example, a barracks now within Parker has a double roof and tin can lid patches over knot holes (Figures 10.54 and 10.55). The Colorado River Indian Tribe's old Head Start school, although lacking the double roof, was once a relocation center building (Figure 10.56). In addition to the relocation center hospital building at Poston II, there is another hospital building a little over 2 miles north of Poston I (Figure 10.57).

Figure 10.60. Kiosk at Poston I.

Interpretation

Along Mohave Road at Poston I there is a large monument and kiosk, complemented by sidewalks, palm trees, sitting areas, and a water fountain (Figures 10.58-10.60). The location next to a fire station, was chosen in part to help deter vandalism. The monument, dedicated in 1992, consists of a 30-foot- high concrete column with a 7-foot-wide hexagonal base shaped like a Japanese stone lantern. The kiosk,

Figure 10.59. Monument at Poston I.

dedicated in 1995, is four-sided with an overhanging pyramidal roof. Both the monument and kiosk have interpretive signs which discuss the history of the relocation, Japanese-American military service, and the Colorado River Indian Tribe reservation (Figures 10.61 and 10.62). The tribe plans to restore the Poston I auditorium and adjacent class-rooms and bring back and restore as many as 16 barracks as part of a heritage park. The Kabuki theater, M.P. post, and other features would also be replicated (Raoul Roko, personal communication, 2000).

Figure 10.61. Plaques at the Poston monument.

Figure 10.62. One of four interpretative signs at the Poston I kiosk.

Chapter 11

Rohwer Relocation Center

The Rohwer Relocation Center was located in Desha County, Arkansas, 11 miles north of McGehee and 110 miles southeast of Little Rock. It was one of two relocation centers in Arkansas – 27 miles south was the Jerome Relocation Center. The relocation center was named after the community of Rohwer, which was located one-half mile south.

Five miles west of the Mississippi River and at an elevation of 140 feet, the relocation center area is intertwined with canals, bayous, creeks, and swampy areas. The forests that once covered the area are now gone, replaced with rice, soybean, and cotton fields and dispersed housing. About 1 mile south of the relocation center, on the east side of State Highway 1, there are Indian mounds, one with a residence on it (Figure 11.1).

Several sources indicate the relocation center reserve encompassed 10,161 acres, but a boundary map for the entire reserve could not be

Figure 11.1. Residence south of Rohwer on top of a suspected Indian mound (another Indian mound is to the left of the house).

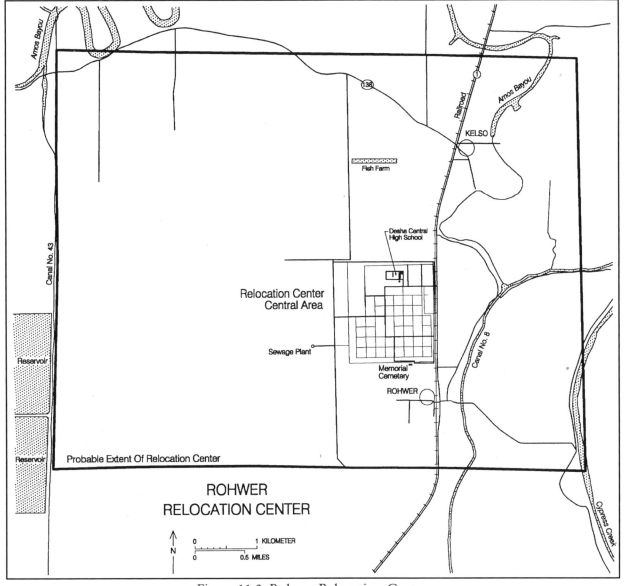

Figure 11.2. Rohwer Relocation Center.

located for this report. However, the central area layout plan includes a vicinity map which may provide clues to the boundary. Twenty full sections and four partial sections around the central area are numbered on the map, whereas the other sections depicted on the map are not numbered. While the total area of these sections exceeds the reported 10,161 acre figure, the relocation center reserve was likely limited to lands within the numbered sections (Figure 11.2).

According to Bearden (1989), half of the relocation center reserve remained under swampy bayou water during the spring. The reserve was mostly on public land meant for subsistence homesteads under the Farm Security Administration; the balance was purchased from local farmers.

The roughly 500-acre central area of the relocation center was along the west side of State Highway 1 and the adjacent Missouri Pacific Railroad. Construction by the Linebarger-Senne Construction Company of Little Rock, Arkansas, began July 1, 1942, and the center was ready for use on September 18, 1942 (Figure

Figure 11.3. Construction underway at the Rohwer Relocation Center (WRA photograph, National Archives).

11.3). The maximum population, reached in November 1942, was 8,475. Evacuees were from California, who endured a three-day train ride from the assembly centers to reach Arkansas. The center closed November 30, 1944.

Rosalie Gould, the former Mayor of McGehee, grew up in the area, and recounts that the Arkansas relocation centers were located in very poverty-stricken areas, probably, she believes, at the insistence of some influential Arkansas senator. In spite of local expectations, the centers did not bring prosperity. Hence, as difficult as conditions were within the relocation center, some local residents envied the evacuees' access to regular meals and health care.

The relocation center at Rohwer was divided into 51 blocks surrounded by a barbed wire fence, a patrol road, and eight watch towers (Figures 11.4 and 11.5). All of the blocks were on a north-south grid. The southern two-thirds of the central area were residential blocks;

Figure 11.4. Watch tower at Rohwer (from Rohwer Reunion Committee 1990).

warehouses were located in the northeast corner just north of the main entrance, which was along the east side. The administration and hospital areas lay to the west of the warehouses, and the military police compound was along the east boundary just south of the main entrance.

East-west roads were designated by letters; north-south roads by numbers. "I" Street (also known as "Eye") was the main entrance road, extending west from the entrance and perpendicular to State Highway 1 and the Missouri Pacific Railroad. There was also an entrance along the west side of the central area near the southwest corner, and the warehouse area had two openings through the fence for access to a railroad siding (Figures 11.6 and 11.7).

There were over 620 buildings at the center. The military police compound (designated Block 30), included 12 buildings. Across the road from the military police compound was the receiving building at the main entrance. The administration area (Block 44) also had 12 buildings when first built, but up to 15 staff apartment buildings were later constructed using evacuee labor (Figure 11.8). The warehouse area (Block 50) had 21 buildings, and the hospital area (Block 47) had 17 buildings. An area north of the warehouses was used for coal storage (Block 51). Blocks 44 and 45, along Eye Street, included the post office, a sawmill, a plumbing shop, and three warehouses. There were also three other warehouses along Eye Street in Blocks 30 and 47. A cannery was located north of the hospital.

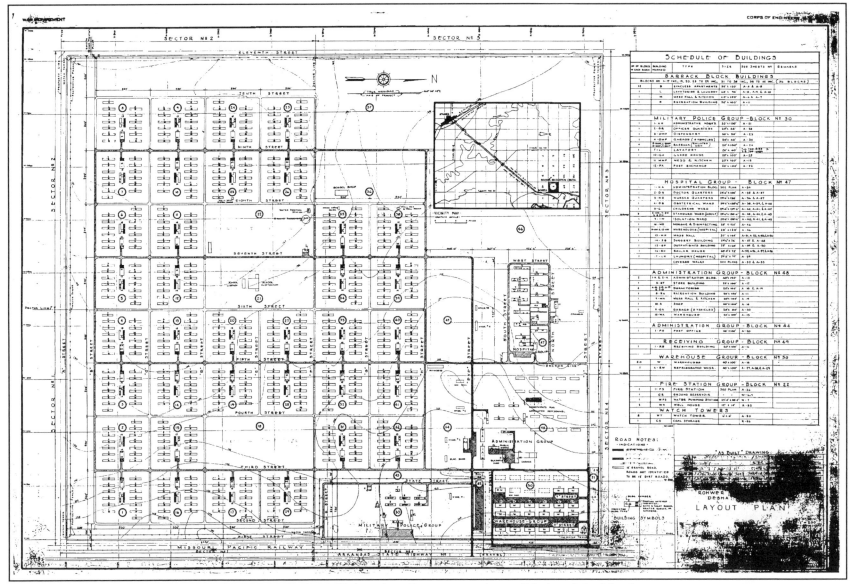

Figure 11.5. Rohwer Relocation Center central area (National Archives).

Figure 11.6. Evacuees unloading boxcar at Rohwer (Tom Parker photograph, Bancroft Library, University of California, Berkeley).

Figure 11.7. Evacuees unloading coal at Rohwer (Tom Parker photograph, Bancroft Library, University of California, Berkeley).

Figure 11.8. Evacuees building staff apartment at Rohwer (Tom Parker photograph, Bancroft Library, University of California, Berkeley).

Figure 11.9. Wooden sidewalk at Rohwer (Charles E. Mace photograph, Bancroft Library, University of California, Berkeley).

Figure 11.10. Drainage ditch in residential block at Rohwer (Gretchen Van Tassel photograph, Bancroft Library, University of California, Berkeley).

Figure 11.11. Evacuee garden at Rohwer (Charles E. Mace photograph, Bancroft Library, University of California, Berkeley).

Figure 11.12. Barracks residence at Rohwer (Gretchen Van Tassel photograph, Bancroft Library, University of California, Berkeley).

Figure 11.13. Farm mules at Rohwer (Tom Parker photograph, Bancroft Library, University of California, Berkeley).

Figure 11.14. Harvesting cucumbers at Rohwer (Charles E. Mace photograph, Bancroft Library, University of California, Berkeley).

The 36 residential blocks were located south of the administration area. They lay within a rectangle eight blocks east-west by six blocks north-south. To combat muddy conditions each block was surrounded by a drainage ditch, and gravel and wooden sidewalks were constructed between the barracks (Figures 11.9 and 11.10). The southwest portion of the residential area was an especially low area, which after rains would become flooded even above the level of the wooden sidewalks. Sometimes buildings had to be sandbagged to prevent them from being flooded (Rohwer Reunion Committee 1990).

Each residential block had twelve 20-foot-by-120-foot barracks, a recreation building, a mess hall, and a combined bathroom and laundry building. Many evacuees planted vegetable and flower gardens to beautify their new homes (Figures 11.11 and 11.12). Recreation buildings were used for stores, churches, movies, girl and boy scout meetings, a toy library, YWCA, judo, boxing, weaving, sewing, and other activities (*Rohwer Outpost* October 1989). All the standard buildings in residential Blocks 31 and 35 were used for elementary and high schools (*Rohwer Outpost* 11/7/42), and Block 35 had an extra building built for school use. Well houses were located in Blocks 23 and 38 of the residential area.

Some of the residential blocks had special functions and therefore had different configurations of buildings, or no buildings at all. Block 21 had only a school auditorium and school library, Block 36 had a school shop, and Block 22 had a fire house, a pumping station, a reservoir, and an unidentified building. Blocks 18, 37, and 45 were open areas.

Outside the fenced central area the evacuees dug ditches and cleared land for farming. The Rohwer and Jerome relocation centers grew 85 percent of their own vegetables (Bearden 1989). In 1943, 610 acres were under cultivation at Rohwer, in 1944, 577 acres (Figures 11.13 and 11.14). The evacuees also raised hogs and chickens for their own consumption. The hog and chicken farm locations are not known, but they likely utilized existing farm buildings within the relocation center reserve.

As at the Jerome Relocation Center, evacuees working outside the fenced area were subject to harassment caused by mistaken identity. Early in the relocation center occupation, evacuee volunteers clearing brush were reportedly taken off to a local jail at gunpoint by local residents who thought they were Japanese paratroopers (Hayashi 1997).

When the relocation center was closed, 120 acres were deeded to the local school district and the rest was sold back to the original farmers or to veterans. The Desha Central High School originally used two of the hospital buildings (Stuart 1979), the high school auditorium, and perhaps other relocation center buildings. However, none of these remain today. Equipment and buildings were also sold to bidders across the country; some barracks are still in use on the Southern Illinois University campus (Hoshiko 1988).

Central (Fenced) Area

Today the relocation center site is partly agricultural fields and partly developed with scattered houses and the Desha Central High School. A few relocation center road segments remain, including portions of Eye, D, F, 6th, and 7th streets. The concrete water reservoir and the hospital boiler room smokestack are the only standing structures.

Hospital, Administration, and Warehouse Areas

The northern third of the central area now includes a residential area and Desha Central High School. Side-by-side near the high school are the foundations from the hospital laundry room and boiler house (Figure 11.15). Adjacent to the boiler house foundation, in apparently stable condition, is a 100-foot-tall red brick smokestack (Figure 11.16).

Figure 11.15. Hospital boiler house foundation at Rohwer.

Another intact slab, that of the hospital mess hall, is just behind one of the many buildings of the high school complex (Figure 11.17).

The present high school auditorium, made of yellow concrete block, looks very similar in form to relocation center buildings (Figure 11.18). However, the current building does not date to the relocation center as has been suggested (Hoshiko 1992). The relocation center auditorium was used by the high school following closure of the center, but it was constructed of wood and burned down in the 1950s (Figure 11.19). According to WRA blueprints, the original auditorium was over 2,000 feet south of the present auditorium.

In the administration area there are now numerous homes, a church, and other buildings (Figure 11.20). Only a few features remain. A short concrete drive north of what was once Eye Street appears to be from the relocation center. Just south of the former Eye Street is the slab and concrete vault of the post office (Figure 11.21). Amongst the houses there are also scattered small concrete slabs and an isolated

Figure 11.16. Hospital boiler house smokestack.

section of sidewalk that may be associated with the relocation center.

In the northeastern portion of the relocation center there are debris and foundation remnants from warehouses. The railroad siding that serviced the relocation center is gone, and the railroad itself has been

Figure 11.17. Concrete slab of the hospital mess hall at Rohwer.

recently abandoned (Figure 11.22). It is posted at all road crossings as owned by Arkansas State Parks.

Residential Area

From "D" Street south, the former residential area is under active rice cultivation; from "D" Street north there is currently scrub growth in fallow fields. The concrete slab latrine and mess hall foundations have been broken up and consolidated within each block to increase the area available for crops (Figure 11.23). The consolidated rubble areas are present at all blocks except 9, 10, 24, and 25, and the few remaining relocation center roads help demarcate the location of blocks within the fields. Each rubble area, roughly 100 feet by 300 feet in size, appears to include at least a portion of an intact slab, as well as fragments of cast iron pipe and bricks. All are overgrown by nearly impenetrable brush, trees, and thorny vines. On a few of the slabs are toppled concrete boxes, whose original use is not evident (Figure 11.24).

Figure 11.18. Desha Central High School auditorium.

Figure 11.19. High school auditorium at the Rohwer Relocation Center (from Nakamura 1994).

Figure 11.20. Residences within the former administration area at Rohwer.

Figure 11.21. Remains of the relocation center post office at Rohwer.

Figure 11.22. Railroad and warehouse area at Rohwer today.

Figure 11.23. Former residential area at Rohwer, now a rice field. Dark vegetation patch is rubble where concrete foundations from the mess hall and bathroom/laundry buildings have been consolidated.

Figure 11.24. Concrete debris on concrete slab in rice field at Rohwer.

Figure 11.25. Concrete water reservoir at Rohwer today.

At Block 21, the rubble mound includes slab foundation debris possibly from the relocation center school auditorium and library. Block 22 is marked by the concrete water reservoir, which is still standing. Measuring 75 feet in diameter by 15 feet tall, it is almost completely hidden by vegetation (Figure 11.25). Just east of the reservoir, at the former location of the relocation center fire station, there is a dense growth of vegetation covering a concrete slab and rubble.

Near the water reservoir, within what was Block 38, there is a well house in the same location as one depicted on WRA blueprints (Figure 11.26). Made of concrete block rather than wood, the building likely rests on the original relocation-center-era concrete slab. According to a local resident, the relocation center water system is still used to supply water for area homes.

Other portions of the relocation center's subsurface utilities remain buried but are currently unused, such as a sewer line exposed by an irrigation ditch (Figure 11.27). The only artifacts seen in the fields were some brick and concrete fragments. No domestic trash dump, or even scattered domestic trash, was observed.

Security Features

No evidence of the original perimeter fence or watch towers remain. In the former military police compound, there is a residence and a fallow field.

Outlying Area

No records or maps of any outlying features other than the relocation center cemetery and sewage treatment plant have been found. A cursory inspection of the surrounding area suggests that no features likely remain.

Figure 11.26. Modern well house at the site of a relocation center well (Block 38).

Figure 11.27. Exposed and displaced sewer pipe at Rohwer.

Figure 11.28. Digester at the sewage treatment plant today.

Sewage Treatment Plant

Now surrounded by rice fields, the sewage treatment plant was located west of the southwest corner of the central area. It is similar in design to the plant at the Jerome Relocation Center, but smaller and with no evidence of filter rock beds (Figures 11.28 and 11.29). Access to the sewage treatment plant is via a dirt road that becomes nearly impassably muddy during wet weather.

Cemetery

The relocation center cemetery, enclosed by concrete fence posts, includes 24 uniform cast concrete headstones, two large concrete monuments, a toppled concrete bench, a flagpole, sidewalks, and two concrete entrance markers facing towards the relocation center, all built by the evacuees (Figures 11.30-11.33). Interestingly, the cemetery is not shown on WRA blueprints. The present approach road was probably part of the former "A" Street, which was part of the patrol

Figure 11.29. Manhole at the Rohwer sewage treatment plant.

road that encircled the outside of the barbed wire perimeter fence (Figure 11.34).

One monument, in the shape of a military tank, is to the Japanese Americans in the 100th Battalion and the 442nd Regimental Combat Team who were killed in Italy and France (Figure 11.35). The second

Figure 11.30. Rohwer Relocation Center cemetery in July 1943 (Charles E. Mace photograph, Bancroft Library, University of California, Berkeley).

Figure 11.31. Rohwer Relocation Center cemetery in June 1944 (Charles E. Mace photograph, Bancroft Library, University of California, Berkeley).

Figure 11.32. Rohwer Relocation Center cemetery today.

Figure 11.33. Rohwer Relocation Center cemetery today.

Figure 11.34. Road to the Rohwer Memorial cemetery.

monument is to those who died in the relocation center (Figure 11.36). It has both Japanese and English inscriptions. The Japanese translates to: "May the people of Arkansas keep in beauty and reverence forever this ground where our bodies sleep." The English inscription reads: "Erected by the inhabitants of Rohwer Relocation Center October 1944." Two recent monuments at the cemetery are discussed below.

Interpretation

Signs along State Highway 1 direct passersby to the Rohwer Memorial Cemetery (Figure 11.37). The cemetery area is very neat and well kept, recently weeded, and has a few new concrete fence posts. In addition to the two relocation-center-era concrete monuments at the cemetery, there are two recent granite monuments (Figure 11.38). One honors the 31 Japanese Americans soldiers from Rohwer who were killed during World War II (Figure 11.39). The second, smaller, monument

Figure 11.35. Monument to the 100th Battalion and 442nd Regimental Combat Team, erected by evacuees during the war.

Figure 11.36. Monument to those who died at the Rohwer Relocation Center, erected by the evacuees in 1944.

commemorates the relocation center, and indicates the cemetery is a National Historic Landmark (Figure 11.40).

The cemetery area was listed on the National Register of Historic Places in 1974 and designated a National Historic Landmark in 1992, due in large part to the efforts of Rosalie Gould, the former mayor of McGehee, who has been very active in researching and preserving the site. Presently, she is working to create a small museum in McGehee to house the various photographs, newspaper articles, and other materials she has collected about the Rohwer and Jerome relocation centers.

Figure 11.37. Sign along State Highway 1.

257

Figure 11.38. Monuments at the Rohwer Cemetery.

Figure 11.39. Recent monument to Japanese American soldiers from Rohwer killed during World War II.

Figure 11.40. National Historic Landmark monument.

Chapter 12

Topaz Relocation Center

The Topaz or Central Utah Relocation Center was located in west-central Utah, in Millard County near the town of Delta, 140 miles southwest of Salt Lake City. Named after Topaz Mountain, 9 miles northwest, the relocation center was briefly known as the "Abraham Relocation Center," after a nearby settlement (Figure 12.1).

The extremely flat terrain of the relocation center lies within the Sevier Desert, part of the Basin and Range province that was once covered by Pleistocene Lake Bonneville. An "Old River Bed" depicted on maps less than a mile west of the site drains northward to the Topaz Slough. The most prominent physical landmark in the vicinity is Smelter Knolls, 4 miles west. Elevation at the Topaz Relocation Center is about 4600 feet and the native vegetation consists mainly of high desert brush.

The 19,800-acre relocation center reserve was a mixture of public domain land, farms acquired by the county for non-payment of taxes, and several privately-held parcels purchased for a dollar an acre (Arrington 1962). Construction of the relocation center was begun July 10, 1942, by the California firm Daley Brothers with a crew of 800.

The relocation center was in operation from September 11, 1942, to October 31, 1945. The maximum population was 8,130; most of the internees were from the San Francisco Bay area. A total of 623 buildings were constructed during

Figure 12.1. Sign at the Great Basin Museum in Delta, Utah.

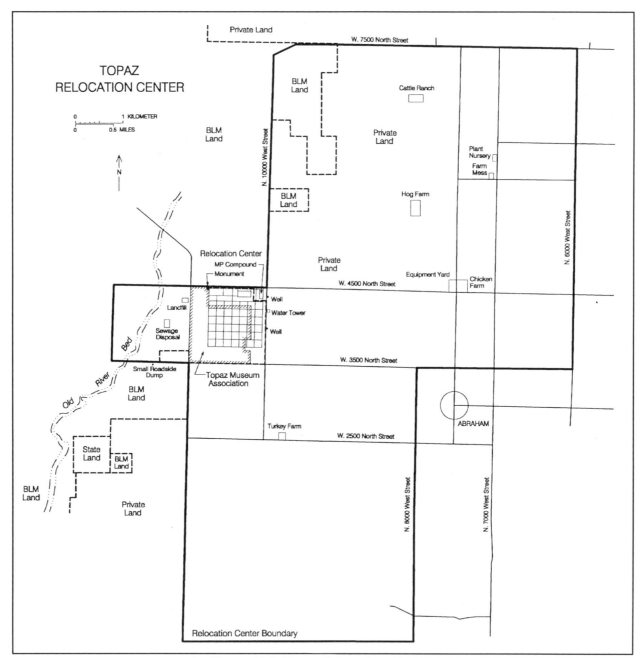

Figure 12.2. Topaz Relocation Center.

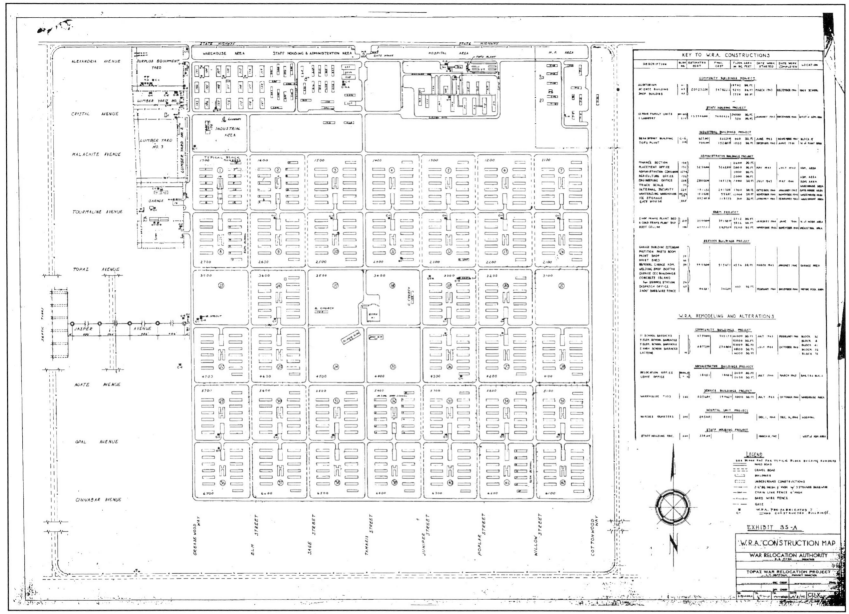

Figure 12.3. Residential and administration area, Topaz Relocation Center (National Archives).

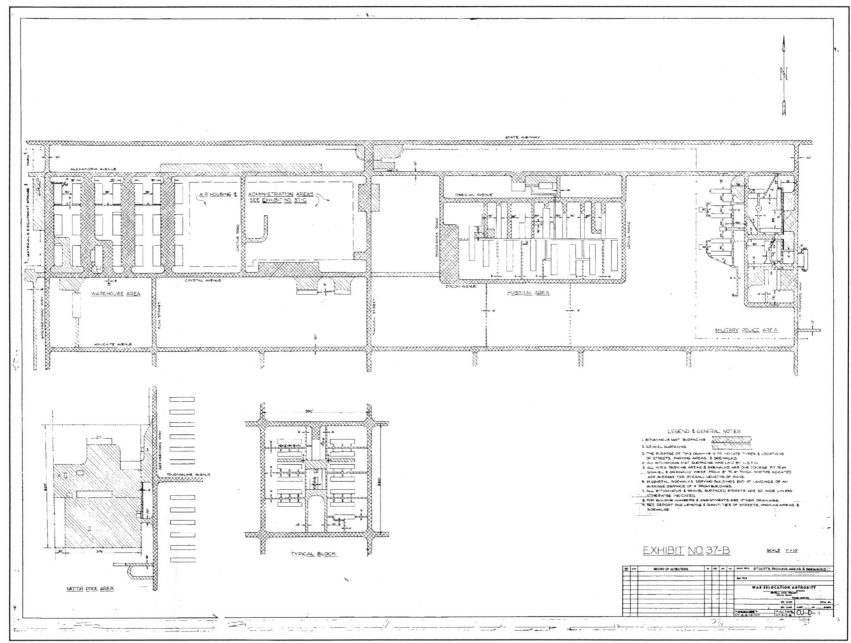

Figure 12.4. Administration area, hospital, and military police compound, Topaz Relocation Center (National Archives).

Figure 12.5. Panorama view of the Topaz Relocation Center (Francis Stewart photograph, Bancroft Library, University of California, Berkeley).

Figure 12.7. Corral at the relocation center hog farm (Tom Parker photograph, Bancroft Library, University of California, Berkeley).

the life of the relocation center (Powell 1972). The nucleus of the facility consisted of a one-square-mile area for residents, administrative personnel, and the military police (Figures 12.2-12.5). This "central area" included 42 blocks, eight for administration and 34 for residences. Each residential block had 12 barracks, a mess hall, a recreation hall, and a combination washroom, shower, toilet, and laundry building. The eight administration blocks included office buildings, staff housing, warehouses, a hospital, and a military police compound. Security features at Topaz included a sentry post at the entrance, a perimeter fence, seven watch towers, and a military police compound.

Some of the buildings at Topaz were imported, recycled from nearby Civilian Conservation Corps (CCC) camps. For example, two buildings were moved from the Antelope Springs CCC camp to Topaz to be used as the Christian and Buddhist churches, and two

Figure 12.6. Irrigation ditch constructed by evacuees (Ray T. Woodhull photograph, Bancroft Library, University of California, Berkeley).

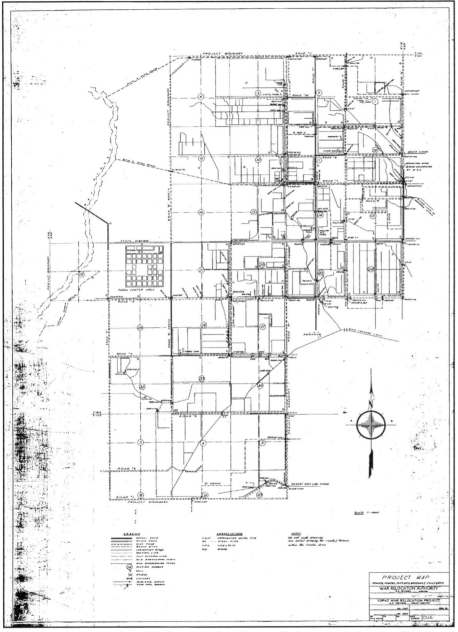

Figure 12.8. Irrigation ditches at the Topaz Relocation Center (National Archives).

garages and other buildings were moved from the Black Rock CCC camp (Kelsey 1996:99). During World War II the head-quarters of the Buddhist Church of America was transferred to Topaz from San Francisco (Ulibarri 1972).

In addition to the typical relocation center array of buildings and other developments, there were also sports fields and facilities, evacuee-constructed ponds and ornamental gardens, victory gardens to grow food, and trees and other vegetation. Over 7,500 trees and 10,000 shrubs were planted during the first 9 months, however nearly all died due to the heat, wind, and alkaline soil (Arrington 1962).

A cemetery was built to the southeast of the central area, but was never used. The bodies of the 144 persons who died at Topaz were instead sent to Salt Lake City for cremation and their ashes were held at the relocation center for burial in the San Francisco area after the war (Arrington 1962).

Much of the 19,800-acre relocation center area was devoted to raising food for the center (Figures 12.6-12.8). Beyond the central fenced area were agricultural fields, irrigation ditches, a farm nursery, a chicken farm, a turkey farm, a cattle ranch, a hog farm, a farm equipment storage yard, and a farm workers kitchen, as well as a sanitary landfill and sewage treatment system.

Even further afield, the CCC camp at Antelope Springs, 90 miles west of Topaz, was converted for use as a recreation site. Remains at the Antelope Springs camp are described in Chapter 16. The Deer Creek and Castle Valley mines in central Utah initially supplied coal to the relocation center. Within a short time, however, a group of Japanese American miners was sent from Topaz to operate the Dog Valley Mine south of Emery. Buildings from the Willow Springs CCC camp were moved to the mine to

Figure 12.9. James Wakasa funeral (Russell A. Bankson photograph, Bancroft Library, University of California, Berkeley).

serve as housing for the miners (Geary 1997).

The administration came up with an elaborate address scheme for the evacuees, apparently to give the outside world the impression that Topaz was a normal city. All roads were given names: east-west roads were named after gem stones and north-south streets were named after plants. Each block was then designated by a four digit number (1100-6700) to which the barracks and apartment number was added, which was then appended to the adjacent street. So mail to Apartment A, Barracks 11, Block 39 would instead be addressed to 6411-A Juniper Street, Topaz, Utah.

However, Topaz was far from being a normal city. On Sunday, April 11, 1943, 63-year-old James Hatsuaki Wakasa was fatally shot in the

Figure 12.10. Aerial view of the Topaz Relocation Center site, 1993 (Bureau of Land Management, Fillmore, Utah).

chest by a military guard (Figure 12.9). Wakasa was near the perimeter fence about 300 feet from a watch tower and was either distracted or unable to hear or understand the guard's warnings. Guards had fired warning shots at others on eight previous occasions. To avoid further incidents, the administration restricted the military in their use of weapons and access to the relocation center. Nevertheless, a guard fired at a couple strolling too close to the fence, a little more than a month later (Taylor 1993:141).

Figure 12.11. Overview of the Topaz site.

Figure 12.13. Rock wall in the administration area.

Figure 12.12. Manhole in Block 4 at the Topaz Relocation Center.

Central (Fenced) Area

Prior to 1998, all of the residential and administrative portions of the relocation center site were owned by a local farmer, Mervin Williams, who lives in a mobile home placed on a concrete slab that was once the Block 28 mess hall foundation. In 1998 the Topaz Preservation Board bought 417 acres from Mr. Williams to protect the relocation center site from development. Mr. Williams retained his home in Block 28, trailers and buildings in the adjacent blocks (35 and 42), and other areas along West 4500 North Street. Presently there are five homes within the former central area of the relocation center.

There are no World War II-era buildings remaining in the central area, but concrete foundations are present at former latrines, mess halls, and warehouses, and at buildings in the administration area (Figure 12.10). Manholes remain and the internal roads are still evident, with some distinguishable by the original asphalt and others surfaced with gravel cinders (Figures 12.11 and 12.12).

Figure 12.14. Topaz fire station (Francis Stewart photograph, Bancroft Library, University of California, Berkeley).

Figure 12.15. Topaz fire station today.

The sentry post location at the main entrance to the relocation center is marked by some building debris and white-washed boulders. The entrance road leads south to a short stone masonry wall which outlines a parking area, with paths leading to the administration building (Figure 12.13). Further south is the fire station slab, a two-bay building with evidence of a shower, toilet, and washroom facilities (Figures 12.14 and 12.15). The only inscriptions seen at Topaz were a few partial names on the concrete entry ramp of the fire station. Numerous other concrete slabs, mostly from warehouses, occur in the administration area, as well as a few small entryway slabs of other building. There is one large concrete slab in the former garage area.

Two concrete slabs remain in the hospital area and there is a concrete coal-storage bin just north of the hospital area (Figure 12.16). From the bin a conveyor fed the coal to the adjacent furnace which generated heat for the hospital buildings. Structural brick and firebrick are still

Figure 12.16. Concrete hopper north of the hospital area.

Figure 12.17. Stove pipes near the hospital location.

Figure 12.19. Stoves on mess hall slab.

Figure 12.18. Latrine and laundry room slab.

Figure 12.20. Concrete sink on latrine and laundry room slab.

Figure 12.21. Rock work at the location of Barracks 1, Block 14.

scattered around, and some parts of the conveyor belt system are still present at the bottom of the bin. Nearby, dozens of stove pipe elbows are concentrated in an old gravel parking lot (Figure 12.17). They were likely collected for recycling after the relocation center closed, but never reused.

In the residential blocks there are concrete slabs from the latrines/laundries and the mess halls, some broken, some intact (Figure 12.18). Where the barracks buildings had been, there are abundant nails, pieces of tar paper, small boards, stove pipe, brick fragments, and ceramic electrical parts. There are still cooking stoves at several of the mess hall foundations in the eastern portion of the site (Figure 12.19). A concrete wash tub was found, broken and loose, on one of the latrine/laundry slabs (Figure 12.20).

Figure 12.22. Rock-lined ditch and culvert.

Figure 12.23. Remnants of baseball backstop in Block 15.

Remnants of raised gravel walkways are common in the barracks area. There was apparently little rock used in landscaping, no doubt due to the paucity of naturally occurring rock in the area. Only a few rock-outlined gardens and one small pond was seen. Other rock work now visible is limited to a rock-lined ditch and culvert at the northwest end of Block 4 (Figure 12.22), and concrete and gravel paths with scattered rocks and boulders at the location of the Buddhist church in Block 17. Much of the details of walkways and paths within the residential area were probably destroyed when the pipes of the water system were dug up for salvage. Other recent ground disturbance has been caused by the construction of ditches to drain surface water.

Very little evidence of athletic fields or other recreational areas was seen. There were no signs of the football field or basketball courts known to have been in Blocks 24 and 25. Baseball backstop remnants were found in Blocks 15, 24, and 25 (Figure 12.23). The area south of

Figure 12.24. Rock and concrete wall at the military police compound.

Figure 12.25. Watch tower foundation and intact portion of the western perimeter fence.

270

Figure 12.26. Topaz Relocation Center landfill.

Figure 12.27. Government-issued ceramics at the Topaz Relocation Center landfill.

Blocks 36 and 37, which contained several baseball fields and other sports facilities, now exhibit only discarded trash and debris.

Security Features

Recently constructed ramps in the northeast portion of the central area has caused extensive disturbance to the military police compound. Very little remains there besides three small concrete slabs, one recently modified by a crude rock and concrete wall (Figure 12.24).

On the west, south, and east sides of the relocation center, portions of the perimeter security fence still remain. Foundations of three of the seven watch towers are still in place (Figure 12.25). At the location of two of the other watch towers, the foundations, though pulled out of place, are nearby. Eight other likely watch tower foundation remnants (large formed-in-place concrete blocks) have been used to make a low wall at the driveway entrance to Mr. Williams's home in Block 28.

Outlying Area

The relocation center landfill is on the west side of the relocation center's residential and administrative area, on federal land currently administered by the Bureau of Land Management. The landfill has suffered extensive vandalism and apparent collecting: there are numerous freshly dug holes, and compared to the other relocation center landfills examined, there are very few Japanese ceramics visible on the surface (Figures 12.26 and 12.27).

Sewage disposal consisted of a large septic system. Besides the remains of a concrete collection box adjacent to Block 22, no tangible remains were observed. From the collection box, sewage was apparently pumped westward to settling ponds.

Many features related to the outlying agricultural facilities, including the chicken, turkey, hog, and cattle farms, the farm kitchen, and an equipment storage area, could be relocated using WRA blueprints

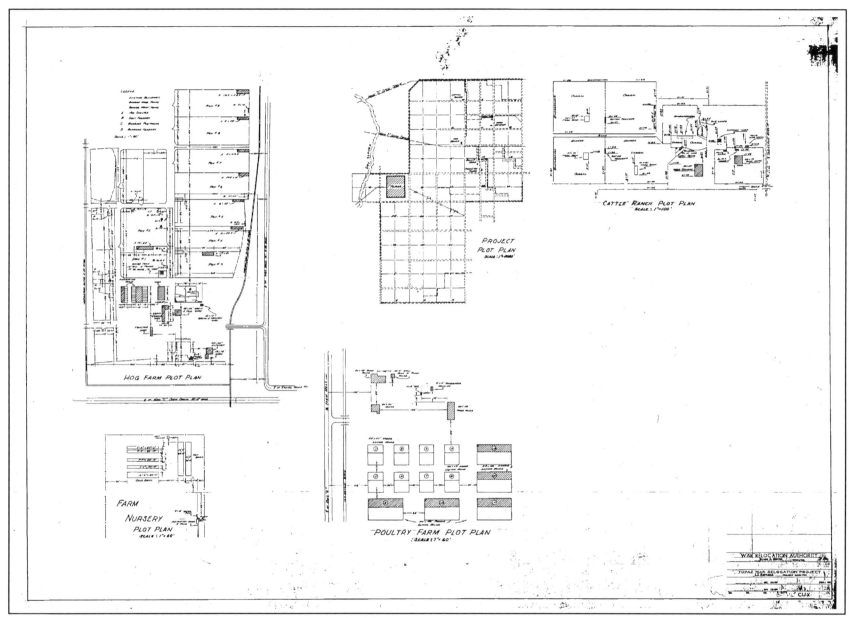

Figure 12.28. Outlying farm buildings, Topaz Relocation Center (National Archives).

Figure 12.29. Farm house at the Topaz Chicken Farm

Figure 12.31. Laying house at the Topaz Chicken Farm.

Figure 12.30. Collapsed laying houses at the Topaz Chicken Farm.

Figure 12.32. Adobe wall at the Topaz Chicken Farm.

Figure 12.33. Building remains at the Topaz Turkey Farm.

Figure 12.35. Farm house at the Topaz Cattle Ranch.

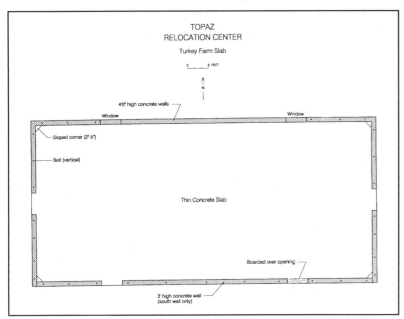

Figure 12.34. Plan map of building remains at the site of the Topaz Turkey Farm.

Figure 12.36. Barn at the Topaz Cattle Ranch.

Figure 12.37. Garage at the Topaz Farm Kitchen.

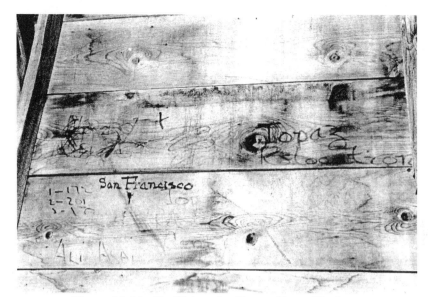

Figure 12.39. Graffiti at the Topaz Farm Kitchen.

Figure 12.38. Barn at the Topaz Farm Kitchen.

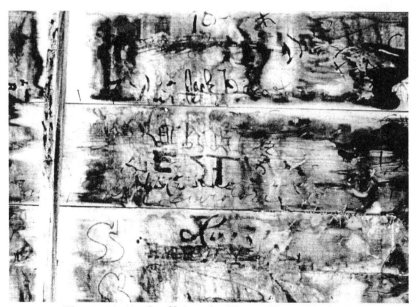

Figure 12.40. Graffiti at the Topaz Farm Kitchen.

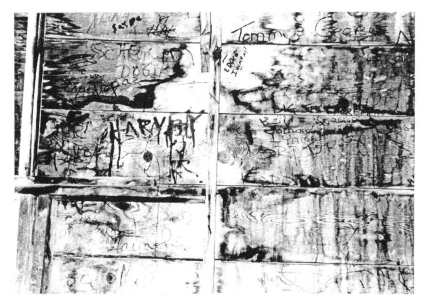

Figure 12.41. Graffiti at the Topaz Farm Kitchen.

Figure 12.42. Monument at the site of the Topaz Relocation Center.

(Figure 12.28). The chicken, hog, and cattle farms and possibly the farm kitchen appear to have incorporated structures from pre-re-location center farms. The farm buildings at the hog farm are still in use by the current owner, Mr. Nelson, but the others are abandoned.

The chicken farm is located 2½ miles east of the residential portion of the relocation center, at the northeast corner of the intersection of 4500 North Street and 7500 West Street. WRA blueprints show a farm house, a bunk house, a generator shed, a feed storage building, a water tank and pump house, eight 22-foot by 45-foot laying houses, and five 22-foot by 100-foot laying houses. The house, bunk house, and some of the laying houses are still standing, although currently not used. The house has a basement and adobe walls with a wire mesh and stucco veneer (Figure 12.29); the bunk house is stucco over wood frame. The laying houses were likely built by the evacuees. Made of adobe block and concrete mortar with wooden roofs, they are in various stages of decay (Figures 12.30-12.32). Located across the road

from the chicken farm was an equipment storage area. Currently the area contains some building debris, a possible structure location, and a couple of small trash piles.

The relocation center turkey farm was located on the north side of 2500 North Street, 0.2 mile east of the intersection of 10000 West Street. Remains at the turkey farm include a single low concrete-walled coop 23½ feet by 50 feet in size (Figures 12.33 and 12.34).

The hog farm was located about 2 miles northeast of the residential area, at the northwest corner of 5500 North Street and 8000 West Street. Presently occupied, buildings there include a house (noted as a kitchen and an attached shed on WRA blueprints), a feed bin, and several smaller structures.

The cattle ranch is about 3½ miles northeast of the residential area of the relocation center, at the northwest corner of 7000 North Street and

8000 West Street. Structures remaining at the cattle ranch include a bunkhouse, a feed storage barn, a chicken shed, a well house, and several corrals (Figures 12.35 and 12.36). Three small shacks noted on WRA blueprints are no longer present.

At the farm kitchen, located 0.2 mile west of the intersection of 6000 North Street and 7000 West Street, there is a barn, garage, shed, and well (Figure 12.37 and Figure 12.38). The barn and garage, certainly in place during use of the relocation center, may have been constructed by the evacuees. Both are made of the same kind of lumber as was commonly used at the relocation centers, and the barn has numerous names, dates, home towns, and other graffiti written by the evacuees on the interior of the west wall (Figures 12.39-12.41). In amongst the graffiti there are several undecipherable Japanese characters. The barn is similar in size and design to a relocation center mess hall, and may be the "Farm Kitchen" itself.

The plant nursery location, depicted on the WRA blueprints as about one-quarter mile north of the farm kitchen, is now a cultivated field.

Interpretation

At the relocation center itself there is a large historic monument and a gravel parking area in what was the northwest portion of the central area. The area is within the former surplus equipment yard, according to WRA blueprints, and is presently part of Mr. Williams's holdings. The monument is a large concrete and rock-veneer block set on a concrete platform (Figure 12.42). Informative interpretative plaques set in the monument contain text describing the history of the relocation center and some historical photographs. Unfortunately, the monument has been vandalized by gunfire, and bullet holes have defaced the plaques and photographs (Figures 12.43 and 12.44).

Figure 12.43. Detail of vandalized plaque.

A portion of a dining hall is at the Delta High School and several barracks that had been sold to homesteading veterans are still in the surrounding vicinity. Some have been extensively remodeled into houses; those that were used as barns retain greater design integrity, but they are generally very deteriorated. In the town of Delta, there is a monument with directions to the relocation center site (Figure 12.45). In addition, the Great Basin Museum in Delta has an extensive display of photographs, artifacts, and other items related to the relocation center, as well as one-third of a barracks from Topaz restored to its original condition (Figure 12.46). Additional relocation center displays are located in the barracks, which is owned by the Topaz Preservation Board. The Board is actively rasing funds to purchase more of the Topaz site and recently received a Getty Foundation Grant to develop a long-term preservation and management plan.

Figure 12.45. Historical marker in Delta city park.

Figure 12.44. Detail of vandalized monument at the site of the Topaz Relocation Center.

Figure 12.46. Restored partial barracks at the Great Basin Museum in Delta, Utah.

278

Chapter 13

Tule Lake Relocation Center

The Tule Lake Relocation Center is in Modoc County, California, 35 miles southeast of Klamath Falls, Oregon, and about 10 miles from the town of Tulelake. The town is spelled as one word and the relocation center as two. The post office designation for the relocation center was Newell, the name of the post office, general store, and gas station at a nearby crossroads.

The relocation center reserve, which encompassed 7,400 acres, is presently a mix of public, state, and private land (Figures 13.1 and 13.2). Situated in the Klamath Valley, the Tule Lake Relocation Center was located within an underdeveloped federal reclamation district, authorized in 1905. The Modoc Project was begun in the Klamath Reclamation District in 1920 to drain Tule Lake for use as farm land. By 1941, 3,500 acres of former lake bed were under cultivation (Jacoby 1996). Large remnants of Tule Lake, now a National Wildlife Refuge, lie within a few miles of the relocation center site.

The lacustrine geology is evident: the relocation center site and surrounding area is flat and treeless, and the sandy loam soil is interspersed with the abundant remains of freshwater mollusks. To the south and west vulcanism is prominent: Tule Lake was just north of lava flows emanating from the Medicine Lake Highlands, the easternmost promontory of the Cascade Range. An 800-foot-high bluff, called the Peninsula, is composed of volcanic tuff that was extruded within Pleistocene Tule Lake. The Peninsula lies just south of the developed central area of the relocation center, and there are other smaller bluffs to the north and east. Lava Beds National Monument includes two areas southwest of the relocation center, one just south of the Peninsula and another, much larger area at the northern end of the Medicine Lake Highlands. Fifty miles south on a clear day 14,000 foot Mt. Shasta is visible (Figure 13.3). At an elevation of 4,000 feet, the winters at Tule Lake are long and cold and the summers hot and dry. The vegetation consists of a sparse growth of grass, tules, and sagebrush.

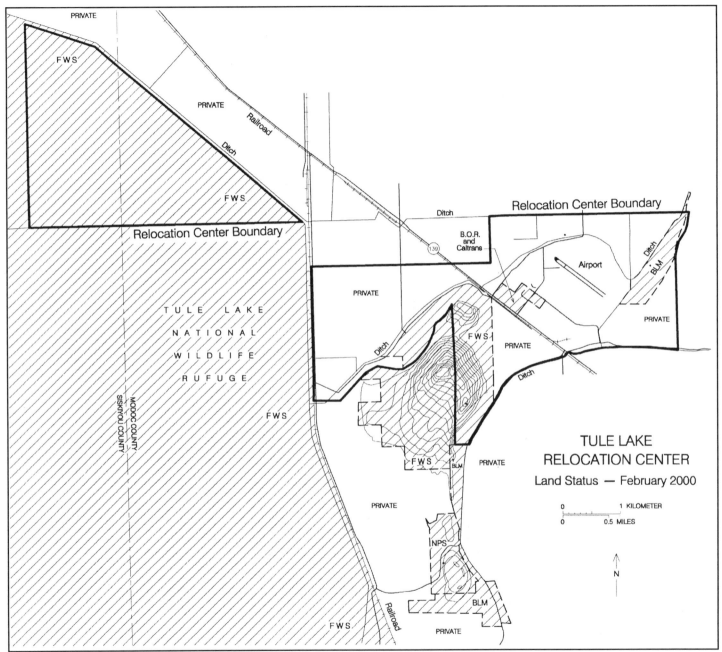

Figure 13.1. Land status, Tule Lake Relocation Center and vicinity.

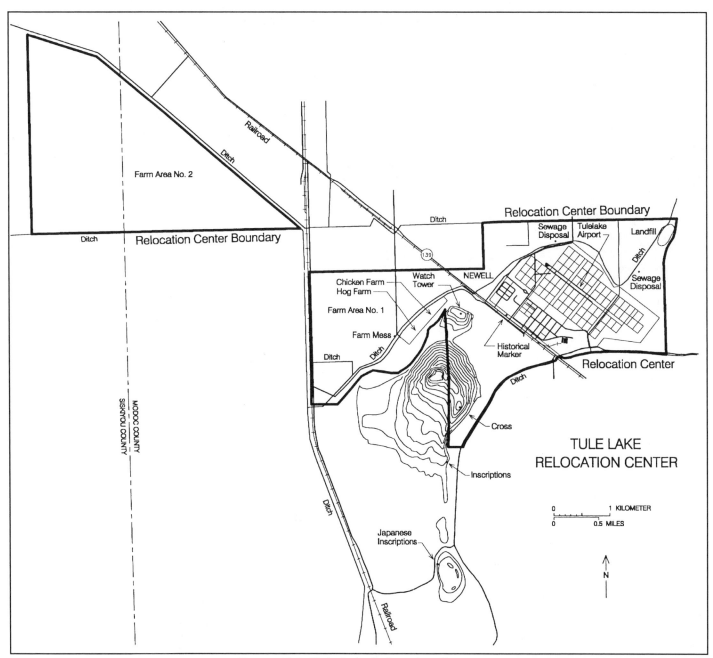

Figure 13.2. Tule Lake Relocation Center.

Figure 13.3. Tule Lake and Mt. Shasta.

Construction of the Tule Lake Relocation Center began April 15, 1942. On May 25, the first Japanese Americans, 500 volunteers from the Portland and Puyallup Assembly Centers, arrived to help set up the relocation center (Jacoby 1996). When the WRA later decided to send the evacuees at the Portland and Puyallup Assembly Centers to Minidoka rather than Tule Lake, some of these first volunteers decided to stay anyway since being the first to arrive they had good jobs. Most of the evacuees at Tule Lake were from the Marysville, Pinedale, Pomona, Sacramento, and Salinas Assembly Centers. In addition, a large number of evacuees were sent directly to the relocation center from the southern San Joaquin Valley without first going to an assembly center.

From the start, the Tule Lake Relocation Center was plagued by problems and discontent. Within 5 months of its opening there was a mess hall strike to protest inadequate food, a farm strike, and a general strike (Kowta 1976). Additional problems arose when, in response to public and congressional criticism, the WRA decided to segregate the "disloyals" from the "loyals" with a poorly-worded questionnaire. Those who answered "no" to the two loyalty questions were considered "disloyal."

When some 35 Nisei from the same block who had applied for repatriation to Japan failed to answer the questionnaire by an arbitrary deadline, the military police surrounded their block and arrested them. Over the next two months over 100 more evacuees were arrested and housed in nearby jails and an old Civilian Conservation Corps (CCC) camp 5 miles west of the relocation center (see Chapter 15). Measured by the questionnaire results, Tule Lake had the highest proportion of disloyals of all the Relocation Centers. While the average number of "no-no's" at other centers was 10 percent, at Tule Lake 42 percent did not answer the questionnaire at all, or answered no to both loyalty questions.

In the summer of 1943 the Tule Lake Relocation Center was converted into a maximum security segregation facility. One of the camps at Poston was originally chosen, but eventually, the disloyals were segregated to the relocation center at Tule Lake, which already housed the highest number of disloyals. The original evacuees at Tule Lake who answered "yes" to the loyalty questions were supposed to choose another relocation center to make room for more disloyals at Tule Lake. Some 6,000 evacuees did move out, but the 8,500 "old Tuleans" who remained included some 4,000 loyals who did not want to move yet again.

New barracks were constructed to house many of the new arrivals and Tule Lake became the largest of the WRA-run centers. By the spring of 1944, over 18,000 people were interned there (Figure 13.4). Additional troops were assigned to Tule Lake, including eight tanks (Drinnon 1987:110). A lighted 6-foot-high chain link "man-proof" fence, topped with barbed wire, as well as more watch towers were

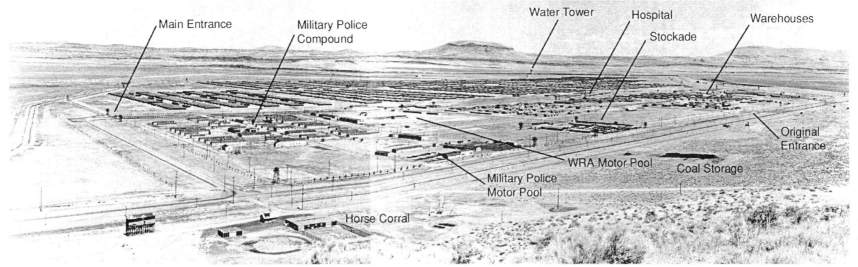

Figure 13.4. Tule Lake Relocation Center, June 1946 (Bureau of Reclamation, Sacramento, California).

added around the relocation center perimeter. Fences and watch towers were also built around the outlying farm fields of the center.

In October 1943 an evacuee farm worker died in a truck accident. To protest the minuscule compensation offered the victim's widow, agricultural workers went on strike. The administration brought in 234 Japanese Americans from other relocation centers to harvest the crops. For their protection, they were housed at the former CCC camp nearby. But the strikebreakers' presence and the fact they were paid about ten times the standard evacuee wage contributed to general discontent.

On November 1, a large crowd assembled in the administration area to protest the sending of center supplies to the strikebreakers. The military police used jeeps mounted with machine guns and tear gas to disperse the crowd and began the arrest of suspected leaders. Most work at the center stopped, and the evacuees boycotted a WRA-called assembly. On November 14 martial law was declared and the military police took over control of the center from the WRA. A fence and five watch towers were constructed between the administration and evacuee residential areas and a stockade was built to isolate those arrested from the rest of the center population (Figure 13.5 and 13.6).

Arrests and unrest continued until over 350 dissident leaders were in the stockade and 1,200 Issei had been sent to Department of Justice internment camps. On January 11 the remaining center residents voted to end the protest. In response to the vote, martial law was lifted on January 15 and the center administration, except for the stockade, was returned to the WRA. On May 23, 1944, control of the stockade was turned over to the WRA. However, tensions still ran high. On May 24, an evacuee was shot and killed during an altercation with a guard, and in June the general manager of the Business Enterprise Association, one of the most stable elements in the evacuee community, was found murdered.

Figure 13.5. Demonstration at Tule Lake (from Weglyn 1976).

Figure 13.6. Fence between the administration and evacuee residential area (Special Collections, J. Willard Marriott Library, University of Utah).

Because many of the evacuees at Tule Lake had renounced their American citizenship, the Tule Lake Center operated until March 20, 1946. At that time the remaining 400 evacuees were transferred to the Crystal City Internment Center in Texas. Custodial administration of the center was transferred to the Bureau of Reclamation on May 5, 1946. The military police compound and one ward of the evacuee residential area were leased to the Tulelake Growers Association for migrant laborer housing (Figure 13.7). The first laborers arrived on May 27. The Growers Association also leased the three large industrial warehouses to store grain.

Some of the buildings and land of the center were distributed to veteran homesteaders and some land was kept by the Bureau of Reclamation. Other buildings were held for later transfer to homesteaders (570 barracks and other buildings), government agencies, and non-profit groups (school and service buildings and over 400 barracks).

The remaining buildings were stripped of their furnishings and removed between July 28 and December 9, 1946 (Figures 13.8-13.10). Around 1963, H.A. and Anna Fletcher bought the military police compound and turned it into a subdivision. Many of the original buildings in the compound remain but have been modified, and some have been demolished.

The construction and layout of the Tule Lake Center followed the WRA's general design for the relocation centers. The central developed area was adjacent to the Central Pacific Railroad and California State Highway 139 (Figure 13.11). The relocation center road grid was aligned with the highway, at about 50 degrees from true north. Roads parallel with the highway were designated 1st through 13th Street; roads perpendicular to the highway were designated 1st through 16th Avenue. Four roads west of 1st Avenue, the last constructed during the initial building of the relocation center, were named Modoc, Siskiyou,

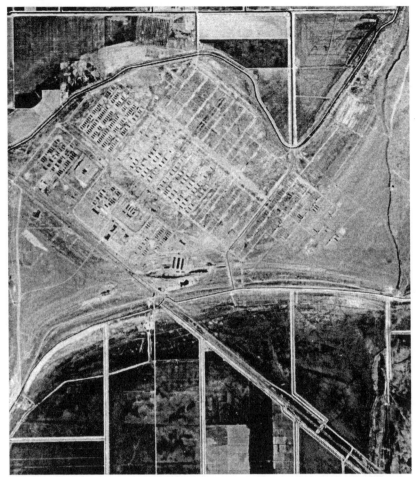

Figure 13.7. 1949 aerial photograph of the Tule Lake Relocation Center, north to top (Bureau of Reclamation, Klamath Falls, Oregon).

Klamath, and Shasta, since they did not fit in with the pre-existing numbering system. Later, for the segregation center, 17th, 18th, and 19th Avenues were added to the east (Figure 13.12).

From west to east along the south side of the central area was the military police compound (designated Block 1), the administration area and hospital (Block 2), and the warehouse and industrial areas

Figure 13.8. Abandoned staff building in the staff area, 1946 (Bureau of Reclamation, Sacramento, California).

(Block 3). The relocation center entrance was originally directly from the highway into the administration area, in the center of the central area. The administration area included four interconnected administration buildings (Figure 13.13), two other office buildings, a store, a mess hall, the director's residence, three staff houses, two dormitories, a laundry, nine recreation buildings, and three garages. Within the same block designation northeast of the administration area was the hospital. It included 19 buildings interconnected with covered walkways.

To the east of the administration area in the warehouse area there were 71 buildings. Many of these were warehouses, others included ten staff houses, three buildings used for an evacuee furniture factory, a bakery,

Figure 13.9. Abandoned evacuee barracks, 1946 (Bureau of Reclamation, Sacramento, California).

Figure 13.10. 1955 aerial photograph of the Tule Lake Relocation Center, north to top (Bureau of Reclamation, Klamath Falls, Oregon).

and a tofu factory. During use of the center seven buildings from the warehouse area were moved to other areas. One was used for a funeral parlor, one for an office, one was split and used for the farm kitchen and a bunk house at one of the sewage treatment plants. Four were moved to the stockade when it was constructed.

East of the warehouse area was the industrial area, which included two railroad spurs, an office, ten warehouses, and a coal shed. Later, a latrine and three large buildings (60 feet by 300 feet) were added. One of the large buildings was a potato warehouse and the other two were to be used for factories, but were instead used for storage.

After Tule Lake was designated a segregation center a new, more secure

entrance, a larger military police compound, a motor pool, and other facilities were built to the west of the original military police compound, which was converted to staff housing. As staff housing, the former military police compound included 27 staff houses, a dormitory, two latrines, two laundries, a warehouse, three garages, and an office. An elementary school for the children of the Caucasian staff was located in the open area between the staff housing and the

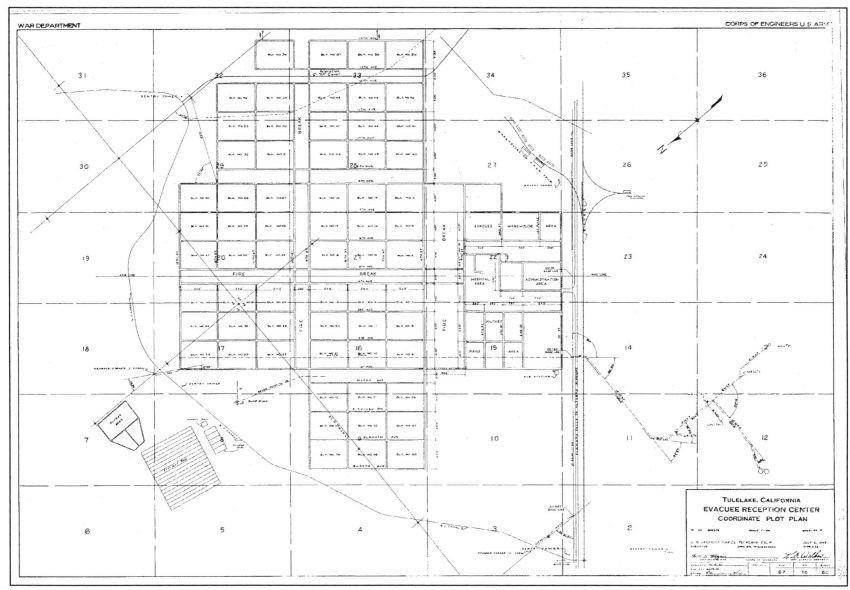

Figure 13.11. Tule Lake Relocation Center central area in 1942 (Bureau of Reclamation, Klamath Falls, Oregon).

Figure 13.12. Tule Lake Relocation Center central area in 1944 (Bureau of Reclamation, Klamath Falls, Oregon).

Figure 13.13. Administration building at Tule Lake (Francis Stewart photograph, Bancroft Library, University of California, Berkeley).

highway. Older children of the Caucasian staff went to high school at the town of Tulelake. The relocation center post office was located at the north end of the staff block to allow access from both sides of the security fence built between the administration area and the evacuee housing.

The new WRA motor pool area, constructed between the staff housing and the new military police compound, included two offices, two repair shops, a gas station, a latrine, a wash rack, two grease racks, a storage shed, and a vehicle shed.

The new military police compound, in the west corner of the central area, housed an entire battalion (31 officers and 900 enlisted men; eventually 1,200 soldiers would be assigned to Tule Lake). The compound included a headquarters building, a military jail, a theater/chapel, a post exchange, a fire station, two classroom buildings, three officers' quarters, an officers' mess hall, an officers' recreation building, 22 enlisted men's barracks, two enlisted men's mess halls, four enlisted men's recreation buildings, five supply rooms, a warehouse, a cold storage building, an ordnance building, and a substation and auxiliary power supply. To the south, the military police motor pool included a gas station, two latrines, a wash rack, a grease rack, two sheds, a motor repair shop, an office, a warehouse, a utility building, and a carpenter and paint shop.

The new entrance to the center was along the northwestern fence between the evacuee area and the new military police compound. Access from the highway was via a road along the outside of the fence. At the new entrance was a vehicle gate, a sentry post, and two pedestrian turnstiles (one on each side of the road). From the gate the road entered the central area and continued east 1,600 feet through a large open area between two security fences to another gate. This inner gate was the farm workers' embarkation area, where there was another sentry post and multiple turnstiles for pedestrians, with gates on either side for vehicles (Figure 13.14), a processing building to one side, and a parcel inspection building on the other.

There were other gates along the perimeter security fence, some with sentry posts (gate houses): one to each of the two sewage treatment plants, the old main gate, two at the railroad spur, and one from the highway to the military police area. There were also four gates along the fence constructed between the administration and the evacuee residential areas.

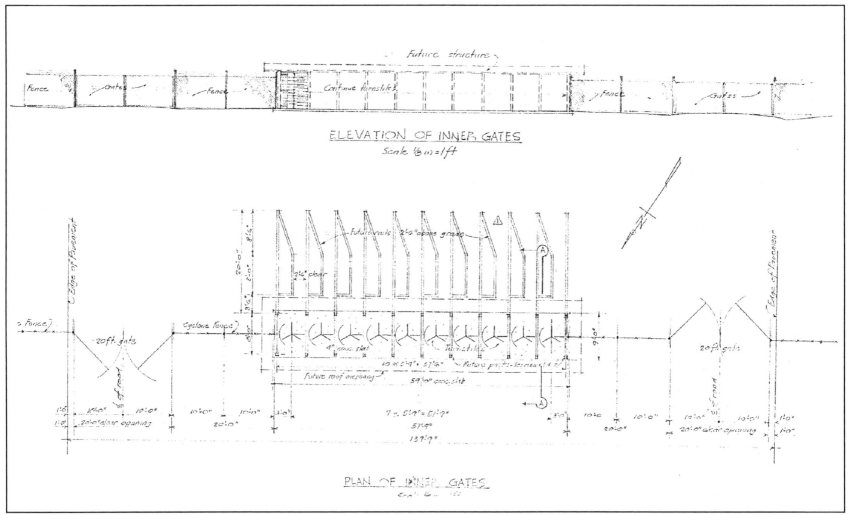

ELEVATION OF INNER GATES
Scale 1/8 in = 1 ft

PLAN OF INNER GATES

Figure 13.14. Detail of inner gate at Tule Lake (National archives).

Unique features of the Tule Lake center were the stockade, a 250-foot-by-350-foot area enclosed by fences and watch towers, and a jail located to the north of the stockade. The stockade watch towers included one original perimeter tower and three others moved from outlying farm areas. The side of the stockade towards the evacuee housing area was paneled to inhibit communication between those within and outside the stockade. Within the stockade fence there were two to five barracks, a mess hall, and a latrine (Drinnon 1987:111).

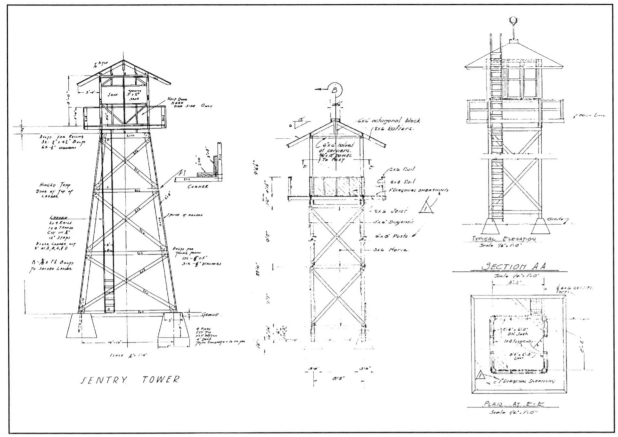

The evacuee residential blocks were located on the northeast side of the central area away from the highway. The evacuee area was separated from the rest of the developed central area by a 400-foot-wide firebreak. The fence that was added between the evacuee residences and the administration areas after the Fall 1943 disturbance was constructed along the south side of the firebreak.

The evacuee residential blocks were divided into eight wards, each bounded on all sides by 200-foot-wide firebreaks. Most wards comprised nine evacuee residential blocks; the exceptions were Ward 6, which had only six blocks, and Ward 8, on the east side, which was composed of 13 blocks. The eastern portion of the evacuee residential area was crossed by a canal.

Figure 13.15. Watch tower designs at Tule Lake, left 1942, middle and right 1943 (National Archives).

Around the perimeter of the relocation center there were originally only six watch towers, but after Tule Lake was converted to a segregation center, there was a total of 19 towers on the perimeter. The newly-constructed towers were of a slightly different design (Figure 13.15). In addition to the lighted 6-foot-high perimeter fence topped with barbed wire, there was a warning fence 50 feet in from the perimeter fence (Figures 13.16 and 13.17). A WRA blueprint depicts the warning fence as about 3½ feet high, constructed of wood posts with wood rails, barbed wire, and warning signs.

The 40 earliest-constructed evacuee residential blocks each had thirteen 20-foot-by-100-foot barracks (Figure 13.18), a mess hall, a recreation building, a men's latrine and shower, a women's latrine and shower, a laundry, and an ironing room. Later, another women's latrine and shower building was added to each of these blocks. Sixteen later-constructed blocks had a combination men's and women's latrine and shower building and a combination laundry and ironing room. After segregation ten more of these types of blocks were added, for a total of 66 residential blocks. Blocks were numbered sequentially, likely in the order they were built,

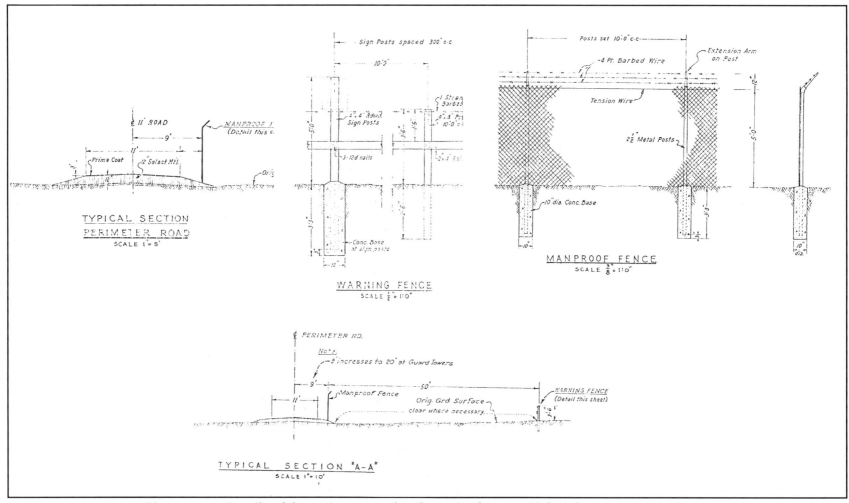

Figure 13.16. Details of the perimeter road and security fences at Tule Lake (National archives).

but with numbers 55 and 60-65 not used.

Block recreation buildings were used for offices, six stores, five canteens, a beauty parlor, a barber shop, four judo halls, eight Buddhist churches, a Catholic church, and three other churches. In the firebreaks there were three fire stations, a fish store, an outdoor stage (*Tulean Dispatch* 4/6/43), and a funeral parlor and cemetery, as well as 31 baseball and softball fields (*Tulean Dispatch* 5/11/43; Figure 13.19), and a sumo wrestling pit between Blocks 18 and 19 (*Tulean Dispatch* 7/2/43).

New school buildings were planned, but only the high school, located

Figure 13.17. Evacuee painting of the lighted perimeter security fence at Tule Lake (Drinnon 1987:95).

Figure 13.19. Baseball game at Tule Lake (Special Collections, J. Willard Marriott Library, University of Utah).

Figure 13.18. Evacuee barracks at Tule Lake (John D. Cook photograph, Bancroft Library, University of California, Berkeley).

in the firebreak between the hospital and evacuee residential area, was ever completed and then not until February 1944. It included an auditorium/gym, a shop, a science and crafts building, a library, an administration building, and four classroom buildings, connected by covered walks. Two of the classroom buildings at the high school were used for an elementary school.

Domestic water was supplied by seven wells, a water treatment plant, and an elevated 200,000 gallon storage tank to the east of the central area, and two 1 million gallon tanks to the south on the Peninsula. Sewage was treated in two plants, the second added after the relocation center was changed to a segregation center and expanded. Each had a sump pump, Imhoff tank, sludge beds (180 feet by 366 feet), and effluent beds (800 feet by 900 feet). Apparently the first plant did not have enough capacity even for the original relocation center population: WRA blueprints show a large pond for holding untreated sewage near it.

There were two farm areas, Farm Area 1 southwest and north of the central area, and Farm Area 2 three miles west of the central area (Figures 13.20-13.24). After segregation each farm was surrounded by a warning fence, a security fence, and 16 watch towers. Farm Area 1, nearest the central area, also had five searchlights. A WRA blueprint notes that large boulders at the base of an adjacent bluff were removed, probably to eliminate cover for possible escapes. A watch tower shown as on WRA blueprints on the Peninsula overlooking Farm Area 1 and the central area was likely a CCC-built fire lookout. After the disturbance in the Fall of 1943, eight of the watch towers at Farm Area 2 were moved to the central area. Five were placed along the fence constructed between the evacuee barracks and the administration area, and three were placed at the stockade.

In 1942, 450 evacuee laborers farmed 837 acres of barley, 570 acres of potatoes, 208 acres of onions, 145 acres of carrots, 152 acres of rutabagas, and other vegetables. The next year, 813 acres in Farm Area 1 west of the relocation center were planted with oats, rye, barley, alfalfa, clover, and mixed vegetables, and 455 acres north of the central area were planted in oats, rye, and alfalfa. In Farm Area 2, over 2,300 acres were planted with barley, mixed vegetables, and potatoes (*Tulean Dispatch* 6/18/43).

To bring Farm Area 2 under cultivation the evacuees had to build a distribution and drainage system which included 13 miles of canals, 8.5 miles of drains, 180 timber gates and other structures, and two small drainage pumping plants (Hayden 1943). In 1945 the evacuees lined 2,920 feet of canal ("M" Canal) through the relocation center, and began construction of a timber bridge with concrete piers, but work was suspended due to lack of labor as evacuees were released (Bureau of Reclamation 1946).

Farm Area 1 also included a farm kitchen and the hog and chicken farms near the base of the Peninsula (Figures 13.25-13.27). At the chicken farm there were 20 coops, granaries, an office, and a processing plant. The hog farm had 26 hog pens, a slaughter house, a well, and a water tank. The farm kitchen was located across the road from the hog farm. Across the highway south of the central area were a horse corral, a coal unloading and storage area (Figure 13.28), water wells, and two water tanks.

Central Fenced Area
Along State Highway 139 within the former central area of the relocation center is the present town of Newell. Within the town many buildings from the relocation center remain at their original locations. While most have been extensively remodeled, some appear relatively unchanged. The greatest number of extant buildings is in the military police compound (see Security Features, below).

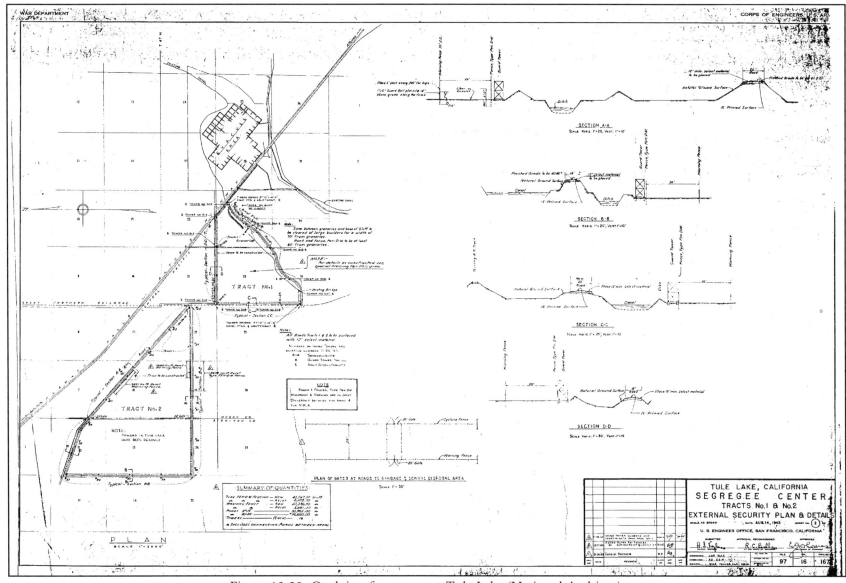

Figure 13.20. Outlying farm areas at Tule Lake (National Archives).

Figure 13.21. Irrigating crops at Tule Lake (Francis Stewart photograph, Bancroft Library, University of California, Berkeley).

Figure 13.22. Irrigation ditch at Tule Lake farm (Francis Stewart photograph, Bancroft Library, University of California, Berkeley).

Figure 13.23. Loading potatoes (Francis Stewart photograph, Bancroft Library, University of California, Berkeley).

Figure 13.24. Field of Chinese cabbage (Bureau of Reclamation, Sacramento, California).

Figure 13.25. Hog farm at Tule Lake (Francis Stewart photograph, Bancroft Library, University of California, Berkeley).

Figure 13.26. Chicken farm at Tule Lake (Francis Stewart photograph, Bancroft Library, University of California, Berkeley).

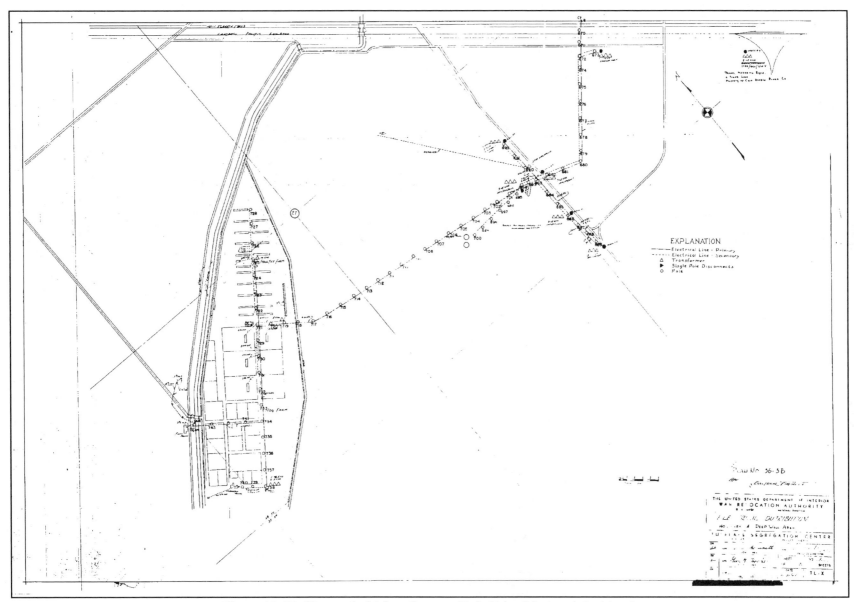

Figure 13.27. Hog and chicken farms at Tule Lake (National Archives).

Figure 13.28. Unloading coal at Tule Lake (Francis Stewart photograph, Bancroft Library, University of California, Berkeley).

Figure 13.29. Overview of the central area at the Tule Lake Relocation Center today.

Outside of the area along the highway nearly all of the central area has been graded to some extent, with most of the concrete slabs either removed or broken up and piled. Some areas are farmed but most of the vicinity is open space apparently used for cattle grazing (Figures 13.29 and 13.30).

Administration, Hospital Area, Staff Housing, and Motor Pool Areas
Outside the evacuee housing area, most of the relocation center road grid is still in place. The present Newell general store was the staff personnel recreation building. The building, with decorative wood floors and an impressive evacuee-built rock fireplace, is relatively unchanged (Figure 13.31). Another building behind the store dates to the relocation center, but these historic buildings are nearly surrounded by more recent houses. None of the other administration or hospital buildings remain.

No relocation center buildings remains in the staff housing area – the location is now the site of a small housing project and a high school. A Caltrans maintenance facility encompasses the relocation center motor pool, and three relocation center buildings are still in use, along with more modern additions.

Warehouse and Industrial Area
Among numerous more recent buildings, three relocation center buildings remain in the warehouse area. There are Japanese inscriptions in pencil on the interior wall of one of the buildings, now privately owned and used as a shop. The writing, some of which is faded, is entirely in phonetic Japanese. The consistent handwriting suggests that one person wrote the entire text, but the lack of organization suggests the writer did not have later readers in mind (Table 13.1; Figure 13.32).

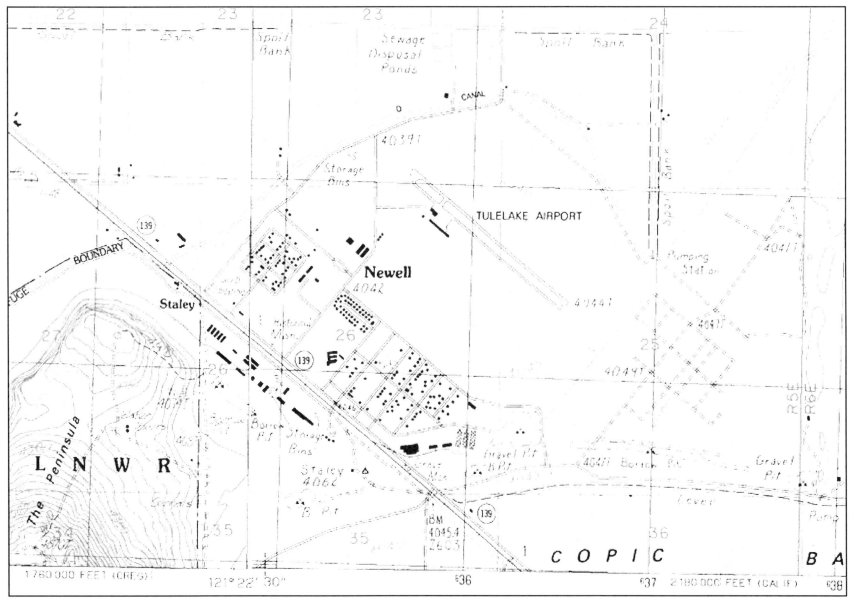

Figure 13.30. Central area at the Tule Lake Relocation Center today (adapted from USGS 7.5' maps Newell and Tulelake, California 1988).

Figure 13.31. Basalt rock chimney at the Newell store.

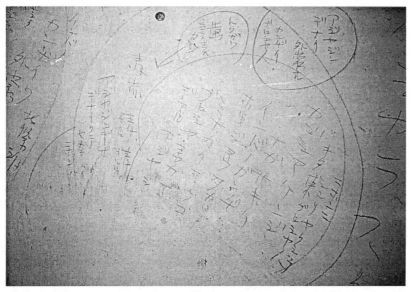

Figure 13.32. Portion of pencilled Japanese text on the wall of a former relocation center warehouse (photograph courtesy of Lava Beds National Monument).

Table 13.1. Translation of Japanese Text on the Interior Wall of a Former Warehouse at the Tule Lake Relocation Center.

The world is not governed fairly.
Takahiro (?) Ikeda is a right-winger, is a whit fig.
The imitations in ...
Kill them (us).
Japanized Japanese.
Not a land of God, nor of Buddha, nor of the stars.
Ever since Hojo came in, Tokugawa and Shimazu rule ...
Duke of Simazu.
Maeda ...
Tokisada Hojo's blood ...
God does not live in today's world.
Blue. Red. Blue (young) county.
Not an Asian.
Russia (?) that invaded Japan ... /People of Kagoshima prefecture /People of Nagasaki prefecture /Gandhi of India is ... /Hojo Takashi (?) ...
Sumire (?) Tokugawa /from Nikolaevsk.
(Hojo, Tokugawa, Shimazu, Maeda, and Ikeda are surnames. The Hojo was a clan which ruled Japan during the late Kamakura period. Simazu, Maeda, and Ikeda were famous lords in the feudal Tokugawa (Edo) period. It is likely that those names are symbolically used to mean something or someone else.)

Japan, the country under the sun.
America, the country of stars.
Longing for the stars.
America.
Asia.
Usami Hachimangu (a shrine's name).

Figure 13.33. Former industrial warehouses at the Tule Lake Relocation Center.

Figure 13.34. Concrete foundation slab of combination men's and women's latrine and shower building in Ward 7.

Within the former industrial area, five relocation center buildings are currently being used by the Newell Potato Cooperative. These include the three large industrial warehouses and two smaller warehouses; all have some modification, including the addition of metal roofs and siding (Figure 13.33). Northeast of the industrial area there is a large borrow pit.

Evacuee Residential Area

In the evacuee residential area, all of the relocation center roads west of the "M" Canal have been obliterated. Most of the evacuee residential area is taken up by the Tule Lake Airport. The vicinity is irrigated and used for grazing and cultivated fields. One area now has a transfer station for recycling waste.

Along a post-relocation center road in the western end of the central area the foundation slabs of some of the communal buildings within two blocks of Ward 7 remain. The size and layout of two of the slabs indicate they were the combined men's and women's latrine and shower building; one of the slabs has been damaged by the new road (Figures 13.34-13.37). Other slabs remain from laundry buildings, and concrete bins for the storage of heating coal are still present (Figure 13.38). Nearby, in a field south of an access road to the airport, there is a segment of basalt and concrete-lined ditch and a culvert from a relocation center road (Figure 13.39).

There are few artifacts in the cleared irrigated areas; these include small intact bottles, jar fragments with 1940s date marks, other glass fragments, a few hotel ware ceramic fragments, abundant coal, lumber fragments, drywall fragments, concrete debris, stove pipe, and animal bone fragments. At the relocation center high school site there are manholes and numerous foundation blocks (Figure 13.40), apparently little disturbed in spite of grazing and other activities in the vicinity.

Blocks built to the east of the original evacuee housing when Tule

301

Figure 13.35. Concrete foundation slab of combination men's and women's latrine and shower building in Ward 7.

Figure 13.36. Metal trough urinal discarded next to men's latrine foundation.

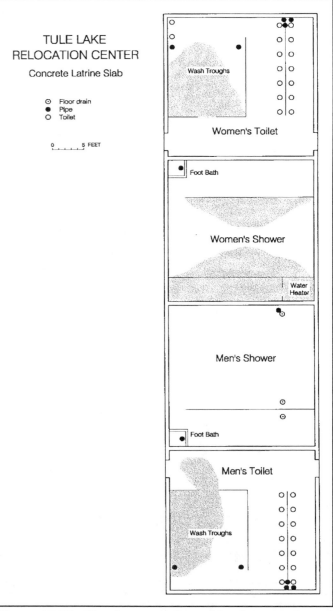

Figure 13.37. Sketch map of combination men's and women's latrine and shower building in Ward 7 (stippling denotes dirt-covered portion of slab).

Figure 13.38. Heating coal storage bin in Ward 7.

Figure 13.40. Concrete footing blocks at the site of the Tule Lake Relocation Center high school.

Figure 13.39. Rock and concrete culvert near the present-day Tule Lake Airport.

Figure 13.41. Typical relocation center road in Ward 8.

303

Figure 13.42. Concrete slab and rubble in Ward 8.

Figure 13.43. Clothesline pole in Ward 8.

Figure 13.44. Manhole in Ward 8.

central area. However, at least one intact 1943 watch tower foundation is present at the hog farm (see Outlying Areas below). The perimeter patrol road on the north and east sides of the central area is still used. Also along the northern perimeter is one of the most poignant features at the site: standing sections of the six-foot-high "man-proof" fence of chain link and barbed wire (Figures 13.46-13.48). The entrance road on the east end of the central area is still in use, and the concrete foundation slabs of the inner and outer sentry buildings and remnants of rock work near the outer sentry post are still present (Figures 13.49-13.51).

Thirty-three World War II-era buildings in the military police compound are currently used for homes or outbuildings (Figures 13.52-13.54). Many of the buildings have been modified, but others apparently have had very little work done on them since the 1940s. The original functions of these houses and outbuildings include 13 barracks, five recreation buildings, three officers' quarters, three supply buildings, two mess halls, two classroom buildings, half of the admin-

Lake was converted to a segregation center (Ward 8) have not been farmed or irrigated, and the road grid is still marked by red cinder roads (Figure 13.41). Slabs and rubble at latrine locations (Figure 13.42), a standing metal clothesline pole (Figure 13.43), and manholes remain, as well as scattered artifacts from the relocation center use.

Security Features

Around the edge of the central area there are pulled foundation blocks of a few of the large watch towers built in 1942 (Figures 13.45 and 13.46). No intact watch tower foundations are present around the

Figure 13.45. Watch tower foundation blocks at Tule Lake.

Figure 13.47. Perimeter fence at Tule Lake.

istration building, the cold storage building, the fire station, and the post exchange (Figures 13.55-13.60). There is a concrete slab foundation at the theater/chapel location and one additional standing building to the south in the military police motor pool area. The original paved roads of the military police compound are all still used

East of the military police compound the jail still stands, abandoned. The jail, within a Caltrans maintenance yard and surrounded by a fence with a locked gate, was documented in 1989 by the Historic American Building Survey (HABS Number CA-2279). No remains of the adjacent stockade are apparent.

The one-story concrete jail is made of steel-reinforced concrete walls and a similar flat concrete roof (Figures 13.61 and 13.62). There are six identical cells in the building, four against the northwest wall and two against the southeast wall. Architectural remnants indicate each cell had six bunks, a toilet and a wash basin (Figure 13.63). There is no evidence of electricity in each cell, but the building was wired.

Figure 13.46. Watch tower foundation blocks and perimeter fence at Tule Lake.

Figure 13.48. Perimeter fence at Tule Lake.

Figure 13.49. Outer sentry post foundation.

Figure 13.50. Rock work near outer sentry post.

Figure 13.51. Inner sentry post foundation.

Apparently a single cast-iron coal burning stove in the entrance room heated the entire building (Figure 13.64).

There are numerous pencilled inscriptions on the jail cell walls. Many are simply doodles, but others include names, dates, and political statements. Some are in Japanese and some are in English (Table 13.2; Figures 13.65-13.66, cover art). It is apparent that in some cases the writer was lying on his bunk since the writing is 90 degrees from the horizontal.

Outlying Area

Many of the outlying features of the relocation center are still evident, including farm fields, irrigation and drainage ditches, the farm kitchen, hog farm, chicken farm, horse corral, landfill, sewage treatment plants, and other features. There are evacuee inscriptions in concrete at the hog farm and in rock at two petroglyph sites.

Farm Fields and Ditches

Around the perimeter and within the central area there are two large concrete-lined irrigation canals, at least one of which ("M" Canal) was lined by the evacuees (Figure 13.67). Other outlying ditches constructed or used by the relocation center are still in use as well. The portion of Farm Area 1 east of the central area is

Figure 13.52. Overview of military police compound, 1946 (Bureau of Reclamation, Sacramento, California).

Figure 13.53. Overview of the military police compound today.

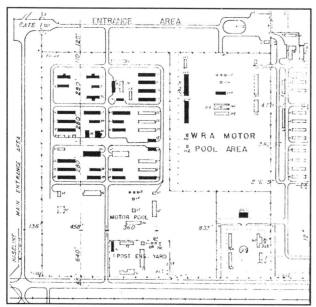

Figure 13.54. World War II-era buildings remaining in the military police compound.

private land still under cultivation; the part of Farm Area 1 north of the central area is apparently used for grazing. Farm Area 2, west of the central area, is now part of the Tule Lake National Wildlife Refuge.

The farm kitchen located within Farm Area 1 is still standing, but abandoned. The building is pretty well overgrown by trees, bushes, and other vegetation (Figure 13.68). Irregular in shape, it appears to be a combination of at least two buildings salvaged and reconstructed at the site. It has a partial concrete slab, an interior bathroom, and an interior door that reads "DIET KITCHEN" (Figure 13.69).

Hog and Chicken Farms

The site of the hog and chicken farms is now within the Tule Lake Wildlife Refuge, which limits access during the nesting season. From the Peninsula overlooking the hog and chicken farms, distinctive patterns in the grass are easily visible showing the outlines of former buildings, fences, and roads (Figures 13.70 and 13.71). Most notable is the red cinder road that was once around the perimeter. There are

Figure 13.55. Building in MP compound.

Figure 13.56. Building in MP compound.

Figure 13.57. Building in MP compound.

Figure 13.58. Former MP fire station.

Figure 13.59. Building in MP compound.

Figure 13.60. Building in MP compound.

intact manholes at the hog farm, and at the southern end of the hog farm there are the concrete foundations of the slaughterhouse, other structures, and a watch tower (Figures 13.72-13.77). There is also a dilapidated well house (Figure 13.78), with inscriptions in its 5-foot-by-5-foot concrete floor (Table 13.3, Figures 13.79 and 13.80).

Horse corral

At the horse corral location, across Highway 139 from the central area, there are two badly weathered concrete slabs (Figure 13.81) and several concrete bases with imbedded metal straps which supported the roof columns of the stable. At the southwest end of the corral there are

several half-buried, in-line creosoted poles apparently delineating that edge of the corral, surrounded by red cinder gravel used for a road. There are more red cinders at the forage shed location (Figure 13.82).

Sewage Treatment Plants and Landfill

Both sewage treatment plants contain the remains of the large multi-chambered concrete Imhoff tanks, measuring approximately 54½ feet by 63 feet by 21 feet high (Figures 13.83 and 13.84). The sludge bed location at Plant No. 2 is indicated by a low berm. Plant No. 1, north of the central area, is owned by the Newell County Water District. Plant No. 2 is located east of the central area.

Figure 13.61. Stockade jail at Tule Lake.

Figure 13.62. Stockade jail at Tule Lake.

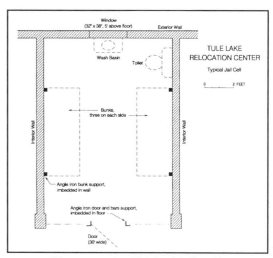

Figure 13.63. Typical jail cell.

Figure 13.64. Heating stove in the stockade jail.

Figure 13.65. Japanese graffiti on the wall of the stockade jail.

Figure 13.66. Japanese graffiti on the wall of the stockade jail.

Table 13.2. Selected Pencilled Inscriptions on the Walsl of the Stockade Jail.

Japanese	"The Great Japanese Empire" (dai nippon teikoku) and the word "window"	Figure 13.65
Japanese	"Down with the United States"	cover art
Japanese	"Yoshida" (surname)	
Japanese	Three times the ideogram for "tadashii;" this is a Japanese/Chinese, way of counting off, as Americans use llll and then a diagonal line; the character has five strokes, so a complete character (all of these are complete) counts off "5"	
Japanese	Right portion of left set reads: "Please be a second when I commit Harakiri" or "Request to assist in committing Harakiri." Left portion of left set reads: "Mondai no kaishaku," meaning "Interpretation of problem." Both portions use the word "kaishaku," though they have different meanings. A Chinese translator translated the right portion as "Today was wrongfully accused of disorder problem" and the left portion as "The explanation of the problem." The upper right character is not clearly written but seems to be the male first name Akira; other characters in that set are illegible.	cover art
Japanese	Right column reads: "September 29, 1945" Middle column reads: "Kawano, Toshio year of 1919" Left column reads: "Kuruma, Iwakuni-city, Yamaguchi Prefecture" Mr. Kawano, a U.S. citizen, was born June 20, 1919, in Honolulu, Hawaii. He was originally sent to Topaz and was transferred to Tule Lake August 20, 1945. He was released November 30, 1945 (Yosh Shimoi, personal communication, 2000).	Figure 13.66
Japanese	Graffiti with parts of names and words in hiragana (one of the Japanese phonetic systems); legible characters include "center," "loyalty," and "useful lecture" (story, information)	
English	When the golden sun has sunk beyond the desert horizon and darkness followed, under a dim light casting my lonesome heart	
English	Show me the way to go to home	cover art
English	Large "5"	
English	20 years old 4315 C-D MAMORU Yoshinota 5/24/45 — 180 days — KU..AMATA 18 " " 1406-4– HAMO YOKOI 6/17/45 — 270 — NA..Ta 3.. " " 580-B MASAKI NISHU 5/24/45 — 180 — KOMA...TO 19 " " 1806-B MASHHAIU YOS...IA — 180 — HUS...U..	
English	H.T. 5/25/45 MON.	cover art

Figure 13.67. "M" Canal today.

Figure 13.68. Tule Lake Relocation Center farm kitchen today.

Figure 13.69. Detail of interior door at the Tule Lake Relocation Center farm kitchen.

Figure 13.70. Hog and chicken Farms in 1943 (National Archives).

Figure 13.71. Overview of the hog and chicken farm areas today.

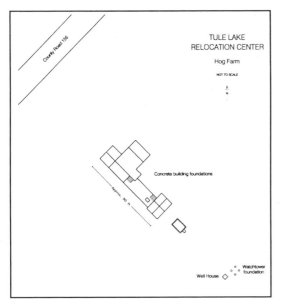

Figure 13.72. Foundation remains at the southern end of the Tule Lake Relocation Center hog farm.

Figure 13.73. Foundation remains at the southern end of the Tule Lake Relocation Center hog farm.

Figure 13.74. Foundation remains at the southern end of the Tule Lake Relocation Center hog farm.

Figure 13.75. Foundation remains at the southern end of the Tule Lake Relocation Center hog farm.

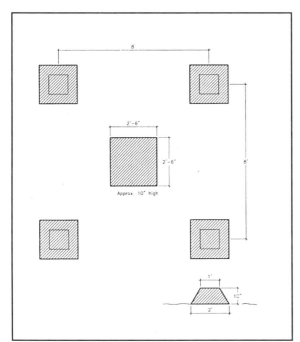

Figure 13.76. Watch tower foundation at the Tule Lake Relocation Center hog farm.

Figure 13.77. Watch tower foundation at the Tule Lake Relocation Center hog farm.

Figure 13.78. Well house at the Tule Lake Relocation Center hog farm.

Figure 13.79. Inscription at well house.

The relocation center landfill is on Bureau of Reclamation land northeast of Sewage Treatment Plant No. 2. It includes at least six parallel trenches with abundant burned and unburned trash (Figures 13.85-13.87). A wide variety and large number of artifacts include large cow bones, abundant glass fragments (food jars, "Coke" bottle fragments from Pittsburg, CA, Bend, OR, and Klamath Falls, OR, and "Mt. Lassen Soda"); hotel ware ceramics fragments (with "Bauer," "Hall," "TEPCO," "USQMC," and "V" basemarks), and some Japanese ceramics (Figures 13.88 and 13.89). Northeast of the trenches, a dense concentration of hotel ware ceramic fragments likely marks a disposal pit (Figures 13.90 and 13.91).

The landfill and surrounding area includes abundant post 1940s trash; for example, bottle dates at the landfill range from 1942 to 1952. More post 1950s trash has been dumped and scattered throughout the area to the south and east of the landfill. There are also many concrete chunks to the south, perhaps from relocation center building slabs, in rocky areas not suitable for farming.

Inscriptions

There are two areas south of the developed central area that have carved Japanese-American inscriptions. One area,

313

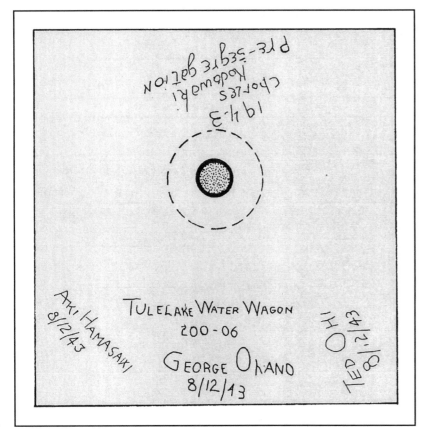

Figure 13.80. Inscriptions in the concrete slab floor of the hog farm well house.

Table 13.3. Inscriptions at the Tule Lake Hog Farm (all in English).

1943 Charles Kodowaki Pre-Segregation	Figures 13.79 and 13.80
TULE LAKE WATER WAGON 200-06	Figure 13.80
George Ohano 8/12/43	Figure 13.80
Ted Ohi 8/12/43	Figure 13.80
Aki Hamasaki 8/12/43	Figure 13.80

looks like it was done with a rotary grinder or similar tool, because the edges are smooth and deep.

The other area with Japanese American inscriptions is at Petroglyph Point (site CA-MOD-1), about 3½ miles south of the central area within a detached portion of Lava Beds National Monument. There are many thousands of glyphs from prehistoric through contemporary on the cliff faces (Figure 13.95). All of the prehistoric glyphs at the site were recorded in 1988 (Lee et al. 1988).

The main petroglyph area has been fenced since before the relocation center's establishment. To the north of the fenced cliff face there are some prehistoric glyphs and hundreds of modern and historic inscriptions in an area about 75 feet long. Most of the World War II-era inscriptions are located in this area, which corresponds to Panels 29 through 32 in the 1988 recording. The cliff face is so crowded with graffiti and over-writing that many individual inscriptions are difficult to read. But identifiable are a few Japanese characters, Japanese American names, 1940s dates, and relocation center addresses (Table

recorded as site CA-MOD-22, is 2 miles south of the central area on an east-facing cliff of the Peninsula (Figure 13.92). The site was originally recorded for a proposed land exchange, and is now BLM land (Gates 1982). Most of the glyphs at CA-MOD- 22 are prehistoric, but there are many historic inscriptions. The World War II-era inscriptions are within a 100 foot-long area, 5 to 10 feet above the ground. They include Japanese American names, 1942 and 1943 dates, a possible relocation center address, and one glyph reading "Tule Lake WRA Center," (Table 13.4; Figures 13.93 and 13.94). One name looks

Figure 13.81. Concrete slabs at the horse corral location.

Figure 13.83. Imhoff tank at Sewage Treatment Plant No. 1.

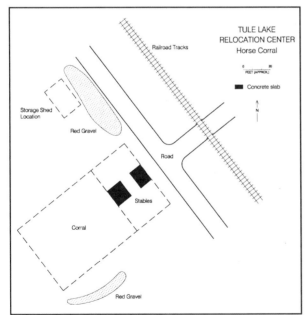

Figure 13.82. Sketch map of the Tule Lake Relocation Center horse corral.

Figure 13.84. Imhoff tank at Sewage Treatment Plant No. 2.

315

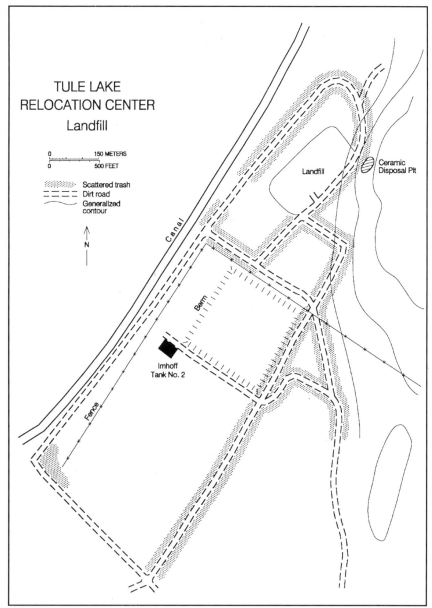

TULE LAKE
RELOCATION CENTER
Landfill

0 ___ 150 METERS
0 ___ 500 FEET

░░░░ Scattered trash
– – – – Dirt road
〜〜〜 Generalized
       contour

N
↑

Canal

Landfill

Ceramic
Disposal Pit

Berm

Imhoff
Tank No. 2

Fence

Figure 13.85. Sketch map of the relocation center landfill vicinity.

13.5, Figure 13.96). Some appear to have been deliberately erased.

Near the north end of the graffiti on the cliff face there are three sets of Japanese inscriptions on a large boulder 25 feet from the cliff face. All appear to echo pro-Japan sentiments (see Table 13.5; Figures 13.97 and 13.98). Some of these inscriptions have been scratched over, as though later visitors attempted to erase them.

Other Features

The relocation center water tanks and most of the wells south of State Highway 139 are still in use. The foundation blocks of the watch tower (CCC fire lookout) on the Peninsula south of Newell are still in place.

Southwest of Newell there is a steel cross on a rock promontory of the Peninsula (Figure 13.99). The original cross of wood was constructed by the evacuees. It deteriorated or was destroyed, and the current cross was placed by the California Japanese Christian Church Federation. A plaque at the base of the cross reads "Tule Lake Christian Ministry Monument – October 2, 1982" and lists the names of the 24 ministers that served the center (Iritani and Iritani 1994).

After Tule Lake was closed the remaining burials at the relocation center cemetery were moved to the Linkville Cemetery in Klamath Falls. There, a small plot contains two grave markers and two other memorials to the Japanese Americans who died at Tule Lake (Figures 13.100-13.104). All are flush to ground. The largest is a brass plaque that is set into a granite slab. It reads: "IN MEMORY OF DECEASED INTERNEES OF TULELAKE RELOCATION CENTER/FLOWERS FADED IN THE DESERT WIND/(11 names)/DEDICATED BY JAPANESE AMERICAN CITIZEN LEAGUE ON SEPTEMBER 10, 1989." The other memorial is a granite slab that reads: "IN MEMORY OF DECEASED/1942–1945/TULELAKE W.R.A." One of grave markers is a small stone which appears to be a natural boulder on which Japanese and English was inscribed. The English text reads: "DEC 6 1942/OUR BABY/J. MATSUBARA." The other grave marker is a

Figure 13.86. Trash-filled trench at the Tule Lake Relocation Center landfill.

Figure 13.87. Trash-filled trench at the Tule Lake Relocation Center landfill.

Figure 13.88. Typical artifacts at the Tule Lake Relocation Center landfill.

Figure 13.89. Typical artifacts at the Tule Lake Relocation Center landfill.

Figure 13.90. Ceramic disposal area at the Tule Lake Relocation Center landfill.

Figure 13.91. Detail of the ceramic disposal area.

Figure 13.92. Overview of CA-MOD-22.

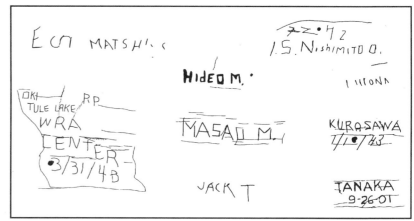

Figure 13.94. World War II-era inscriptions at CA-MOD-22.

Table 13.4. World War II-era Inscriptions at Rock Art Site CA-MOD-22 (all in English).

KUROSAWA 1/10/43	Figure 13.93
OKI RP TULE LAKE WRA CENTER 3/31/43	Figure 13.94
E... MATSHI...	Figure 13.94
Hideo M.	Figure 13.94
42 I.S. Nishimito O. ...ona	Figure 13.94
MASAO M.	Figure 13.94
JACK T	Figure 13.94
TANAKA 9-26-01	Figure 13.94

Figure 13.93. Inscription at CA-MOD-22.

Figure 13.95. Petroglyph Point, Lava Beds National Monument.

Table 13.5. Selected Inscriptions at Petroglyph Point, Lava Beds National Monument.

Main cliff face		
Japanese	"dawn" (?)	Figure 13.96a
Japanese	"August 8"	Figure 13.96b
Japanese	"Inoue" (surname)	Figure 13.96b
Japanese?	unknown	Figure 13.96c
English	...T ...TA 45	Figure 13.96d
English	43 MAXINE	Figure 13.96e
English	B.S. UMEZU 1105-A 2/11/45	Figure 13.96f
English	BETTY YAMASHIRO	Figure 13.96g
English	CLARA O. YOKOTA 1103-C	Figure 13.96h
English	ALVA 1945	Figure 13.96i
Japanese	"Oyama" (surname)	Figure 13.96j
Japanese	"Iwashita" (surname?)	Figure 13.96j
English	YFK 1113-D 8/21/...	
English	JO 42	
Detached Boulder		
Japanese	"Japanese Patriot" "Japanese Empire"	Figure 13.97a
Japanese	"Loyalty and patriotism"	Figure 13.97b
Japanese	Last syllable in the word for "Japan."	Figure 13.97c

319

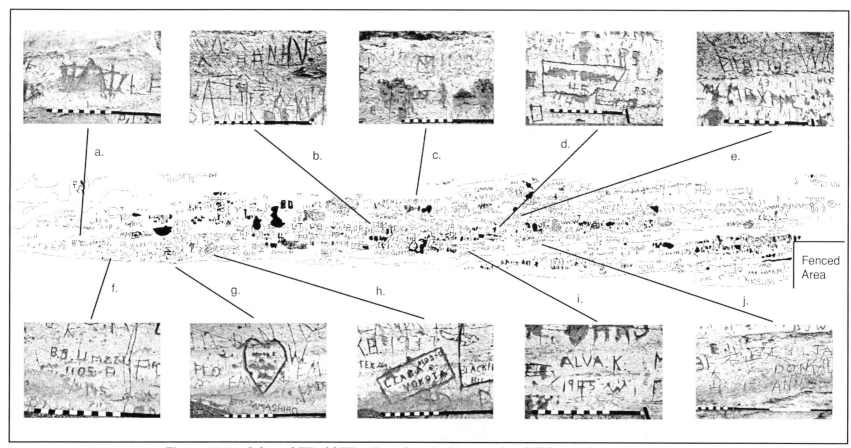

Figure 13.96. Selected World War II-era inscriptions on the cliff face at Petroglyph Point.

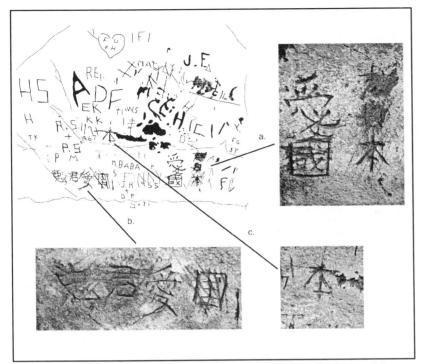

Figure 13.97. Japanese inscriptions on a detached boulder at Petroglyph Point.

Figure 13.98. Detached boulder at Petroglyph Point with Japanese inscriptions.

Figure 13.99. Cross on promontory southeast of Newell.

Figure 13.100. Linkville Cemetery, Klamath Falls, Oregon.

Figure 13.101. Memorial plaque at the Linkville Cemetery.

Figure 13.102. Memorial at the Linkville Cemetery.

Figure 13.103. Grave marker at the Linkville Cemetery.

Figure 13.104. Grave marker at the Linkville Cemetery.

Figure 13.105. Monument along State Highway 139.

Figure 13.106. Detail of state historic marker.

shaped concrete piece which contains only Japanese characters translated as "The grave of Kouzo Hamao/Died in June 5th Showa 18(?)/ Sixty-six(?) years old." Both of these grave markers are about 15 inches long. The Matsubara baby is included in the list on the brass plaque, but Kouzo Hamao's name is not.

Interpretation

A large monument of basalt rock and concrete along the north side of State Highway 139 commemorates the relocation center. The monument, dedicated in 1979, incorporates multiple levels of rock walls, a concrete apron, and a state historical marker (Figures 13.105 and 13.106).

In the Caltrans maintenance yard at Newell is the Harvey Yoshizuka Sand House (Figure 13.107). Built in the 1980s, it was named for a young evacuee at the relocation center who is now an engineer working for Caltrans. As an aside, much of the exterior filming of the 1970s television movie "Farewell to Manzanar" was done at Tule Lake.

The Bureau of Reclamation office in Klamath Falls has historical photographs, a large set of blueprints (see Appendices), and other files from the relocation center. They also have a couple of office chairs that were made at the Tule Lake evacuee-operated furniture factory.

There is a small exhibit about the Tule Lake Center at the county fairgrounds museum (Cohen 1994), and Lava Beds National Monument maintains a small collection of ceramics and other artifacts from the relocation center (Figures 13.108 and 13.109). An interesting item in the Lava Beds collection are some metal pieces that would go over the lower end of a roof rafter (the end showing under the eaves) embossed with Japanese characters that translate as "May happiness come here."

Figure 13.107. The Harvey Yoshizuka Sand House at the Caltrans maintenance yard in Newell.

Figure 13.108. Japanese ceramics from the Tule Lake Relocation Center in the Lava Beds National Monument collections.

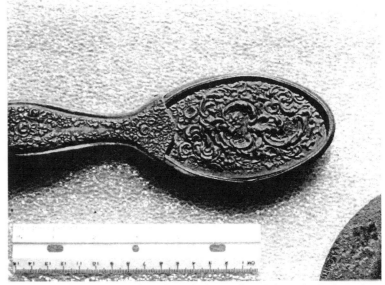

Figure 13.109. Ornate hair brush from the Tule Lake Relocation Center in the Lava Beds National Monument collections.

Chapter 14

Citizen Isolation Centers

After the riot at the Manzanar Relocation Center in December 1942, the War Relocation Authority (WRA) decided to remove so-called troublemakers from the relocation centers. An isolation center was established at an abandoned Civilian Conservation Corps (CCC) Camp at Dalton Wells, near Moab, Utah, which had been vacant only 15 months (Figures 14.1 and 14.2). The Dalton Wells camp was used as-is, with no fence or other improvements. Like the relocation centers the isolation center was run by the WRA, headed by Ray Best, who would later be the director of the Tule Lake Segregation Center.

On January 11, 1943, sixteen men from Manzanar were the first arrivals at Moab. Within a few months others from Manzanar and the other relocation centers were also sent to the isolation center, for "crimes" as minor as calling a Caucasian nurse an old maid (Drinnon 1987:104). No formal charges had to be made, transfer was purely at the discretion of the relocation center director (Myer 1971:65). This led to indiscriminate incarceration. For example, thirteen leaders of two separate Young People's Associations at the Gila River Relocation center were sent to Moab. The administration was having troubles with one of the groups and sent the leaders of both on the mistaken assumption that they were related.

Conflict between those opposed to the relocation and sympathizers carried over from the relocation centers to the isolation center. Further, living conditions were much harsher than in the relocation centers so protests over treatment and conditions continued. To further segregate the population seven inmates at the isolation center were transferred to the Grand County jail in Moab.

At its peak the Moab facility held 49 men (Louthan and Pierson 1993). On April 27, 1943, the inmates were moved to an abandoned Indian

Figure 14.1. Dalton Wells CCC Camp in 1937 (from Louthan 1993).

Figure 14.2. Administration buildings at the Dalton Wells CCC Camp (from Louthan 1993).

Figure 14.3. Leupp Isolation Center (Harry Ueno photograph, from Drinnon 1987).

boarding school at Leupp, Arizona (Figures 14.3 and 14.4). The transfer to Leupp was ostensibly "for the purpose of bringing together the families of those persons sent to [Moab]." However, "incorrigibles" were to be placed in an isolated, fenced area of the camp (WRA Report cited in Louthan et al. 1994), and no families were ever transferred to Leupp.

Most of the Moab inmates were moved to Leupp by bus. Five of those held in the Grand County jail, however, were forced to make the 11-hour trip each confined in a four by six foot box on the back of a flatbed truck. On arrival at Leupp, four inmates were transferred to jail in

Figure 14.4. Mess hall at the Leupp Isolation Center (Harry Ueno photograph, from Embrey et al. 1986).

the nearby town of Winslow for a few days before being placed in a jail occupied by six others at Leupp (Embrey et al. 1984). The prison atmosphere at Leupp was enforced by four guard towers, a cyclone fence topped with barbed wire, and the 150 military police who outnumbered the inmates by more than 2 to 1 (Negri 1985).

More evacuees were transferred to Leupp, for such infractions as drawing pictures that did not meet administration approval, leading a work walk-out, or trying to form a union. Francis Frederick, in charge of internal security at the isolation center, remarked in a letter to a friend "What [the WRA] call dangerous is certainly questionable" (Drinnon 1987).

When Ray Best transferred to Tule Lake and was replaced by Paul Robertson, conditions at Leupp improved as the new director became aware of the injustice and illegality of the incarceration (Louthan and Pierson 1993; Negri 1985). On December 2, 1943, the Leupp facility was closed and the 71 inmates present were transferred by train to the segregation center at Tule Lake (Myer 1971:77). The transfer was to have taken place a month earlier, but it was delayed when the military police had to be called in to control demonstrations at Tule Lake.

Moab Isolation Center, Utah

The site is at Dalton Wells, Utah, east of U.S. Highway 191, about 13 miles north of the town of Moab. At the highway, low concrete pillars flank the entry road (Figure 14.5). Cottonwood and tamarisk trees to the east (between the highway and Courthouse Wash) mark the camp location (Figure 14.6). The area shows recent use for stock grazing, with corrals, sheds, troughs, and water tanks.

Historical photographs show 18 board-and-batten buildings, including eight barracks, at the camp in the 1930s. Later photographs show three or four additional buildings. As is common at CCC camps, the Moab camp is divided into three sections: an administration area, a support area, and a barracks area. The administration area is to the north of the current access road and the support and barracks areas are to the south.

In the administration area probable building locations are indicated by small concrete slabs, barren leveled areas, large cottonwood trees, and other remains. South of the slabs and trees there are rock alignments and rock rubble at what may have been the camp flagpole location. A retaining wall on the east side of the administration area and a concrete well box are likely from the CCC era. Near the well is a more recent well with windmill supports.

In the support area, along the east side of the camp along the wash, there are large concrete foundations for what appears to be a generator building, a garage, and a blacksmith shop (Figures 14.7 and 14.8). A concrete loading dock along the wash has collapsed.

Figure 14.5. Concrete entrance pillars, Moab Isolation Center.

Figure 14.6. Administration area, Moab Isolation Center.

Figure 14.7. Concrete slab in support area, Moab Isolation Center.

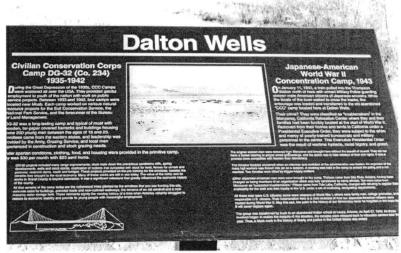

Figure 14.8. Historical marker at the site of the Moab Isolation Center (Photograph courtesy of the Dan O'Laurie Canyon Country Museum).

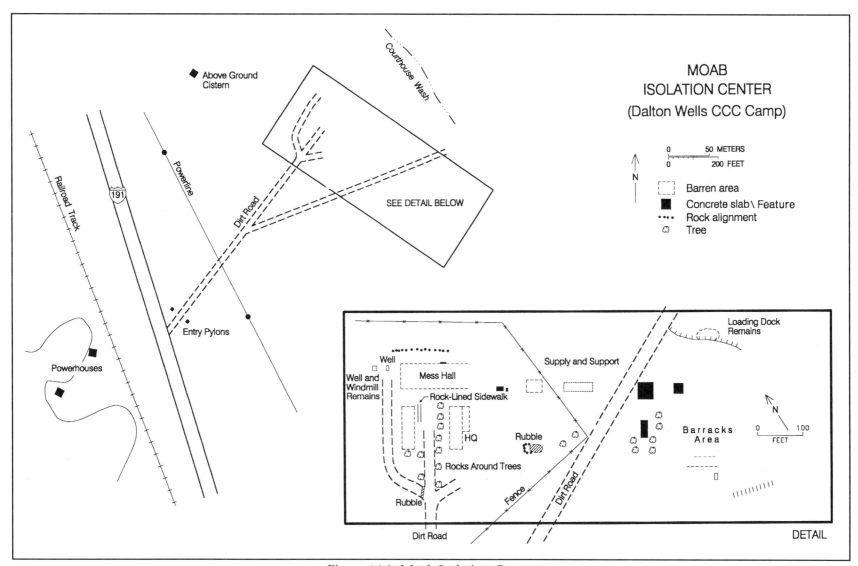

Figure 14.9. Moab Isolation Center.

In the barracks area there is little indication of former buildings and the area is partly covered by a pond and its berm. There is, however, what appears to be a concrete floor trough for a laundry room, overgrown with vegetation. It may be associated with a much larger buried slab. A single rock alignment was found along a road that once connected the barracks and administration areas.

Outlying remains associated with the camp include a CCC-built concrete and rock cistern to the north and two explosives sheds dug into the hillside west across the highway from the camp (Figure 14.9). The site was listed on the National Register of Historic Places in 1994 for its association with the New Deal CCC work program and the World War II Japanese American relocation. There is no historical marker at the site, but the Dan O'Laurie Canyon Country Museum in Moab has a photograph on display of the camp with the simple caption: "1937 – Dalton Wells Civilian Conservation Corps Camp – It was a prison for Japanese-American Citizens in 1943." In 1995 a historical marker was placed at the isolation center site by the Grand County Historical Commission.

Figure 14.10. Leupp Boarding School (Museum of Northern Arizona Photo Archives, date unknown).

Leupp Isolation Center, Arizona

The Leupp Isolation Center, in northeastern Arizona about 30 miles northwest of Winslow, was located at an abandoned Indian boarding school on the Navajo Indian Reservation. Historical photographs show the boarding school, built in the 1920s, with substantial red sandstone buildings which housed 500 Navajo children (Figure 14.10; Drinnon 1987). The school was closed in early 1942 apparently due to its location in the flood plain of the Little Colorado River (Negri 1985). Today the area, now called "Old Leupp," has just a few residences and a presbyterian church. The current town of Leupp is about 2 miles northwest.

Catherine "Tink" Borum, now of Winslow, Arizona, provided information about the Leupp community that helped confirm the site's location. Her parents ran the trading post in Old Leupp, and they lived on the second floor of that building (Figure 14.11). She was nine years old on April 15, 1943, the day the first soldiers came to Leupp. The military consisted of one captain, two second lieutenants and 150 troops. The trading post continued to operate during this time, selling to the soldiers as well as to Indians.

In the 1940s the main road from U.S. Route 66 entered (Old) Leupp from the south, ran through Leupp, and went on to the Sunrise trading post near the current town of Leupp. The raised road bed south of Leupp is now part of a protective levee system (Figure 14.12), but the concrete bridge abutments at the Little Colorado River are still in place.

Figure 14.11. Leupp Trading Post (Museum of Northern Arizona Photo Archives, date unknown).

Figure 14.12. Old highway south of Old Leupp.

Figure 14.13. Former superintendent's residence at Old Leupp.

Figure 14.14. Sidewalk remnants at the Leupp Isolation Center.

Figure 14.15. Concrete slab at the Leupp Isolation Center.

Figure 14.16. Water tower foundation blocks at the Leupp Isolation Center (block in foreground is inscribed with the name "KNOX").

The only building left at the boarding school is the superintendent's house (Figure 14.13). Other remains there include sidewalks, foundations, and a few manholes (Figures 14.14-14.16). No remains of the sentry building, guard towers, or barbed wire fence built by the WRA are present. According to Ms. Borum, the military leveled all the buildings with bulldozers when they abandoned the site. Debris from the destruction and removal of buildings was perhaps used to build new levees, or reinforce existing ones.

Vegetation is taking over much of the former boarding school, but in the central portion of the site, where the majority of the buildings would have been, there are scattered remnants of concrete and sandstone foundations (Figures 14.17 and 14.18). To the northeast there are three foundations identified by Ms. Borum as the teacher's residence, dining hall, and laundry (Figure 14.19). The former trading post, in use as recently as 1972, has been destroyed by vandals. Remains there include concrete, sandstone, bricks, and mortar (Figure 14.20).

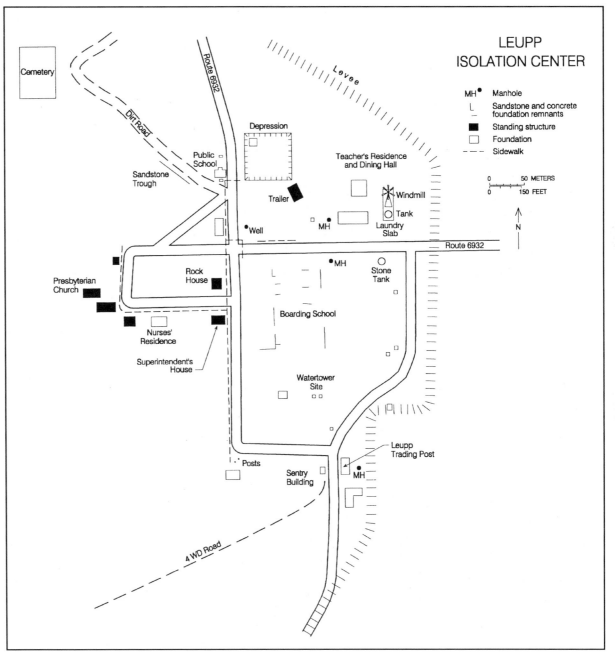

Figure 14.17. Leupp Isolation Center.

Figure 14.18. Site of the Leupp Isolation Center.

Figure 14.19. Foundation of the dining hall at the Leupp Isolation Center.

Figure 14.20. Leupp Trading Post today.

Chapter 15

Additional War Relocation Authority Facilities

In addition to the relocation centers and isolation centers, the War Relocation Authority (WRA) used at least three other facilities, all former Civilian Conservation Corps (CCC) camps. Antelope Springs, Utah, was used as a recreation area for the Topaz Relocation Center to make difficult conditions more bearable. Cow Creek and Tulelake, California, were emergency short-term housing used to defuse tense situations when conditions had already gotten out of hand.

Antelope Springs, Utah

Antelope Springs, a WRA recreation area for the evacuees at the Topaz Relocation Center (Figure 15.1), was originally the Antelope Springs CCC Camp (designated DG-29), established in the summer of 1935 at the foot of Swasey Peak. The CCC enrollees built range improvements such as roads, fences, and cattle tanks. According to Kelsey (1997) the CCC camp included 20 buildings (Figures 15.2-15.4). Along

the main road were an Army office, a truck shed and motor pool, and another building. North of the road were a dispensary and first aid building, a grazing service building (office and quarters), and an Army officers' quarters. South of the road were four barracks, a recreation hall, a mess hall and commissary, two toilets, a shower building, a cement vault, a supply building, and two other buildings. The camp was closed in late 1939 or early 1940 when the enrollees and most of the buildings were moved to a CCC camp at Black Rock, Utah (Kelsey 1997). It is not known how many buildings remained at the camp after the closure. However, in 1942 two buildings were moved from the Antelope Springs camp to the Topaz Relocation Center for use as churches.

Upon its conversion to a WRA recreation area in 1943, Antelope Springs provided a respite from the alkali flats of the Topaz Relocation Center, 90 miles east. Youth groups from the relocation center such as boy scouts and girl scouts enjoyed camping, swimming, and hiking

Figure 15.1. Composite photograph of Japanese American children at Antelope Springs (Bancroft Library, University of California, Berkeley).

Figure 15.2. Barracks area at the Antelope Springs CCC Camp (from Kelsey 1997).

Figure 15.3. Truck shed and motor pool at the Antelope Springs CCC Camp, Swasey Peak in background (from Kelsey 1997).

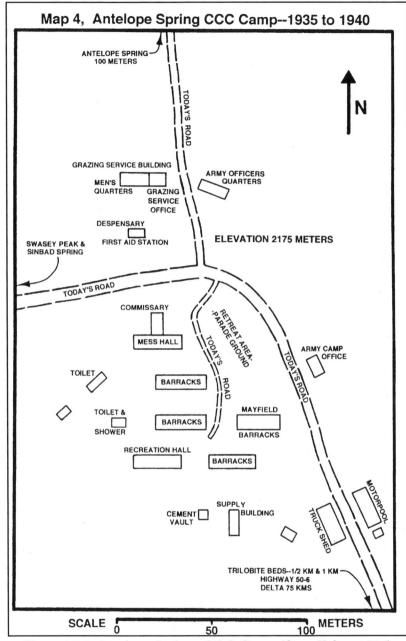

Map 4, Antelope Spring CCC Camp--1935 to 1940

ANTELOPE SPRING—
100 METERS

N

TODAY'S ROAD

GRAZING SERVICE BUILDING

MEN'S
QUARTERS

GRAZING
SERVICE
OFFICE

ARMY OFFICERS
QUARTERS

DESPENSARY
FIRST AID STATION

ELEVATION 2175 METERS

SWASEY PEAK &
SINBAD SPRING

TODAY'S ROAD

COMMISSARY

MESS HALL

RETREAT AREA-
PARADE GROUND

TODAY'S ROAD

TODAY'S ROAD

ARMY CAMP
OFFICE

TOILET

BARRACKS

TOILET &
SHOWER

BARRACKS

MAYFIELD

BARRACKS

RECREATION HALL

BARRACKS

MOTORPOOL

CEMENT
VAULT

SUPPLY
BUILDING

TRUCK SHED

TRILOBITE BEDS--1/2 KM & 1 KM
HIGHWAY 50-6
DELTA 75 KMS

SCALE 0   50   100 METERS

Figure 15.4. Antelope Springs CCC Camp (from Kelsey 1997).

at Antelope Springs, which was located in a sparse pinyon and juniper forest at an elevation of 7,400 feet. Evacuees could also get passes to roam the mountains which extended up to 9669 feet at Swasey Peak (Tunnell and Chilcoat 1996).

Today the Antelope Springs site is on public land administered by the Bureau of Land Management (BLM). There is a large commercial trilobite quarry ("U Dig It") and numerous smaller fossil quarries less than 1 mile southeast on State land along the way to Antelope Springs. A dirt road from the main graded road to a working water faucet provides easy access to the site.

No features or artifacts specifically from the Japanese American use of the site are apparent. The location of a swimming hole at Antelope Springs in WRA photographs archived at the Bancroft Library (see Figure 15.1) could not be positively identified. However, numerous remains of the CCC camp are still present (Figure 15.5). The most obvious is a small 6-ft-high adobe-walled building used as the cement vault (Figure 15.6). There are also six concrete slab foundations, three of which appear to have been for toilet buildings and one for a shower building (Figure 15.7 and 15.8). Concrete and rock walls at one of the toilet building foundations look like they were added after the original building was removed (Figure 15.9). Other features at the site include a small trash-filled depression (Feature 1 on Figure 15.7), two 2-ft-square concrete slabs (Features 2 and 5), a retaining wall and building pad at the former truck shed and motor pool location (Feature 3), a structure pad at a former water tank (Feature 6), and a pecked inscription on a boulder reading "JULY 14, 1936/JIMMIE GISSOM/ COLUMBIA, KY" (Feature 5; Figure 15.10). Other remains include concrete slab remnants at the location of the CCC-era Army officers' quarters, small holes and depressions, building pads, terraces, rock steps, rock alignments, and a gravel walkway.

Figure 15.5. Overview of the Antelope Springs CCC Camp today.

Figure 15.6. Remains of adobe building at the Antelope Springs CCC Camp.

Artifacts seen at the site include scattered glass fragments (including "Coke" bottle fragments and a bottle base with an Obear-Nester Glass Company hallmark [post 1915]), plain and decorated white ware ceramic fragments (one with a Limoges China Co., Sebring, Ohio, hallmark [1900-1955]), sanitary seal cans, lumber, and chicken wire (Figure 15.11). In the northwest portion of the site there are small amounts of coal, slag, and building rubble. There is a small area of early- to mid-twentieth century trash east of the site, some or all of which may relate to the historical use of the Antelope Springs camp.

Cow Creek, Death Valley, California

Between December 1942 and February 1943, 65 Japanese Americans from the Manzanar Relocation Center lived at Cow Creek, a former CCC camp adjacent to the headquarters of Death Valley National Monument (Figure 15.12). From 1933 to 1936 there were two CCC camps at the monument headquarters area, separated by a small wash. One camp was named Cow Creek, the other Funeral Range. Each camp had four barracks, a mess hall, an infirmary, a recreation building, a latrine, a shower, and a laundry. Truck shops and a motor pool were located between the camps. In 1936 most of the Cow Creek camp was destroyed by a fire. The camp was reconstructed on the same side of the wash as the Funeral Range camp, with both camps consolidated into one larger camp named Cow Creek.

When the WRA moved the 65 evacuees from Manzanar to Death Valley, the Cow Creek camp and the adjacent park headquarters and utility yard included about 35 buildings (Figure 15.13). These 65 evacuees included "outspoken patriots" (Myer 1971:64) who were on a reported death list for supporting the relocation center administration after the Manzanar Riot. Their removal from the relocation center was considered necessary for their protection. For three days they were housed in the military police compound at Manzanar until the Death Valley accommodations were arranged. They were then loaded into

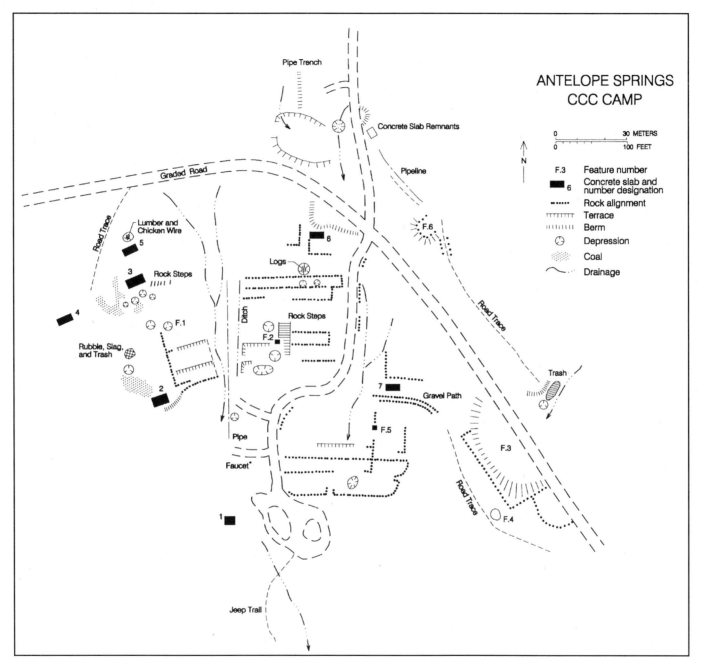

Figure 15.7. Sketch map of the Antelope Springs CCC Camp.

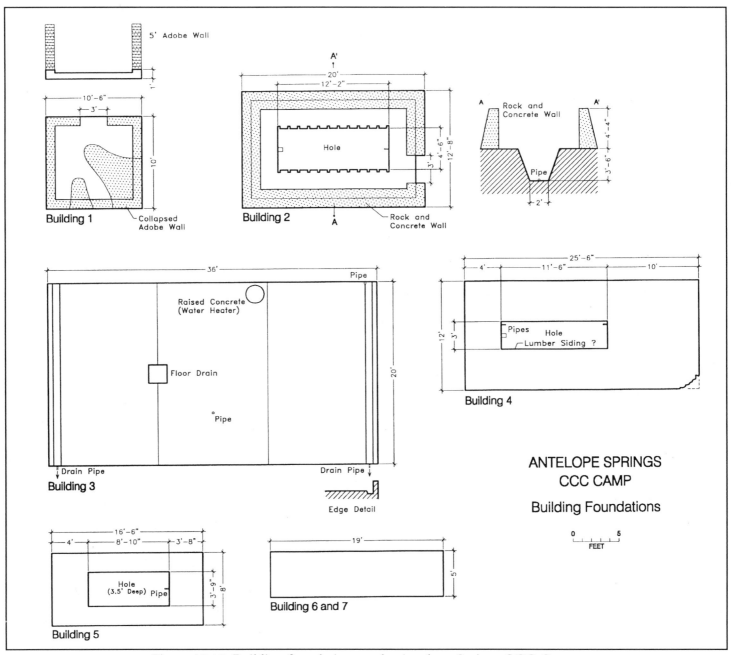

Figure 15.18. Building foundations at the Antelope Springs CCC Camp.

Figure 15.10. Historic inscription at the Antelope Springs CCC Camp (Feature 4).

Figure 15.9. Remains of Building 2 at the Antelope Springs CCC Camp.

Figure 15.11. White ware ceramic fragments at the Antelope Springs CCC Camp.

Figure 15.12. Headquarters area at Death Valley National Monument in 1935 (from Merritt 1987).

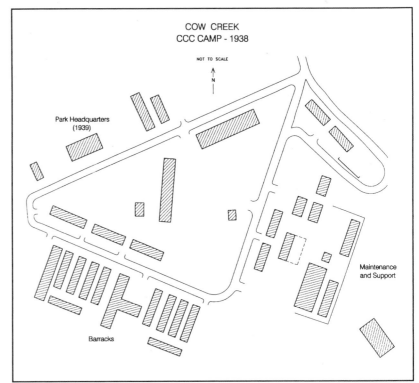

Figure 15.13. Cow Creek CCC Camp, 1939 (adapted from Greene 1988).

Army trucks and transported to Death Valley along with bedding, dishes, and a week's worth of food. The caravan consisted of two passenger cars, a jeep, six army transports, and three open trucks, including one loaded with hay bales for stuffing mattresses (Uyeno 1973). Personal belongings were sent later.

The WRA had use of six barracks, a mess hall, a library, an infirmary, and a cottage for a staff member, his wife, and a nurse (Figures 15.14-15.19). Up to 12 soldiers and 10 staff members stayed at the camp (Merritt 1987; Oda 1980). Food and other supplies were trucked in from Manzanar each week. Once when the supply truck from Manzanar was several days late, wild burro meat was served.

Figure 15.14. Unloading supplies at Cow Creek (Special Collections, University of California, Los Angeles).

Figure 15.15. Cow Creek during the Japanese American internment (Special Collections, University of California, Los Angeles).

Figure 15.16. Military police officer (note pre-WW II lace-up boots) and T.R. Goodwin, superintendent of Death Valley National Monument (Special Collections, University of California, Los Angeles).

Figure 15.17. Fire-fighting equipment brought to Cow Creek from Manzanar (Special Collections, University of California, Los Angeles).

Figure 15.18. Infirmary at Cow Creek (from Merritt 1987).

Figure 15.19. Japanese American children at Cow Creek (from Merritt 1987).

Figure 15.20. Departure for Chicago (from Oda 1980).

The relocated evacuees cleaned and repaired the CCC buildings to make them more liveable. The shower room was divided into men's and women's sides, and a CCC-built swimming pool was cleaned out and filled for use. A boiler house, which had not been used for quite awhile, burned down the second night the evacuees reused it.

The new Cow Creek residents did volunteer work for the park; they worked in the park sign shop, on the water supply system, and did general clean-up and other projects. Within three months all of the Japanese Americans at Cow Creek had been placed in jobs outside the West Coast and released (Figure 15.20). On January 14, the first family

left for a teaching job, and on February 15 and 16 the last 31 were taken under army escort to Las Vegas to board a train for jobs back east.

Today, the entire area along the south side of the wash where the central portion of the Funeral Range camp and second Cow Creek camp where the Japanese American evacuees were housed is now a maintenance yard and an abandoned mobile home residential area. No evidence remains of its former use. Most of the CCC-era buildings were torn down in 1954 when they became too dilapidated to maintain. However, 10 of the 35 buildings present in the 1940s still remain in the surrounding area, and provide an idea of what the camp would have looked like when the Japanese Americans were there (Figure 15.21 and 15.22).

The buildings remaining include the park headquarters built in 1939, two buildings from the original Cow Creek CCC Camp built on the north side of the wash in 1933, seven buildings in the utility yard built by the CCC between 1935 and 1938, and a machine shop built in 1942. Intermingled with these are a few modern buildings and seven World War II-era surplus metal Quonset huts. The park headquarters, now used for park offices, is a one-story, seven-room building with adobe walls (Figure 15.23). The other buildings at Cow Creek today include the former infirmary and an office/recreation building, both now used as warehouses (Figure 15.24). The office/recreation building is 1200 square feet, wood frame, divided into three rooms. The infirmary is also wood frame, two rooms, 840 square feet. It still has an original sink, cabinet, and ceiling, but in 1956 its tarpaper siding was removed and batten strips were added (Greene 1988).

Other CCC-built buildings include three warehouses, an oil house, a shop, and two other unidentified buildings in a utility yard enclosed by a 6-foot-high adobe wall. All are still used by park maintenance (Figure 15.25). Five of the buildings are of similar adobe brick

Figure 15.21. Overview of the Cow Creek area today.

Figure 15.23. Office/recreation building (left) and infirmary at Cow Creek today.

Figure 15.22. The old park headquarters today.

Figure 15.24. Garage (known as the "I-Hall" by park staff) in the utility area at Cow Creek today (cf. Figures 15.14 and 15.17).

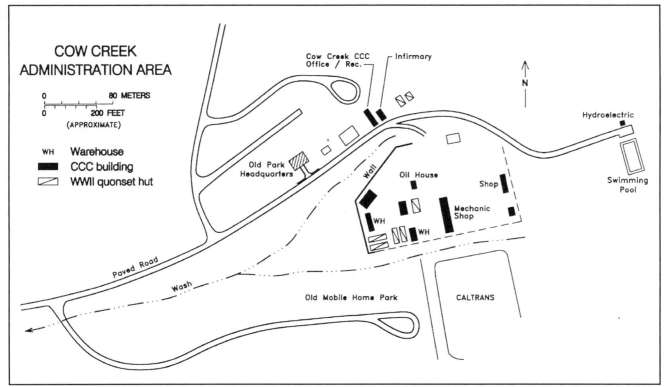

Figure 15.25. Cow Creek Administration Area, Death Valley National Park.

men from the Tule Lake Center who had refused to answer the WRA's loyalty questionnaire were arrested. The men were held at the Tulelake CCC Camp, as well as at local jails. Some were later returned to the Tule Lake Relocation Center, but many were transferred to other facilities run by the Justice Department and the U.S. Army (Turner 1982). The second group of Japanese Americans housed at the Tule Lake CCC Camp arrived in October 1943 when evacuee farm workers at the Tule Lake Relocation (Segregation) Center went on strike. To break the strike the administration brought in 234 Japanese Americans from other relocation centers who received higher wages to harvest crops. For their protection, the workers were housed outside the relocation center at the CCC camp.

The Tulelake CCC Camp (designated BF-3), built between 1935 and 1938, included 30 buildings (Figures 15.26 and 15.27). All of the buildings were wood frame with board and batten siding. The administration, barracks, mess hall, and hospital were grouped around a courtyard, with the service area and related structures to the south. Because both times the WRA used the CCC camp were of fairly short duration, it seems likely that few changes were made at the CCC camp for the evacuees.

construction, built after the fire of 1936 to be more fireproof. One building of wood frame construction has exterior walls of "novelty siding," a somewhat fancy version of clapboards popular in the late 1930s. To the east of the utility yard is the CCC-built swimming pool still in use; a nearby adobe shed built in 1939 that housed a hydroelectric generator is now used for storage.

Tulelake, California

Two different groups of Japanese American evacuees were temporarily held at a CCC camp located five mile west of the Tule Lake Relocation Center. Over several months beginning in March 1943, over 100

Figure 15.26. Tulelake CCC Camp in 1940 (Tule Lake National Wildlife Refuge).

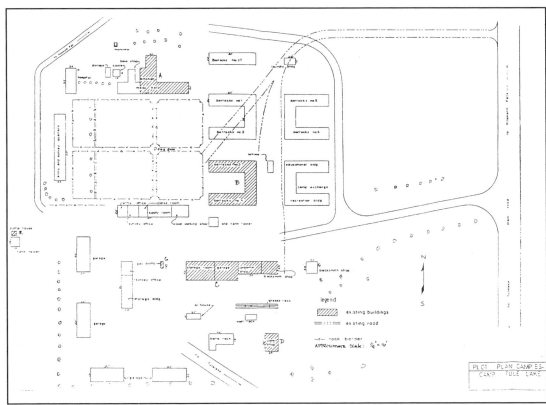

Figure 15.27. Tulelake CCC Camp, remaining buildings shaded (Tule Lake NWR).

However, alterations did occur later during World War II when the CCC camp was converted for use as a Prisoner of War (POW) camp in May 1944 (Figure 15.28). A double fence was constructed to form a compound around the barracks and mess hall. Four guard towers with searchlights were built at the corners, and a patrol road, gate, and sentry post were also added for security. The laundry building was enlarged and a latrine, septic tanks, and a sewage system were added. A guard house was built within a separately fenced area within the fenced compound. Two CCC garages, the oil house, and the water tower were removed from within the fenced compound. Outside the fenced compound two military barracks, a mess hall and kitchen, a latrine, and a new water tower were added.

About 150 Italian POWs lived in tents while setting up the POW camp, while their guards were housed in a high school gym in the nearby town of Tulelake. The Italians were shipped out and in June 250 German POWs arrived. The POW camp reached its peak population, of 800, by October. The POWs were used by local farmers and by the Bureau of Reclamation to clear area canals of moss and algae (Figure 15.29).

In May 1946 the camp was turned over to the Fish and Wildlife Service. Some of the buildings were moved for use elsewhere, but most of the buildings were razed as they were considered unsafe. Three barracks moved to the Sacramento National Wildlife Refuge in 1949 have since been destroyed as well (Pinger n.d.).

Today five of the original CCC buildings which were used by the WRA remain at the site (Figure 15.30, see also Figure 15.27). The buildings, which include the mess hall and kitchen, a barracks, a garage, a paint shop, and a pump house, are presently abandoned and in poor condition (Figures 15.31-15.33). The mess hall/kitchen and paint shop have concrete slab foundations. The western section of the mess hall and kitchen was removed when the building was converted into a living quarters. The U-shaped barracks was converted for use as a sign shop. The garage has undergone no major alterations, but the pump house was completely rebuilt in 1952. The paint shop was converted to a lumber drying shed in 1963, and now has sheet metal

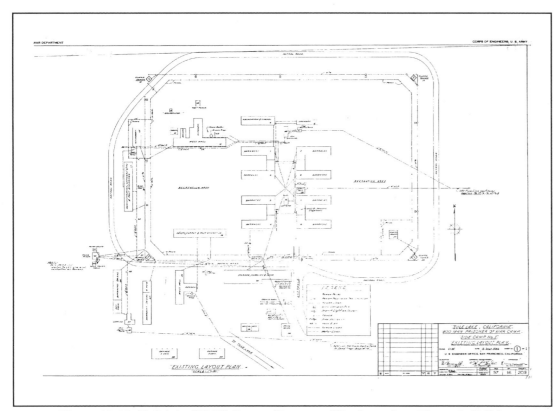

Figure 15.28. Tulelake POW Camp (Bureau of Reclamation, Klamath Falls).

Figure 15.29. German POWs held at Tulelake take a break from work to pose for a group photograph (Bureau of Reclamation, Sacramento).

Figure 15.30. Overview of the Tulelake CCC Camp today.

Figure 15.31. Mess hall/kitchen at the Tulelake CCC Camp today.

Figure 15.32. Barracks building at the Tulelake CCC Camp today.

Figure 15.33. Garage at the Tulelake CCC Camp today.

Figure 15.34. Scattered lumber at the Tulelake CCC Camp, remaining buildings in background.

siding. The other buildings appear to retain their original wood board-and-batten siding.

In addition to the buildings, there is a 1930s gas pump, with two posts and a partial roof (Pinger n.d.). The site is 2 miles south of State Highway 161 on land now within the Tule Lake National Wildlife Refuge. A barbed wire range fence prevents public access to the buildings. Other than the standing buildings there is little evidence of CCC or World War II-era features (Figure 15.34). According to Dave Menke of the Tule Lake National Wildlife Refuge staff, the current plan is to demolish the remaining buildings.

Chapter 16

Assembly Centers

Although Executive Order 9066 authorized the evacuation of all persons of Japanese ancestry from the West Coast, at the time it was signed there was no place for the Japanese Americans to go. When voluntary evacuation proved impractical, the military took over full responsibility for the evacuation: on April 9, 1942, the Wartime Civilian Control Agency (WCCA) was established by the military to coordinate the evacuation to inland relocation centers. However, the relocation centers were far from ready for large influxes of people. For some, there was still contention over the location; for most, their placement in isolated undeveloped areas of the country exacerbated problems of building infrastructure and housing. Since the Japanese Americans who lived in the restricted zone were perceived to be too dangerous to go about their daily business, the military decided it was necessary to find temporary "assembly centers" to house the evacuees until the relocation centers could be completed.

The assembly centers would require open space for housing, the immediate availability of water and power, and a geographic context that would make it easy to confine and separate the evacuees from the general population. In addition, to expedite the evacuation and eventual transfer to the relocation centers, facilities had to be centrally located with access to roads and railroads. Within 28 days, 17 assembly centers were prepared for use. Nine were at fairgrounds, two were at horse racetracks (Santa Anita and Tanforan, California), two were at migrant workers camps (Marysville and Sacramento, California), one was at a livestock exposition hall (Portland, Oregon), one was at a mill site (Pinedale, California), and one was at an abandoned Civilian Conservation Corps camp (Mayer, Arizona). In addition, the "reception centers" under construction near Parker Dam in Arizona (Poston) and in the Owens Valley of eastern California (Manzanar), originally set up to expedite the voluntary evacuation, were also employed as assembly centers. Both would later be designated relocation centers as well.

The assembly centers were surrounded by barbed wire fences. Armed military police, housed in a separate compound, patrolled the perimeter. Existing structures were adapted for use as offices, infirmaries, warehouses, and mess halls. At the racetracks, stables were cleaned out for use as living quarters and at the Portland Assembly Center over 3,800 evacuees were housed under one roof in a livestock pavilion subdivided into apartments. However, housing for the most of the evacuees consisted of hastily constructed "Theater of Operations"-type barracks buildings grouped into blocks with separate communal bathrooms and dining halls.

Most of the barracks were built directly on the ground or supported by wooden foundation blocks; 2- by 4-inch floor joists supported wooden floors. In a few assembly centers, some barracks had concrete or asphalt floors. Walls were made of horizontal boards covered with 30 lb. felt or one-ply roofing paper. Gable roofs (or shed roofs as at the Puyallup Assembly Center) were constructed with 2- by 4-inch rafters sheathed with boards and a single layer of roofing. The barracks buildings were divided into 20 ft by 20 ft rooms with wooden partition walls extending from the floor to the top of the outside wall line, leaving open a space above the interior walls to the roof. Each room had one door and two or more windows (American Red Cross 1942).

Beginning May 26, 1942, some 500 evacuees a day were transferred from the assembly centers to the relocation centers. Slowed by construction delays at the relocation centers and the lack of certain supplies (DeWitt 1943), transfers dragged on over a five-month period and were not completed until October 30, 1942.

Fresno Assembly Center, California
The Fresno Assembly Center was located at the Fresno County Fairgrounds. Occupied from May 6 to October 30, 1942, it was the last assembly center to close. It held a total of 5,344 evacuees (with a

Figure 16.1. Oblique aerial view of the Fresno Assembly Center (from DeWitt 1943).

Figure 16.2. Grandstand at the Fresno County Fairgrounds today.

maximum of 5,120 at a time) from the central San Joaquin Valley and Amador County. Over 100 barracks served by six sets of communal buildings were located within the infield of the fairgrounds racetrack, and four contiguous blocks with 20 barracks each were located adjacent to the fairgrounds (Figure 16.1).

There are no assembly center remains or any historical marker at the site. Most of the fairgrounds has been changed so extensively from its 1942 appearance that it is difficult to determine whether any fair buildings present during the assembly center use still remain (Figure 16.2).

Marysville Assembly Center, California

The Marysville Assembly Center was located at a migrant workers' camp about 8 miles south of Marysville. It was also known as the Arboga Assembly Center after the nearby small community of the same name. Occupied from May 8 to June 29, the assembly center housed a total of 2,465 evacuees (2,451 maximum at a time) from Placer and Sacramento counties. In July, soldiers occupied the center (*Marysville Appeal-Democrat* 7/16/1942).

Construction was begun March 27 and the center was considered ready for occupancy by April 16. However, the arrival of the evacuees was delayed: late rains had left pools of water and rough roads necessitating further grading and filling. The assembly center had 160 buildings, including 100 barracks, five dining halls, and two infirmary buildings (Figure 16.3). There were 15 fire hydrants and the military police had their own barracks and headquarters just outside the entrance (*Marysville Appeal-Democrat* 5/4/1942).

Today the assembly center site lies south of Broadway one-quarter mile east of Feather River Boulevard, northwest of the Lake Golf and County Club (Figure 16.4). The area is now privately owned farm

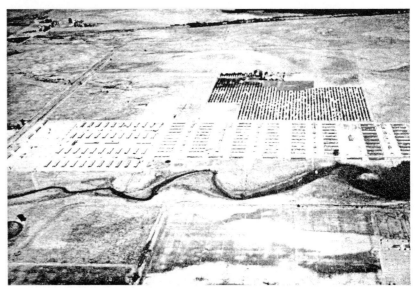

Figure 16.3. Oblique aerial view of the Marysville Assembly Center (from DeWitt 1943).

fields and residences and there is no historical marker at the site (Figure 16.5). The assembly center site itself lies on two properties, with two separate owners.

Most of the assembly center site is encompassed in the northern parcel along Broadway. On that property there is a single house and associated sheds, none of which appear to be from the World War II era. There is also a silted-over 25- by 30-foot slab of uncertain age and some scattered pipe and concrete in the field area, and exposed pipes and concrete rubble along the bank of Clark Slough on the western edge of the site (Figure 16.6). Frank Makamura of Marysville, who had been interned at the assembly center, indicated that the Japanese American Citizen's League had an interest in placing a plaque on the property but had been unable to get agreement from the owner. The property owner has since passed away, and at the time of this report, the property was for sale.

353

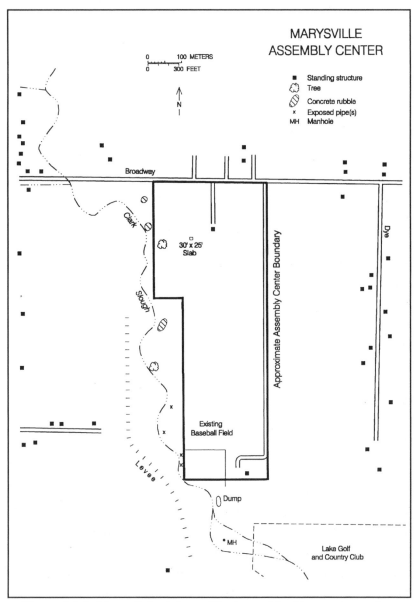

Figure 16.4. Map of the Marysville Assembly Center site today.

Figure 16.5. Site of the Marysville Assembly Center today.

The 1942 aerial photograph indicates that barracks and other buildings were also located on the second parcel, located to the south. According to that property owner, old water pipes were dug up when he recently built his house (Nathan Mayo, Personal Communication, 1996). Also on the southern property, just south of the original assembly center boundary, there are small trash scatters likely related to the assembly center. These include a small area adjacent to the slough with about 250 small fragments of white and buff hotel ware ceramics, some of which have the U.S.Q.M.C. base mark indicating army-issue (Figures 16.7 and 16.8). In the dry slough bank just west of the ceramics were noted 30 sanitary seal cans, a rubber boot sole, over 20 amber and clear glass fragments, and a few white glass fragments. Additional trash may be buried and the area may have been the assembly center dump.

Later trash (post-1950) is also present nearby, including over 40 church-key opened steel beverage, sanitary seal, and condensed milk

Figure 16.6. Concrete rubble at the site of the Marysville Assembly Center.

Figure 16.7. Hotel ware ceramics at the site of the Marysville Assembly Center.

cans, a bed frame, and a clear round whiskey bottle base embossed with a 1951 date code.

The World War II-era deposit is significant in that it is the only known assembly center dump. In fact, it may be the only assembly center dump still extant: the urban setting of most of the assembly centers suggests trash deposits must have been destroyed by later development or the trash may have been originally hauled off to local city dumps. Excavation and analyses may provide interesting comparisons with later relocation center dumps.

Mayer Assembly Center, Arizona

The Mayer Assembly Center, 75 miles northwest of Phoenix, utilized a former Civilian Conservation Corps (CCC) camp identified as Camp F-33-A. With only 245 people, it had the smallest population of any assembly center, and also the shortest occupation, May 7 to

Figure 16.8. Hotel ware ceramics at the site of the Marysville Assembly Center.

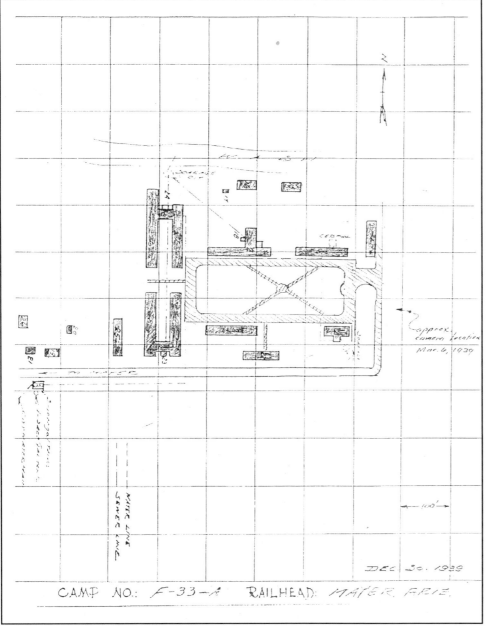

Figure 16.9. Map of CCC Camp No. F-33-A, Mayer, Arizona, 1939 (Prescott National Forest files).

June 2. All of the evacuees were from southern Arizona.

A July 1941 inventory of the CCC camp lists 26 buildings, including four 50-person barracks, a headquarters, a mess hall, an officers quarters, a recreation hall, two garages, a warehouse, a supply building, a blacksmith shop, a school building, an oil house, a shop, an infirmary, two bath houses, two pit latrines, and a flush toilet (Figures 16.9 and 16.10). Before the CCC camp was built, the land had been previously used for farming.

All of these buildings were likely still present when the assembly center opened May 7, 1942. A newspaper article reported that the evacuees were "establishing gardening and [a] recreational facility" prior to being transferred to the Poston Relocation Center (*Prescott Evening Courier* 6/5/42).

Nothing remains of the assembly center today; State Highway 69 from Phoenix to Prescott crosses the site of the assembly center at the current town of Mayer (Figure 16.11). Construction of the highway, along with stores, restaurants, offices, and other businesses, have obliterated all traces of the assembly center. However, local residents confirmed the location of the CCC Camp and that the evacuees did have gardens while they were there.

Merced Assembly Center, California

The Merced Assembly Center, in the central San Joaquin Valley, was within the town of Merced at the

Figure 16.10. CCC Camp No. F-33-A, Mayer, Arizona, 1939 (Sharlot Hall Museum Library/Archives, Prescott, Arizona).

Figure 16.11. Site of the Mayer Assembly Center today.

Figure 16.12. Oblique aerial view of the Merced Assembly Center (from DeWitt 1943).

county fairgrounds. Occupied from May 6 to September 15, it housed a total of 4,669 people (with a maximum of 4,508 at one time) from the northern California coast, west Sacramento Valley, and the northern San Joaquin Valley. Historical photographs show about 200 buildings at the assembly center, most located south of the fairgrounds proper (Figure 16.12).

A State of California historical marker is located at the main pedes-

trian entrance to the fairgrounds (Figure 16.13). Some fair buildings visible on the 1942 aerial photograph may remain, but there have been extensive changes at the site. Behind (south of) the fairgrounds the former barracks area is now a gravel parking lot. Eleven concrete foundations there may be from the assembly center: the slabs are in poor condition, but most measure approximately 20 ft by 100 ft, the

Figure 16.13. Monument at the Merced County Fairgrounds.

Figure 16.14. Concrete slabs at the Merced County Fairgrounds.

standard barracks size (Figures 16.14 and 16.15). Concrete floors for temporary barracks were unusual, if not unique, given the assembly centers' hasty construction. The only relocation center with concrete barracks floors was Granada, where, coincidentally, the internees at Merced were transferred.

Pinedale Assembly Center, California

This assembly center was located 8 miles north of downtown Fresno on vacant land near an existing mill-workers housing area (Figure 16.16). The area is now within the Fresno city limits, north of Herndon Road 1 mile west of Blackstone Avenue.

Occupied from May 7 to July 23, the Pinedale Assembly Center housed a total of 4,823 evacuees, with a maximum of 4,792 at a time. The evacuees were from Sacramento and El Dorado counties, and

Figure 16.15. Concrete slab at the Merced County Fairgrounds.

Oregon and Washington. Ten barracks blocks, each with 26 buildings, were constructed for the evacuees, and a separate block was built for the military police and administration.

The large industrial/warehouse complex visible in the 1942 aerial photograph is still present, which provided confirmation of the assembly center location (Figure 16.17). However, the site of the assembly center is now a subdivision; the architectural style and mature vegetation suggest the housing development dates to the 1950s or 1960s (Figure 16.18). There is no historical marker at the site. Subdivision roads appear to generally follow the assembly center roads.

Pomona Assembly Center, California

The Los Angeles County Fairgrounds (Fairplex) was the site of the Pomona Assembly Center. There is no historical marker at the site. Used from May 7 to August 24, the assembly center held a total of

Figure 16.16. Oblique aerial view of the Pinedale Assembly Center (from DeWitt 1943).

5,514 persons, with a maximum population of 5,434 at one time.

Evacuees confined at Pomona were from Los Angeles, San Francisco, and Santa Clara counties. Over 300 barracks were constructed at the center, along with eight H-shaped buildings with combined bathroom, shower, and laundry facilities (Figures 16.19 and 16.20). Four baseball fields are visible on the 1942 aerial photograph.

The grandstand and other fair buildings on the 1942 aerial photograph remain (Figure 16.21). The barracks area of the assembly center is now used for the fair midway, other events, and parking. Eight stable buildings are in the same location as on the aerial photograph. Since they are constructed of metal and somewhat modern looking, these may not be the same stables in use at the time of the assembly center. Further, although evacuees were housed in stables at Santa Anita and Tanforan, it is not clear if stables at other assembly centers were used for housing, too. Currently people caring for the horses live in small

Figure 16.17. Warehouses near the site of the Pinedale Assembly Center.

Figure 16.18. Site of the Pinedale Assembly Center today.

Figure 16.20. Pomona Assembly Center (National Archives Photograph).

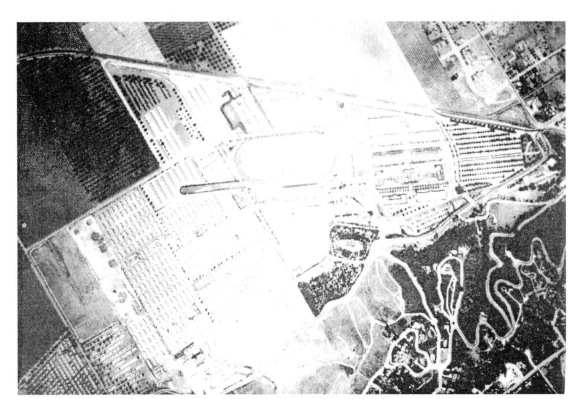

Figure 16.19. 1942 aerial photograph of the Pomona Assembly Center (from DeWitt 1943).

Figure 16.21. Grandstand at the Los Angeles County Fairgrounds (Fairplex) today.

Figure 16.22. Former barracks building at the Los Angeles County Fairgrounds (Fairplex).

housing units at the ends of the stables.

One current building at the fairgrounds looks like those built by the military for the assembly center (Figure 16.22). The 20 foot by 100 foot building was likely moved to its present location from elsewhere within the fairgrounds, since no building is shown in this location on the 1942 aerial photograph. It appears to be only slightly modified. Two towers near the Fairplex racetrack and stables do not appear to be guard towers remaining from the assembly center use. Their great height, small windows, and metal superstructure suggest that if they were they have been greatly modified (Figure 16.23).

Portland Assembly Center, Oregon

The Portland Assembly Center was centered around the 11-acre Pacific International Livestock Exposition Pavilion. A total of 4,290 people from northeast Oregon and central Washington were interned there

Figure 16.23. Racetrack media tower at the Los Angeles County Fairgrounds (Fairplex).

Figure 16.24. Oblique aerial view of the Portland Assembly Center (from DeWitt 1943).

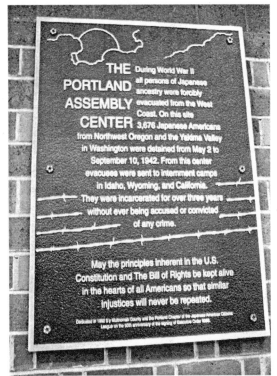

Figure 16.25. Historical marker inside the Portland Exposition Center.

Figure 16.26. Portland Assembly Center (National Archives photograph).

Figure 16.27. Portland Exposition Center today.

Figure 16.28. Portland Assembly Center (National Archives photograph).

Figure 16.29. Interior of the Portland Exposition Center.

between May 2 and September 10, 1942. Over 3,800 evacuees were housed under one roof in the pavilion, which was subdivided into apartments, a kitchen, and dining hall. Outlying buildings included a hospital, a laundry, other support facilities, and the military police compound. The North Portland Harbor, a branch of the Columbia River, is just north of the assembly center (Figure 16.24).

The assembly center site, now the Portland Exposition Center, is in nearly continuous use with trade shows, exhibits, and other events. A memorial plaque in the entrance lobby on the east side of the pavilion describes the role of the center in World War II (Figure 16.25). The front column facade at the original entrance on the north side of the pavilion has been removed. The north entrance is now for emergency use only, since it opens directly onto Marine Drive, a busy multi-lane road (Figures 16.26 and 16.27).

World War II-era photographs of the assembly center dining hall show the current ceiling trusses and columns, which have since been painted black (Figures 16.28 and 16.29). The assembly center buildings surrounding the exposition hall are gone, replaced by asphalt parking lots for exhibitors and the general public. Quonset huts visible in the aerial photograph are gone as well, replaced by more parking lots. Where support buildings once stood, west of Force Avenue, there are now stockyards for farm animal exhibitions.

Puyallup Assembly Center, Washington

Used from April 28 to September 12, 1942, the Puyallup Assembly Center was located in a small rural community about 35 miles south of Seattle. Also known as "Camp Harmony," the assembly center was built on the grounds and surrounding acres of the Western Washington State Fairgrounds. In addition to the usual stables, racetrack, and other buildings common at the other assembly centers, there was a rollercoaster (Figure 16.30). The assembly center housed a total of

Figure 16.30. Oblique aerial view of the Puyallup Assembly Center (from DeWitt 1943).

7,628 Japanese American evacuees from Washington and Alaska, with a maximum of 7,390 at a time.

Construction of the assembly center, which would effectively double the city's population, was reported as a major event in the local paper:

"With a suddenness that marks all U.S. military moves these days, construction of housing facilities on a scale large enough to accommodate 8,000 Japanese was begun Saturday morning on the 40 acre parking lot of the Western Washington Fair here, after an order for building the project had been given out by the army officers just a few hours previously. Approximately 1,000 men are now employed on the job, which has been ordered completed within a month. Yesterday afternoon more than 40 of the 15 by 40 foot buildings were nearly completed. According to one source,

Figure 16.31. Sculpture at the Puyallup Fairgrounds.

approximately 165 such structures will be needed to house evacuated Japanese who will be brought here from areas designated by the army." (*Puyallup Press*, 4/3/42).

Another contemporary observer was not impressed with the quality of construction or design:

"At the Puyallup fairgrounds ... all was a madhouse of swarming carpenters. Boxlike buildings were being

Figure 16.32. Commemorative plaque at the Puyallup Fairgrounds.

thrown together on a large field that was formerly the parking lot. First the grass was scraped off the surface of the field with steam shovels. Then 2 by 4s were laid on the ground and planks nailed onto them. Then walls with one tiny window every twenty feet in the rear wall, no windows on the side, and a small door (no window in it) at the front. Over all a tarpaper roof. There will be approximately 40 rows of these rabbit hutches. Four hutches to a row, six rooms to a hutch. Each room is about 20 feet square and separated from the next room by a partition that runs up

Figure 16.33. View from the grandstand of barracks at the Puyallup Assembly Center (National Archives photograph).

Figure 16.34. View from the grandstand at the Puyallup Fairgrounds today.

Figure 16.35. Cover of the Souvenir Edition of the Camp Harmony Newsletter (University of Washington, Special Collections).

Figure 16.36. Wooden frame roller coaster at the Puyallup Fairgrounds today.

part way to the roof. Each room is to house a Japanese family. If there is an average of 5 persons to a family, our arithmetic says 4800 people will be living in these boxes this summer." (Conard 1942).

Barracks filled all available space at the fairgrounds, including beneath the grandstand, within the circle of the racetrack, and in parking lots that extended into adjacent neighborhoods. The assembly center was divided into four distinct and separate areas designated Districts A-D. Movement between the districts, which were divided by fences, was restricted. District A was the first to open and housed about 2,000 people, District B housed 1,200, District C housed 800, and District D, which included the racetrack, administration, and bachelor's barracks, housed 3,000.

The assembly center site, still used as a fairgrounds, is in continual use for exhibits, trade shows, and concerts, as well as the annual Puyallup Fair. The fairground administration building is in the same location as in the 1940s, but is apparently recent as the current building is much larger and taller. A sculpture and two plaques in a courtyard outside the fair administration building honor the evacuees (Figures 16.31 and 16.32). The plaques, on a short concrete pedestal, indicate the monument was dedicated by the governor and lists contributors. The sculpture, by George Tsutakawa, is a steel cylinder about 10-foot high which depicts several human figures. Within the fairgrounds the barracks and horse racetrack are gone. The grandstand burned in the 1970s, and was replaced by the present concrete and steel grandstand. The infield now has a covered stage for shows and concerts (Figures 16.33 and 16.34).

Other former barracks areas outside the fairgrounds, now parking lots, show no evidence of their former use. The southern end of the original site, where the assembly center hospital was located, is now completely obliterated by State Highway 512. The grading to accommodate this freeway-sized multi-lane road changed the topography completely. The wooden frame roller coaster, along the western boundary of the fairgrounds next to 5th Street, is still in use (Figures 16.35 and 16.36).

Sacramento Assembly Center, California

Constructed at a migrant workers camp 15 miles northeast of downtown Sacramento, this assembly center was also known as Walerga. It was occupied for 52 days, from May 6 to June 26, and held a total of 4,770 persons, with a maximum at one time of 4,739. Evacuees were from Sacramento and San Joaquin counties. Aerial photographs indicate there were 11 blocks with over 225 buildings (Figures 16.37 and 16.38); one block was likely devoted to the military police and administration.

Figure 16.37. Oblique aerial view of the Sacramento Assembly Center (from DeWitt 1943).

Figure 16.39. Ramada and historical marker at Walerga Park.

Figure 16.38. Sacramento Assembly Center (National Archives photograph).

Figure 16.40. Historical marker and grove of cherry trees at Walerga Park.

Figure 16.41. Oblique aerial view of the Salinas Assembly Center (from DeWitt 1943).

Figure 16.42. Salinas Assembly Center (Clem Albers photograph, Bancroft Library, University of California, Berkeley).

The assembly center area is now bisected by Interstate 80 and covered by recent housing subdivisions in what is now the "Foothill Farms-North Highlands" area of Sacramento. There is a historical marker, a ramada, and a small grove of cherry trees at a small neighborhood park and playground (Walerga Park) at the northwest corner of Palm Avenue and College Oak Drive, within what once was the assembly center (Figure 16.39). The monument incorporates a small concrete slab that may be a remnant assembly center foundation (Figure 16.40).

Salinas Assembly Center, California

Occupied from April 27 to July 4, the Salinas Assembly Center was built at a rodeo grounds at the north end of the town of Salinas. It housed a total of 3,608 evacuees from the Monterey Bay area. The maximum population at one time was 3,594. Over 165 buildings are depicted in the aerial photograph, which shows barracks to the north and east of the rodeo grounds proper, six buildings within the racetrack infield, and perimeter guard towers (Figures 16.41 and 16.42).

The site now encompasses the California Rodeo Grounds, a small neighborhood park (Sherwood Park), and the Salinas Community Center. The grandstand and auxiliary buildings present in the 1942 aerial photograph remain, but the main area of assembly center barracks is now a golf course. In the rear courtyard of the Salinas Community Center there is a State of California historical marker commemorating the assembly center and a small fenced Japanese garden (Figures 16.43 and 16.44). Another historical marker indicates that the assembly center was later used to train a Filipino army unit during World War II. The courtyard is perhaps most known for its cowboy hat sculpture "Hat in Three Stages of Landing" (Figure 16.45).

Figure 16.43. Historical marker at the site of the Salinas Assembly Center.

Figure 16.44. Japanese garden in the courtyard of the Salinas Community Center.

Figure 16.45. Two of the "Three Hats" in the courtyard of the Salinas Community Center.

Santa Anita Assembly Center, California

Located at the world-famous Santa Anita Racetrack (Figures 16.46 and 16.47), the Santa Anita Assembly Center was the longest occupied assembly center, used for 215 days, from March 27 to October 27. It was also the largest assembly center, housing a total of 19,348 persons from Los Angeles, San Diego, and Santa Clara counties, with a maximum at one time of 18,719. Those interned lived in hastily constructed barracks and in existing stables, with 8,500 in converted horse stalls (Figures 16.48 and 16.49).

The assembly center was divided into seven districts: District 1 had 21 stable buildings converted into barracks, District 2 had 20 stable building, District 3 had 19 stable buildings, District 4 had four stable buildings and 113 freshly-built military barracks, District 5 had 161 barracks, District 6 had 160 barracks, and District 7 had 155 barracks (Lehman 1970). Bachelors were housed in the grandstand building. There were six recreation buildings, six showers, six mess halls (referred to by color; Blue, Red, Green, White, Orange, Yellow), a hospital, and a laundry (Figure 16.50; *Santa Anita Pacemaker* various issues 1942). There was a large warehouse and an automobile storage yard in the

Figure 16.46. Santa Anita Assembly Center (National Archives photograph).

Figure 16.47. Construction underway at the Santa Anita Assembly Center (National Archives photograph).

Figure 16.48. Newly-constructed barracks at the Santa Anita Assembly Center (National Archives photograph).

Figure 16.49. Converting horse stalls into housing at the Santa Anita Assembly Center (National Archives photograph).

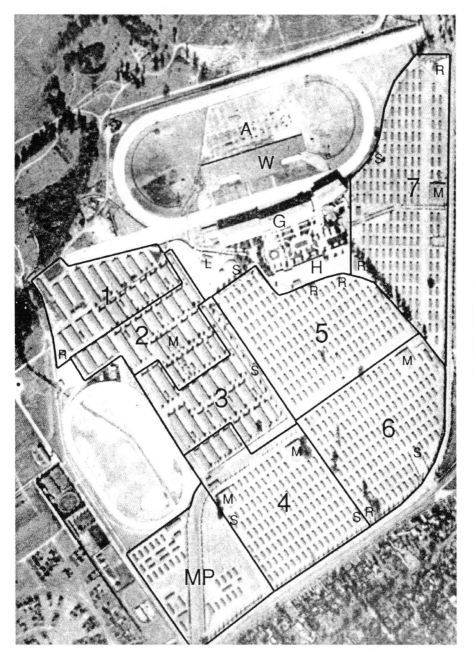

Figure 16.50. 1942 aerial photograph of the Santa Anita Assembly Center; A - automobile storage, G - grandstand (housing), H - hospital, L - laundry, M - mess hall, MP - military police and administration area, R - recreation building, S - showers, W - warehouse, 1-6 - barracks districts (adapted from DeWitt 1943).

racetrack infield and the grandstand seating area was used for a camouflage net factory which employed the Japanese Americans.

There is no historical marker at the site. The areas where the assembly center barracks had been (Districts 4-7) are now paved parking lots, and the District 3 and 4 stables and the military police compound are now a large shopping mall (Santa Anita Fashion Park). However, the massive grandstand and other racetrack buildings present in the 1940s remain (Figures 16.51 and 16.52), as do the horse stalls of Districts 1 and 2. The stables, of wood, are the same as in aerial and historical photographs (Figures 16.53 and 16.54). Security personnel at the stables mentioned that Japanese Americans occasionally return to see their former homes. There are presently as many people (stable workers and their families) as horses living in the stall area.

Figure 16.51. Santa Anita Assembly Center (National Archives photograph).

Figure 16.52. Grandstand building at the Santa Anita Racetrack today.

Figure 16.53. Stables at the Santa Anita Racetrack today.

Figure 16.54. Stable residence at the Santa Anita Racetrack today.

Figure 16.55. Oblique aerial view of the Stockton Assembly Center (from DeWitt 1943).

Figure 16.56. Stockton Assembly Center (National Archives photograph).

Figure 16.57. Historical marker at the entrance to the San Joaquin County Fairgrounds in Stockton.

Stockton Assembly Center, California

The Stockton Assembly Center was at the San Joaquin County Fairgrounds. Occupied for 161 days from May 10 to October 17, it held a total of 4,390 evacuees from San Joaquin County, with a maximum population at one time of 4,271. In the racetrack infield there were 125 barracks and another 40 barracks were on the east side of the fairgrounds (Figures 16.55 and 16.56).

No assembly center or fairground buildings visible in the 1942 aerial photograph remain, but many of the residences and businesses in the vicinity are still present. There is a State of California historical marker at the main pedestrian entrance of the fairgrounds (Figure 16.57).

Tanforan Assembly Center, California

The Tanforan Assembly Center was located at the Tanforan Racetrack in San Bruno, 12 miles south of San Francisco. Occupied from April

Figure 16.58. Oblique aerial view of the Tanforan Assembly Center (from DeWitt 1943).

Figure 16.60. Converted horse stalls and barracks at the Tanforan Assembly Center (National Archives photograph).

28 to October 13, the assembly center held 8,033 evacuees (with a maximum of 7,816 at a time) from the San Francisco Bay area. The assembly center had about 130 barracks, half within the racetrack infield. In addition, stables were used to house evacuees, as at Santa Anita (Figures 16.58-16.60).

The racetrack, opened in 1899, burned down in 1964 and the area is now a shopping mall (Tanforan Mall). At the southwest entrance of the mall there is a large statue of a racehorse and jockey and a group of historical markers (Figure 16.61). One marker has a brief description of the racetrack and assembly center (Figure 16.62). Other markers commemorate the first airplane flight from a ship, the racehorse Seabiscuit, and an early developer.

Figure 16.59. Guard tower at the Tanforan Assembly Center (National Archives photograph).

Figure 16.61. Tanforan Mall.

Figure 16.63. Oblique aerial view of the Tulare Assembly Center (from DeWitt 1943).

Figure 16.62. Historical marker at the Tanforan Mall.

Figure 16.64. Grandstand at the Tulare Fairgrounds today.

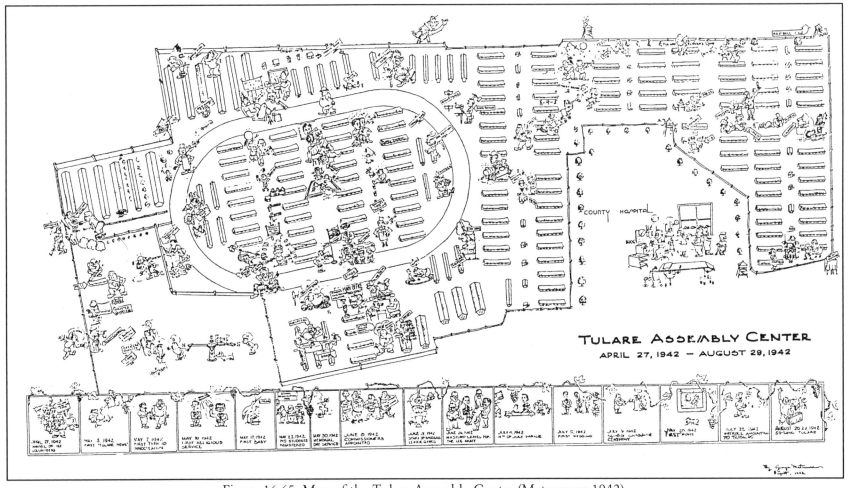

Figure 16.65. Map of the Tulare Assembly Center (Matsumare 1942).

Tulare Assembly Center, California

The Tulare Assembly Center was located in the southern San Joaquin Valley in the town of Tulare at the county fairgrounds. Occupied from April 20 to September 4, it housed 5,061 evacuees (with a maximum at one time of 4,978) from Los Angeles and Sacramento counties and the southern California coast. There were about 100 barracks within the fairgrounds proper and another 55 barracks to the south of the fairgrounds adjacent to the county hospital (Figure 16.63). There were eight mess halls and eight sets of communal buildings for bathrooms, showers, and laundries. Administration offices were in the grandstand and surrounding buildings, the assembly center hospital was northwest of the grandstand, and the military police compound was in the northern portion of the fairgrounds.

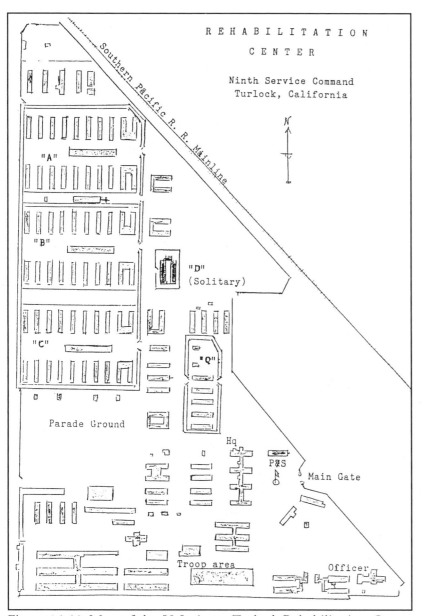

Figure 16.66. Map of the U.S. Army Turlock Rehabilitation Center (from Santos n.d.).

Figure 16.67. Oblique aerial view of the Turlock Assembly Center (from DeWitt 1943).

The grandstand and several buildings in the northeastern corner of the fairgrounds visible in the 1942 aerial photograph are still present (Figure 16.64). The buildings, larger than the barracks, were probably part of the fairgrounds originally. However, a 1942 map (Figure 16.65) confirms they were incorporated into the assembly center. No buildings or features constructed specifically for the assembly center are present, and there is no historical marker at the site.

Turlock Assembly Center, California

The Turlock Assembly Center was at the Stanislaus County Fairgrounds in the town of Turlock. Occupied from April 30 to August 12, it held a total of 3,699 evacuees from the Sacramento River delta and Los Angeles areas. The maximum population at one time was 3,662. After September 14, 1942, the assembly center was used as a U.S. Army Rehabilitation Center where army prisoners received special training and discipline prior to being restored to military duty.

A study of the rehabilitation center lists 150 barracks, 31 latrines, 18 bathhouses, a canteen, an administration building, three hospital buildings, a grandstand, single-pole guard towers, several open sheds, other structures, and a 40-acre victory garden (Figure 16.66; Santos n.d.). The 1942 aerial photograph suggests most of these facilities were also present for the assembly center (Figure 16.67 and 16.68). Oddly enough, the maximum number of army prisoners held at the facility was 1,500. More than twice as many Japanese Americans were confined in the same area, a testament to the crowded and inadequate conditions of the assembly centers.

The fair buildings visible in the 1942 aerial photograph remain, but there is no evidence of any assembly center structures, and no historical marker at the site (Figure 16.69). There are a few possible remodeled barracks to the south of the fairgrounds in an adjoining housing development.

Figure 16.68. Turlock Assembly Center (National Archives photograph).

Figure 16.69. Entrance of the Stanislaus County Fairgrounds in Turlock.

Chapter 17

Department of Justice and U.S. Army Facilities

Most Japanese Americans interned during World War II were held in facilities run by the War Relocation Authority (WRA) and Wartime Civilian Control Agency (WCCA) described in previous chapters. However, other facilities were also used to imprison Japanese Americans during the war. In all, over 7,000 Japanese Americans and Japanese from Latin America were held in internment camps run by the Department of Justice and the U.S. Army. Eight of these facilities were visited for this project.

After the attack on Pearl Harbor and prior to Executive Order 9066 on February 19, 1942, about 4,000 individuals from all over the U.S. were detained by the FBI. Over half of these were Japanese immigrants who were long-term U.S. residents denied U.S. citizenship by discriminatory laws. These Issei, now classified as "enemy aliens," were first sent to temporary detention stations, then transferred to locations known generally as "Justice Department Camps." The camps were run by the Immigration and Naturalization Service, part of the Department of Justice. After hearings, most of the Issei were then sent to U.S. Army internment camps where they remained through May 1943. After that time the internees were returned to Department of Justice control for the duration of the war.

Published literature provides few details about the Japanese American experiences at these facilities. Weglyn (1976:176) notes that most of the U.S. Army and Department of Justice internment camps were considered temporary, and even a complete listing of the camps and internees is not available. Weglyn collected information on the distribution of relief goods sent by the Japanese government through the Red Cross to estimate relative numbers of persons of Japanese ancestry held at various locations. However, as Weglyn notes, these camps often included not only Japanese American Issei who were long-term residents of the United States, but also persons of Japanese ancestry from Latin America.

Figure 17.1. Air view of Ellis Island, 1933 (California Museum of Photography, University of California, Riverside).

Temporary Detention Stations

The Issei who were apprehended by the FBI as soon as the U.S. entered the war were first held at various "temporary" locations prior to being sent to more permanent facilities. The temporary detention stations were located at Angel Island, San Pedro, Sharp Park, and Tuna Canyon in California, and Ellis Island, New York, East Boston, Massachusetts, Cincinnati, Ohio, and Seattle, Washington (Weglyn 1976). The two most prominent locations were the immigration stations at Ellis Island and Angel Island.

Ellis Island, a mostly artificial island of about 27 acres in Upper New York Bay, has been government property since 1808. Between 1892 and 1941 it served as the chief entry station for immigrants to the United States. During World War II it was used as a detention center to hold enemy aliens awaiting hearings. In December 1941 Ellis Island held 279 Japanese, 248 Germans, and 81 Italians, all removed from the East Coast (Figure 17.1). Thereafter several hundred detainees, mostly German and Italian nationals, were brought to Ellis Island each month. Most were transferred or released within 1 to 4 months,

Figure 17.2. Detainee barracks at the Angel Island Immigration Station (Angel Island Foundation).

however some were held for up to 2 years. In February 1944 there were only three Japanese Americans still being held there and in June 1944 only one Japanese American (Jacobs 1997). The immigration center is now run as a museum by the National Park Service.

The Angel Island immigration station is known as the "Ellis Island of the West." The 740-acre island is in the western part of San Francisco Bay. The immigration station, on the north side of the island, was opened in 1910 to handle an expected flood of European immigrants after the opening of the Panama Canal (Figure 17.2). Instead, the vast majority of immigrants were from Asia, including 175,000 Chinese and 100,000 Japanese. The immigration station was closed in 1940 after the administration building burned down. The property was then turned over to the U.S. Army, which used it as a POW processing center. For a short time one of the barracks at the facility was used to house enemy aliens. Buildings remaining at the site today include a detention barracks, two military barracks, a guard tower, a hospital building, and the power plant. Today a museum is located in the

Figure 17.3. Crystal City Internment Camp (National Archives photograph).

Figure 17.4. Housing at Crystal City (National Archives Photograph).

detention barracks. It includes a re-creation of one of the dormitories featuring some of the many poems carved into the walls by Chinese immigrants. The second floor of the barracks has several inscriptions written by Japanese and German POWs (Quan 1999). The Angel Island Immigration Station Foundation is working to preserve, renovate, and interpret the site.

Department of Justice Internment Camps

Eight internment camps run by the Department of Justice held Japanese Americans. Three of these were in Texas, two were in New Mexico, and one each was in Idaho, Montana, and North Dakota. Most of these facilities held only men, but Seagoville in Texas housed single women and families, and Crystal City, also in Texas, held families. Kooskia, in Idaho, was a highway construction camp. All of these facilities were guarded by Border Patrol agents, rather than military police as at the relocation and assembly centers.

Crystal City, Texas

The Crystal City facility, located next to a town of the same name, was originally a Farm Security Administration migratory labor camp for

2,000 people. When it was converted to an internment camp, Crystal City was expanded to house 3,500 people, and a fence and guard towers were added (Figure 17.3). Internee facilities included apartments with shared bathrooms, three-room cottages, and one-room shelters, all within a 290-acre area (Walls 1987; Figure 17.4).

Although the internment camp was originally intended only for persons of Japanese ancestry and nationality, 35 German aliens and their families were the first to arrive, in December 1942. The German imprisonment (and that of one Italian family) at Crystal City was to be temporary while other facilities were being prepared for them. These first internees helped in the construction at the Crystal City camp. The first Japanese U.S. resident aliens arrived at Crystal City in March 1943. Rather than relocate the Germans the camp was divided into separate sections for each ethnic group.

The peak population of the Crystal City camp was around 4,000, of whom two-thirds were of Japanese ancestry. About 600 of these were from Hawaii and 660 from Peru. Because of the unwilling presence of the Japanese Peruvians, the camp was not closed until late 1947. The Peruvian government did not want the Japanese Peruvians returned, most did not want to go to Japan, and the U.S. government who brought the Japanese Peruvians to the U.S. claimed they were illegal immigrants who could not be released. Eventually the Japanese Peruvians left for jobs at Seabrook Farms in New Jersey, as many Japanese Americans had done previously.

Today the town of Crystal City has grown around the internment camp site, which is now owned by the school district. A local landmark present during the internment still stands, though it has been moved from the town park to the town hall (Figures 17.5 and 17.6). This statue of the cartoon character Popeye was erected in 1932 as a symbol of the self-proclaimed "Spinach Capital of the World."

At the internment camp site there are three schools, athletic fields, a small airport, city social services buildings, and a recently built low-income housing project on the site. A monument commemorating the internment, a large engraved granite block (Figures 17.7 and 17.8), is located on a former cottage foundation. There are five other cottage foundations in the immediate area (Figure 17.9). Other possible camp remains at the site include a few scattered foundations (Figure 17.10), a well (Figure 17.11), and some road alignments.

An elementary school building is in the same location and in the same configuration as the former German internee elementary school (Figure 17.12). One of the more interesting features remaining is that of the camp's large concrete swimming pool, now filled in with dirt and overgrown with vegetation (Figures 17.13 and 17.14). Access to the eastern portion (rear) of the camp site is restricted by the airport and private land. This area would have likely had the hog farm, landfill, and sewage disposal facilities, as well as a picnic area known to be on the nearby Nueces River.

Figure 17.5. Popeye monument in 1939 (Russell Lee photograph, Library of Congress).

Figure 17.6. Popeye monument today.

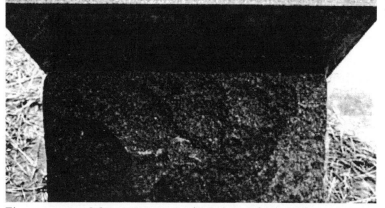

WORLD WAR II
CONCENTRATION CAMP
1943 — 1946

DUE TO CIRCUMSTANCES BEYOND THEIR CONTROL AND CONSEQUENCES OF A WAR BETWEEN THE UNITED STATES AND JAPAN, PEOPLES OF JAPANESE ANCESTRY, BOTH NATIONALS AND U.S. CITIZENS ALIKE WERE ARBITRARILY AND WITHOUT JUSTIFICATION, INCARCERATED IN A CONCENTRATION CAMP AT THIS LOCATION DURING WORLD WAR II.

THIS MARKER IS SITUATED ON AN ORIGINAL FOUNDATION OF A TWO-FAMILY COTTAGE AS A REMINDER THAT THE INJUSTICES AND HUMILIATIONS SUFFERED HERE AS A RESULT OF HYSTERIA, RACISM AND DISCRIMINATION NEVER HAPPEN AGAIN.

DEDICATED BY THE SONS, DAUGHTERS, AND FRIENDS OF THE FAMILIES WHO WERE DETAINED IN THIS CAMP, WITH THE COOPERATION OF THE CITY OF CRYSTAL CITY AND THE CRYSTAL CITY INDEPENDENT SCHOOL DISTRICT.

NOVEMBER 1985

Figure 17.7. Monument at the site of the Crystal City Internment Camp.

Figure 17.8. Overview of monument and slab foundations at the Crystal City Internment Camp.

Figure 17.9. Foundation of three-room cottage at the Crystal City Internment Camp.

Figure 17.10. Concrete slab at the site of the Crystal City Internment Camp.

Figure 17.11. Well and concrete slab at the site of the Crystal City Internment Camp.

Figure 17.12. Elementary school at the former location of the Crystal City Internment Camp German School.

Figure 17.13. Swimming pool at the Crystal City Internment Camp (National Archives).

Figure 17.14. Remains of the concrete swimming pool at the Crystal City Internment Camp today (shallow "wading pool" end).

Figure 17.15. Kenedy Alien Internment Camp (from Walls 1987).

Figure 17.16. Residential neighborhood at the site of the Kenedy Internment Camp.

Figure 17.17. Concrete pillars at the site of the Kenedy Internment Camp.

Kenedy, Texas

The Kenedy Internment Camp originally was a Civilian Conservation Corps (CCC) camp. The adjacent town of Kenedy made a vigorous lobbying effort to bring the internment camp to Kenedy after the CCC camp was disbanded. For the internment camp, over 200 additional buildings, watchtowers, and a 10-foot-high fence were constructed on the 22-acre site (Figure 17.15). Administrative offices were across a road from the camp proper. A 32-acre vegetable farm nearby was worked by Japanese internees. German internees ran a slaughterhouse.

The first internees arrived in April 1942. These prisoners, 464 Germans, 156 Japanese, and 14 Italians, had been living in Latin America. The U.S. Government had convinced the countries of Latin America to send these people, who had retained their original citizenship, to the U.S. so they could be exchanged for Allied prisoners held by Japan. By 1943 there were about 2,000 internees at the camp. The 705 of Japanese ancestry included some long-term residents of the U.S. The internees were transferred to other facilities and the Kenedy facility was used to house German POWs in September 1944. After July 1945, Kenedy housed several hundred Japanese POWs, including the first Japanese prisoner captured in the war (from a midget submarine at Pearl Harbor).

The internment camp is mentioned on the town of Kenedy's historical marker, located downtown. The Kenedy Chamber of Commerce provides directions to the site, which is now a residential area (Figure 17.16). The local library has "POW camp" file which consists mostly of newsletters in German by a POW group and local newspaper articles about the camp. They also have a report by a local high school student on the town's history that includes information on the camp. The report indicates that not much remains of the camp except a fountain built by the Japanese civilian internees, now in a residential backyard (Garcia 1991). Next door to the property with the fountain there is some concrete rubble used for a retaining wall that may have been recycled from camp building foundations. Along the main road on the south side of the current residential area there are two short concrete pillars which are also probably from the camp (Figure 17.17). Located on either side of a road on two different properties, they likely marked the south entrance to the camp administrative area.

Kooskia, Idaho

The Kooskia facility was a highway construction camp in a remote area of north-central Idaho near the small hamlet of Lowell, 40 miles east of the town of Kooskia. The internment camp was located at an old Civilian Conservation Corps (CCC) camp on the Clearwater National Forest that had been previously converted into a prison camp. Although some of the internees held camp jobs, most of the all-male,

Figure 17.18. Caucasian staff and Japanese American internees take a break at the Kooskia Internment Camp (from Wegars 1999b).

paid internee crew were construction workers for the present U.S. Highway 12 (Lewis and Clark Highway) along the Lochsa River, between Lewiston, Idaho, and Lolo, Montana. At least 256 Japanese aliens, 24 male and three female Caucasian civilian employees, and one Japanese American interpreter lived at the Kooskia camp between May 1943 and May 1945 (Figure 17.18). The internees were from Alaska, California, Colorado, Hawaii, Idaho, Kentucky, Louisiana, Minnesota, Nevada, New York, Ohio, Oregon, Texas, Utah, and Washington, and included at least 27 from Peru, two from Mexico, and two from Panama (Gardner 1981; *Minidoka Irrigator* 5/1/43; Wegars 1999a, 1999b, personal communication, 2000).

The site of the Kooskia Work Camp is still within the Clearwater National Forest, near milepost 104 of U.S. Highway 12 and about ½

Figure 17.19. Site of the Kooskia Internment Camp today.

Figure 17.20. Concrete slab at the Kooskia Internment Camp.

mile west of Apgar campground on the north side of Canyon Creek. Very little evidence remains of the former camp (Figure 17.19). There is a 20 foot by 30 foot concrete slab from the water tank, several leveled earthen terraces, some rock features, and a few introduced tree species (Figures 17.20 and 17.21). However, the area is heavily wooded and lush, so vegetation may hide additional features. In addition, some of the rocks in recent campfire rings may have been "recycled" from camp features.

Fort Lincoln, North Dakota

Known today as the United Tribes Technical College, the one-time Fort Lincoln Internment Camp lies five miles south of Bismarck, North Dakota. The brick buildings which are presently used by the college were built in 1903 by the army as a military base. In the 1930s Fort Lincoln became the state headquarters of the CCC, which put up numerous prefabricated wooden buildings at the fort. During World

War II, the CCC barracks buildings and two brick army barracks were fenced and used to house internees (*Bismarck Tribune* 8/4/41; Vyzralek n.d.; Figures 17.22 and 17.23).

The first internees held at Fort Lincoln were Italian and German seamen who had been on Italian and German commercial ships in U.S. waters in 1939 when the war started in Europe. Eight-hundred Italians arrived in April, but soon left for Fort Missoula, Montana. Shortly after the first Japanese American Issei arrived in 1942, they were transferred to other camps, leaving the Germans the sole internees there until February 1945. At that time 650 Japanese Americans were brought in, about half of them so-called "recalcitrants" from camps at Tule Lake, California, and Santa Fe, New Mexico. These internees had renounced their American citizenship and were to be sent to Japan after the war. The rest of the new arrivals were Japanese nationals to be repatriated after the war (Fox 1996).

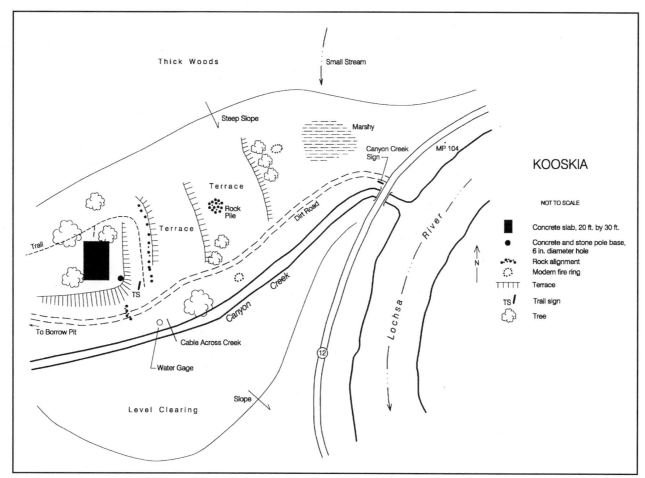

Figure 17.21. Sketch map of the Kooskia Internment Camp.

389

Within the camp the Japanese and German barracks were separated, but the internees were allowed to mingle. Use of the camp laundry was alternated, and each group had separate areas of the mess hall and kitchen, divided initially by a partition, and then only by a line on the floor. The camp hospital had fifty beds, and was staffed by two part-time Public Health Service doctors and two nurses. In addition, both the Japanese and Germans maintained their own infirmaries and dispensaries with internee doctors (Fox 1996).

After the war, Fort Lincoln was designated the headquarters for the Garrison Division of the U.S. Army Corps of Engineers, serving as the planning center for the Garrison Dam Project. The Fort was declared surplus by the U.S. Army in 1966, remodeled, and used as a Job Corps Training Center in 1968. When the Corps closed, United Tribes obtained the use of the property as its campus.

Figure 17.22. Fort Lincoln Internment Camp (from Fox 1996)

Today most of the old brick army buildings are still present, including the barracks used to house internees (Figure 17.23 and 17.24). However, all of the wooden CCC buildings have been removed and there is now married-student housing in the former soccer field and CCC barracks area (Figure 17.25). A stone entry gateway is at the college entrance along State Highway 1804, one-quarter mile south of the Bismarck Airport (Figures 17.26 and 17.27). Articles in the local newspaper indicate that some former internees have returned to visit the site (Bismarck Tribune September 27, 1979 and August 2, 1996). There is no marker or memorial at the site.

Fort Missoula, Montana

Fort Missoula is an old U.S. Army post located just outside the town of Missoula, Montana. The fort was used as a regional headquarters for the CCC in the 1930s and was turned over to the Department of Justice in 1941. Two Mission-style Army barracks and most of the CCC camp facilities were fenced for use as internee housing, and

guard towers were added (Benedetti 1997; Long 1991; Van Valkenburg 1995; Figures 17.28-17.30).

The first internees at the camp were 25 Japanese American Issei from Salt Lake City who arrived on December 18, 1941. By the end of 1941 there were 633 Issei held at the fort. By April 1942 there were 2,003 men, roughly half Japanese Americans and half Italian nationals. The average age of the Japanese Americans was 60 (Van Valkenburg 1995). Several internees died soon after their arrival, one even on his first day at Fort Missoula (Glynn 1994). All of the Issei internees were given cursory hearings and most were then transferred to other internment camps or relocation centers. During their stay a few volunteered for work on local farms. By the end of 1942 only 29 Japanese Americans were left at the fort.

After the last Japanese Americans left, the Italian national population rose to over 1,200. Like the Japanese Americans, the Italians worked on local farms, but also fought forest fires and worked in Missoula

Figure 17.23. Guard tower at the Fort Lincoln Internment Camp (from Fox 1996).

Figure 17.24. Army barracks at Fort Lincoln today.

until they were released following Italy's surrender in 1943. In March 1944, 258 persons of Japanese ancestry from Hawaii were temporarily held at Fort Missoula before being transferred to Santa Fe, New Mexico (Figure 17.33). In July 1944 the facility was officially closed.

Today the 32-acre fort is listed on the National Register of Historic Places. There are still several officers' homes along a tree-lined street and other structures at their original locations (Figure 17.32). Along U.S. Highway 93, about one mile east, the original stone entry posts remain, although the fort access road has been relocated. Within the original fenced internment area, the two large army barracks are now used by the Forest Service and the U.S. Army Reserve (Figure 17.33).

In a vacant field east of the former army barracks there are several foundations from other army buildings, manholes, and a fire hydrant, but no remnants of the CCC barracks once present (Figures

17.34-17.36). Most of the CCC barracks were torn down in the 1950s or relocated. Several were moved to the Montana State Fair in 1954 and are still in use (Van Valkenburg 1995). One has been returned to the fort museum grounds and will be used for exhibits about the internment (Historical Museum at Fort Missoula 1999; Figure 17.37). Next to the relocated barracks is a guard tower cabin and a monument dedicated to those interned without trial at the site (Figures 17.38-17.40). Both the monument and guard tower cabin were placed as Eagle Scout projects. The fort museum, the old quartermaster depot, currently has an exhibit on the internment and a second guard tower cabin.

Fort Stanton, New Mexico

Established in 1855, Fort Stanton is in an isolated portion of New Mexico, 35 miles north of Ruidoso. In 1899 the fort was transferred to the Merchant Marine for use as a tuberculosis sanatorium. During World War II the fort was used as an internment camp, mostly for

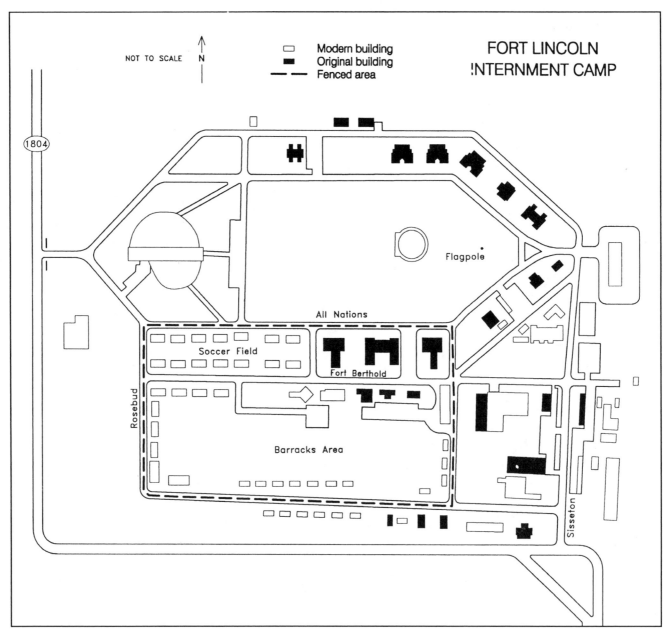

Figure 17.25. Fort Lincoln Internment Camp.

Figure 17.26. North half of stone entry gate at Fort Lincoln.

Figure 17.27. South half of stone entry gate at Fort Lincoln.

German nationals. In 1953 the fort was transferred to the State of New Mexico, which until recently used it as a minimum security women's prison.

The first internees held at the fort were the German crew of the German luxury liner Columbus which was scuttled off the coast of Cuba in 1939. Since the U.S. was not at war with Germany at the time the internees were considered "distressed seaman paroled from the German Embassy." They were housed in a deserted CCC barracks across from Fort Stanton, and cultivated a 60-acre farm. When the U.S. entered the war the Department of Justice brought in border patrol agents as guards and the barracks was surrounded with a barbed-wire fence (Banks 1998).

The Department of Justice also established a small disciplinary camp at Fort Stanton for "incorrigible agitators" which they named "Japanese Segregation Camp #1." The camp served the same function, but for non-citizens, as the citizen isolation centers at Moab and Leupp run by the WRA. Culley (1991) indicates that 58 Japanese Americans were incarcerated there. Actually only 17 Japanese aliens (six were once U.S. citizens) were interned at this camp, they were transferred to the San Pedro Detention Station in California on September 20, 1944. The other 41 alien men were Japanese American volunteers from the Santa Fe Internment Camp who, in August 1945, were transferred to Fort Stanton at the request of the Officer in Charge at Fort Stanton, to provide assistance in the crating, packing, and removal of property from that camp. They returned to Santa Fe when the work was completed in November 1945 (Tom Akashi, personal communication, 2000). The exact location of the segregation camp and whether there are any remains left is not known.

Santa Fe, New Mexico
In February 1942 the Department of Justice acquired an 80-acre site from the New Mexico State Penitentiary that included a CCC camp built in 1933 to house 450 men. By March the CCC camp was

Figure 17.28. Fort Missoula Internment Camp (from Glynn 1994).

Figure 17.29. CCC barracks at Fort Missoula (National Archives photograph).

Figure 17.30. Fenced army barracks at Fort Missoula (from Fox 1996).

Figure 17.31. Internees at Fort Missoula (from Glynn 1994).

Figure 17.32. Abandoned buildings at Fort Missoula.

Figure 17.33. Former army barracks at Fort Missoula.

Figure 17.34. Slab foundation at Fort Missoula.

Figure 17.35. Concrete post supports and slab at Fort Missoula.

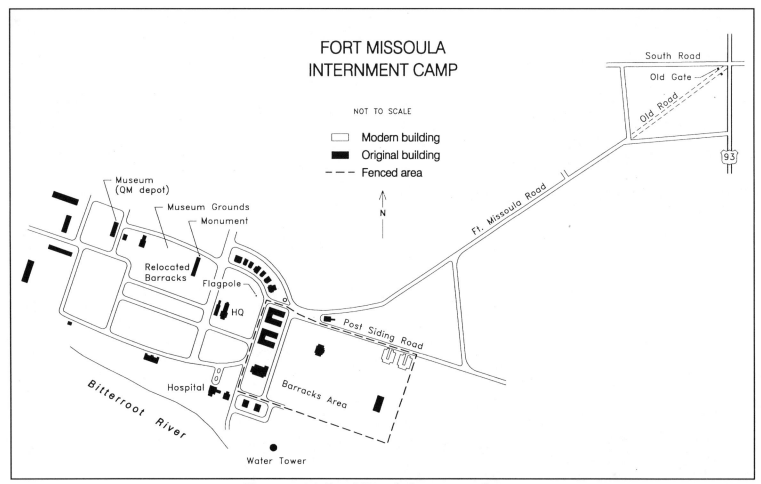

Figure 17.36. Fort Missoula Internment Camp.

Figure 17.37. Relocated CCC barracks (future exhibit building) on Fort Missoula Museum grounds.

Figure 17.38. Guard tower at Fort Missoula (from Fox 1996).

Figure 17.39. Guard tower cabin at Fort Missoula today.

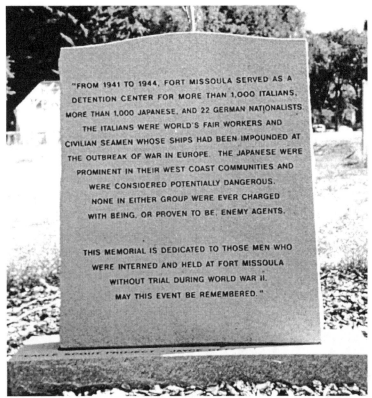
Figure 17.40. Internment monument at Fort Missoula.

back to the Department of Justice. The Santa Fe camp was then expanded and by June 1945 it held 2,100 Japanese American men whose average age was 53.

Many of the new arrivals were from the Tule Lake Segregation Center and had renounced their U.S. citizenship. This included 366 of what the government considered the most active pro-Japan leaders at Tule Lake. In March 1945 a riot at Santa Fe began when the "Tuleans" were requested to turn in their sweat shirts with rising sun motifs. After the leaders of the protest were removed to Fort Stanton, a crowd gathered, rocks were thrown, and tear gas and clubs were used to break up the crowd. Over 350 internees were put in a stockade and 17 more were sent to the Fort Stanton segregation camp. There were no further disturbances at the camp even after another 399 internees from Tule Lake arrived.

After the end of the war the Santa Fe facility was used as a holding and processing center for other internment camps. As late as March 1946, 200 Japanese American men were transferred to Santa Fe from Fort Lincoln. However, by May only 12 of these remained. The camp closed shortly thereafter and all property was sold as surplus (Thomas et al. 1994). Today the camp site is within a residential subdivision. At the Rosario Cemetery, ½ mile east of the camp site, there are graves from two Japanese American men who died during the internment (Narvot 1999a). A State History Museum committee has proposed placing a plaque paid for with private funds at Frank Ortiz City Park overlooking the site, but as of 1999 local opposition has delayed the plaque's installation (Narvot 1999b).

Seagoville, Texas
Located outside of Dallas, the Seagoville facility was originally built as a federal prison for women (Figure 17.41). In 1942 it was converted into an internment camp to house 50 female Japanese American

expanded to house 1,400 men. Housing included wood and tarpaper barracks and 100 "Victory Huts." All but 14 of the victory huts were later replaced by standard Army barracks (Culley 1991).

The camp originally held 826 Japanese American Issei, all men from California. One died at the camp, 523 were transferred to relocation centers, and 302 were transferred to U.S. Army custody. The last internee left the Santa Fe Internment Camp on September 24, 1942. The camp was then used to house German and Italian nationals until February 1943 when the U.S. Army transferred all civilian internees

Figure 17.41. Seagoville Internment Camp (from Walls 1987).

language teachers removed from the West Coast. The two-story brown brick buildings at the prison included six dormitories with 40 to 68 rooms each, an auditorium, a school, a vocational arts center, and a hospital. At first there was no fence at the camp, but later a high fence and 50 small plywood huts for family quarters were added to accommodate Japanese families brought from Latin American countries (Walls 1987). Today the facility is a low-security prison for about 850 men. The buildings retain much of the look and feel of the World War II installation.

U.S. Army Facilities

At least 14 U.S. Army facilities held Japanese Americans during World War II. Most were within the coterminous United States, but there were also four small internment camps in Hawaii and a temporary detention camp at a military base in Alaska. Only one of the U.S. Army internment camps, Camp Lordsburg in New Mexico, was built specifically for the internment of Japanese Americans. Another, at

Stringtown, Oklahoma, was at a state prison, and the remainder were located on existing military bases.

Camp Lordsburg, New Mexico

The Lordsburg Internment Camp is infamous as the location of the shooting under questionable circumstances of two critically ill Japanese American internees by a sentry on July 27, 1942 (Weglyn 1976:312). Construction of the Lordsburg camp began in February 1942. In July, 613 Japanese American Issei men were transferred to Lordsburg from the Fort Lincoln Internment Center in Bismarck, North Dakota. Eventually 1,500 Japanese were interned at the New Mexico camp. By July 1943 all of the Japanese Americans were gone and Italian POWs were brought in; up to 4,000 were held at Lordsburg between 1943 and 1945 (Thomas et al. 1994). The facility was closed by February 1946.

The internment camp site is located along "P.O.W. Road" about 3 miles east of the town of Lordsburg (Figure 17.42). The area is posted with "no trespassing" signs in both English and Spanish (Figure 17.43). There are three residences on the former camp site (Figure 17.44). The owner of one of the residences confirmed that the private property, which has three owners, was the location of the camp. The owners posted the "no trespassing" sign because people looking for camp remains had frequently wandered around without permission. The camp water tank and an adjacent water treatment building are on one property (Figures 17.45 and 17.46); an adjacent property contains a hospital building (Figure 17.47), now used as a residence and another building now used for storage (Figure 17.48). A small concrete vault-like building and a decorative U.S. seal made of pebbles embedded in concrete is on the third property (Figures 17.49 and 17.50). One of the other owners once tried to move the decorative seal to his property but the current owner of the property on which it is located objected.

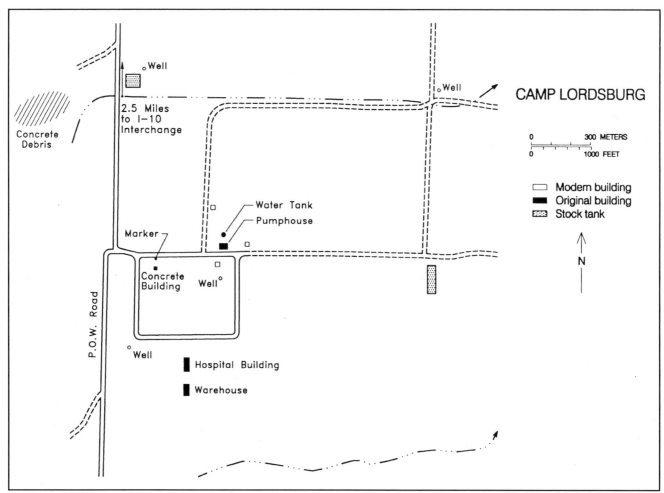

Figure 17.42. Lordsburg Internment Camp.

Figure 17.43. P.O.W. Road, Lordsburg, New Mexico.

Figure 17.44. Sign at the Lordsburg Internment Camp.

and POWs had returned to visit recently, but such visitors were more common years ago (Robert Lowery, personal communication, 1998).

Fort Sill, Oklahoma

Near Lawton, Oklahoma, Fort Sill held some 350 Japanese American Issei who had been first interned at Fort Missoula (Van Valkenberg 1995). It was at Fort Sill that a Japanese Hawaiian internee, distraught over leaving his wife and 12 children behind, was shot and killed by a guard while trying to escape. He was crying "I want to go home, I want to go home" as he climbed the barbed wire fence in broad daylight (Saiki 1982).

The Fort Sill Military Reservation is now the headquarters of the U.S. Army Field Artillery. The old fort area established in 1869 is now a National Historic Landmark. It is not clear where on the expansive military base the Japanese Americans were held, but the current fort archeologist noted that in "Area 2400" southwest of Sheridan and Hunt Roads a German POW camp was located (Spivey, personnel communication, 1999). It seems likely that the POW camp and Japanese American internment camp were one and same, as at other U.S. Army facilities. The area has been cleared for the most part and some new buildings have been constructed in the area (Figure 17.53). It is not known if slab foundations still present at the site date to the internment.

Besides the large structures, not much of the camp is left. A mining company purchased the land in the early 1970s and removed all of the foundation slabs to prepare for building a subdivision, which never materialized. Concrete rubble used for retaining walls for loading ramps at a borrow pit about ½ mile northwest of the site may have been salvaged from the camp (Figures 17.51 and 17.52). Large upturned concrete blocks at a road intersection ½ mile south of the site may have been guard tower foundations. Some former internees

Figure 17.45. Water tank and water treatment building at the site of the Lordsburg Internment Camp.

Figure 17.46. Detail of the water tank at the site of the Lordsburg Internment Camp.

Figure 17.47. Hospital building at the site of the Lordsburg Internment Camp.

Figure 17.48. Warehouse south of hospital building at the Lordsburg Internment Camp.

Figure 17.49. Small concrete building at the Lordsburg Internment Camp.

Figure 17.50. Detail of decorative seal at the Lordsburg Internment Camp.

Figure 17.51. Concrete blocks used for retaining wall northwest of the Lordsburg Internment Camp.

Figure 17.52. Concrete debris northwest of the Lordsburg Internment Camp.

Figure 17.53. Area 2400, Fort Sill, Oklahoma.

Figure 17.54. Inmate housing at the Stringtown Internment Camp today.

Stringtown, Oklahoma

A sub-prison was established on 8,000 acres of land 5 miles north of Stringtown, Oklahoma, in 1933, to relieve the overcrowding at the Oklahoma State Penitentiary. The sub-prison utilized tents and temporary buildings to house 350 inmates as they built fences, roads, towers, and barracks for the facility. In July, 1937, the prison was transformed into the Oklahoma State Technical Institute, which emphasized training inmates to be skilled workers as part of the rehabilitation process. During World War II the facility became an internment camp for enemy aliens (primarily Japanese Americans), and later it became a POW camp for German naval prisoners. Near the end of the war the facility became a state venereal disease hospital, but in 1945 it again became a sub-prison for the Oklahoma State Penitentiary. It is currently a medium security facility, the Mack Alford Correctional Center, named for its warden from 1973 to 1986 (Anonymous n.d.).

In 1988 the facility suffered a riot in which two of the three original inmate housing units were destroyed. The remaining housing unit is still used (Figure 17.54). Also still used is the administration building (Figure 17.55), chapel, gym, and other auxiliary buildings (Figure 17.56). German writing was discovered on the wall of a kitchen when it was recently torn down. Translated it reads "Why be happy, why be outside .... is our work .... life ... whoever play acts can never reckon with himself ... whoever does not ... If there be a thing more powerful than fate, it is the courage which bears it quietly ... and you are so right. The world is quite pitifully wicked and each man in it an evil doer – you and I are naturally not – you and I don't know it all."

Alaska and Hawaii

Family members of Alaskan Japanese American Issei already impris-

Figure 17.55. Administration building at the Stringtown Internment Camp today.

oned were held for a short time at Fort Richardson while enroute to the Puyallup Assembly Center in Washington. Fort Richardson is nine miles north of downtown Anchorage, Alaska.

In Hawaii, Sand Island in Honolulu was the major detention camp for the initial housing and processing of the 5,000 Japanese Americans detained under martial law (Figure 17.57). There were also small detention camps such as the Kalaheo stockade on the island of Kauai, and Haiku camp on the island of Maui. About 1,500 of those incarcerated in Hawaii were later transferred to mainland internment camps, but the majority were released. On the island of Oahu, a permanent internment camp ringed with barbed wire and guard towers was built. Named Honouliuli, it held 284 Kibei under armed guard (Saiki 1982). In November 1944 the camp was closed. Sixty-seven of the internees were then sent to the mainland, the others were paroled provided they would sign releases holding the U.S. government blameless for their incarceration (Weglyn 1976).

Figure 17.56. Guard tower at the Mack Alford Correction Center (Stringtown).

Other U.S. Army Sites

In February 1942, 170 Issei were transferred from the Sand Island Internment Camp in Hawaii to Camp McCoy, a former CCC Camp nine miles west of Tomah, Wisconsin. The internees were soon dispersed to other camps and the facility was converted into a training camp for the 100th Infantry Battalion, the all-Nisei Hawaii National Guard unit removed from Hawaii. Fort McCoy is currently used by the Wisconsin Army National Guard and a state-run "at-risk" residential youth program. Many of the original buildings remain at the site (Figure 17.58). A monument at the site commemorates its use as a training camp.

Figure 17.57. Sand Island Internment Camp (from Ogaawa and Fox 1991).

A segregated military base, Camp Forrest, Tennessee, held Japanese Hawaiians transferred from Camp McCoy. At Camp Forrest five men each were housed in small newly-built huts. Some Japanese Hawaiians and about 40 Issei from Fort Missoula were held at Fort Sam Houston along with 300 Alaskan Eskimos. Barracks were tents, surrounded by a barbed wire enclosure. After nine days the internees were transferred to Camp Lordsburg. Camp Livingston, Louisiana, held over 800 persons of Japanese ancestry (Weglyn 1976). Four hundred of these were from the West Coast, 354 were from Hawaii, and 160 were from Panama and Costa Rica.

The distribution of a small quantity of Japanese relief goods (green tea, soya, and bean mash) destined for Camp Florence, Arizona, and Fort Meade, Maryland, from the exchange ship M.S. Gripsholm in June 1942 and December 1943 suggests there were Japanese nationals being held at these two locations (Weglyn 1976).

Camp Florence opened in August 1942 to house Italian POWs. In May 1945 they were replaced by German and Austrian POWs. Designed to hold 5,000 prisoners the facility had a peak population of 13,000 guarded by 1,200 troops. No information on any Japanese held at the camp has been located. McFarland State Historical Park in Florence has a display about the camp that includes numerous photographs (John Pelton, personal communication, 2000). No further information about Fort Meade was obtained.

Figure 17.58. Camp McCoy today (from Badger Challenge 1999).

Chapter 18

Federal Bureau of Prisons

No Japanese American was ever charged and convicted of sabotage or spying during World War II. However, over a hundred Japanese Americans who sought to challenge the internment were convicted and sentenced to terms in federal prisons. These cases, highlighted in recent research (see, for example, work by Abe n.d.; Erickson 1998a, 1998b; Uyeda 1993), belie the perception that the Japanese American community passively accepted the relocation and internment.

Gordon Hirabayashi, Minoru Yasui, and Fred Korematsu challenged the government's actions in court. Minoru Yasui had volunteered for military service after the Japanese attack on Pearl Harbor and was rejected because of his Japanese ancestry. An attorney, he deliberately violated the curfew law of his native Portland, Oregon, stating that citizens have the duty to challenge unconstitutional regulations. Gordon Hirabayashi, a student at the University of Washington, also deliberately violated the curfew for Japanese Americans and disregarded the evacuation orders, claiming that the government was violating the 5th Amendment by restricting the freedom of innocent Japanese Americans (Figure 18.1). Fred Korematsu changed his name, altered his facial features, and went into hiding. He was later arrested for remaining in a restricted area (Davis 1982:118). In court, Korematsu claimed the government could not imprison a group of people based solely on ancestry.

All three lost their cases and the Supreme Court upheld the convictions of Hirabayashi and Yasui in June of 1943 and that of Korematsu in December 1944. Yasui spent several months in jail and was then sent to the Minidoka Relocation Center. Korematsu was sent to the Topaz Relocation Center while

Figure 18.1. Gordon Hirabayashi in 1942 (Seattle Times Photograph).

Figure 18.2. Trial of 63 Japanese American draft resisters from the Heart Mountain Relocation Center (from NJAHS 1995).

Figure 18.3. Draft resisters just released from McNeil Island wearing government-issued suits (from Uyeda 1993).

Figure 18.4. Japanese Americans imprisoned at the Catalina Federal Honor Camp at their first reunion in 1946 (photograph courtesy of Kenji Taguma).

awaiting trial. Hirabayashi refused bail since he then would have been sent to a relocation center; he therefore spent several months in the King County jail in Washington. After the Supreme Court decision Hirabayashi served the remaining 3 months of his sentence at the Catalina Federal Honor Camp in Arizona.

Other protests by Japanese Americans were connected with military service. When the war began, many of the Japanese Americans who were in the military were dismissed, and U.S. citizens of Japanese ancestry were classified as enemy aliens ineligible for military service. However in May 1942, the 100th Infantry Battalion was formed in Hawaii, where the majority of Japanese American residents were not interned. The prohibition against other Japanese Americans serving in the military was lifted in early 1943, and the draft was re-instated for Japanese Americans on January 20, 1944. The all-Nisei 442nd Regimental Combat Team joined the 100th Infantry Battalion in Europe in June 1944. Over 33,000 Nisei served in World War II, with over 6,000 of them in the Pacific Theater (NJAHS 1995:70, 77).

However, there were protests over the internment both within and outside the military. In March 1944, 106 Nisei soldiers at Fort McClellan in Alabama refused to undergo combat training while their families were held behind barbed wire without trial. Twenty-eight were court-martialed and sent to Leavenworth prison with sentences from 5 to 30 years (Nakagawa 1999; NJAHS 1995:76-77).

More than 300 internees refused to be drafted into the military until their constitutional rights as citizens were restored (Figures 18.2-18.4). The resisters did not object to the draft, in itself, but hoped that by defying the conscription orders they would clarify their citizenship status. If they were to share in the rights and duties of citizens, why did the government forcibly incarcerate them and their families? If their loyalty was in question, why were they being drafted?

At least two federal judges agreed with the resisters' position. Charges against 26 resisters from the Tule Lake Segregation Center were dismissed by Judge Louis Goodman, who said in his decision "It is shocking to the conscience that an American Citizen be confined on the grounds of disloyalty and then while so under duress and restraint, be compelled to serve in the Armed Forces or prosecuted for not yielding to such compulsion" (*Associated Press* 1944). Some 100 resisters from the Poston Relocation Center were fined 1 cent each, the judge deciding that the imprisonment of the relocation center itself was sufficient punishment (Weglyn 1976:303). However, other resisters were sentenced to up to 3 years in federal prisons. Young draft resisters from the Heart Mountain Relocation Center were sent to the McNeil Island Federal Penitentiary in Washington; older men were sent to the Leavenworth Federal Penitentiary in Kansas. Draft resisters from Granada and other relocation centers were sent to the Catalina Federal Honor Camp in Arizona. The draft resisters were pardoned in 1947 by President Harry S. Truman. However, the questions of whether citizens must "prove" loyalty when their rights have been revoked, and how citizens can best stand up for civil rights, have still not been resolved.

Figure 18.5. Catalina Federal Honor Camp, ca. 1945 (photograph courtesy of the Coronado National Forest).

Catalina Federal Honor Camp, Arizona

The Catalina Federal Honor Camp is located in the Santa Catalina Mountains, northeast of Tucson, Arizona. The camp was established in 1939 within the Coronado National Forest to provide prison labor to build a highway that would allow Tucson residents easier access to the cooler elevations of the mountain. In the 1940s the Honor Camp included four barracks, a mess hall, a laundry, a powerhouse, a store-

Figure 18.6. Catalina Federal Honor Camp, ca. 1945 (photograph courtesy of the Coronado National Forest).

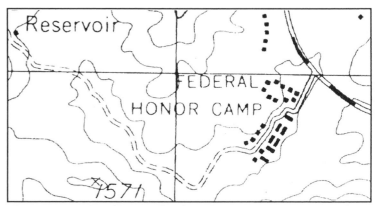

Figure 18.8. Catalina Federal Honor Camp in 1954 (from USGS Bellota Ranch, Arizona 1:50,000).

Figure 18.7. Baseball field at the Catalina Federal Honor Camp (photograph courtesy of Coronado National Forest).

Figure 18.9. Site of the Catalina Federal Honor Camp today (James A. McDonald photograph).

Figure 18.10. Rock walls near the location of the administration building at the site of the Catalina Federal Honor Camp.

room, a garage, a vocational shop, and a classroom. In addition, there was an administration building, ten masonry and five frame cottages for the prison personnel, and water supply and sewage disposal systems (Bureau of Public Roads 1951:22; Figures 18.5 and 18.6). Other facilities included a chicken and turkey farm and a baseball field (Figure 18.7). On a 10-acre farm below the mountain the inmates raised vegetables.

During World War II many of the prisoners at the Honor Camp were draft resisters and conscientious objectors. After the Supreme Court upheld his convictions for disobeying curfew and relocation orders, Gordon Hirabayashi completed his sentence there. Some 45 Japanese American draft resisters were also sent to the Honor Camp to serve their sentences. The majority of the resisters were from the Granada Relocation Center in Colorado; others came from Poston and Topaz. In contrast to Gordon Hirabayashi, who had to hitchhike from Seattle

Figure 18.11. Basement in the staff housing area at the site of the Catalina Federal Honor Camp.

Figure 18.12. Retaining wall along Soldier Canyon Creek, Catalina Federal Honor Camp.

Table 18.1. Archeological Features at the Catalina Federal Honor Camp, Coronado National Forest (keyed to Figure 18.13).

1. Rock and concrete bridge/ford.
2. Rock work and culvert.
3. Foundation remains and level area.
4. Foundation remains and level area.
5. Concrete slab.
6. Level area with an imbedded pipe.
7. L-shaped concrete trough.
8. Concrete slab.
9. Concrete and rock post foundation.
10. Concrete slab foundation.
11. Concrete box.
12. Concrete slab foundation of house.
13. Rubble.
14. Concrete valve box.
15. Floor tiles and large segment of concrete foundation.
16. Possible water tank location.
17. Rock bridge or culvert.
18. Large concrete slab.
19. Small cemented rock post (?) with iron pipe.
20. Concrete slab with pipes.
21. Concrete basketball court.
22. Volleyball or tennis court.
23. Small concrete slab.
24. Bleachers and dugout area, with inscriptions in concrete wall cap "1957," "ETO," "IGM," "MANUEL FLOREZ," "ER."
25. Subterranean structures.
26. Subterranean structures.
27. Concrete slab foundation of mess hall and kitchen.
28. Shuffleboard courts.
29. Concrete work, possibly for miniature golf.
30. Rock and concrete retaining wall.
31. Stone and concrete foundation.
32. Retaining wall with inscription "1962."
33. Concrete slabs and rock retaining wall.
34. Water pipe support posts.
35. Concrete slab.
36. Concrete and rock retaining walls.
37. Bridge support with inscription: "8-3-51."

38. Concrete slab and concrete retaining wall.
39. Concrete slab.
40. Level area/slope cut.
41. Rock-lined drainage ditch.
42. Concrete and rock foundation.
43. Concrete slab, scratched in floor: "Kidds AUG. 17, 1971 MONDAY NITE."
44. Post or tower foundation, with inscription: "May 1950."
45. Rock and concrete patio area.
46. Terraces and steps.
47. Rock work and stone tree planter in patio area.
48. Concrete slab foundation of house.
49. Concrete slab foundation of house.
50. Concrete slab foundation of house.
51. Stairway with elaborate terraced retaining walls and non-native trees. Graffiti spray painted on wall "KEITH M. 1987."
52. Main gate, rock and concrete walls.
53. Concrete slab foundation of house.
54. Concrete slab foundation of house.
55. Rock and concrete retaining walls.
56. Rock and concrete power pole support.
57. Rock and concrete power pole support.
58. Concrete slab.
59. Concrete slab.
60. Foot path.
61. Eroded area along footpath showing buried pipes (two water, one sewer).
62. Flat area with concrete slab.
63. Prehistoric bedrock metates.
64. Prehistoric petroglyphs.
65. Weir box, inscription "FRED DIE."
66. Concrete slab foundation of house.
67. Concrete slab foundation of house.
68. Concrete slab foundation of house.
69. Concrete slab foundation of house.
70. Concrete slab foundation of house.
71. Stone bridge and retaining wall.
72. Leveled area with some concrete.
73. Concrete slab.

74. Concrete slab.
75. Concrete slab.
76. Concrete basement.
77. Bridge supports.
78. Bridge supports and retaining walls, with inscription: "T.N.R. 5/20/65."
79. Bridge supports.
80. Supports for possible foot bridge or aqueduct.
81. Concrete support for radio tower.
82. Post or tower foundation, with inscription: "May 1950."
83. Concrete supports.
84. Concrete base.
85. Manhole and collection box.
86. Baseball field location (borrow pit).
87. Concrete slab.
88. Leveled area and rock berm.
89. Rock and concrete water storage structure with wood roof.
90. Concrete box.
91. Rock and concrete walls with overflow pipe.
92. Valve and rock work and pipe, "MILWAUKEE VALVE CO., INC./1148-1158/125 S.W.P. 200 W.O.G."
93. Pipeline bridge.
94. Pipeline bridge.
95. Foot bridge supports and pipeline along cliff face.
96. Concrete slabs and level area.
97. Bridge supports.
98. Concrete block.
99. Concrete slab.
100. Concrete slab and rocks.
101. Culvert and rock walls.
102. Rock and concrete work at Bug Springs.
103. Water tank remains.
104. Trash scatter in disturbed area.
105. Masonry dam on Sycamore Creek.
106. Pipeline(s).
107. Pipeline supports.
108. Leveled area on hillside.

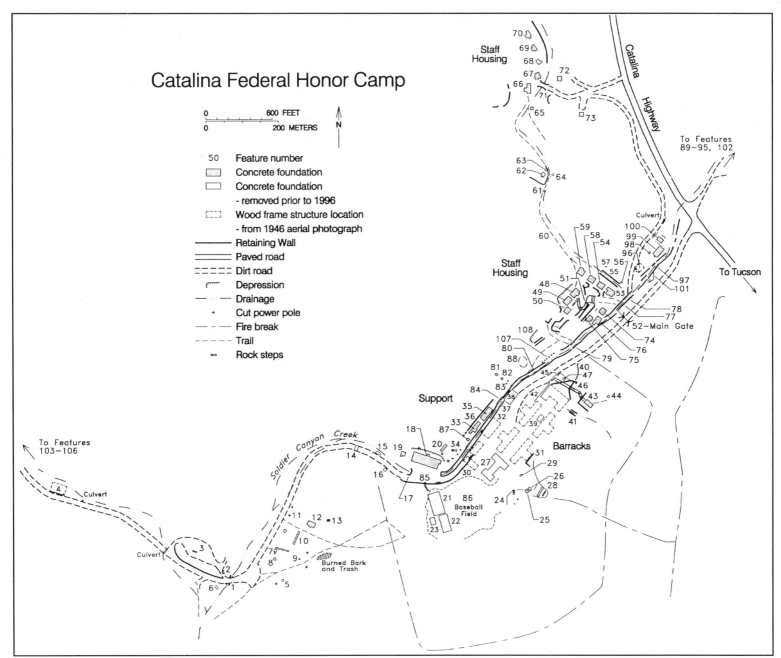

Figure 18.13. Sketch map of the Catalina Federal Honor Camp.

Figure 18.14. Dedication of the Gordon Hirabayashi Recreation Site, November 1999.

Figure 18.15. Resisters and other dignitaries cutting ribbon at the Gordon Hirabayashi Recreation Site dedication (left to right: Joe Norikane (Granada), Hideo Takeuchi (Granada), Ken Yoshida (Topaz), John McGee (USFS), Gordon Hirabayashi (Seattle), Jim Kolbe (US Congress), Harry Yoshikawa (Denver), Takashi Hoshizaki (Heart Mtn), Noboru Taguma (Granada), and Yosh Kuromiya (Heart Mtn).

to Tucson to serve his sentence, the resisters were transferred to the Honor Camp in leg irons and under armed guard. Ironically, security at the Honor Camp was far less stringent than it was in the Relocation Centers: instead of fences and guard towers, the perimeter of the Honor Camp was marked by white painted boulders. The inmates broke rocks with sledge hammers, cleared trees, and drilled holes for dynamite for the road work, as well as worked to maintain the camp and grow food and cook for the prison population.

After the highway was completed in 1951, the camp was used for juvenile offenders; inmates ran a logging and sawmill operation and a sign shop. In 1967 the camp was turned over to the state of Arizona, which used the camp as a youth rehabilitation center until 1973. All of the buildings were razed in the mid-1970s, but over 100 features, including concrete foundation slabs and rock walls, remain (Figures 18.8-18.13; Table 18.1; Farrell 1986). The Coronado National Forest is developing the old prison site into the "Gordon Hirabayashi Recreation Site" named in honor of its most famous prisoner (Figures 18.14-18.16). The site serves as a campground and trail head, and will include

interpretive signs which will focus on prisoners' experiences and the Constitutional issues raised by the internment during World War II.

Leavenworth Federal Penitentiary, Kansas

The Leavenworth Federal Penitentiary, 15 miles northwest of Kansas City, Kansas, is located on 1,583 square acres with 22.8 acres inside the penitentiary walls (Figure 18.17). Construction of the prison began in 1897, using labor from the nearby U.S. Army Disciplinary Barracks at Fort Leavenworth. Inmates of the Army Disciplinary Barracks, in fact, were also the first to be incarcerated at the prison, in 1903. The first cell house opened in 1906, and the prison was completed in the mid-1920s.

Older draft resisters from the Heart Mountain Relocation Center were

Figure 18.16. Sign at the site of the Catalina Federal Honor Camp.

Figure 18.17. Leavenworth Federal Penitentiary today.

incarcerated at Leavenworth, as well as the seven leaders of Heart Mountain's Fair Play Committee who were convicted of counseling others to resist the draft. The 28 solders from Fort McClellan who protested the internment and other discrimination were also sent to Leavenworth, but civilian and military prisoners were kept separate. Today Leavenworth is the largest maximum security prison in the United States, housing about 2,000 inmates.

McNeil Island Federal Penitentiary, Washington

The McNeil Island Federal Penitentiary was on an island in the southern portion of Puget Sound 10 miles southwest of Tacoma. The island was originally settled in the late 1800s. When the Federal Penitentiary was built in the 1920s and 1930s, it incorporated some of the original buildings. For instance, the chaplain's house was originally a settler's house. If not for the fences and guard towers, the penitentiary

Figure 18.18. McNeil Island Federal Penitentiary in 1937 (National Archives photograph).

Figure 18.19. Cell House #1, McNeil Island Federal Penitentiary (National Archives photograph).

Figure 18.20. Cell House #2, McNeil Island Federal Penitentiary (National Archives photograph).

Figure 18.21. Prison buildings at the McNeil Island Federal Penitentiary (National Archives photograph).

might have resembled a small town: in addition to cell houses, it included a boat dock, a ferry landing, a boathouse, ship sheds, a dry dock, a hospital, officers' quarters, bachelor officers' quarters, a warden's house, automobile garages, a library, a reservoir, a utility building, a cannery, warehouses, a workshop, a school for employees' children, a machine shop, farms, a farm dormitory, a farm kitchen, a cattle ranch, and a poultry farm (Figures 18.18-18.21).

Younger draft resisters from the Heart Mountain Relocation Center were incarcerated at McNeil Island. Gordon Hirabayashi was also incarcerated here, along with numerous other conscientious objectors, including Jehovah's Witnesses. Like the Catalina Honor Camp, McNeil Island was a work prison, and inmates held a variety of jobs, including canning fish, clearing land, and farming. Today McNeil Island is a medium-security state correctional facility housing about 1,000 male inmates.

References Cited

Abe, Frank
  n.d.   *Conscience and the Constitution: A Story of Japanese America.* Video documentary in post production. Independent Television Service, San Francisco, California.

Adachi, Ken
  1976   *The Enemy that Never Was.* McClelland and Stewart, Toronto.

American Red Cross
  1942   Report of the American Red Cross Survey of Assembly Centers in California, Oregon, and Washington. In Papers of the U.S. Commission on Wartime Relocation and Internment of Civilians. Part 1, Numerical file archive, Reel 10.

Anonymous
  n.d.   Mack Alford Correctional Center. MS on file, Mack Alford Correctional Center, Stringtown, Oklahoma.

Arrington, Leonard J.
  1962   *The Price of Prejudice: The Japanese-American Relocation Center in Utah During World War II.* The Faculty Association, Utah state University, Logan.

Badger Challenge
  1999   Badger Challenge, A Program Overview. <http://www.badgerchallenge.com/program.htm>.

Bailey, Paul
  1971   *City in the Sun: The Japanese Concentration Camp at Poston, Arizona.* Westernlore Press, Los Angeles.

Baker, Lillian
  1991   *The Japanning of America: Redress and Reparations Demands by Japanese Americans.* Webb Research Group, Medford, Oregon.

  1994   *Dishonoring America: The Falsification of World War II History.* Webb Research Group, Medford, Oregon.

Banks, Phyllis Eileen
  1998   Fort Stanton and Its Past. Southern New Mexico Online <wysiwyg://11/http://www. Zianet.com/snm/ftstant. htm>.

Bearden, Russell
  1989   Life Inside Arkansas's Japanese-American Relocation Centers. *Arkansas Historical Quarterly* 48(2):169-196.

Benedetti, Umberto
  1997   *Italian Boys at Fort Missoula, Montana, 1941-1943.* Pictorial Histories, Missoula, Montana.

Bureau of Public Roads
  1951   Final Construction Report, Arizona Forest Highway Project 33, Catalina Highway, Coronado National Forest, Pima County, Arizona. U.S. Department of Commerce, Bureau of Public Roads, Division Seven. MS on file, Coronado National Forest, Tucson, Arizona.

Burton, Jeffery F.
  1996   Three Farewells to Manzanar: The Archeology of Manzanar National Historic Site, California. *Western Archeological and Conservation Center Publication in Anthropology* 67. National Park Service, Tucson, Arizona.

Chuman, Frank
  1976   *The Bamboo People: The Law and Japanese Americans.* Japanese American Research Project, Chicago, Illinois.

Cohen, Irene J.
  1994   Manzanar: A Japanese American Relocation Center Memorial. Master's thesis, School of Architecture, University of Illinois, Urbana-Champaign.

Commission on Wartime Relocation and Internment of Civilians (CWRIC)
1982 *Personal Justice Denied.* U.S. Government Printing Office, Washington, D.C.

Conard, Joseph
1942 Japanese Evacuation Report #8. Seattle Office of the American Friends Service Committee, April 2, 1942. Hoover Institution Archives, Joseph Conard, Collection, Box 3, Notebook.

Conley, Curt
1982 *Idaho for the Curious: A Guide.* Backeddy Books, Cambridge, Idaho.

Culley, John J.
1991 The Santa Fe Internment Camp and the Justice Department Program for Enemy Aliens. In *Japanese Americans: From Relocation to Redress,* edited by Roger Daniels, Sandra C. Taylor, and Harry H.L. Kitano, pp. 57-71. University of Washington Press, Seattle.

Daniels, Roger
1989 *Concentration Camps: North America, Japanese in the United States and Canada During World War II.* Robert E. Krieger, Malabar, Florida.

1991 Introduction. In *Japanese Americans From Relocation to Redress,* Revised Edition, edited by Roger Daniels, Sandra C. Taylor, and Harry H.L. Kitano, pp. 132-133. University of Washington Press, Seattle.

1993 *Prisoners Without Trial: Japanese Americans in Worold War II.* Hill and Wang, New York.

Daniels, Roger, Sandra C. Taylor, and Harry H.L. Kitano
1991 *Japanese Americans From Relocation to Redress,* Revised Edition. University of Washington Press, Seattle.

Davis, Daniel S.
1982 *Behind Barbed Wire: The Imprisonment of Japanese Americans During World War II.* E.P. Dutton, New York.

DeWitt, John B.
1943 Final Report, Japanese Evacuation from the West Coast 1942. U.S. Government Printing Office, Washington, D.C.

Drinnon, Richard
1987 *Keeper of Concentration Camps: Dillon S. Myer and American Racism.* University of California Press, Berkeley.

Effland, Richard W., and Margerie Green
1983 Cultural Resource Assessment for the Gila River Farms Indian Community, GRIC. MS on file, Archaeological Consulting Services, Ltd., Phoenix, Arizona.

Embree, John F.
1943 The Relocation of Persons of Japanese Ancestry in the United States: Some Cases and Effects. *Journal of the Washington Academy of Science* 33(8):238-242.

Embrey, Sue Kunitomi, Authur A. Hansen, and Betty Kulberg Mitson
1986 *Manzanar Martyr: An Interview with Harry Y. Ueno.* Japanese American Oral History Project, California State University, Fullerton.

Erickson, Jim
1998a WWII Internees' Lives in Catalinas Examined: Renowned Japanese-American Looks Back. *Arizona Daily Star,* August 30, 1998.

1998b Forty-five Japanese Americans Lent Muscles to Build Highway. *Arizona Daily Star,* August 31, 1998.

Farrell, Mary M.
1986 Mount Lemmon Highway Staging Ground Cultural Resources Clearance. MS on file, Coronado National Forest, Tucson, Arizona.

Finnerty, Margaret.
1991 *Del Webb : A man, A Company.* Heritage Publishers, Flagstaff, Arizona.

Fox, Steve
1996   Fort Lincoln Internment Camp, 1941-1946.
        <http://humboldt1.com/~stfox/lincoln.html>.

Gardiner, C. Harvey
1991   The Latin American Japanese and World War II. In *Japanese Americans From Relocation to Redress*, Revised Edition, edited by Roger Daniels, Sandra C. Taylor, and Harry H.L. Kitano, pp. 139-141. University of Washington Press, Seattle.

Garcia, Marvin
1991   The History of Kenedy. English Honors Paper, Kenedy High School, Kenedy, Texas.

Gardener, Harvey C.
1981   *Pawns in a Triangle of Hate: The Peruvian Japanese and the United States.* The University of Washington Press, Seattle.

Garrett, Jessie A., and Ronald C. Larson
1977   *Camp and Community: Manzanar and the Owens Valley.* Japanese American Oral History Project, California State University, Fullerton.

Gates, Gerald R.
1982   Tule Lake National Wildlife Refuge Land Exchange Archaeological Reconnaissance Report (ARR 05-09-17 [CY-82]). MS on file, U.S. Fish and Wildlife Service, Tulelake, California.

Geary, Edward A.
1997   A History of Emery County, Chapter 6: Hard Times, Good Times, 1920-1945. Utah Centennial History Series.

Girdner, Audrie, and Anne Loftis
1969   *The Great Betrayal: The Evacuation of the Japanese-Americans During World War II.* MacMillan, London.

Glynn, Gary
1994   *Montana's Home Front During World War II.* Pictorial Histories, Missoula, Montana.

Gorman, Michael
1985   Heart Mountain Relocation Center National Register of Historic Places – Nomination Form. Wyoming Recreation Commission, Cheyenne.

Greene, Linda
1988   Cow Creek Historic District National Register of Historic Places – Nomination Form. Denver Service Center, National Park Service, Denver, Colorado.

Hansen, Arthur A.
1977   "Gila River Relocation Center." In *Transforming Barbed Wire*, edited by Rick Noguchi, pp. 7-9. Arizona Humanities Council, Phoenix.

Hayashi, Masumi
1997   American Concentration Camps. <wysiwyg://10/http://www.csuohio.edu/art_photos/index.html>.

Hayden, B.E.
1943   Annual Report and O & M Report of the Klamath Project, Oregon-California, for Calendar Year 1943. U.S. Department of the Interior, Bureau of Reclamation.

Hersey, John
1988   A Mistake of Terrifically Horrible Proportions. In *Manzanar: Commentary by John Hersey, Photographs by Ansel Adams,* by John Armor and Peter Wright, pp. 1-66. Times Books, New York.

Hirabayashi, Gordon K.
1991   The Japanese Canadians and World War II. In *Japanese Americans From Relocation to Redress*, Revised Edition, edited by Roger Daniels, Sandra C. Taylor, and Harry H.L. Kitano, pp. 139-141. University of Washington Press, Seattle.

Hirabayashi, Lane Ryo, and James Hirabayashi
1984   A Reconsideration of the United States Military's Role in the Violation of Japanese-American Citizenship Rights. In *Ethnicity and War*, edited by Winston A. Van Horne and Thomas V. Tonnesen, pp. 87-110. University of Wisconsin, American Ethnic Studies Coordinating Committee, Milwaukee.

Historical Museum at Fort Missoula
1999 Fort Missoula Alien Detention Center. <http://www.
      montana.com/ftmslamuseum/alien.htm>.

Hoshiko, Mike
1988 Putting Rohwer, Arkansas on the map. Pacific Citizen Holiday
      Issue, December 23-30, 1988.

Ichioka, Yuji
1989 *Views from Within: The Japanese American Evacuation and
      Resettlement Study*. Asian American Studies Center, University of
      California, Los Angeles.

Inouye, Mamoru
1997 *The Heart Mountain Story: Photographs by Hansel and Otto Hagel of
      the World War II Internment of Japanese Americans*. Privately
      published, Mamoru Inouye, Los Gatos, California.

Iritani, Frank, and Joanne Iritani
1994 *Ten Visits: Accounts of Visits to all the Japanese American Relocation
      Centers*. Japanese American Curriculum Project, San Mateo,
      California.

Irons, Peter
1983 *Justice at War: The Story of the Japanese American Internment Cases*.
      Oxford University Press, New York.

1989 *Justice Delayed: the Record of the Japanese American Internment
      Cases*. Wesleyan University Press, Middletown, Connecticut.

Jacobs, Arthur D.
1997 World War II - The Internment of German American Civilians.
      <http://www.netzone.com/~adjacobs/>.

Jacoby, Harold Stanley
1996 *Tule Lake: From Relocation to Segregation*. Comstock Bonanza
      Books, Grass Valley, California.

Japanese American Curriculum Project (JACP)
1973 *Wartime Hysteria: The Role of the Press in the Removal of 110,000
      persons of Japanese Ancestry during World War II, a Gathering of
      Actual Newspaper and Magazine Clippings*. Japanese American
      Curriculum Project, San Mateo, California.

Japanese American National Museum Quarterly
1994 Heart Mountain Mystery Rocks Donated to Museum. *Japanese
      American National Museum Quarterly*, Summer 1994.

Kelsey, Michael R.
1996 *The Story of Black Rock, Utah*. Kelsey Publishing, Provo, Utah.

1997 *Hiking, Climbing & Exploring Western Utah's Jack Watson's Ibex
      County*. Kelsey Publishing, Provo, Utah.

Kowta, Makoto
1976 "Tule Lake War Relocation Project." In Archaeological
      Overview for the Mt. Dome and Timbered Craters Regions,
      North Central California, by Janet Friedman, Appendix I. MS
      on file, California Historic Resource Information System,
      California State University, Chico.

Larson, Thomas K., Dori M. Penny, Michael Andrews, and James O. Rose
1995 Cultural Resources Investigations at the Heart Mountain
      Relocation Center, Wyoming. Paper presented at the Society for
      Historic Archaeology 28th Annual Conference on Historical
      and Underwater Archaeology, Washington, D.C.

Lee, Georgia; Hyder, William D., and Benson, Arlene
1988 The Rock Art of Petroglyph Point and Fern Cave, Lava Beds
      National Monument. MS Lava Beds National Monument.

Lehman, Anthony L.
1970 *Birthright of Barbed Wire: The Santa Anita Assembly Center for the
      Japanese*. Westernlore, Los Angeles.

Leighton, Alexander H.
1945 *The Governing of Men: General Principles and Recommendations
      Based on Experience at a Japanese Relocation Camp*. Princeton
      University Press, Princeton, New Jersey.

Long, Wallace
1991　*The Military History of Fort Missoula.* Historical Museum at Fort Missoula.

Louthan, Bruce, Lloyd M. Pierson, and Kurt Wall
1994　Dalton Wells CCC Camp/Moab Relocation Center National Register of Historic Places – Nomination Form. Office of Historic Preservation, Salt Lake City, Utah.

Mackey, Mike
1998　A Brief History of the Heart Mountain Relocation Center and the Japanese American Experience. <http://www.nwc.when. edu/library/hmdp/history. htm>.

Madden, Milton Thomas
1969　A Physical History of the Japanese Relocation Camp Located at Rivers, Arizona. Master's Thesis, History Department, University of Arizona, Tucson.

Manzanar Committee
1998　*Reflections in Three Self-Guided Tours of Manzanar.* Manzanar Committee Los Angeles, California.

Masaoka, Mike
1944　Final Report. F:PT 6.115, JERS, Bancroft Library, University of California, Berkeley.

Merritt, Ralph P.
1946　Project Director's Final Report. War Relocation Authority, Manzanar Relocation Center, California (UCLA Special Collections).

Merritt, Ralph P., Jr.
1987　Death Valley–Its Impounded Americans. *Death Valley '49ers Encampment Keepsake* 49.

Mitson, Betty E., and Arthur A. Hansen
1974　Voices Long Silent: An Oral Inquiry into the Japanese American Excavation. Cal State Fullerton Japanese American Project.

Myer, Dillon S.
1971　*Uprooted Americans: The Japanese Americans and the War Relocation Authority During World War II.* University of Arizona Press, Tucson.

Nakagawa, Martha
1999　'DB Boys,' An Untold WWII Story. *Pacific Citizen,* November 11, 1999.

Nakamura, Robert A.
1994　*Something Strong Within.* Japanese American National Museum, Los Angeles.

Nakano, Takano Ujo and Leatrice Nakano
1980　*Within the Barbed Wire Fence: A Japanese Man's Account of His Internment in Canada.* University of Toronto Press, Toronto.

National Japanese American Historical Society
1995　*Due Process: Americans of Japanese Ancestry and the United States Constition.* National Japanese American Historical Society, San Francisco.

Navrot, Miguel
1999a　Japanese Internees to be Honored. *Albuquerque Journal,* April 18, 1999.

1999b　Monument Plans Sock Survivors. *Albuquerque Journal,* August 11, 1999.

Negri, Sam
1985　Forgotten Arizona Compound Housed Japanese-American "Troublemakers." *Arizona Republic,* August 4, 1985.

Nelson, Douglas W.
1970　Heart Mountain: The History of an American Concentration Camp. M.A. thesis, University of Wyoming.

Nishimoto, Richard S.
1995　*Inside an American Concentration Camp: Japanese American Resistance at Poston, Arizona.* University of Arizona Press, Tucson.

Noguchi, Rick
    1997   *Transforming Barbed Wire: The Incarceration of Japanese Americans in Arizona During World War II.* Arizona Humanities Council, Phoenix, Arizona.

Nudd, Jean
    1992   Japanese Internment Camps in Arizona: Sources for Original Documents. *Casa Grande Valley Histories* 1992, pp. 29-41. Casa Grande Valley Historical Society.

Oda, James
    1980   *Heroic Struggles of Japanese Americans: Partisan Fighters from Americas Concentration Camps.* Privately printed, James Oda, North Hollywood, California.

Ogaawa, Dennis M., and Evarts C. Fox, Jr.
    1991   Japanese Internment and Relocation: The Hawaii Experience. In *Japanese Americans From Relocation to Redress*, Revised Edition, edited by Roger Daniels, Sandra C. Taylor, and Harry H.L. Kitano, pp. 135-138. University of Washington Press, Seattle.

Okihiro, Gary Y.
    1973   "Japanese Resistance in America's Concentration Camps." *Amerasia Journal* 2 (Fall 1973):20–34.

Page, George
    1986   Salvage Estimates – Two Wood Frame Buildings, Heart Mountain War Relocation Camp, Ralston, Wyoming. MS on file, Bureau of Reclamation, Montana Project Office, Billings.

Penny, Dori M., Thomas K. Larson, Jim C. Miller, and Keith H. Dueholm
    1990   Results of a Cultural Resource Inventory of Five Bureau of Reclamation Parcels in Park County, Wyoming. MS on file, Bureau of Reclamation, Montana Project Office, Billings.

Pinger, Julie
    n.d.   Documentation for a Determination of Eligibility – Camp Tulelake. MS on file, U.S. Fish and Wildlife Service, Tulelake, California.

Powell, Kent
    1972   Topaz War Relocation Center National Register of Historic Places – Nomination Form. Utah State Historical Society, Salt Lake City.

Quan, Daniel
    1999   Angel Island Immigration Station: Immigration History in the Middle of San Francisco Bay. *Cultural Resource Management* 22(8):16-19.

Residents of the Minidoka Relocation Center
    1943   *Minidoka Interlude.* Published by the Residents of the Minidoka Relocation Center, Hunt, Idaho.

Rose, James O.
    1992   An Assessment of the Heart Mountain Relocation Center, Park County, Wyoming. MS on file, Bureau of Reclamation, Montana Project Office, Billings.

Russell, Scott C., Karolyn Jackman Jensen, and Jon S. Czaplicki
    1995   The Historic Archaeology and Ethnohistory of a World War II Japanese-American Relocation Center in Central Arizona. Paper presented at the Society for Historic Archaeology 28th Annual Conference on Historical and Underwater Archaeology, Washington, D.C.

Saiki, Patsy Sumie
    1982   *Ganbare! An Example of Japanese Spirit.* University of Hawaii Press, Honolulu.

Sakoda, James M.
    1989   The "Residue:" The Unsettled Minidokans, 1943-1945, In *Views from Within: The Japanese American Evacuation and Resettlement Study*, edited by Yuji Ichioka, pp. 247-286. Asian American Studies Center, Los Angeles.

Santos, Robert LeRoy
    n.d.   The Army Needs Men: An Account of the U.S. Army Rehabilitation Center at Turlock, California, 1942-1945. MS on file, University Library, California State University, Stanislaus.

Sawyer-Lang, Monique
1989 Recovery of Additional Information from the Gila River Farms Expansion Area: A Study of a Japanese-American Relocation Center. Cultural Resources Report 53. Archaeological Consulting Services, Ltd.

Seabrook, John
1995 The Spinach King. *The New Yorker* February 20-27, pp. 222-235.

Simmons, Thomas H., and R. Laurie Simmons
1993 Granada Relocation Center National Register of Historic Places – Nomination Form. State Historic Preservation Office, Denver, Colorado.

Smith, Lorayne O.
1987 40 Years Ago Veterans Settled Hunt Project. *Times-News*, June 14, 1987.

Smith, Page
1995 *Democracy on Trial: The Japanese American Evacuation and Relocation In World War II.* Simon and Schuster, New York.

Spencer, Robert F.
1992 The Relocation Center at Rivers, Arizona: Concentration Camp or Community? *Casa Grande Valley Histories* 1992, pp. 7-20. Casa Grande Valley Historical Society.

Spicer, Edward H., Asael T. Hansen, Katherine Luomala, and Marvin K. Opler
1969 *Impounded People: Japanese-Americans in the Relocation Centers.* University of Arizona Press, Tucson.

Stanley, Jerry
1994 *I am an American: A True Story of Japanese Internment.* Crown Publishers, New York.

Stuart, Colburn Cox
1979 *Inside View Japanese American Evacuee Center at Rohwer, Arkansas, 1941-1945.* Desha County Historical Society, McGehee, Arkansas.

Sullivan, Mary, Monique Sawyer-Lang, Richard W. Effland Jr., and Margerie Green
1987 An Archaeological Survey of the Gila River Farms Expansion, Pinal County, Arizona. MS on file Archaeological Consulting Services, Ltd.

Suzuki, Peter T.
1981 "Anthropologists in the Wartime Camps for Japanese Americans." *Dialectical Anthropology* 6 (August 1981):23–60.

Tajiri, Vincent
1990 *Through Innocent Eyes: Writings and Art from the Japanese American Internment by Poston I Schoolchildren.* Keiro Services, Los Angeles.

Tamir, Orit, Scott C. Russell, Karolyn Jackman Jensen, and Shereen Lerner
1993 Return to Butte Camp: A Japanese American World War II Relocation Center. Cultural Resources Report 82. Archaeological Consulting Services, Ltd.

Taylor, Sandra C.
1993 *Jewel of the Desert: Japanese American Internment at Topaz.* University of California Press, Berkeley.

tenBroek, Jacobus, Edward N. Barnhart, and Floyd W. Matson
1954 *Prejudice, War, and the Constitution: Causes and Consequences of the Evacuation of the Japanese Americans in World War II.* University of California Press, Berkeley.

Thomas, Dorothy Swaine
1952 *The Salvage: Japanese American Evacuation and Resettlement.* University of California Press, Berkeley.

Thomas, Gerald W., Monroe L. Billington, and Roger D. Walker
1994 *Victory in World War II: The New Mexico Story.* Rio Grande Historical Collections, New Mexico State University Library, Las Cruces.

Tunnell, Michael O., and George W. Chilcoat
1996 *The Children of Topaz: The Story of a Japanese-American Internment Camp Based on a Classroom Diary.* Holiday House, New York.

Turner, Denise
    1989   Symms Speaks at Hunt Camp Dedication. *Times-News*, August 2, 1989.

Turner, Stanton B.
    1982   A History of the Tule Lake Basin. Tule Lake Historical Research Project: 1981-1982. MS on file, U.S. Bureau of Reclamation, Klamath Falls, Oregon.

Ulibarri, Richard O.
    1972   Utah's Ethnic Minorities: A Survey. *Utah Historical Quarterly* 40(3):210-232.

USDI, BOR
    1946   Klamath Project, Annual History for 1945, Volume 34. USDI, BOR, Klamath Falls, Oregon.

    1947   Klamath Project, Annual History for 1945, Volume 35. USDI, BOR, Klamath Falls, Oregon.

Uyeda, Clifford I.
    1993   Nisei Draft Resisters. *Nikkei Heritage* 5(4):4-7.

Uyeno, Tad
    1973   Point of No Return. *Rafu Shimpo*, October 10, 1973.

Van Valkenburg, Carol
    1995   *An Alien Place: The Fort Missoula, Montana, Detention Camp 1941-1944.* Pictorial Histories, Missoula, Montana.

Vyzralek, Frank E.
    n.d.   Fort Lincoln. MS on file, North Dakota State Historical Society, Bismarck.

Walls, Thomas K.
    1987   *The Japanese Texans.* Institute of Texan Cultures, Austin.

Webber, Bert
    1992   *Silent Siege – III: Japanese Attacks on North America in World War II – Ships Sunk, Air Raids, Bombs Dropped, Civilians Killed.* Webb Research Group, Medford, Oregon.

Wegars, Priscilla
    1999a A Real He-Man's Job: Japanese Internees and the Kooskia Internment Camp, Idaho, 1943-1945. Paper presented at the Society for Historic Archaeology 32nd Annual Conference on Historical and Underwater Archaeology, Salt Lake City, Utah.

    1999b The Kooskia (Idaho) Japanese Internment Camp, 1943-1945. Asian American Comparative Collection <http://www.uidaho.edu/LS/AACC/kooskia.htm>.

Weglyn, Michi
    1976   *Years of Infamy: The Untold Story of America's Concentration Camps.* Morrow Quill, New York.

Weik, Shirley
    1992   Introduction. *Casa Grande Valley Histories* 1992, pp. 1-6. Casa Grande Valley Historical Society.

Welch, James M., Robert G. Rosenberg, and Michael A. Nash
    1988   Class III Cultural Resource Inventory of Shoshone Municipal Water Supply Project, Park and Big Horn Counties, Wyoming. MS on file, Frontier Archaeology, Cheyenne, Wyoming.

Wilson, Marjorie
    1978   Japanese Relocation Center at Rivers National Register of Historic Places – Nomination Form. Arizona State Parks Board, Phoenix.

Yamaguchi, Jack T.
    1989   *This was Minidoka.* Pollard Printing Group, Tacoma, Washington.

Relocation Center Drawings in Records Group 210, National Archives, Cartographic Division (Washington, D.C.)

Complied by Irene J. Cohen

Gila River Relocation Center

Electrical Distribution and Telephone Lines – Butte Unit

Electrical Distribution and Telephone Lines – Canal Unit

Gila River Project Area Plan – Agricultural Development

Plan of Center Area – Canal Unit (1" = 200')

Plan of Center Area – Butte Unit (1" = 200')

Road System and Location Map (1" = 5,000')

Sewer System Layout

Title Page and Index

W.R.A. Construction (Site Plans with Dates and Construction Costs)

Water and Gas Distribution – Butte Unit

Water and Gas Distribution – Canal Unit

Granada Relocation Center

Electrical Distribution System Layout Plan (1" = 200')

Granada Relocation Area Field Map (Crops) (3" = 1 Mile; Faded Blueline)

Project Area (3" = 1 Mile)

Temporary Buildings Site Plan (1" = 200'; Contour Map)

Utility System – Water Supply, Storage, and Distribution Layout (1942)

Utility System – Water Supply, Storage and Distribution (1942)

Utility Systems – Sewers

Heart Mountain Relocation Center

Plan of Center Area (1" = 400'; Includes Buildings)

Area Map 1" = 5000' (Dark, Hard to Read)

Map of Heart Mountain Relocation Project (1" = 2000')

Layout Plan (With Key to Roads and Buildings)

Water Supply System General Plan

Electrical Distribution System

Sewer System – General Plan

Jerome Relocation Center – Folder 1
(General Including Evacuee Barracks)
Administration Headquarters for MP Group
Administration Group Dormitory
Administration Group Store
Administration Building for Admin Group
Administration Group Dormitory
Denson Cemetery Layout Plan (1" = 15')
Drainage Layout
Evacuees Barracks Building – Foundation Plan, Floor Plans,
    Sections
Evacuees Barracks Building – as Built (1/4" = 1')
Evacuees Mess Hall and Kitchen (Plan, Sections, Furnishings,
    Elevation)
Evacuees Lavatory and Laundry (Elevation)
Evacuees Lavatory and Laundry (Plans, Details)
Evacuees Lavatory and Laundry (Plumbing)
Evacuees Lavatory and Laundry
Evacuees Mess Hall and Kitchen
Evacuees Mess Hall and Kitchen (Building Section, Long Elevation,
    Details)
Evacuees Lavatory and Laundry
Fire Station
Framing – as Built
Garages for Administration and MP Groups, Watch Towers, Well
    Pump
Guard House for Military Police Group Plans, Elevation, Sections
Kitchen and Mess Hall for Admin. Groups and MP Group
Layout Plan (1" = 200'; W/building Schedule and Location Map)
Map of Land Developed by WRA – Roads and Bridges,
    (1" = 1/2 Mile)
Military Police Barracks

Misc. Details: Typical Closet for Evacuee Barracks; Screened
    Ventilators, and Kitchen Store Room
Officers Quarters and Dispensary for MP Group, Plans, Elevation,
    Lecture Room
Piping Detail of Two Hot Water Tanks in Evacuees Lavatory and
    Laundry
Post Exchange
Post Office
Post Office Vault and Interior Equipment Details
Receiving Building Plans, Elevations Sections
Recreation Building for Evacuees Blocks and for Admin. Group
Refrigerated Warehouse
Refrigerated Warehouse
Refrigerated Warehouse
Typical Details for All Buildings (Sections Mostly)
Typical Details for All Buildings (Windows, Doors, Porches, Etc.)
Typical Details for All Buildings
Warehouse for Warehouse Group and Shop for Admin.
Warehouse for Admin. Group

Jerome Relocation Center – Folder 2
(Hospital and Related)
Admin Building – Hospital Group
Children's and Isolation Wards, Obstetrical Ward, Electrical Work
Construction Details – Hospital Group
Covered Walks – Hospital
Cross – Sectional Details of Piping for Sewage Treatment Plant
Doctors and Nurses Quarters – Plumbing, Heating, and Electrical
Doctors Quarters – Plans and Elevations
Fire Stops and Covered Walk Ramp – Hospital Group
Hospital Mess Plumbing and Heating Work
Hospital Boiler House Equipment Foundations
Hospital Mess Roof Truss Details
Hospital Boiler House – Misc. Details

Hospital Boiler House – Plans, Elevations

Hospital Boiler House and Misc. Details

Hospital Mess – Plans, Elevations, Etc.

Hospital Mess Misc. Details

Isolation and Children's Ward Plans, Elevations, Section, Hospital Group

Isolation and Children's Ward Plumbing and Heating

Laundry Building Hospital Group

Mess Building

Morgue and Disinfecting Building and Hosp. Warehouse 46

Nurses Quarters – Plans and Elevations

Obstetrical Ward – Plumb and Heating

Obstetrical Ward Plans and Elevations, Hospital Group

Optional Roof Truss for Hosp. Mess Hall – Details, Elevation

Outpatients Building – Plumb, Heating, Electrical

Outpatients Building – Plans, Elevations, Section

Sprinkler System for Standard Ward Building

Sprinkler System for Isolation Ward, Children's Ward, Obstetrical Ward, Hospital

Sprinkler System for Covered Walks – Hospital Group

Standard Ward Building – Plumbing and Heating Plan Hospital Group

Standard Ward Plans and Elevation

Standard Ward Building – Plumbling and Heating Plan (Hospital Group)

Standard Ward Plans and Elevations

Standard Ward Building – Electrical Plan

Standard Ward Building – Electrical Plan, Hospital Group

Steam Distribution System.

Surgery Building – Plumb, Heating, Electric

Surgery Building – Hospital Group (Plans, Elevation)

Well and Pump Line Installation Details

Jerome Relocation Center – Folder 3
(Water, Sewage, and Utilities)

Aerial Electrical Distribution System. Neutral Grid and Grounding System

Aerial Electrical Distribution System. Pole Schedule

Aerial Electrical Distribution System. 13.2 KV. Const. Det

Aerial Electrical Distribution System – Sector No. 2

Aerial Electrical Distribution System. 13.2 KV. Constr. Det.

Aerial Electrical Distribution System. Sector No. 4

Aerial Electrical Distribution System – Sector No. 3

Aerial Electrical Distribution System – Sector No. 1

Composite Plan – Utility Distribution – Sector No. 1

Composite Plan – Utility Distribution – Sector No. 2

Composite Plan – Utility Distribution – Sector No. 3

Composite Plan – Utility Distribution – Sector No. 4

Fire Alarm and Tel System – Pole Lines

Sanitary Sewers – Detailed Layout – Sector No. 4 (1" = 100")

Sanitary Sewers – Detailed Layout – Sector No. 1

Sanitary Sewers – Detailed Layout – Sector No. 3

Sanitary Sewers – General Layout

Sanitary Sewers – Detailed Layout Sector No. 2

Sewage Treatment Plant Prelim. Sedimentation Tanks

Sewage Treatment Plant Filter Beds

Sewage Treatment Plant Final Sedimentation Tanks

Sewage Treatment Plant Sludge Digester

Sewage Treatment Plant Operation Diagram

Sewage Treatment Plant – Sludge Drying Beds

Sewage Treatment Plant – Sewage Pumping Station No. 1

Sewage Treatment Plant – General Layout

Transformer Station – Location Layout

Water Distribution System – Water Pumping Station

Water Distribution System. – Water Reservoir

Water Distribution System – Detailed Layout – Sector No. 2
Water Distribution System – Detailed Layout, Sector No. 4
Water Distribution System – Detailed Layout, Sector No. 3
Water Distribution System – Detailed Layout, Sector No. 1
Water Distribution System – General Layout

Manzanar Relocation Center

Boundary Map (4" = 1 Mi.)
Camp Layout (1" = 200', Incl. Building Legend)
Construction Plot Plan (WRA Construction, Remodeling)
Electrical System and Fire Alarm Telephone
Irrigation Map
Land Improvements (Roads, Airport, Etc; 1" = 100)
Manzanar Relocation Area (1" = 2,000"; Small Sheet)
Sanitary Sewer System
Water Distribution System

Minidoka Relocation Center

Basic Construction by U.S. Engineers: Center Plan (1" =300';
    Includes Building Key and Vicinity Map)
Electrical Distribution – Detail Layout
General Plan (1" = 200' Incl. Buildings, No Key)
Lateral 21.3 Location and Farm Units Served by Lateral
Minidoka Relocation Project (1" = 1/4 Mi)
W.R.A. Construction and Remodeling (1" = 300', Includes Key)

Poston Relocation Center

Canal System (1" = 2000')
Electrical Distribution
Electrical Distribution System – Unit I
Electrical Distribution System – Unit II
Electrical Distribution System – Unit III
Hog Farm Area
Key Map – WRA Colorado River Indian Reservation

Parker Warehouse Area
Poston – Unit I (1" = 300')
Poston – Unit II (1" = 300') and Typical Block (1" = 100')
Poston – Unit III (1" = 300') and Typical Block (1" = 100')
Roads and Land Improvements (1"= 2000')
Sewer System – Unit I
Sewer System – Unit II
Sewer Layout – Unit III
Telephone System Cables and Terminals – Unit I
Telephone System Cables and Terminals – Unit II
Telephone System Cables and Terminals Unit III and Typical Block
    (1" = 100')
Water Distribution System – Unit I
Water Distribution System – Unit II
Water Distribution System – Unit III
Water Distribution System Parker Warehouse Area

Rohwer Relocation Center

Aerial Electrical Distribution. System. – Sector No. 1
Aerial Electrical Distribution. System. – Sector No. 2
Aerial Electrical Distribution. System. – Sector No. 3
Aerial Electrical Distribution. System. – Sector No. 4
Aerial Electrical Distribution. System. – Neutral Grid and
    Grounding
Composite Plan – Utility Distribution – Sector No. 1
Composite Plan – Utility Distribution – Sector No. 2
Composite Plan – Utility Distribution – Sector No. 3
Composite Plan – Utility Distribution – Sector No. 4
Layout Plan and Vicinity Map (1" = 200')
Sanitary Sewers – Detailed Layout – Sector No. 1
Sanitary Sewers – Detailed Layout – Sector No. 2
Sanitary Sewers – Detailed Layout – Sector No. 3
Sanitary Sewers – Detailed Layout – Sector No. 4
Sanitary Sewers – General Layout

Sewage Treatment Plant – General Layout
Water Distribution System – Detailed Layout Sector No. 1
Water Distribution System – Detailed Layout Sector No. 2
Water Distribution System – Detailed Layout Sector No. 3
Water Distribution System – Detailed Layout – Sector No. 4
Water Distribution System – General Layout

Topaz Relocation Center

Center Plot Plan – Buildings Planned
Electrical Distribution in Topaz
Hospital Water, Sewer and Sprinkler System (1" = 30')
Land, Fencing, Irrigation and Drainage
Other Investments by WRA (Structures, i.e. Playground Equipment, Flagpole)
Plot Plans for Hog Farm, Poultry Farm, Cattle Ranch
Project Map – Roads, Fences, Ditches, Bridges and Culverts (1'= 1,500')
Project Map – (Small Sheet, No Scale)
Project Plot Plan – Water Lines

Road Layout, Elevations, Typical Sections
Sewer System
Sketch of Irrigation System Showing Culverts in Center (Small Sheet)
Staff Housing – Water, Oil and Sewer Lines (1" = 30')
Streets, Parking Areas and Sidewalks, Hospital Block (1" = 10')
Streets, Parking Areas and Sidewalks in Administration and Appointed Personnel Housing Areas (1"=30')
Construction Buildings (Includes Key)
Utility Area – Water, Sewer, and Road Layout
WRA Construction Map
Warehouse 109 (Large Scale)
Warehouse and MP Areas, and Typical Telephone System
Water Map (Including Detail of Water Tower)

Tule Lake Relocation Center

Camp Area Water Lines
Electrical Distribution – Hog Farms and Deep Well Area
Electrical Distribution System
Master Plot Plan (1" = 300'; Includes Key to Buildings)
Master Area Plot Plan (1" = 600'; Buildings, No Key)
Sewer Lines and Manholes
Utilities Layout

Appendix B

Tule Lake Relocation Center Drawings at the Bureau of Reclamation, Klamath Falls (Oregon) Office

40' x 100' Mess Hall – Military Police Area

Addition to Administration Building

Additional Construction – Preliminary (1943)

Additional Housing, Mess Hall, Combined Men's and Women's Latrine Building – Architectural, Plumbing

Additional Housing, Mess Hall, Combined Men's and Women's Latrine Building – Details

Additional Housing, Plot Plan – Fence and Perimeter Road

Additional Housing, Sewage Collection System – Plan

Additional Housing, Water Distribution System – Plan

Additional Housing – Building Location Plan and Streets

Additional Housing – Notes and Lists of Drawings

Additional Housing – Recreation Building, Architectural and Electrical Plan, Electrical Plans

Additional Housing, Family Barracks, Laundry and Ironing Building – Details

Additional Utilities, Bar Screen Chamber

Additional Utilities, Changes and Additions to Protective Lighting

Additional Utilities, Effluent and Sludge Beds

Additional Utilities, Imhoff Tank – General

Additional Utilities, Imhoff Tank – Structural Details

Additional Utilities, Pump Station

Additional Utilities, Pump Station – Installation

Additional Utilities – General Plan

Administration Building and Turnstile Canopy – Plans, Elevations, and Details

Auxiliary Power House and Electrical Details

Boiler House

Boiler House – Plan and Details

431

Appendix C

Selected Relocation Center Drawings

This appendix contains a sample of Corps of Engineers construction plans for various buildings in the relocation centers. Included are:

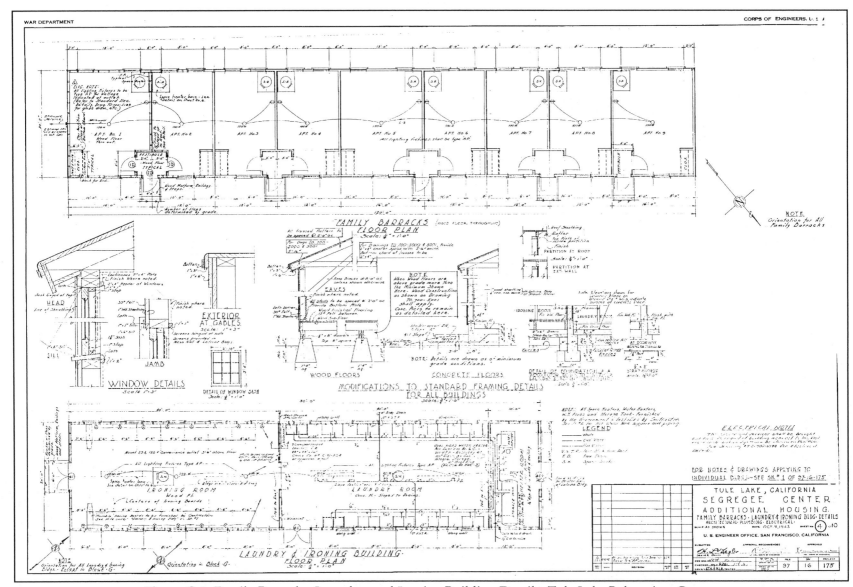

Figure C.1. Family Barracks, Laundry, and Ironing Building Details, Tule Lake Relocation Center.

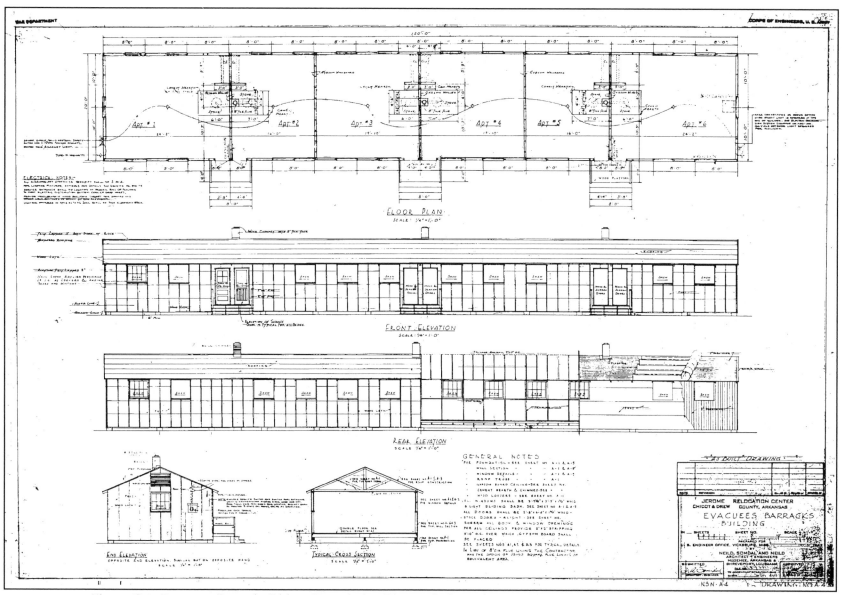

Figure C.2. Evacuees Barracks Bldg – Foundation Plan and Floor Plans and Sections, Jerome Relocation Center.

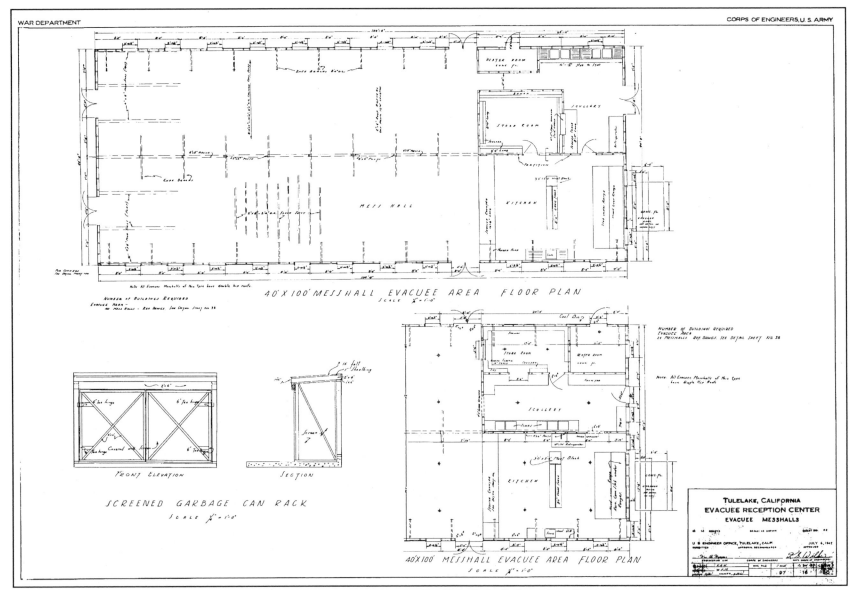

Figure C.3. Evacuee Mess Halls, Tule Lake Relocation Center.

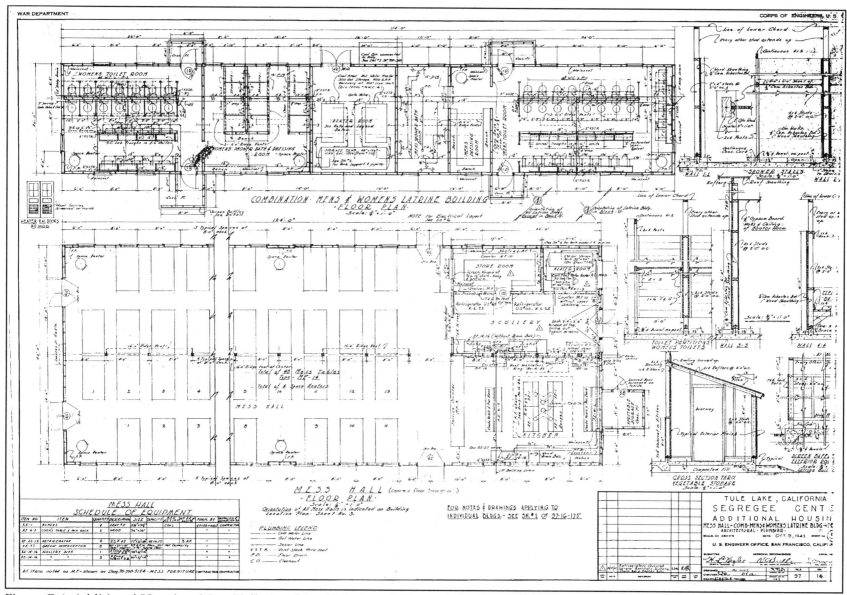

Figure C.4. Additional Housing, Mess Hall, Combined Men's and Women's Latrine Building – Architectural, Plumbing, Tule Lake Relocation Center.

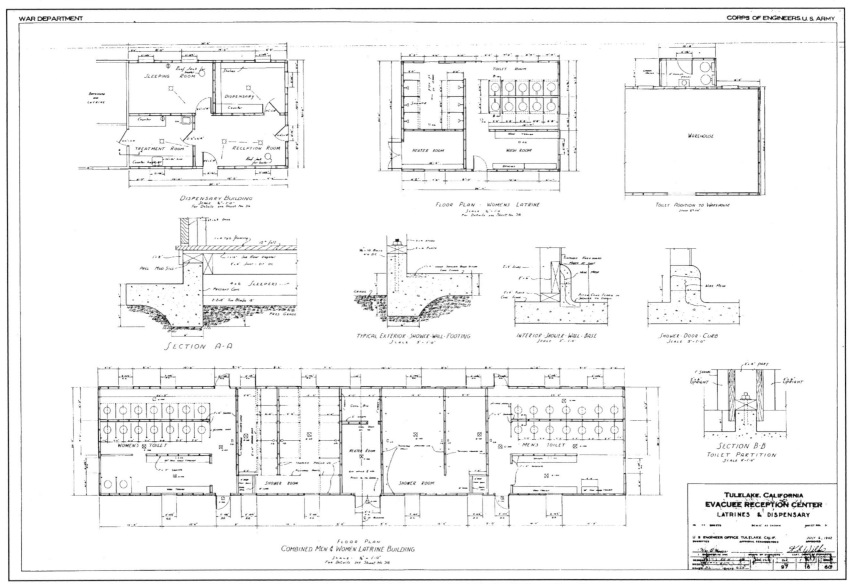

Figure C.5. Latrines and Dispensary, Tule Lake Relocation Center.

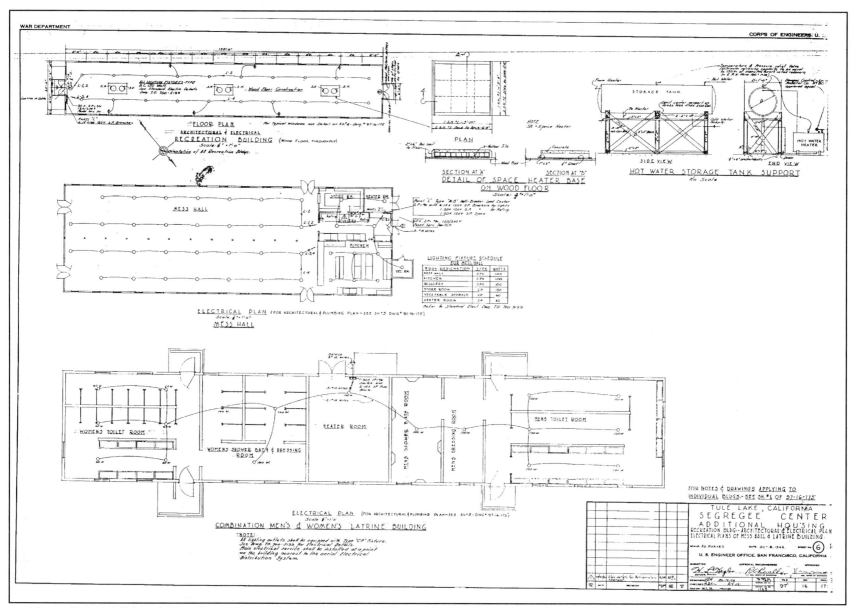

Figure C.6. Additional Housing – Recreation Building, Architectural and Electrical Plan, Electrical Plans, Tule Lake Relocation Center.

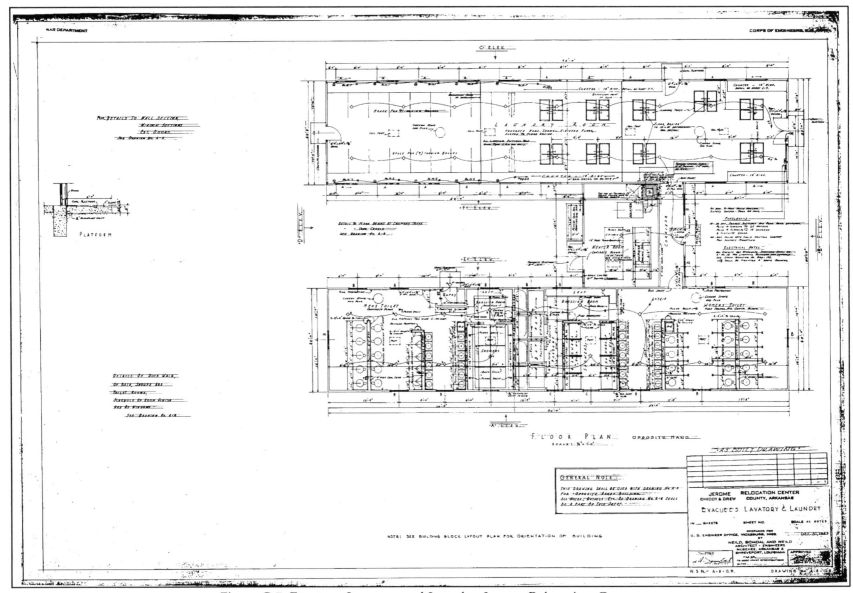

Figure C.7. Evacuees Lavatory and Laundry, Jerome Relocation Center.

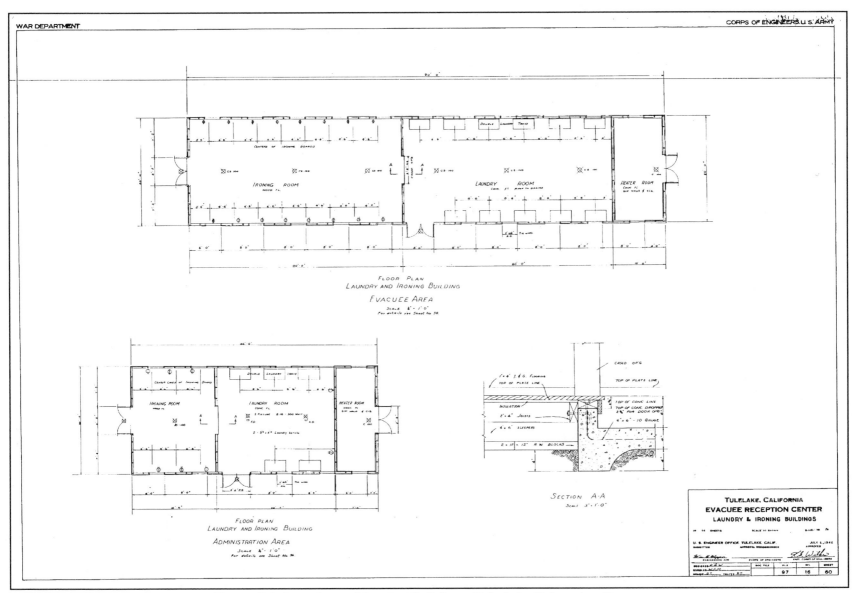

FLOOR PLAN
LAUNDRY AND IRONING BUILDING

EVACUEE AREA

SCALE ⅛" = 1'0"
For details see Sheet No. 58.

FLOOR PLAN
LAUNDRY AND IRONING BUILDING

ADMINISTRATION AREA

SCALE ⅛" = 1'0"
For details see Sheet No. 58.

SECTION A-A
SCALE 3" = 1'0"

TULELAKE, CALIFORNIA
EVACUEE RECEPTION CENTER
LAUNDRY & IRONING BUILDINGS

U. S. ENGINEER OFFICE TULELAKE, CALIF.

Figure C.8. Laundry and Ironing Buildings, Tule Lake Relocation Center.

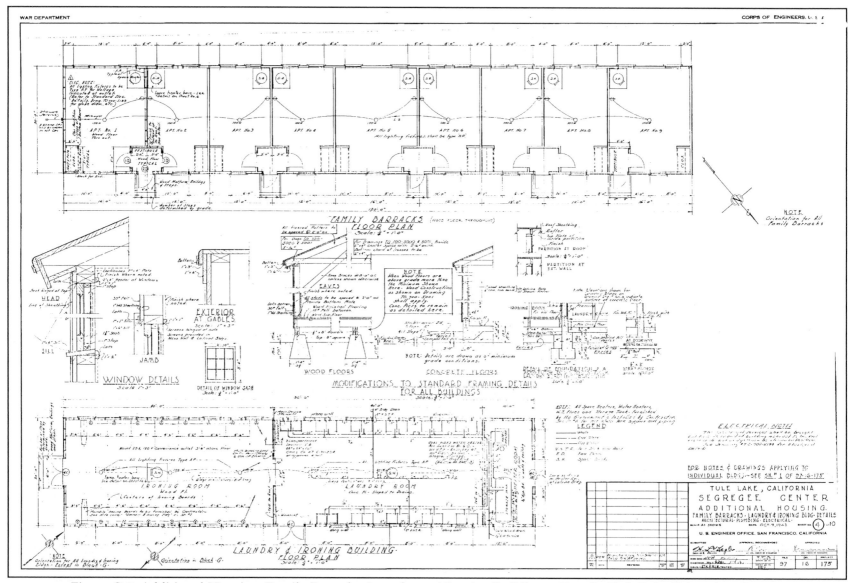

Figure C.9. Additional Housing, Family Barracks, Laundry and Ironing Building – Details, Tule Lake Relocation Center.

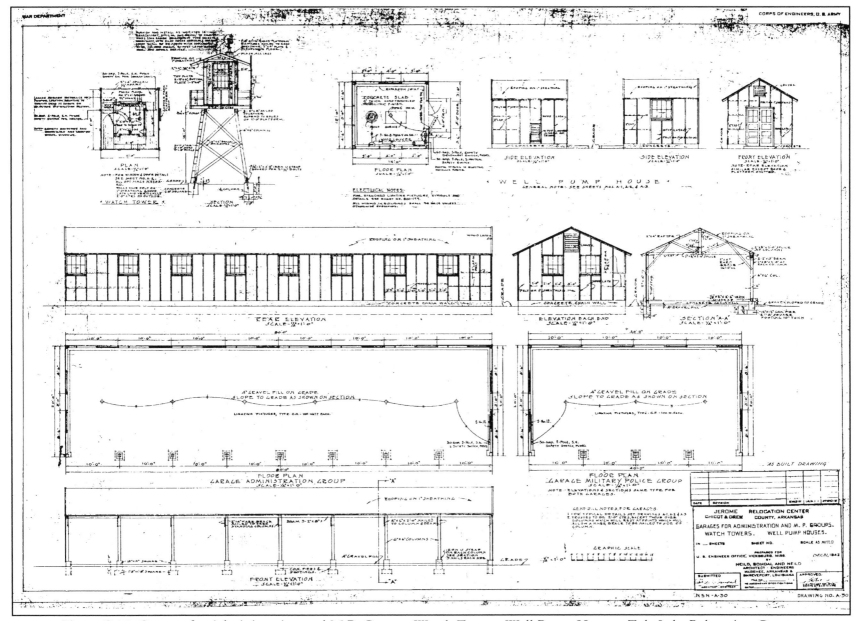

Figure C.10. Garages for Administration and M.P. Groups, Watch Towers, Well Pump Houses, Tule Lake Relocation Center.

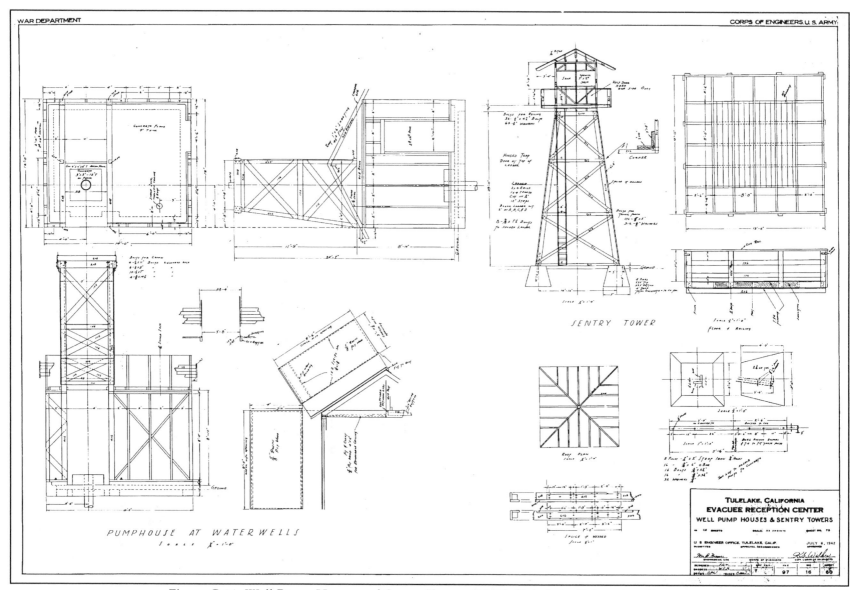

PUMPHOUSE AT WATERWELLS

SENTRY TOWER

TULELAKE, CALIFORNIA
EVACUEE RECEPTION CENTER
WELL PUMP HOUSES & SENTRY TOWERS

Figure C.11. Well Pump House and Sentry Towers (1942), Tule Lake Relocation Center.

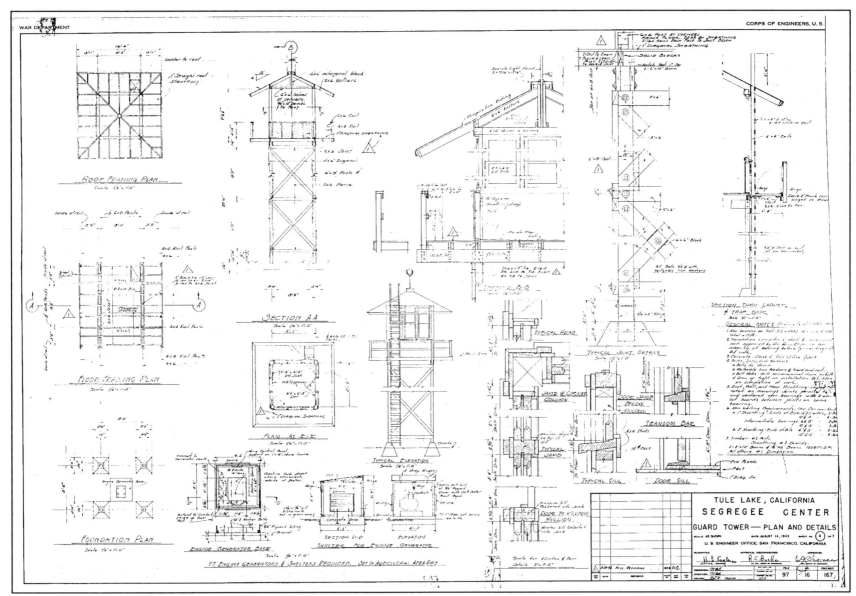

Figure C.12. Guard Tower – Plan and Details (1943), Tule Lake Relocation Center.

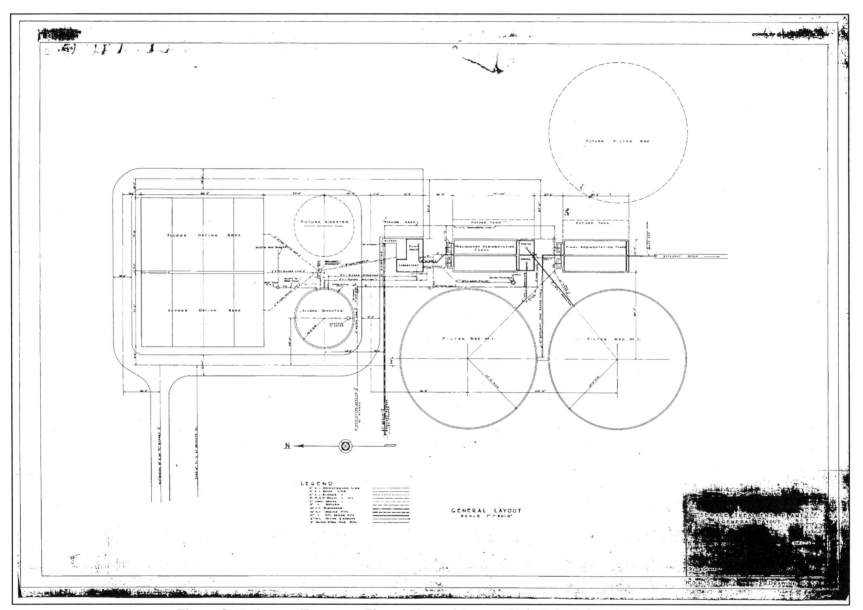

Figure C.13. Sewage Treatment Plant – General Layout, Tule Lake Relocation Center.

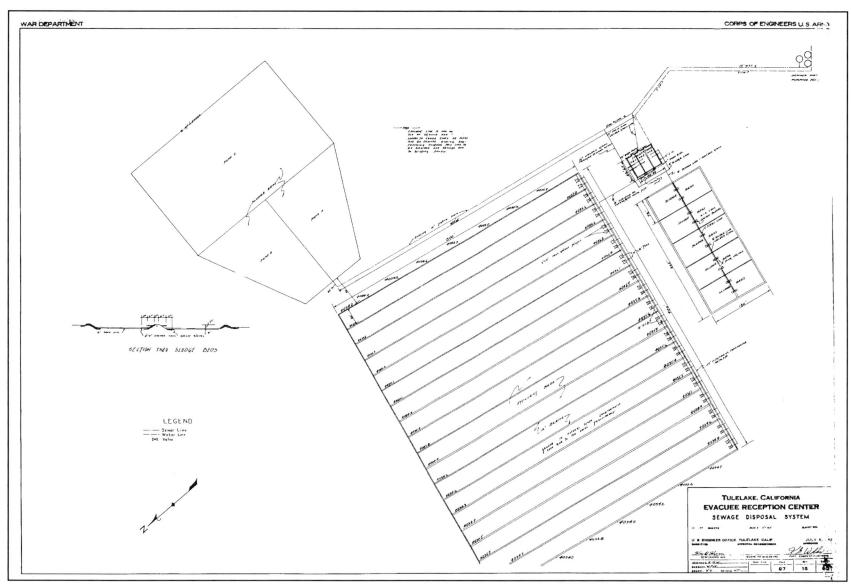

Figure C.14. Sewage Disposal System, Tule Lake Relocation Center.